# The Impact of Humanism
## on Western Europe

*Affectionately dedicated to*
*Denys Hay*
*by all the contributors to this book*

# The Impact of Humanism on Western Europe

---

*Edited by*
*Anthony Goodman*
*and*
*Angus MacKay*

**LONGMAN**
London and New York

**Longman Group UK Limited,**
Longman House, Burnt Mill, Harlow,
Essex CM20 2JE, England
and Associated Companies throughout the world.

Published in the United States of America
by Longman Inc., New York

© Longman Group UK Limited 1990

First published 1990

**British Library Cataloguing in Publication Data**
The Impact of humanism on Western Europe
  1. Europe. Humanism
  I. Goodman, Anthony   II. MacKay, Angus
  144'.094

**ISBN 0-582-05281-5 CSD**
**ISBN 0-582-50331-0 PPR**

**Library of Congress Cataloging-in-Publication Data**
The Impact of humanism on Western Europe/edited by Anthony Goodman
  and Angus MacKay.
       p.   cm.
    Bibliography: p.
    Includes index.
    ISBN 0-582-05281-5. – ISBN 0-582-50331-0 (pbk.)
      1. Humanism – Europe.  I. Goodman, Anthony, 1936–   . II. Mackay.
  Angus, 1939–
  B778.I46   1989                                      89-2326
  144'.094 – dc19                                         CIP

Set in Linotron 202 10½/12pt Bembo Roman

Produced by Longman Singapore Publishers (Pte) Ltd.
Printed in Singapore

# Contents

# Contents

# The Contributors

*Sydney Anglo* is Professor Emeritus, University College of Swansea.

*Peter Burke* is Reader in Cultural History at the University of Cambridge, and Fellow of Emmanuel College, Cambridge.

*James K. Cameron* is Professor of Ecclesiastical History at the University of St Andrews.

*Sir Geoffrey Elton* is Regius Professor Emeritus of Modern History at the University of Cambridge, and Fellow of Clare College, Cambridge.

*Anthony Goodman* is Reader in the Department of History at the University of Edinburgh.

*Anthony Grafton* is Professor of History at Princeton University.

*George Holmes* is Chichele Professor of Medieval History at the University of Oxford, and Fellow of All Souls College, Oxford.

*Jeremy N. H. Lawrance* is Lecturer in the Department of Hispanic Studies at the University of Manchester.

*Angus MacKay* is Professor of Medieval History at the University of Edinburgh.

*Jean-Claude Margolin* is Professor at the Centre d'Etudes Supérieures de la Renaissance, Université François Rabelais, Tours.

*Peter Matheson* is Professor in the Department of Church History at the University of Otago.

*Lewis W. Spitz* is Professor of History at Stanford University.

*Richard Tuck* is Lecturer in History at the University of Cambridge, and Fellow of Jesus College, Cambridge.

# Introduction

When we originally planned this book we had two specific and inter-related purposes in mind: the first was to produce a book of studies coherently organized and focused on the problem of assessing the impact of humanism on Western Europe; the second was to invite internationally prestigious scholars to contribute to the volume in honour of Denys Hay. Readers acquainted with those collections of essays which are normally referred to as *Festschriften* will, we hope, immediately understand the logic underlying our plans. For when a scholar is given the accolade of a *Festschrift*, it is usually because his or her eminence derives precisely from the fame and reputation of numerous and far-reaching publications in various different fields of scholarship. Thus the essays published in his or her honour tend to reflect these different interests, and the end result is often a book which lacks the unity of a central theme. In this sense, Professor Hay posed us exactly the same problem. If we had tried to produce a volume of essays reflecting all the interests contained in his numerous publications, this book would also have contained contributions on such fascinating topics as the nature of medieval frontier societies (an interest springing from his background as a Northumbrian), the profit motives of participants in the Hundred Years War, western historiography from the chroniclers down to the foundation of learned journals, and even the Ministry of Munitions and the design and development of weapons in twentieth-century Britain.

The impact of humanism on Western Europe, on the other hand, is one of the themes closest to Denys Hay's heart, and it is of course in this field that his numerous books and articles have had their greatest impact, as the select list of his publications, which only contains those items relevant to this book, makes abundantly clear. But perhaps not clear enough? His *The Italian Renaissance in its Historical Background*, for example, has been translated into German, Italian, and even Japanese, thus breaking out of the geographical confines of the book in his honour!

How successful, then, have we been in our aim to produce a coherent book rather than a random series of essays? Readers and reviewers, of course, will judge for themselves, but we should perhaps explain some of the principles we adopted in our preparation. First of all we invited the contributors to submit wide-ranging studies rather than in-depth research papers relating to restricted topics. These studies were divided into two groups: those which deal with themes across Western Europe as a whole (chapters 1–5), and those which deal with the impact of humanism on specific countries (chapters 6–11). This means, of course, that the same problems are frequently seen from different angles, but we believe that this is an advantage. Furthermore, not all readers have the same interests: the hispanist, for example, will turn to chapter 10, the reformation historian to chapter 2 – but both will no doubt 'gut' the other chapters as well.

Secondly, in drawing up editorial guidelines for the contributors we urged that the task of assessing the impact of humanism on each particular 'theme' or country should be interpreted in the broadest sense possible, although, of course, by its very nature the topic relates most closely to the institutions and culture of the ruling groups in society, where the Renaissance had its first impact, and which were the milieux in which it generated change in society.

Thirdly, we did not ask for the definitive 'last word' on each theme or country. Instead, we advised: 'Chapters should take the form of a survey. Contributors should try and give a clear picture or "summing up" of the present position in historical studies *vis-à-vis* the topic or geographical area they are dealing with.'

Finally, we made a point of allowing the contributors a great deal of flexibility, urging them for example to stray outside the guidelines if they wished to make a particularly important point. Indeed Peter Burke immediately pointed out that there was no intellectual justification for excluding Poland and Hungary from his study of the spread of Italian Humanism, and so we agreed that even the concept of Western Europe should be loosely defined so that the contributors of the thematic chapters could, if they so wished, include 'Eastern Europe' in their discussions.

In the event each contributor approached his task in the spirit laid down by our guidelines, and we are very grateful to them for fulfilling such a difficult remit. No doubt they have done so in very diverse and, at times, stimulatingly contradictory ways. However, we hope that readers of this book, and in particular Denys Hay, will enjoy the fruits of this collaborative effort by an international team of eminent historians.

Anthony Goodman
Angus MacKay

## Acknowledgements

We owe thanks for his help to Dr. Peter Sharratt of the Department of French, University of Edinburgh.

# Denys Hay

Denys Hay was born in 1915 and educated at the Royal Grammar School, Newcastle upon Tyne and Balliol College, Oxford. His first academic appointments, respectively in 1938 and 1939, were at the University of Glasgow and University College, Southampton. He served in the R.A.S.C. from 1940 to 1942 and was seconded to the Cabinet Office as a War Historian from 1942 to 1945. In 1945 he became a Lecturer in the History Department, University of Edinburgh, and in 1954 was appointed to its Chair in Medieval History. He was Vice-Principal of the University, 1971–75. He retired from the Chair in 1980, and from 1980 to 1982 held the Chair of History in the European University at Badia Fiesolana near Florence. Denys Hay has been Literary Director of the Royal Historical Society from 1955 to 1958 and Editor of *The English Historical Review* from 1958 to 1965. He was President of the Historical Association, 1967–70, and of the Ecclesiastical History Society, 1980–81. In 1970 he was elected Fellow of the British Academy and in 1981 an Honorary Vice-President of the Royal Historical Society. His pre-eminence as a historian has been reflected in his international appointments and distinctions. He was Visiting Professor at Cornell University in 1963; Senior Fellow at the Newberry Library, Chicago in 1966 and Visiting Professor at the University of Virginia in 1980. He has received Honorary Doctorates from the University of Newcastle in 1970 and the University of Tours in 1982; in 1974 he was elected an Honorary Foreign Member of the American Academy of Arts and Sciences. In 1980 he was appointed Commendatore all' Ordine del Merito della Republica Italiana. His scholarly work has always been blessed with the support and help of his wife, Gwyneth. They have three children, two daughters and a son.

## Denys Hay's Publications on the Renaissance

Note: This select list only includes those studies which have a bearing on the Renaissance. Translations of Professor Hay's books into foreign languages are omitted.

'The Manuscript of Polydore Vergil's *Anglica Historia'*, *English Historical Review*, LIV (1939).

'Pietro Griffo. An Italian in England: 1506–1512', *Italian Studies*, 2 (1939).

'The *Narratio Historica* of P. Vincentius, 1553', *English Historical Review*, LXIII (1948).

'The Life of Polydore Vergil of Urbino', *Journal of the Warburg and Courtauld Institute*, XII (1949).

*The Anglica Historia of Polydore Vergil, A. D. 1485–1537*, ed. with a trans. (Camden Series, LXXIV: 1950).

'The Historiographer Royal in England and Scotland', *Scottish Historical Review*, XXX (1951).

*Polydore Vergil: Renaissance Historian and Man of Letters* (Oxford, 1952).

*From Roman Empire to Renaissance Europe* (1953); retitled as *The Medieval Centuries* (1964).

Ed., R. K. Hannay, *The Letters of James V* (HMSO: Edinburgh, 1954).

*Europe: The Emergence of an Idea* (Edinburgh, 1957; 2nd edn 1968).

'Introduction' to *The New Cambridge Modern History*, I. *The Renaissance (1493–1520)* (Cambridge, 1957; 2nd edn 1975).

'Literature: The Printed Book', in *The New Cambridge Modern History*, II, *The Reformation (1520–1559)*, ed. G. R. Elton (Cambridge, 1958).

'Schools and Universities', in *The New Cambridge Modern History*, II, *The Reformation (1520–1559)*, ed. G. R. Elton (Cambridge, 1958).

'Italy and Barbarian Europe', in *Italian Renaissance Studies*, ed. E. F. Jacob (1960).

'Flavio Biondo and the Middle Ages', *Proceedings of the British Academy*, XLV (1960).

*The Italian Renaissance in its Historical Background* (Cambridge, 1961; 2nd edn 1977).

'History and Historians in France and England during the Fifteenth Century', *Bulletin of the Institue of Historical Research*, XXXV (1962).

*The Renaissance* (BBC Publications, 1963).

Ed., *The Renaissance Debate* (New York–Toronto–London, 1965).

'The Concept of Christendom', in *The Dark Ages*, ed. D. Talbot Rice (1966).

'The Background to the Reformation', in *The Reformation Crisis*, ed. J. Hurstfield (1965).

'The Early Renaissance in England', in *From the Renaissance to the Counter-Reformation: Essays in Honor of Garrett Mattingly*, ed. C. H. Carter (New York, 1965).

*Europe in the Fourteenth and Fifteenth Centuries* (1966; second edn 1989).

'Fiat Lux', in *Printing and the Mind of Man*, ed. J. Carter and P. H. Muir (1967).

'Florence and its History', in *The City of Florence* (BBC Publications, 1967).

'A Note on More and the General Council', *Moreana*, 15 (1967).

Ed., *The Age of the Renaissance* (1967; repr. 1986).

Aeneas Sylvius Piccolomini, *De Gestis Concilii Basiliensis Commentarium Libri* II, ed. and trans. (with W. K. Smith) (Oxford, 1967).

'The Church of England in the Later Middle Ages', *History*, LIII (1969).

'The Italian View of Renaissance Italy', in *Florilegium Historiale; Essays Presented to Wallace Ferguson*, ed. J. G. Rowe and W. H. Stockdale (Toronto, 1971).

'The Place of Hans Baron in Renaissance Historiography', in *Renaissance Studies in Honor of Hans Baron*, ed. A. Molho and J. A. Tedeschi (Florence, 1971).

'Sir Thomas More's *Utopia*: Literature or Politics?', *Rendiconti dell'Accademia Nazionale dei Lincei*, 175 (1972).

'Idea of Renaissance', in Scribner's *Dictionary of the History of Ideas: Studies of Selected Pivotal Ideas*, IV (New York, 1973).

*Italian Clergy and Italian Culture in the Fifteenth Century* (The Society for Renaissance Studies: 1973).

'The Church in Italy in the Fifteenth Century', *Irish Historical Studies*, IX (1974).

'Renaissance Europe: The Historical Background' in *Literature and Western Civilization*, III, ed. D. Daiches and A. Thorlby (1974).

'England and the Humanities in the Fifteenth Century', *Itinerarium Italicum*, ed. H. A. Oberman and T. A. Brady (Leiden, 1975).

'Muratori and the British Historians', *L. A. Muratori Storigrafo: Atti del Convegno Internazionale di Studi Muratoriani*, ed. S. Bertelli (1975).

'1500 –1700: The Bibliographical Problem. A Continental S. T. C.?', in *Classical Influences on European Culture .. 1500–1700*, ed. R. R. Bolgar (Cambridge, 1976).

*Annalists and Historians. Western Historiography from the Eighth to the Eighteenth Centuries* (1977).

*The Church in Italy in the Fifteenth Century* (Cambridge, 1977).

'New work on Florentine History', *History*, 63 (1978).

'Storici e Rinascimento negli ultimi venticinque anni', in *Il Rinascimento: Interpretazioni e Problemi* (Rome–Bari, 1979).

'Renaissance Education and its Influence on the "Governors"', in *Per Federico Chabod* (1901–1960), I (Lo Stato e il Potere nel Rinascimento), ed. S. Bertelli (Perugia, 1980).

'Religion North and South: Christendom and the Alps on the Eve of the Reformation', in *Società, Politica e Cultura a Carpi ai Tempi di Alberto III Pio* (Padua, 1981).

'Scholarship, Religion and the Church', *Studies in Church History* (1982).

'Scotland and the Italian Renaissance', *Renaissance and Reformation in Scotland: Essays for Gordon Donaldson*, ed. I. Cowan and D. Shaw (Edinburgh, 1983).

'Did Politics Change in the Late Middle Ages and Renaissance?' in *Studies in Medieval History Presented to R. H. C. Davis*, ed. H. Mayr-Harting and R. I. Moore (London, 1985).

'The Historian's interest in early Printing', in *Bibliography and the Study of 15th-Century Civilisation*, ed. L. Hellinga and J. Goldfinch (British Library Occasional Papers 5, 1987).

*Renaissance Essays* (London and Ronceverte, 1988).

*Italy in the Age of the Renaissance 1380–1530*, with John Law (1989).

## Chapter One

# The Spread of Italian Humanism

### PETER BURKE

### I

The aim of this chapter is to offer a general and comparative account of one of the most famous episodes, or movements, in the intellectual history of Western (and, indeed, East-Central) Europe – the discovery, by scholars and writers, of Italian humanism, and the rediscovery, thanks in large part to the Italian humanists, of the culture of the classical Greek and Roman world.

As is so often the case with key terms in intellectual history, 'humanism' does not lend itself to precise definition, nor is it easy to say exactly what is meant by its 'spread'.

The problem with 'humanism', a term coined by the Germans at the beginning of the nineteenth century, and first used in English (according to the Oxford English Dictionary) by Matthew Arnold, is that it is commonly employed in two very different ways, one of them precise and narrow and the other rather wide and vague. Humanism in the wide sense is associated with the belief in the dignity of man, and, more generally, with human or secular (as opposed to other-worldly) values. In North-Western Europe, as in the Italy of Giannozzo Manetti and Pico della Mirandola, the dignity of man was the subject of treatises, notably the *Diálogo de la dignidad del hombre* by Fernán Pérez de Oliva (published in 1546, after the death of the author) and the *Excellence et dignité de l'homme* by Pierre Boaystuau (published in 1558). However, the ideas expressed in these treatises are relatively traditional and conventional and would scarcely justify the employment of a phrase such as 'the humanist movement'.

Reacting against the wider definition popular at the beginning of the century, historians tend nowadays to use the term 'humanism' in a rather narrow sense, to refer to the men known in fifteenth-century Italy as *humanistae*, in other words the teachers of the *studia humanitatis* or 'humanity' (as opposed to divinity), generally defined to include grammar, rhetoric, ethics, poetry and history. In English, French and Spanish the word 'humanist' was occasionally employed in the sixteenth century, for example in the *Vocabulario del humanista* published in 1569 by a Spanish university teacher, Lorenzo Palmireno.

This precision has its price. Restricting the term 'humanist' to the professional university teachers of the Renaissance involves excluding some individuals who were very much concerned with the recovery of classical culture; the lawyer Thomas More, for example, the patrician Willibald Pirckheimer, the country gentleman Michel de Montaigne, and, above all, Erasmus, who occasionally took tutoring jobs but did not make teaching his profession, risking poverty for the sake of independence. There seems therefore to be a good case for a middle-of-the-road definition of humanism, neither too wide nor too narrow to be useful, as the movement to recover, interpret and assimilate the language, literature, learning and values of ancient Greece and Rome; while a humanist is someone actively involved in the movement, whether a professional teacher, churchman, royal councillor, or whatever.

The terms 'spread', 'diffusion', 'impact' or indeed 'reception' also raise problems. Like much of the historian's vocabulary, they are of course metaphors, dead or at any rate sleeping, and sometimes inappropriate for the tasks they are required to perform. The mechanical image of 'impact', the hydraulic metaphor of 'flow' (humanism spreading like an oil slick), or even the more human images of 'borrowing', passing something from hand to hand ('reception') or handing it down ('tradition') are too crude to cope with the process of cultural change.

Even in the case of material objects, from the axe-heads and pots studied by archaeologists to Renaissance manuscripts or statuettes, it is necessary to investigate demand as well as supply, to examine such problems as selective borrowing ('filtering'), unevenly-distributed receptiveness, and the changes in the use, and hence the meaning of objects in the course of their passage from one socio-cultural environment to another.[1] As for ideas, they have the habit of changing while in transit, or, more exactly, of being re-interpreted by the borrowers and adapted to local situations, so that the message received may well differ very considerably from the message originally transmitted. It is

---

1. One of the few serious studies of these problems is the work of a Swedish geographer: T. Hägerstrand, *Innovation Diffusion as a Spatial Process* (Eng. trans. Chicago, 1967).

for this reason that historians of the reception of the Renaissance may
have something to learn from what is known among students of literature as 'Reception Theory', which emphasises the creative role played
by receivers and the need to keep an eye on their 'horizon of
expectations'.[2]

The moral of this discussion is that an essay on the spread of Italian
humanism abroad, or, to vary the metaphor, its 'dissemination' (Italian
seeds transplanted into new environments with varying results), must
necessarily deal not only with the routes or channels of diffusion and
the institutions which encouraged or hindered it, but also with the ways
in which what we call Italian humanism was perceived in other parts
of Europe in the fifteenth and sixteenth centuries, and with the extent
to which and the manner in which it was assimilated by different
individuals or groups in different parts of Europe, translated into local
idioms.[3] To discuss these questions is the task of the present chapter.
The ideas of Tuscan humanists were subject to similar processes of
adaptation as they spread through Italy, from Venice to Palermo, but
this problem will not be considered here, any more than the equally
important problem of Italian responses to ideas, books and individuals
from other parts of Europe.

## II

With these problems in mind, it may still be helpful to start this survey
in the time-honoured manner by considering the importance of the
most direct and personal means of diffusing humanism: travel to and
from Italy. Appendix 1 lists some Italian scholars who were active
abroad from the beginning of the fifteenth century to the end of the
sixteenth. Given the difficulty of defining humanism, let alone the gaps
in the evidence, such a list can make no pretence to completeness or
indeed to objectivity. It may, however, provide a useful general
impression of the geography and chronology of the Italian humanist
diaspora. On the geographical side, it does at least show the misleading
implications of the customary contrasts between the Italian and
'Northern' Renaissances, since Italian teachers can be found not only
in France, the Empire, the Netherlands and Britain, but in southern
parts such as Spain and Hungary.

As for the chronology of the movement, the special importance of
the second half of the fifteenth century will be obvious enough, with

2. J. H. Jauss, *Towards an Aesthetic of Reception* (English trans., Manchester, 1982)
3. Brief general discussions of the theme include P. O. Kristeller, 'The European
Diffusion of Italian Humanism' (1962), reprinted in his *Renaissance Thought II* (New
York, 1965), pp. 20–68 and R. Weiss, *The Spread of Italian Humanism* (1964).

twenty-five expatriate Italians to contrast with eight between 1400 and 1449, twelve between 1500 and 1549, and six between 1550 and 1559 (when other countries had plenty of humanists of their own, and in any case parts of Northern Europe were torn apart by civil wars).

Why did these scholars go to England, France, Poland and so on? Why did they leave Italy? What did they do abroad? What difference did their presence make, and how did scholars and writers respond to them in the countries they visited? In some cases at least, evidence bearing on these questions has survived. In the early fifteenth century, a group of humanists left Italy to attend two councils of the Church, in Constance and Basel. Poggio Bracciolini, Antonio Loschi and Pier Paolo Vergerio the elder all attended the Council of Constance as papal secretaries, while Ambrogio Traversari and Enea Silvio Piccolomini attended the Council of Basel, the former as papal nuncio, the latter, who was still in his mid-twenties, as secretary to Cardinal Capranica. For Poggio, who found he had nothing to do at Constance, the importance of his visit abroad was doubtless his discovery of a manuscript of Quintilian, 'filthy with dust' in the library of the monastery of St Gallen.[4]

For the German churchmen, on the other hand, the councils were important (so it has been argued) because they offered 'an opportunity to see the rhetorically schooled Italians in action'.[5] One might add that others besides German churchmen were impressed by these five Italians – the Frenchman Nicholas of Clamanges and the Pole Mikolaj Lasocki, for example, who made the acquaintance of Poggio; the Emperor Frederick III, who took up both Vergerio (who never returned to Italy) and Enea Silvio (who served him for some years as secretary and wrote his treatise on the education of children for the emperor's brother Ladislaus); and János Vitéz, the humanist archbishop of Esztergom. The latter's intellectual development seems to have been influenced by his contacts with Vergerio and also with Enea Silvio.

Generally speaking, the expatriate humanists were not missionaries and they did not particularly want to leave Italy. What geographers call the 'push' factor was more important than the 'pull' of foreign countries. Filippo Buonaccorsi, better known by his nickname 'Callimaco', who became a prominent figure at the Polish court in the late fifteenth century, arrived in 1470 from Rome after a conspiracy against Pope Paul II in which he had been involved proved unsuccessful. Another unsuccessful conspiracy, against the Medici this time, forced Luigi Alamanni to flee from Florence in 1522, to the court of Francis I, where

---

4. Poggio Bracciolini, *Lettere*, ed. H. Harth, 2 (Florence, 1984), p. 155.

5. L. Spitz, 'The Course of German Humanism', in *Iter italicum*, ed. H. Oberman and T. Brady (Leiden, 1975). pp. 392 f.

he made a successful career for himself as poet and diplomat. Jacopo Corbinelli also fled to the French court, in 1566, after another anti-Medici conspiracy, and found employment teaching the future King Henry III Latin and Italian.

From the 1540s onwards, a number of Italian intellectuals went into exile for religious reasons. Which of them should be counted as humanists it is not easy to decide, but a good case could be made for Celio Secundo Curione, who fled to Switzerland in 1542, as it could for the Sozzinis, who left a generation later.[6] Curione, apparently a secret Anabaptist, taught classics at Basel and translated Guicciardini's *History of Italy* into Latin. His friend Pier Paolo Vergerio the younger, who arrived in Switzerland in 1544, may also be described as a humanist, or at least as an ex-humanist, a former member of Bembo's circle and a university lecturer.[7]

Some Italian humanists travelled abroad in search of manuscripts, like Poggio in France, Angelo Decembrio in Spain, or Pandolfo Collenuccio in Germany. Some were sent abroad on missions: Bibbiena visited France and Castiglione Spain as diplomats in papal service, while Polydore Vergil originally came to England as a collector of Peter's Pence. A larger group went abroad to teach. The university of Paris attracted (among others) Gregorio Tifernate, Filippo Beroaldo the elder, Pico della Mirandola (for a brief visit), and Girolamo Aleandro. Oxford and Cambridge had their Italian lecturers, respectively Stefano Surigone of Milan and Lorenzo Traversagni of Savona. Lucio Marineo and Pietro Martire d'Anghiera taught in Spain, Jacopo Publicio and Cataldo Parisio in Portugal. These visitors generally taught the *studia humanitatis*, more especially rhetoric and poetry.

It has been observed that 'with the exception of the elder Beroaldo and Girolamo Aleandro, no first-rate humanist went to teach outside Italy or served at a foreign court'.[8] To this short-list of the first-rate I would be inclined to add Andrea Alciati of Milan, a humanist lawyer who taught at Avignon and Bourges. The general point remains valid, but the welcome given to the second-rate is precious evidence of contemporary interest in Italian humanists. Leading scholars received pressing invitations from various quarters, like Romolo Amaseo of Bologna, who was asked to teach in England and Poland but preferred to remain in Italy. Later in the century, Fulvio Orsini and Carlo Sigonio were also invited to Poland. From the point of view of the reception of humanism, what we should like to know is who invited

---

6. The debt of sixteenth-century Italian heretics to the humanist tradition is empha-sised in D. Cantimori, *Eretici italiani del Cinquecento* (Florence, 1939).

7. On him, A. J. Schutte, *P. P. Vergerio* (Geneva, 1977), especially chapter 1.

8. Weiss, *Spread of Italian Humanism*, p. 70.

these scholars, and why. The surviving information is patchy but in some cases at least it is possible to give details.

A few rulers were personally interested in attracting Italian humanists to their courts, to teach their children, look after their books, and praise their achievements in classical Latin. An outstanding example is King Matthias Corvinus of Hungary, who reigned from 1458 to 1490, and had been educated by humanists (János Vitéz and Grzegorz of Sanok) before coming to the throne. Matthias tried to attract Ficino to Hungary. The attempt was unsuccessful, but a friend of Ficino's, Francesco Bandini, did enter the king's service. Matthias also invited Galeotto Marzio of Narni (who had already visited Hungary to see his old friend Janus Pannonius) to Buda to look after his library and write his biography; he appointed Taddeo Ugoletto of Parma to succeed Marzio as royal librarian; and he commissioned Antonio Bonfini of Ascoli (who had brought himself to the notice of Queen Beatrice while she was still in Italy), to write a history of Hungary. Bonfini's *Decades* followed classical models and incidentally traced the king's ancestry back to a Roman consul, Marcus Valerius Corvinus.[9]

Francis I is an even more famous example of royal interest in Italian humanism. The king brought the Greek scholar Janos Lascaris from Italy to be his librarian. He commissioned Alamanni's epic, *Gyrone il cortese*, engaged Italians as tutors for his sons, and gave money to Giulio Camillo, who visited the court in 1530, to finance his work on the art of memory.[10] Francis did not need to commission a history of France in the humanist style, because one of his predecessors had already done so. The work of Paolo Emili of Verona, this *History of the French* was published in the 1520s. Henry VII may not be in the class of Matthias or Francis as a Renaissance patron, but he did have 'a weakness for cultivated Italians', made Pietro Carmeliano his Latin secretary, and commissioned Polydore Vergil (who confessed to having been 'most courteously received by the king'), to write a history of England, the equivalent of Emili on France and Bonfini on Hungary.[11]

Some local aristocrats, clerical and lay, also encouraged Italian humanists to pursue careers abroad. The humanist archbishop of Lwów, Grzegorz of Sanok, helped Callimaco on his arrival in Poland. Another humanist archbishop, János Vitéz of Esztergom, encouraged

---

9. T. Klaniczay, ed., *Rapporti Veneto-Ungheresi all'epoca del Rinascimento* (Budapest, 1975). Other Italian humanists who visited Hungary in the reign of Matthias are Aurelio Brandolini, Bartolemeo Fonzio and Raffaele Maffei.

10. The Italians employed as tutors at the French court were Girolamo Fondulo and Benedetto Tagliacarne. On Camillo and his 'memory theatre', see F. Yates, *The Art of Memory* (1966), p. 130.

11. D. Hay, *Polydore Vergil* (Oxford, 1952), pp. 3–4.

Matthias's interest in humanism and is described (with some exaggeration) by Vespasiano da Bisticci as having brought 'the most learned men of Italy' to Hungary. Cardinal Wolsey tried to entice Amaseo to England.

As for the lay aristocracy, the well-known English example of Humphrey duke of Gloucester, who invited Leonardo Bruni to England and gave his patronage to Tito Livio Frulovisi, does not stand alone. Two Italian humanists were brought to Spain by noblemen who had made their acquaintance abroad; Pietro Martire d'Anghiera by the count of Tendilla, ambassador to Rome, and Lucio Marineo by the admiral of Castile, who had discovered him while visiting Sicily.

What did these patrons want from Italian humanists? What did they expect? How did other Europeans respond? To find answers to these questions, it is necessary to take a somewhat indirect route, looking at some foreign visitors to Italy and at their reactions to humanist culture. Appendix 2 lists 132 such visitors; scholars, writers, and patrons. They are of course no more than a small proportion of the foreign visitors to Italy in the period – pilgrims, soldiers, merchants, diplomats, artists and so on. The curve of development is worth noting: fourteen visitors in the first half of the fifteenth century, 44 between 1450 and 1499, a peak of 63 between 1500 and 1549, declining to 30 or so between 1550 and 1599.

What did these visitors do in Italy? A fair number of them attended university – Pavia, Ferrara, Bologna and especially Padua. William Grey, John Tiptoft and Janus Pannonius were among the foreigners who studied with the leading humanist Guarino of Verona, while the Polish cleric Mikolaj Lasocki sent his nephews to Guarino to be educated.[12] A few foreign visitors are known to have visited Florence and met the humanists there. In the early 1490s, Johan Reuchlin and Jacques Lefèvre d'Etaples both went to Florence to meet Pico and Ficino. (John Colet 'never did meet Ficino' when he was in Italy, although he corresponded with him later).[13] Poliziano's lectures also attracted some foreign students, among them Thomas Linacre and the Portuguese humanists Aires Barbosa and Henrique Caiado.

In a few cases, we know that students who went, or were sent to Italy to study a traditional subject (generally law) in a traditional way, changed their mind after an encounter with the humanists. The Netherlander Rudolf Agricola, for example, who went to Italy in 1468, at the age of twenty-four, began by studying law at Pavia but later moved

---

12. Guarino, *Epistolario*, ed. R. Sabbadini, 3 vols. (Venice, 1915–19), 2, no. 716; cf no. 817.

13. S. Jayne, *John Colet and Marsilio Ficino* (Oxford, 1963).

to Ferrara to engage in the *studia humanitatis*. Henrique Caiado was also supposed to have been studying law, not listening to Poliziano. Ulrich von Hutten and Conrad Mutianus both abandoned law while they were in Italy; Hutten discovered Lucian and Mutianus discovered Plato. Willibald Pirckheimer's father seems to have been exceptional in advising his son 'to go to lectures on the *studia humanitatis*', but then Pirckheimer senior had himself studied in Italy.[14]

Other foreigners went to Italy on diplomatic missions in the course of which they made friends with Italian humanists and acquired new ideas as well as books; Robert Gaguin, for example, in the 1480s, Sir Thomas Wyatt in the 1520s, and Diego Hurtado de Mendoza in the 1540s. Justus Lipsius, who became one of the leading classical scholars in Europe, visited Rome in 1567 in the retinue of Cardinal Granvelle. One wonders what the discovery of Italian humanism meant to Granvelle, a cultivated man and an important patron of scholars. Come to that, one would love to know what difference their 'visits' to Italy (not to say invasions) made to the intellectual interests of Charles VIII, Louis XII, Francis I and Charles V. At least two Frenchmen who served in Italian campaigns returned with a life-long interest in humanism, Christophe de Longueil and Symphorien Champier.

In a few cases only have the visitors left us records of their reactions to Italy. One of these articulate travellers is Erasmus, whose first visit lasted from September 1506 to July 1509. A letter of 1506 explains that he went to Italy to learn Greek. Years later, he laid more emphasis on the opportunity to visit libraries and scholars (he did in fact make the acquaintance of Aldus Manutius, Marcus Musurus, Janos Lascaris, Girolamo Aleandro and Filippo Beroaldo the younger). Towards the end of his life, he declared that he had already wanted to visit Italy when he was seventeen, and contrasted the Italian learning of that time with the 'horrid barbarism' of the North.[15]

A few more testimonies of this kind have survived. Rudolf Agricola wrote from Pavia telling a friend that 'the holiest, greatest and most serious men of genius' were to be found in Italy.[16] The Portuguese humanist Osorio reminisced about visiting Italy in his youth 'for the sake of training my mind' (*excolendi ingenii gratia*); he studied under Amaseo at Bologna.[17] Among the English visitors, Thomas Starkey, who studied at Padua, explained that 'I went straight into the country of Italy, as to the place most famed both with great learning and good

---

14. Quoted in Spitz, 'The Course of German Humanism', p. 406.

15. *Epistolae*, ed. P. S. Allen, vol. 1, no. 433; vol. 3, no. 267; vol. 11, no. 177.

16. Quoted in J. H. Overfield, *Humanism and Scholasticism in late medieval Germany* (Princeton, 1984), p. 89.

17. J. Osorio, *De gloria* (1543; in *Opera*, 4 vols., Rome, 1592, I, p 118).

and just policy'.[18] Richard Pace tells us that his patron, the bishop of Winchester, 'sent me to Italy to study the liberal arts at the university of Padua' and that he applied himself to 'the humanities' (*literis human-ioribus*).[19] Thomas Hoby, the translator of Castiglione's *Courtier*, learned his Italian in Padua in 1548, and also attended some lectures 'in humanitie'.[20]

Among the French visitors (who included Rabelais and Joachim Du Bellay), the responses of Jacques-Auguste de Thou and Michel de Montaigne are the best documented. De Thou, who became a distinguished French magistrate and man of letters, visited Italy in his youth, in the suite of the French ambassador to Venice, and he made a point of meeting the most famous humanists of the day: Carlo Sigonio in Bologna, Piero Vettori in Florence, and Fulvio Orsini in Rome. Montaigne, despite his suspicion of the humanists' concern with words, paid a visit to the tomb of Pietro Bembo in Padua, and in Rome found time to look at ancient manuscripts as well as ancient ruins. He also took the opportunity to acquire a number of books by Italian men of letters. It is time to examine the role of the book in the dissemination of humanism.

## III

One way of assessing responses to Italy on the part of foreign visitors is to see what kinds of book they took home with them. The Florentine bookseller Vespasiano da Bisticci, who worked in a humanist milieu, included a number of foreigners among the 'illustrious men' whose lives he recorded, among them William Grey bishop of Ely, János Vitéz archbishop of Esztergom, and the Spanish nobleman Nuño de Guzmán. Vespasiano naturally emphasised their interest in books, in other words manuscripts (he hated the new-fangled printing-press). He tells us that when Grey arrived in Florence, 'He ordered many books, which were transcribed for him', and that when he returned to England, 'he founded a very noble library'. The archbishop of Esztergom collected 'a magnificent library', and many books which he had failed to find else-where 'he caused to be transcribed in Florence regardless of cost'. Guzmán 'often sent scribes to Florence at his own expense to copy various books' and so 'collected a fine library'.[21]

---

18. T. Starkey, *A Dialogue between Reginald Pole and Thomas Lupset*, ed. K. Burton (1948), preface.

19. R. Pace, *De fructu qui ex doctrina percipitur* (1517; with English trans., New York, 1967), pp. 39, 125.

20. *A Booke of the Travaile and Life of me Thomas Hoby*, ed. E. Powell (1902), p. 8.

21. Vespasiano da Bisticci, *The Vespasiano memoirs. Lives of the illustrious men of the XVth century*, trans. W. G. and E. Waters. (1926) pp. 185–6, 189, 434.

The advantage of choosing these three men is that in these cases it is possible to verify Vespasiano's statements from other sources, and to add details. Some of Grey's manuscripts are still to be found in Balliol College Oxford, and they include not only classical texts but works by such leading Italian humanists as Biondo, Bruni, Guarino, Poggio and Valla.[22] The contents of the library of János Vitéz have been reconstructed by a Hungarian scholar, and they prove to include texts by nine Italian humanists.[23] Nuño de Guzmán's collection has been lost, but something is known about the Italian books he procured for his relative the marquis of Santillana (the famous poet), and they included works by Leonardo Bruni, Pier Candido Decembrio, Giannozzo Manetti and Lorenzo Valla.[24]

Although the influence of Italian humanism could have been communicated through less direct channels, the presence of texts by Italian scholars in foreign libraries may be taken as a sort of litmus test of the interests of the owners. The test should be most reliable in the case of relatively small libraries, whose owners were likely to be familiar with all their books. The library of Beatus Rhenanus, for example, contained books by no fewer than fifteen Italian humanists, which is not too surprising in the case of a leading German scholar who had studied with Andrelini in Paris, although Beatus does not seem to have visited Italy himself.[25] Given the common assumption that (as Bacon put it) 'histories make men wise', it was perhaps only to be expected that intellectual rulers such as Erik XIV of Sweden and James VI of Scotland should have owned a number of Italian humanist histories. Both kings had works by Giovio and Sabellico in their libraries (in Erik's case the copy is annotated in the royal hand). Erik also possessed Bruni's *History of Florence* and Emili's *History of France*, while James had copies of Biondo's *Rome Restored* and the histories of Italy by Guicciardini and Sigonio.[26] Henry III of France also owned Emili and Guicciardini.[27]

---

22. R. Weiss, *Humanism in England during the Fifteenth Century* (Oxford, 1941; second ed., 1957), p. 94.

23. K. Csapodi-Gárdonyi, *Die Bibliothek des Johannes Vitéz* (Budapest, 1984). The humanists are Biondo, Boccaccio, Ficino, Fonte, Marzio, Pius II, Poggio, Publico and Vergerio.

24. M. Schiff, *La bibliothèque du marquis de Santillane* (Paris, 1905), nos. 52–54.

25. G. K. Knod, *Aus der Bibliothek des Beatus Rhenanus* (Leipzig, 1889). The fifteen were Andrelini, Beroaldo, Ficino, Filelfo, Guarino, Battista Guarino, Leto, Perotti, Pico, Platina, Poggio, Sabellico, Valla, Vergerio and Polydore Vergil.

26. 'Concept till inventarium öfver Konung Erik XIV.s Böcker', *Handlingar rörende Skandinaviens Historia*, 27 (1845), pp. 380–90; cf. G. Annell, *Erik XIV.s Etiska Föreställningar* (Uppsala, 1945); G. F. Warner ed., 'The Library of James VI', *Publications of the Scottish History Society*, 15 (1893), pp. xi–lxxv.

27. F. Boucher, *Société et mentalités autour de Henri III*, 4 vols. (Lille-Paris, 1981), p. 864.

It is a little more surprising to find an advocate at the Parlement of Paris, a certain Jean Le Féron, owning almost as many humanist texts as Beatus Rhenanus, while Thomas Cranmer possessed works by eleven Italian humanists, including Crinito and Vergerio on education, Ficino's letters, and Platina's *History of the Popes*.[28] More striking still is the fact that the Spanish architect Juan de Herrera, who died in 1597, owned not only Italian books on art and architecture but also what the inventory calls Alberti's 'moral works', Biondo's *Rome Triumphant*, Camillo on memory and Zarlino on music. However, Herrera had studied humanities in his youth at the University of Valladolid.[29]

Public and private collections of books attest a growing acquaintance with Italian humanism in university circles. In 1467, for example, Vienna university library acquired Valla's *Elegantiae*, Biondo's *Rome Restored*, and Barzizza's *Letters* (a book which is known to have gone through at least fifteen editions before 1500).[30] In Cambridge in 1473, 'the would-be student of the new learning' would have found nothing relevant in the University Library 'save a single copy of the *De Remediis* of Petrarch', but the situation was soon to change and the libraries of the university and the colleges still contain thirty-seven sixteenth-century copies of Valla's *Elegantiae* and forty-six of Platina's *Popes*.[31]

As for private libraries, if it is possible to generalise from the example of Cambridge, we may conclude that foreign students and teachers frequently owned books by Italian humanists. A recent study of the books mentioned in Cambridge inventories in the sixteenth and early seventeenth centuries reveals forty-three references to Valla's *Elegantiae*, nineteen to Platina's *History of the Popes*, ten to Ficino and seven to Pico.[32] Although it was Valla's *Annotations on the New Testament* which made the biggest impression on Erasmus, it was, understandably, his *Elegantiae*, a Latin grammar, which had the widest diffusion. It was one of the first books to be printed at the press at the Sorbonne set up in 1470, and it went through at least forty-five editions outside Italy in just over a century.[33] As for Platina, his 'far from

28. R. Doucet, *Les bibliothèques parisiennes au 16e siècle* (Paris, 1956); G. E. Duffield ed., *The Work of Thomas Cranmer* (Appleford, 1964), ch. 10.

29. J. Ruiz de Arcante, *J. De Herrera* (Madrid, 1936), pp. 153–70.

30. Overfield, *Humanism and Scholasticism*, p. 128; *Gesamtkatalog der Wiegendrucke*, 3 (Leipzig, 1928), nos 3675–89.

31. T. Oates, *History of Cambridge University Library* (Cambridge 1986), p 29; H. M. Adams, *Catalogue of the Books Printed on the Continent of Europe 1501–1600 in Cambridge Libraries*, 2 vols. (Cambridge, 1967).

32. E. Leedham-Green, *Books in Cambridge Inventories*, 2 vols. (Cambridge, 1987), 2, pp. 343, 618, 624, 770.

33. This minimum has been arrived at by conflating the editions mentioned in Adams with those in the Bibliothèque Nationale and the British Library. The century runs from c. 1471 to 1577.

uncritical' history of the popes was of obvious interest to the Protestant academics of Cambridge, Basel, and elsewhere.[34]

The importance of non-Italian editions of Italian humanist texts deserves emphasis. Most of the copies of works by Valla, Biondo, Ficino and other Italian thinkers and scholars to be found in public or private libraries outside Italy had in fact been printed outside Italy, most of them by a small group of printers who specialised in texts of this kind. Obvious names to cite are Bade and Estienne in Paris, Gryphius in Lyons, and Amerbach, Froben and Petri in Basel. These families played a crucial role as intellectual middlemen between Italy and Northern Europe and they were themselves actively involved in the humanist movement. Josse Bade, for example, had studied with Battista Guarino at Ferrara before setting up shop in Paris. Bade's daughter married Robert Estienne, who wrote books as well as printing them and was on friendly terms with leading French humanists such as Budé and Vatable.[35] Sebastian Gryphius, a German who settled in Lyons, employed Dolet and Rabelais to help him with his publication of classical and humanist texts. Johann Froben of Basel was the friend of Erasmus and the employer of Beatus Rhenanus. Bonifacius Amerbach, also of Basel, studied under Alciati before becoming a printer and he was a friend and disciple of Erasmus, indeed his heir in the legal as well as the intellectual sense. Less is known about the life of Henric Petri, but in the course of a long business career in Protestant Basel he did publish the works of at least ten Italian humanists.[36]

## IV

A student at St Andrews in 1478, a certain Gilbert Haldane, owned a copy of Guarino's *Praecepta de studendi ordine*, which might be translated, a little freely, as 'How to Study'.[37] This example may serve as a reminder that many if not all the editions of Italian humanists discussed above were intended to be used in schools and universities.

The contribution of the schools to the spread of the concepts, methods and values of Italian humanists was obviously crucial but is naturally impossible to measure. Discussions of the subject are generally limited to a few model schools for which the evidence is relatively

---

34. D. Hay, *Annalists and the Historians* (1977), p. 105.

35. E. Armstrong, *Robert Estienne* (Cambridge, 1954; reprint Sutton Courtenay, 1986).

36. Cardano, Crinito, Ficino, Leoniceno, Petrarch, Pico, Pius II, Pomponazzi, Sabellico, Valla. He also published Aretino and Guicciardini in Latin translations. On Italian humanism and Basel printers, P. G. Bietenholz, *Der italienische Humanismus und die Blütezeit des Buchdrucks in Basel* (Geneva, 1959).

37. J. Durkan and A. Ross, *Early Scottish Libraries* (Glasgow, 1961), p. 110.

precise; the schools of Vittorino da Feltre in Mantua, Guarino of Verona in Ferrara, St Paul's in London, the Collège de Guyenne in Bordeaux, and the Gymnasium at Strasbourg.

St Paul's school was founded by John Colet about 1509, and its statutes are a kind of manifesto opposing 'literature' to barbarism and 'blotterature'. Colet had visited Italy, as we have seen, he was in touch with the humanists there and so was his first high master, William Lily, a former pupil of Pomponio Leto. The Collège de Guyenne was reorganised in 1534 and its teachers included two men who would become famous scholars, George Buchanan and Marc-Antoine Muret. As for Strasbourg, its gymnasium was under the direction of the humanist Johann Sturm for more than forty years, 1538–81, and its teachers included the expatriate Italian Protestants ('humanists' in some respects at least), Pietro Martire Vermigli and Girolamo Zanchi. In 1545 the school had 644 pupils.[38]

It would not be difficult to extend this list of humanist schools. The 'Valla test' would allow us to add, among others, the grammar school at Auch and Cardinal College, Ipswich (a short-lived foundation of Cardinal Wolsey's). Specialists in East-Central Europe have pointed out the importance of St Elizabeth's in Wrocław from the late fifteenth century onwards, and of the school of the Virgin Mary at Buda between 1480 and the Turkish conquest of Hungary in 1526.[39] The schools headed by distinguished humanists included Deventer under Alexander Hegius and Westminster under William Camden. In the case of sixteenth-century France, it has recently been argued that the municipal schools of Amiens, Béziers, Chartres, Grenoble, Mende, Narbonne, Nimes, Rennes, Sens, Troyes, Vienne and elsewhere inculcated humanist values, and it would no doubt be possible to extend the list much further.[40]

It remains difficult to say how seriously the teachers took Italian humanism (let alone how seriously the students took the teachers). In these respects, Renaissance universities are somewhat better documented.

The traditional picture of the European universities of the fifteenth and sixteenth centuries is not one of the spread of Italian humanism, but of resistance to it. We have the humanists themselves to thank for this picture, immortalised in the *Epistles of Obscure Men* and in *Pantagruel*. They had a point, which will be discussed in more detail in the

---

38. A. Schindling, 'Die humanistische Bildungsreform in der Reichstädten Strassburg, Nürnberg und Augsburg' in W. Reinhard ed., *Humanismus in Bildungswesen des 15 und 16 Jahrhunderts* (Weinheim, 1984).

39. G. Bauch, *Das Schutwesen in Breslau* (Breslau, 1909); I. Mészáros, *XVI századi városi iskoláink* (Budapest, 1981).

40. G. Huppert, *Public Schools in Renaissance France* (Urbana and Chicago, 1984).

next section, but they did of course exaggerate for comic and polemical effect. The academic career of Rabelais himself, who taught at Montpellier, is a reminder not to identify all the inhabitants of French universities with the most violent opponents of humanism. There were, as we have seen, Italian humanists teaching in Paris, Heidelberg, Oxford, Vienna and elsewhere, and they were of course appointed to these posts by the local academics. Some of the foreigners who discovered humanism in Italy returned to teach in universities at home.

In some universities, such as Erfurt, we find the *studia humanitatis* introduced into the curriculum at a relatively early stage. In Cracow, the arts faculty was reformed in 1449 by Jan Dąbrowski, who was an admirer of the educational programme set out by P. P. Vergerio in his treatise *De ingenuis moribus*.[41] Orations in praise of the *studia humanitatis* were delivered at the university of Heidelberg in 1456, by Peter Luder, who had recently returned from a long stay in Italy, and at the university of Vienna two years later, by Georg Peurbach.[42] Yet humanists and humanism seem to have remained on the periphery of the universities.

One sign of the continuing resistance to humanism, as well as of the efforts to break it, is the foundation of new institutions to teach what the humanists recommended – new universities and new colleges, in which the pressure of tradition was lower than elsewhere. A few examples are well known: Vienna, Wittenberg, Alcalá, Oxford, Louvain, and Paris.

At the university of Vienna, an autonomous college of poets and mathematicians was founded by the Emperor Maximilian in 1501 at the request of the 'arch-humanist' Conrad Celtis.[43] The university founded at Wittenberg in Saxony in 1502 was not, apparently, intended as a new kind of institution and it was originally organised on traditional lines, but within a few years a small group of humanists came to play an important role there, which continued long after Wittenberg became the first Protestant university. Georg Spalatin (adviser to the Elector of Saxony and a friend of Luther's) and Philip Melanchthon (appointed professor of Greek at Wittenberg, thanks to Luther's support, in 1518) were committed to the ideals of humanism as well as Protestantism.[44]

The new university of Alcalá, which opened in 1508, was modelled on the university of Paris, but as at Wittenberg the humanists were able

---

41. Zarebski, 'L'Italia nel primo umanesimo polacco', in M. Brahmer ed., *Italia, Venezia e Polonia tra umanesimo e rinascimento* (Warsaw, 1967), pp. 35–57.

42. Overfield, *Humanism and Scholasticism*, pp 65–9.

43. L. W. Spitz, *Conrad Celtis, the German Arch-Humanist* (Cambridge, Mass., 1957), pp 68–70.

44. E. G. Schwiebert, 'New Groups and Ideas at the University of Wittenberg', *Archiv für Reformationsgeschichte*, 49 (1958), pp 60–78; M. S. Grossmann, *Humanism in Wittenberg, 1485–1517* (Nieuwkoop, 1975).

to play an unusually important part, and the new foundation included the college of San Ildefonso, with its chairs in the three languages of the Bible, Hebrew, Greek and Latin. The chair of Latin was occupied by the distinguished humanist Antonio Nebrija, an admirer of Poliziano and Pico who had spent nearly a decade in Italy.[45] San Ildefonso seems to have been the model for the trilingual college at the university of Louvain, founded in 1517 by the provisions of the will of Jérôme de Busleyden, a leading statesman and churchman and a former student at the university of Padua (the subject he studied was law, but his later interests suggest that the humanists there had some influence on him).[46] In the same year, the English bishop Richard Foxe founded Corpus Christi College at Oxford, with lecturers in the humanities (*lector artium humanitatis*), Greek, and theology (rather than Hebrew), a rough parallel to the Louvain foundation.[47] Finally Francis I, encouraged by the leading humanist Guillaume Budé, in 1530 appointed *lecteurs royaux* in Latin, Greek and Hebrew, as a fifth column (or as the humanists would have said, a 'Trojan horse') within the university.[48]

Personal contacts with Italian humanists and the study of their books do not exhaust the channels through which their ideas 'flowed', and academic milieux were not the only ones in which these ideas were discussed or put into practice. Among the institutions which deserve a place in this survey are academies, courts, chanceries and monasteries.

Academies were small discussion groups, more or less formally organised, including amateur and professional scholars, writers and philosophers. Modelled on Italian groups such as Ficino's Platonic Academy just outside Florence and Leto's academy in Rome, these groups included the literary clubs (*sodalitates*) founded at Heidelberg and Vienna by the poet Conrad Celtis, and the court academies associated with Charles IX and Henry III of France.[49] Unfortunately their discussions were rarely recorded. The same goes for the less academic salons whose members discussed neoplatonism. If the poems of Du Bellay and Ronsard are anything to go by, these discussions owed little more than their initial inspiration to Italian humanists such as Ficino.[50]

The existence of palace academies is a reminder that courts as well

---

45. M Bataillon, *Erasme et l'Espagne* (Paris, 1937); B. Hall, 'The Trilingual College of San Ildefonso', *Studies in Church History*, 5 (1969), pp 114–46.

46. H. de Vocht, *Jerome de Busleyden* (Turnhout, 1950).

47. J. K. McConica ed., *The History of the University of Oxford*, 3 (Oxford, 1986), p 21.

48. R. Knecht, *Francis I* (Cambridge, 1982), pp 238–9.

49. Spitz, *Celtis*, pp 45f; F. Yates, *French Academies of the Sixteenth Century* (1947); R. J. Sealy, *The Palace Academy of Henry III* (Geneva, 1981).

50. R. V. Merrill and R. J. Clements, *Platonism in French Renaissance Poetry* (New York, 1957).

as schools and universities helped spread some at least of the ideals of Italian humanists. Erasmus was doubtless exaggerating when he described the court of Henry VIII as 'the seat and citadel of humane studies', but it has already been suggested that Matthias of Hungary, the Emperor Maximilian, Francis I, and other monarchs could and did do a good deal for them.

An associated institution, which deserves closer study from this point of view is the chancery. The art of writing an eloquent letter in good classical Latin was increasingly appreciated by rulers and by the aristocracy, with the result that humanists were employed as secretaries and that chanceries became settings for the transmission of Renaissance rhetoric. In the early fifteenth century, in the chancery of the duke of Berry, for example, Jean de Montreuil was able to show the skills he had learned from his Italian friends Salutati and Poggio.[51] In the later fifteenth century, János Vitéz, who was chancellor to King Matthias, introduced to the royal secretaries the classical models of letter-writing which he had doubtless learned in his student days in Italy. Piotr Tomicki, whose enthusiasm for Italy earned him the nickname 'the Italian', made similar innovations a few years later in the chancery of the king of Poland. Charles V's chancellor, Mercurino de Gattinara, made good political use of the rhetorical skills of the Spanish humanist Alonso de Valdés.

Like the universities, the monasteries of the Renaissance have had rather a bad press. Despite Poggio's notorious remarks about classical manuscripts left to gather dust in monastic libraries, let alone Erasmus's haste to leave the cloister of Steyn, it would seem that convents might on occasion offer a favourable environment for the *studia humanitatis*, at least when they had abbots like John Whethamstede of St Albans (a friend of Humphrey duke of Gloucester and a collector of Italian books), and Johannes Trithemius of Sponheim and Würzbürg, a friend of Celtis, Pirckheimer and Reuchlin and a considerable scholar in his own right.[52] It was, incidentally, as an abbess that Willibald Pirckheimer's sister Charitas was able to sustain her humanist interests.

## V

The preceding pages have attempted to assemble evidence, as precise as the surviving sources permit, for foreign interest in the achievements of Italian humanists. The attempt risks giving an exaggerated impression of this interest, which was not shared by all the scholars and

51. E. Ornato, *Jean Muret et ses amis* (Paris, 1969), p 81n.
52. Weiss, *Humanism in England*, pp 30–8; N. Brann, *The Abbot Trithemius* (Leiden, 1981).

writers of Europe at this time. Visitors to Italy did not necessarily return converted to humanism, and scholars with works by humanists in their libraries often owned books by scholastic philosophers as well and might have preferred their ideas. Some scholars were ignorant of the existence of the humanists, others indifferent to them, others openly opposed to their work. It is important not to forget the existence of this opposition, which was as much an obstacle to the dissemination of their ideas as the physical difficulties of communication.

The opposition was strong, or at least extremely vocal, in a number of European universities. In Vienna in the 1450s, a certain Conrad Söldner launched an attack on the philology of Guarino and Valla, complaining that 'the Italians are occupied in studies of this kind of vanity'.[53] The famous *Letters of Obscure Men* reminds us that in the early years of the sixteenth century the value of the study of poetry and Hebrew were questioned (or more exactly, attacked with violence) by men in leading positions in some German universities, from Cologne to Leipzig. The existence at Oxford of a group hostile to Greek studies, calling themselves 'Trojans', can be documented from Thomas More's famous reply to them in 1518.[54] At the university of Louvain in the 1520s, a certain Frans Tillemans, lecturing on Scripture, denounced what he called the errors of recent scholars, in other words the emendations to the Vulgate put forward by Valla, Lefèvre and Erasmus.[55] At the university of Paris in the 1530s, the theologians of the Sorbonne, led by Noel Beda, tried to prevent the newly-appointed *lecteurs royaux* from lecturing on Scripture.[56]

This academic opposition was part of a larger movement, or, if 'movement' is too precise a term in this context, a wave of hostility to innovation and to foreigners, especially Italians. This xenophobia seems to have been particularly strong in courts where Italians were numerous, from France under Catherine de' Medici to Poland under Zygmunt August. As the Protestant Reformation made more and more converts, hostility to the two Romes, pagan and papist, tended to merge, and the criticism of humanists to become louder.

This is not to say that the Reformation put an end to the humanist movement. Luther was no enemy of the *studia humanitatis*. Indeed, he encouraged Melanchthon's efforts to give the university of Wittenberg a humanist curriculum, and he believed that the revival of antiquity was

---

53. Overfield, *Humanism and Scholasticism*, pp 120–3.
54. E. F. Rogers ed., *The Correspondence of Sir Thomas More* (Princeton, 1947), pp 111–20.
55. J. Bentley, 'New Testament Scholarship at Louvain in the Early Sixteenth Century', *Studies in Medieval and Renaissance History*, 2 (1979), pp 51–79.
56. M. A. Screech, *Rabelais* (1979), p 44.

a necessary precondition of the Reformation.[57] Calvin, who had undergone a humanist training (as his commentary on Seneca shows), became suspicious of *les sciences humaines*, as he called them, as examples of vain curiosity, but it remained perfectly possible for scholars such as Henri Estienne or François Hotman to combine their humanist interests with their allegiance to the reformed religion.[58]

In Catholic Europe the story is similar. The Counter-Reformation did not put an end to the humanist movement. It is true that the humanists suffered a major defeat at the Council of Trent in 1563, in the sense that the Vulgate was reaffirmed to be the official translation of the Bible, rather than being replaced by a new translation from the original Greek and Hebrew. The notorious Index of Prohibited Books, which was promulgated after the Council, included works by a number of Italian humanists, as well as Erasmus.

In that sense the Trojans triumphed, but their triumph was not complete and it would be unwise to assume that 1563 marked a sharp break with the humanist past. The classics continued to appear in new editions edited by scholars of the calibre of Justus Lipsius and Isaac Casaubon, and to be taught in grammar schools from Rome to Geneva. The importance of the classics in the curriculum of Jesuit schools is well known.[59] It has been argued that the Jesuits offered the shadow rather than the substance of the *studia humanitatis*. 'They recognised that humanism had come to stay. So they mastered it, drained it of its dangerous content, and turned it into decorative learning for the Roman Church and the Christian Prince.'[60]

However, this interpretation (like the traditional view of Erasmus and other northerners as 'Christian' humanists) rests on the now discredited view of the 'real' humanists as essentially pagan or at least worldly. If, however, it is agreed that Petrarch, Salutati, Valla, Ficino and Pico were all concerned to adapt the classical tradition to fit Christianity, it is harder to draw any sharp line between them and the Jesuit (or indeed Calvinist) scholars of the late sixteenth century. Carlo Borromeo, the famous reforming archbishop of Milan, interested as he was in Christian stoicism, now seems closer to humanism than he did fifty years ago, while the great classical scholar Justus Lipsius now seems closer to the Counter-Reformation.

---

57. On Luther and humanism, A. G. Dickens, *The German Nation and Martin Luther* (1974), ch 3.

58. D. R. Kelley, *The Beginning of Ideology; Consciousness and Society in the French Reformation*, (Cambridge, 1981), especially, pp 150–8.

59. F. de Dainville, *L'éducation des jésuites* (Paris, 1978).

60. H. R. Trevor-Roper, *Renaissance Essays* (1985), p 229.

The Jesuits and the Calvinists were of course extremely selective in what they borrowed or appropriated from the classical tradition. My point is – to return to the beginning of this essay – that everyone is selective and that we all interpret new ideas and new information in terms of what we already have. This is not to say that the ideas and methods of the humanists did not seem new; for some people they were, as we have seen, extremely exciting and for others, extremely dangerous. However, in the course of their spread and acceptance these ideas and methods came to be incorporated in the daily routine of teaching, assimilated to what was 'known' or believed already, and, in a word, domesticated. It would seem to be no accident that it was 'the most medieval of Petrarch's works, *De remediis*' which was most popular in fifteenth-century France (as well as being, as we have seen the only work by that author in Cambridge University Library in 1473).[61] The 'civic' humanist Leonardo Bruni was much admired outside his own republican environment, but he was known for his treatise on education rather than for his panegyric on the city of Florence. The anti-papal sonnets of Petrarch naturally took on a new meaning after the Reformation, when they were translated by Protestants.[62] It is also likely that Platina's *History of the Popes* (which had considerable appeal, as we have seen, in English academic circles), came to be viewed as an example of proto-Protestantism. In a similar way, when the Italian Protestant refugee Celio Secundo Curione published his Latin translation of Guicciardini in 1566, he restored the notorious passage on the rise of the Papal States which had been suppressed in the Italian edition, and the passage took on a new significance in the light of the suppression and indeed in the light of the Council of Trent, which had just come to an end.

It is this process of domestication which explains the need felt by many historians of the fifteenth and sixteenth centuries to coin various compound terms such as 'legal', 'medical', 'pragmatic' and even 'chivalric' humanism, hybrid phrases which refer to the many attempts at synthesis between old and new. Despite the contempt of Petrarch, Valla and other humanists for Aristotle and his medieval followers, the 'schoolmen' (*scholastici*), it is not difficult to find eclectic thinkers who try to reach some sort of accommodation between humanism and scholasticism.[63]

---

61. N. Mann, 'Petrarch's Role as Moralist in Fifteenth-Century France', in A. Levi, *Pagan Virtue and the Humanism of the Northern Renaissance*, The Society for Renaissance Studies, Occasional Papers no. 2 (1974), pp 6–28.

62. On translations into Dutch, French and English, C. J. Rasmussen, 'Quietnesse of Minde', *Spenser Studies* I (1980), pp 3–28.

63. Recent studies of such attempts at compromise include C. Schmitt, *Aristotle and the Renaissance* (Cambridge, Mass., 1983), especially ch 4.

There is nothing wrong in talking about the 'spread' of Italian humanism, provided that we remember that this term is a metaphor; or in describing or even mapping its uneven 'penetration' of the different parts of Europe, noting, for example how early it reached Hungary or how late it reached Sweden. What would be a mistake would be to assume that the package of concepts, methods and values we now call 'humanism' was accepted or rejected as a whole. This essay has tried to suggest that the package broke open in transit and that some of its contents were put to uses which might well have surprised Leonardo Bruni or even Lorenzo Valla.

# Appendix I
## Italian humanists abroad (the date is of the first known visit abroad)

| | | | |
|---|---|---|---|
| 1411 | Loschi in Germany | 1487 | P. M. d'Anghiera in Spain |
| 1414 | Poggio and Vergerio in Germany | 1487 | Bonfini in Hungary |
| | | 1488 | Andrelini in Paris |
| 1431 | Enea Silvio in Scotland | 1489 | Fontius in Hungary |
| 1432 | Guiniforte Barzizza in Spain | 1489 | Brandolini in Hungary |
| | | 1493 | Collenuccio in Germany |
| 1436 | Frulovisi in England | c. 1502 | P. Vergil in England |
| 1454 | Surigone in England | c. 1505 | Ammonio in England |
| 1456 | Tifernate in France | 1508 | Aleandro in Paris |
| c. 1458 | A. Decembrio in Spain | 1518 | Bibbiena in France |
| 1465 | Marzio in Hungary | 1518 | Alciati in France |
| 1465 | Publicio in Portugal | 1522 | Alamanni in France |
| 1469 | Callimaco in Poland | 1525 | Castiglione in Spain |
| 1470s | Vitelli and Lorenzo da Savona in England | 1526 | Navagero in Spain |
| | | 1530 | Camillo in France |
| 1476 | Beroaldo in Paris | 1542 | Curione in Switzerland |
| 1477 | R. Maffei in Hungary | 1547 | P. M. Vermigli and Ochino in England |
| c. 1478 | Traversagni in England | | |
| 1480 | Ugoletti in Hungary | 1549 | Vergerio in Switzerland |
| 1481 | Carmeliano in England | 1552 | Cardano in Britain |
| 1483 | Emili in France | 1570s | Patrizzi in Spain |
| 1484 | Balbo in France | 1574 | F. Sozzini in Switzerland |
| 1484 | Marineo in Spain | 1577 | Bruno in France |
| 1485 | Cataldo Parisio in Portugal | 1578 | F. Sozzini in Poland |
| 1485 | Pico in France | | |
| 1486 | E. Barbaro in Netherlands | | |

# Appendix 2
## foreign scholars in Italy

1417 Nicholas of Cusa
1428 Pedro of Portugal
1430 Heimberg
c. 1430 Ludziska
1434 Luder
1437 Laubing, Grzegorz of
      Sanok
1439 Nuño de Guzmán
c. 1439 Margarit
1444 Eyb
1445 Grey
1446 Flemmyng
c. 1447 Alfonso de Palencia
1447 Janus Pannonius
c. 1450 Peurbach, Roth
1455 Váradi
1456 Free
1458 Tiptoft
1458 Tendilla
1460 Nebrija
c. 1460 Regiomontanus
1463 Schedel
c. 1463 Luder
c. 1468 Agricola
1469 J. Pirckheimer
1469 Herbenus
1469 Fichet
1470 Wolf, Karoch
c. 1470 Marulić
1471 Gansfort
c. 1475 Barbosa, J. Amerbach
1480 Urswick
1482 Reuchlin
1482 Peutinger
1484 Gaguin
c. 1486 J. Badius
1486 Buschius
1487 Celtis, Núñez, Linacre
1488 Grocyn, W. Pirckheimer
1489 Teixeira
1491 Lefevre
c. 1492 Lily
1492 Wolf jr
1493 Colet
c. 1494 Mutian, Cayado

1495 Grünpeck
1496 Copernicus
c. 1498 Pace, Tomicki
c. 1500 Bérauld, Brodarics,
        Krzycki, Oecolampadius
1501 Budé, Busleyden
c. 1503 Tunstall
1505 Dantiscus
1506 Erasmus
1506 Lemaire
1506 Tory
c. 1506 Longolius
1507 Bovillus
1509 Champier, Paracelsus
1511 Agrippa
1513 Laski
c. 1513 B. Amerbach
c. 1514 L. de Baif
1515 Aventinus, Glareanus,
     Hutten, Lupset, Sepúlveda
c. 1516 Oldendorp
1519 Pole
1522 Heresbach
c. 1524 Finé
c. 1525 Osorio
1526 Dolet
1527 Wyatt, Widmanstetter
1528 J. Colin
c. 1532 Pole, Starkey, Morison
1534 Gois
1534 Rabelais
1535 Danès
1535 Agustin
1535 Guevara
1536 O. Magnus
c. 1536 Vesalius
c. 1537 H. Junius
1538 Janicki
c. 1538 Holanda
1539 Caius
1540 López de Gómara
c. 1540 T. Smith, Crato
c. 1543 Górnicki
1544 Erastus
1545 Laguna, Thomas

1546    Pibrac
c. 1546    Languet
c. 1547    Amyot
1548    Pasquier, Hoby
1550    Dudith
c. 1550    H. Estienne, Lambin
1553    Sambucus
1554    Muret
1554    Gohorry
1554    Lotichius
1555    Boissard, T. Wilson
1556    Warszewicki
c. 1555    Bornemisza, Cheke
c. 1556    Kochanowski

1557    Brantôme
c. 1560    Goslicki
1563    Dee, J. J. Scaliger
c. 1563    Zamojski
1566    Cujas
1566    Severinus
c. 1567    Lipsius, Sęp-Szaryński
1573    Monau, Sidney, de Thou
c. 1574    Chappuys
c. 1576    Zlataric
1577    Melissus
1580    Montaigne
1588    Jessenius

*Chapter Two*

# Humanism and Reform Movements

## PETER MATHESON

### I

'Erunt omnes θεοδίδακτοι' ('all will be taught by God').[1] Luther's assertion, pegged to a scriptural base, with the key-concept in Greek, sums up the difficulty of relating humanism to the sixteenth-century reform movements. How does one relate culture to faith; Teachers and Poets and Editors and Scholars to Liturgists and Catechists and Pastors and Theologians; educative processes to the alleged workings of God or Satan? Which category is the inclusive one within which the other is being interpreted: humanism or reform? How can we trace the impact of humanism on reform when the interaction of both is so intimate and constant and subtle? Was humanism a John the Baptist movement which preceded and paved the way for reform?[2] Was it a 'third force' side by side with Catholicism and Protestantism?[3] Were the *Spirituali*, or Catholic evangelicals in France or Italy, first and foremost humanists, or Catholics, or even crypto-Protestants?[4]

Such questions may remind us that sixteenth-century men and women moved within a conceptual universe unimaginably different

---

1. *D. Martin Luthers Werke. Kritische Gesamtausgabe* (Weimar, 1883–; henceforth *WA*), *WA* 8, 424/6; cf. John 6[45].

2. Maurer's fine treatment of the young Melanchthon, for example, has 'The Humanist' as the title of vol. I, 'The Theologian' of vol. II; W. Maurer, *Der Junge Melanchthon* (Göttingen, 1967–9).

3. F. Heer, *Die Dritte Kraft: der europäische Humanismus zwischen den Fronten des konfessionellen Zeitalters* (Frankfurt A. M., 1959).

4. P. McNair, *Peter Martyr in Italy: an anatomy of apostasy* (Oxford, 1967).

from our own, and that early modern historians have tended 'to use whatever part of the vocabulary of recent history was not hopelessly *mal à propos* for matters which it could be stretched into covering, and to disregard or fail to organise whatever that vocabulary could not be forced to cover'.[5] The 'fairly shopworn' concepts of humanism and Reformation have come under constant criticism of late.[6] At present, moreover, no agreed framework for the interaction of humanism and the various reform movements – Catholic, Protestant and Radical – exists,[7] and some of the bolder attempts to get beyond a piecemeal treatment carry little conviction.[8]

To begin with, it may be helpful to remember that to relate humanism to reform movements is not to compare like with like, and that a degree of dissymmetry will be evident throughout. Humanists existed, but did 'humanism'? Renaissance historians, not least Denys Hay himself,[9] have insisted that it certainly did not exist as a coherent system of doctrine, or code of values, or series of Five-Year Plans. Humanism convoked no synods, composed no confessions, despatched no commissars to nudge the deviant towards conformity.

Many humanists, like Henricus Cornelius Agrippa (1486–1535), with his interest in the occult and the Cabbala, were too individualistic to relate to any of the major reform movements, or like Johannes Aventinus (1477–1534), whose critical historical works ended up on the Index, were a thorn in the flesh to any and every orthodoxy. Such organisation as the humanists possessed was always inchoate and provisional. Their networks of friendships and correspondences, of sodalities or reading-parties were as fragile as the personal, spiritual, scholarly interests which held them together. They lived precariously

---

5. J. H. Hexter, *Reappraisals in History*, (Chicago, 1979), p. 270.

6. Cf. John Bossy's warning about the use of 'reformation', in *Christianity in the West 1400–1700* (Oxford, 1985); one echoed by many Protestant scholars.

7. Good surveys in S. Ozment, *Reformation Europe: A Guide to Research. Centre for Reformation Research*, (St. Louis, 1982); A. Buck; 'Uberlegungen zum gegenwärtigen Stand der Renaissanceforschung', *Bibliothèque d'Humanisme et Renaissance*, 43 (1981), pp. 7–38; *Itinerarium Italicum: The Profile of the Italian Renaissance in the mirror of its European Transformations*, ed. H. Oberman and T. Brady. (Leiden, 1975); 'Humanismus', article by L. W. Spitz in *Theologische Realenzyklopädie*, XV (Berlin, 1986) esp. pp. 651 ff.

8. Arguing that both humanism and the Reformation challenged the ontological basis of inherited culture William Bouwsma claims that to cope with the resultant anxiety a new approach emerged: 'In both nominalism and humanism, the word, now humanised, created its own cosmos out of crude experience' (W. J. Bouwsma, 'Anxiety and the Formation of Early Modern Culture', in *After the Reformation*, ed. B. C. Malament (Manchester, 1980), p. 234).

9. Definitions of humanism should not be taken as an invitation to confused assumptions about the 'dignity of man' etc.; 'England and the Humanities in the Fifteenth Century', in *Itinerarium Italicum*, p. 306.

on the patronage of the powerful or had to snatch such time and energy as they could spare from other work. Humanism earned no one a living. The humanist moved incognito under the robes of Monk or Councillor, Merchant or Preacher, Lawyer or Scholastic Theologian.

Thus there is nothing comparable with the institutionally anchored outreach of the 'magisterial' Reformations or with the precisely articulated confessional or disciplinary literature of Catholic or Protestant reform. Even the Radical reformers, with their covenants and bans, were well organised by comparison! Thus it is no easy matter to trace the impact of this (agreeably non-totalitarian) humanism on the worship and piety, the creeds and paedagogic systems of the reformers.

Its importance, moreover, can easily be over-estimated. Many humanists, after all, were uninterested in reform. They were 'Poets' or Artists or Musicians, Grammarians or Ciceronians, addicted to good letters and convivial company, to *Pura Locutio* rather than *Vera Intentio*. Certainly there had been a groundswell of moral and religious concern among many humanists in the closing decades of the fifteenth century,[10] but if we define the humanists, in Kristeller's minimalist terms, as those enamoured of the literature and values of the Classical world, and seeking to reflect and propagate them in their own life and work, there is no necessary reason why they should evince any interest in moral or religious reform.

The converse is also true. The tone of countless reform tracts, with their ethical rigorism and torrid polemic and sheaves of biblical quotations, betrays virtually no trace of humanist ideas.[11] Mystical, apocalyptic, ascetic, revivalist and legalist tributaries flowed into the main-stream of reform as much as humanist ones. It was often the simple peasant, the poor, the unlearned, who preached and welcomed 'the Gospel', while the learned, the powerful, the élite (*dye abgescheydenen*) disdained it. The apocalyptic preaching of a Savonarola may have made Pico della Mirandola's hair stand on end, but surely in spite of, not because of his humanism. Classical allusions are scattered throughout Sebastian Brant's *Ship of Fools* but its ascetic, eclectic world is scarcely that of humanism.[12] The rigorist reform programmes of Cardinal Carafa or the devotional tracts of Menno Simons reflect Catholic and Radical programmes which are equally innocent of humanist influences. The fire in the belly of the commoner, of Herr and Frau

---

10. Lewis Spitz refers to 'its practical, didactic and moralistic nature' in Germany: 'The Course of German Humanism,' in *Itinerarium Italicum*, p. 397.

11. One example among many is O. Brunfels, 'Von dem Evangelischem Anstoss/wie und in was gestalt das wort Gottes uffrur mache,' in *Flugschriften des frühen 16. Jahrhunderts*, ed. H. J. Köhler etc. (Zug, 1978).

12. Lewis Spitz, however, sees it as 'a humanistic work' with 'a classical rhetorical structure', 'The Course of German Humanism', *op. cit.*; p. 398.

Omnes, was lit by concern for the common weal, for divine righteousness, for a caring clergy, for a more egalitarian, lay-orientated Church. 'Every Christian has the same power as the Pope!'[13] The scholarly interests of an Erasmus, the Latin or Neo-Latin culture of humanist circles, may have coincided with theirs in the campaign against scholasticism and clerical obscurantism and 'superstition', and in the advocacy of a pure Gospel, but they diverged at countless other points. Reform was indeed married to humanism but it was far from being a monogamous relationship.

The leisurely life-style of the reforming bishop of Carpentras, Jacopo Sadoleto,[14] with its Classical (and Augustinian) ideal of an *otium* devoted to learned reflection, betrays the aristocratic or patrician milieu in which much humanism flourished. At a less exalted level, Johann Egranus, the humanist and mildly reformist preacher of St Mary's, Zwickau, with his criticism of indulgences and of the cult of St Anne, but also his aloofness and social conservatism, may be quite as typical of humanist reformers as the impatient zeal of Martin Bucer in Strasbourg or Oecolampadius in Basel. Humanism tended to be an urban or courtly affair, embraced by the young and hopeful, or by those of some substance in society, by the better endowed monasteries and the more progressive universities. It may be impossible to limit its appeal to a certain 'class' in society, but it lacked the populist character of the early Lutheran movement, except where, as in South West Germany and Switzerland, it joined hands with religious revival and social reform.[15]

Yet when all that can be said by way of qualification has been said it remains true that neither the Catholic, nor the Lutheran nor the Reformed renewals of Church piety, praxis and doctrine are conceivable without the input and impact of humanist tools, skills and perspectives. E. W. Kohls speaks of the Erasmian reform movement flowing almost without a break into the evangelical movement.[16] P. G.

---

13. Hans Maurer ('Karsthans'), quoted in Franziska Conrad's pioneering study of peasant religiosity in Alsace, *Reformation in der bäuerlichen Gesellschaft: zur Reception reformatorischer Theologie in Elsass* (Veröff. d. Instituts fur europäische Geschichte, Mainz, 116; Stuttgart, 1984), p. 77; cf. also P. Blickle, *Gemeindereformation: die Menschen des 16. Jahrhunderts auf dem Weg zum Heil* (Oldenbourg-Munich, 1985).

14. R. M. Douglas, *Jacopo Sadoleto, 1477–1547; Humanist and Reformer* (Cambridge, Mass., 1959).

15. One suspects that A. G. Dickens, *The German Nation and Martin Luther*, (1974) will become a classical treatment of this; Robert Scribner has demonstrated that the verbalism of humanism had to be supplemented by image and ritual if the masses were to be reached; *For the Sake of Simple Folk: Popular Propaganda for the German Reformation* (Cambridge, 1981).

16. 'Erasmus und die werdende evangelische Bewegung des sechzehnten Jahrhunderts', *Scrinium Erasmianum. Mélanges historiques*, ed. J. Coppens, (Leiden, 1969), I, p. 206.

Bietenholz agrees that there was a natural alliance between the Erasmian emphasis on inner piety and Luther's doctrine of justification by faith, creating a sort of silent majority which came to believe that 'the truth cannot be suppressed; and what upright people decide in the stillness of their hearts will have its weight for future generations, too'.[17] The tarring of Erasmian reform movements with a Lutheran brush in Spain and their consequent suppression in the 1530s is an indirect attestation of the correctness of this view. Yet Catholic reform itself, in Italy, in England, Germany, the Netherlands and Spain also owed a massive debt to humanism; and not least because the synthesis had been so generally and attractively incorporated in the person of Erasmus himself. The older view that there was a sharp discontinuity between humanist and Protestant concerns no longer seems to carry conviction.[18] Within the Radical Reformation the situation is more complex; among the anti-trinitarians and the *spirituali* such as Juan de Valdés one actually finds some of the best examples of a near fusion of humanist and reformist concerns;[19] but there is also a sharply anti-intellectualist current, summed up by the widespread slogan '*die gelehrten – die verkehrten*': 'the learned – the perverted'.

What then, were the areas in which the humanist contribution to reform was most clearly seen? For decades, first of all, they had been quietly accustoming people to the secular pursuit of holiness.[20] The exaggerated claims for the influence of the Brethren of the Common Life in propagating a lay, humanist spirituality north of the Alps may no longer be acceptable,[21] but their contribution as editors of Classical

---

17. Erasmus/Reuchlin, 8/11/1520, Ep. 1155/15 ff, quoted in Bietenholz, 'Luther und die Stillen in Land,' *Bibliothèque d'Humanisme et Renaissance*, 47 (1985), pp. 27–46; cf. P. Lefèvre, 'La lecture des oeuvres d'Érasme au sein du bas clergé durant la première moitié du XVI siècle' (*Scrinium Erasmianum* I, 84–91) who argues for a similar smooth transaction from Erasmian to evangelical views in Hainault.

18. Apart from a fairly isolated voice like that of Georget Livet who argues that the forces unleashed by the love of good letters rapidly 'connurent un cheminement d'agressivité exclusive et violente manifestée hors de l'humanisme chrétien', the 'temps humain' of the Old Church being replaced by Luther's 'temps divin' ('Humanisme Allemand Réforme et Civilisation Européenne', in *XVIII<sup>e</sup> Colloque International de Tours: L'Humanisme Allemand (1480–1540)* (Humanistische Bibliothek Reihe I, Bd. 38; Munich/Paris, 1979), pp. 16, 18).

19. A good English translation by A. M. Mergal of *A Dialogue on Christian Doctrine, One Hundred* and *Ten Considerations,* and *The Christian Alphabet* in G. H. Williams, A. M. Mergal (eds.) *Spiritual and Anabaptist Writers* (Library of Christian Classics, XXV, 1957), pp. 297–390.

20. *The Pursuit of Holiness in late medieval and Renaissance Religion,* ed. C. Trinkaus, with H. Oberman (Leiden, 1974).

21. Cf. the revisionist work of R. R. Post, *The Modern Devotion, Confrontation with Reformation and Humanism* (1968).

texts, for example, cannot be doubted. Secondly, the gradual shift from a scholastic, or philosophically-based theology to a 'positive' one, based on the Scriptures and other early Christian literature, was contributed to by countless humanists. The emergence of 'Biblical humanism' at the turn of the century was a most astonishing phenomenon. The platform was laid here for an alternative culture. Given the intense difficulty of the Hebrew language, for example, or of Pauline thought, or of the linguistic, historical, and hermeneutical problems of understanding the Bible, there are few more surprising and dramatic events in cultural history than this breakthrough to a fresh, contextual approach to the Scriptures. John Colet, Dean of St Paul's in London, with his historical, personal approach; Jacob Wimpheling (1450–1528) drawing on the Classics; Jacques Lefèvre, combining careful scholarship with a mystical and devotional sensitivity, the Hebraist and Cabbalist Reuchlin (1455–1522), and many others, all paved the way for the reform programmes of Erasmus, Luther and the Radicals – for their extraordinary, single-minded concentration on the Bible.

Thirdly, the close collaboration between the humanists and the new printing presses provided the reformers with their libraries, with the editions and translations of the Greek and Latin Classics, of the Early Christian Fathers, of Judaic and Rabbinic writings. Here, speaking for many, is the young Thomas Müntzer writing to his bookseller in Leipzig in 1520: 'Tell me how much I owe you for the chronicle of Eusebius, and what the price is of the collected works of Jerome, and of the letters and sermons of Saint Augustine . . . I would be very indebted if you would send me the acts of the Council of Constance and at the same time the acts of the Council of Basel, unbound'.[22] Zwingli's passion for buying books is typical. John à Lasco, the Reformed theologian of Polish descent, at home in the sacred and secular literature of the Greek, Latin and Hebrew Classics, acquired in 1525 the rights to Erasmus' library.[23]

Then, again, the Hebrew and Greek languages of the Law and the Prophets, of the Gospels and Epistles, painfully acquired without benefit of good dictionaries and grammar, were seen, as by Luther, as the sheath of the Spirit. The ideal of the *vir trilinguis* was cordially embraced by Zwingli. Probably the only major Protestant reformer without considerable language skills was John Knox! Likewise the Catholic Reformers of Spain, France, Italy laid great emphasis on access

---

22. Thomas Müntzer/Achatius Glov, 3/1/1520, G. Franz (ed.), *Thomas Müntzer: Schriften und Briefe* (Gutersloh, 1968), p. 353 (my translation); since 1489 editions of Augustine, Ambrose, Cassiodorus, Jerome, Tertullian etc. had been appearing.

23. J.-C. Margolin, 'Laski, lecteur du "Nouveau Testament" d'Erasme,' *Scrinium Erasmianum*, I, 95 f.

to the original text. The unmuddied springs of God's unique self-revelation could, it was believed, be opened up by means of the new humanist philology and literary skills.

Thus Biblical humanism and the call for reform began to fuse. By the early 1520s even rural congregations in Southern Germany were demanding the pure preaching of Scripture.[24] In the cities a regular cult of the exegetical sermon developed, the Renaissance adulation of the Greek and Latin Classics being transferred to Christianity's Apostolic Classics. Ciceronianism and Biblicism were fruits from the same tree.

Among Erasmians such Biblicism was tempered by respect for the Church Fathers and the *consensus fidelium*. McConica speaks of the 'essentially social character of the activity of the Holy Spirit' for Erasmus, the sense that the scholar has to temper his individual judgement to the corporate identity and wisdom of the Church.[25] This is true also of many of the *spirituali*, though for Juan de Valdès and his followers, who have little time for the institutional Church, it is replaced by a more mystical vein.[26] Calvin, on the other hand, is quite clear that he is authorised by Scripture to speak as he does, and is no mere 'poet or orator'.[27] This implacable assurance of possessing divine authority points, perhaps, to some of the dangers of the humanist principle of returning 'ad fontes'. In the chaste, largely Scriptural formulations of the Council of Trent, on the other hand, the indirect influence of the humanist critique of scholasticism can be traced, but the authority of Scripture is within the context of tradition and the *magisterium*.[28]

Thus, in its new humanist dress, the Church took on a 'younger' look, the pure, virginal innocence of apostle and martyr, of Alexandrian scholar or North African bishop, while at the same time being linked to the *paideia* of the Ancients, and so more universal and

24. Cf. F. Conrad, *op. cit.*, *passim*.

25. He quotes Erasmus' judgement that Oecolampadius spoke wisely about the Eucharist; 'adderem etiam pium, si quid pium esse posset quod pugnat cum sententia consensuque Ecclesiae . . .' J. K. McConica, 'Erasmus and the Grammar of Consent', *Scrinium Erasmianum* I, 81,96; cf. Allen VI, 1636, p. 206.

26. Valdès' *Christian Alphabet*, for example, has no section on the Church; *Spiritual and Anabaptist Writers* (Library of Christian Classics, XXV) ed. by G. H. Williams (1957), pp. 357–90.

27. Like Ezekiel his exhortations are not like those of 'quelque Poëte ou Orateur', but are to be obeyed as the word of God; Preface to the *Duae Epistolae*, in E. Droz, *Chemins de l'Hérésie*, I, p. 137.

28. *Enchiridion Symbolorum Definitionum et Declarationum de rebus fidei et morum*, ed. H. Denzinger and, A. Schönmetzer (Rome, 1963) p. 364 f; Jean Delumeau actually argues that 'The Council fathers could be said to have had Erasmian leanings', a judgement which would have greatly surprised them; *Catholicism between Luther and Voltaire: a new view of the Counter-Reformation* (1977), p. 10.

generous in its cultural and intellectual appeal. The myth, at least, was convenient. It offered an alternative pattern of piety and churchmanship to that of late medieval populism and scholasticism. Its critical edge against superstition was sharp, its credentials appeared compelling, its ethos positive and constructive.

In practice, of course, the humanists may often have read the Church Fathers largely from a literary or cultural point of view, assuming too readily that the latter shared their own rather uncritical enthusiasm for the Classical world.[29] The fashionable 'Augustinianism' of many humanists cut little theological ice. Martin Greschat, for example, argues that their understanding of Christianity tended to be consistently reductionist.[30] The truth behind this rather schematic view may be that the humanists' scholarly programmes benefited from the alliance with reform as much as the reverse. Both stood to gain from a weakening of the hold of scholastic theology and the traditional forms of monastic and university life which fostered it. Positively, the transition from the sodalities of the humanists, with their love of Scripture and the Fathers, to Catholic or Protestant reform often seemed natural, if not inevitable. The 'violence' of scholasticism[31] was simply replaced by a method of study more appropriate to Scripture. What Juan de Valdès meditated on in the morning with his select group of disciples in Naples, Peter Martyr would preach on publicly in the afternoon.[32] Perhaps the best example of this natural drift from humanist scholarship to popular evangelism is the 'Prophecy' of Zwingli's Zürich, a systematic training in the Hebrew, Greek and Latin texts of Scripture, widely copied elsewhere.[33]

At the heart of the alliance between humanism and reform lies a common concern for education, to whose theory and practice the humanists had contributed so much – an education often imaginatively conceived, for women as well as men, ordinary folk as well as the university student or Latin school pupil, of the laity as well as the cleric. For Thomas More or Philip Melanchthon the idea of a disciplined, holistic education appears much the same: it is to prepare one for service to the commonwealth and for the true worship of God. The enlightened prince or magistrate would spread the new learning to his

---

29. A. Buck argues that the Church Fathers used the Classics *victoris iure*, and were considerably misunderstood by the humanists; *op. cit.*, p. 33.

30. M. Greschat, 'Humanistisches Selbstbewusstsein und reformatorische Theologie', *XVIII*ᵉ *Colloque International de Tours* (Munich, 1979), p. 372–86.

31. *Quod violentum est studium, maxime philosophiae*, Luther on scholastic speculations, *WA*, Br I, 17⁴⁰⁻⁴, quoted in H. Junghans, *Der Junge Luther und die Humanisten* (Göttingen, 1985), p. 163.

32. P. McNair, *op. cit.*, p. 150.

33. Cf. G. R. Potter, *Zwingli*, (Cambridge, 1976), pp. 221–4.

grateful subjects through school and pulpit. Society's hierarchies and harmonies would be affirmed but purified. The leading Swiss humanist, Glareanus (1488–1563), who spent his life editing the Classics, and liberally endowed scholarships to promote the cause of Catholic reform, is typical of many others. Martin Luther's passionate advocacy of good libraries in every town, of teaching children music and poetry and all the arts of learning as '*lust und spiel*', 'fun and games', rests on the conviction that the devil prefers ignorance and that these present times are a 'true year of gold', a rich harvest of scholarship being providentially provided to coincide with the recovery of the Gospel.[34] Our modern distinction between education and piety has scant relevance to the sixteenth century.

The old contrast between the piety of Erasmus, coming from his *Devotio Moderna* roots, and his Renaissance scholarship;[35] or between the sober religious form of humanism in the North of Europe and its more sensual, worldly form in Italy,[36] can no longer be sustained. It was precisely the piety of a Colet, an Erasmus, a Bucer or Melanchthon which owed most to humanism. The cult of relics and miracles was replaced by a cult of inwardness, of the word. Bullinger's *De Origine Erroris* (1539) developed a whole theology of history, based on a decline from original purity and innocence to an elaborate, outward system of ceremonies.[37] Perhaps Erasmus' greatest contribution to reform was this advocacy of a *pietas litterata*, an educated innocence, a faith centred on a teaching Christ. It has been argued that the roots of this go right back to the Italian Renaissance's emphasis on the *imago Dei*,[38] the inherent dignity of the human as the image of the divine.

Erasmus himself, after all, was hailed as the regenerator, not only of education and piety, but of theology as well, not least in Spain and England, and his own writings lend not a little support to this claim.

---

34. *To the Councilmen of all cities in Germany that they establish and maintain Christian schools, Luther's Works* 45, (Philadelphia, 1962), pp. 347–78.

35. P. Mestwerdt, *Die Anfänge des Erasmus: Humanismus und 'devotio moderna'*, ed. H. von Schubert (Leipzig, 1917).

36. An exaggerated German nationalism lies behind much of this thesis; illuminating in this regard is a sad article by the fine historian Willy Andreas in a secondary school reader at the height of the Third Reich, which sees the Reformation as a break-through (*Aufbruch*) of the German spirit, whose specific characteristics gained the upper hand in Northern humanism: 'Es war die Volkseigenart selber, die sich darin durchsetzte'; Andreas, 'Der deutsche Mensch der Reformation,' *Saat in die Zeit, VII: Ein Lesewerk für Höhere Schulen*, ed. A. Grotz (Düsseldorf, 1940), p. 54; for a recent, positive view of the interaction of the Italian and the Northern Renaissance, cf. C. Trinkaus, *The Scope of Renaissance Humanism* (Ann Arbor, 1983).

37. Heinrich Bullinger, *De origine erroris in divorum et simulachrorum cultu* (Basel, 1529).

38. Cf. C. Trinkaus, *In Our Image and Likeness: Humanity and Divinity in Italian Humanist Thought*, vols I–II, (Chicago, 1970).

From quite an early stage humanists had found themselves brushing with the language, the logic, the 'proofs' of scholastic theology, forced to defend their own literary or scholarly interests, their freedom to pursue authentic text or accurate translation, not to mention correct interpretation, of Aristotle or Plato or Pythagoras. Their preference for a non-philosophical, non-speculative theology had, at least in part, the aim to separate the two realms, to allow Aristotle, for example, to be studied for his own sake, not as the philosophical pillar of a theological edifice. Figures as diverse as Pomponazzi, Lefèvre, the young Luther, shared this aim. Much of the 'attack' on the theology of the schools sought to free the Classical – and to some extent the Hebraic or Rabbinic inheritance – from its domestication, and had little specific interest in developing a new 'theology'.

## II

The 'fronts' between the humanists and the scholastics were seldom clearly defined. Many scholastics were open to humanist influences, were eager to improve their Latinity, welcomed the reformist edge of satires like Reuchlin's *Sergius* on the cult of relics, or themselves actively pursued humanist studies. In the early years of the century humanistic scholastics like Jodokus Trutvetter, Rector of Erfurt in 1501, were far from uncommon. It was a new mood, a new way of 'doing theology', the *via rhetorica* rather than the *via dialectica* that the humanists helped to create. They showed little aptitude or inclination for constructing alternative systems of doctrine or patterns of salvation or forms of churchmanship.

Yet – and here is the rub – as one follows the widening circle of humanist concerns: from grammar and good letters to education, piety and theology, to the grandiose utopias which mirrored the folly of the present and the potential for the future, it becomes progressively more difficult to maintain a consistently minimalist definition of humanism. The conservative features of More's *Utopia*[39] may have been much emphasised of late – its ascetic and monastic aspects – but there is also a growing recognition of the point made long ago by J. H. Hexter that the thoroughly practical component in the humanist concerns found considerable fulfilment in the Calvinist experiments with a godly

---

39. In a recent article, not distinguished for its elegance of diction, Peter Kaufman argues that More's *Utopia*, far from being the 'capstone of the humanist position and protest' against churchly regimentation, 'was a gentle ecclesial remonstrance', a 'muted recognition of the frontiers of humanist spirituality' ('Humanist Spirituality and Ecclesial Reaction: Thomas More's "Monstra"', *Church History* 56 (1987), pp. 33, 37).

society in Geneva and elsewhere.[40] It is clear that, in a multitude of often surprising ways, the new wine of humanism burst through the containers of the received wisdom.

What is much less clear, and quite unresolved in current historiography, is whether the role of humanism in converting the *causa Lutheri* into a national and trans-national *causa Reformationis* was a largely instrumental one, or whether there was a grand humanist design for reform, with its own priorities and presuppositions. Lewis Spitz speaks for many when he dismisses as an outdated cliché the idea that humanists and reformers were opposed to one another, but he identifies at the same time a 'broad chasm' separating the religious assumptions of classical and Christian humanism from those of the Protestant reformers on such matters as the freedom of the will, law and gospel, sin and grace.[41]

Few church historians can be convinced that humanism was not distinguished by a particular anthropology, often characterised as confident, individualistic and moralistic. In his study of the young Melanchthon, for example, Wilhelm Maurer talks of Erasmus' ideal of a moral utopia.[42] At times confessional triumphalism is evident as when the Reformation is described as the 'fate' (Schicksal) of humanism, being an 'infinitely more radical alternative' to it.[43] Humanism is also frequently chastised for its indifferentism in doctrinal matters.[44]

There are, however, genuine issues at stake. While there is little or nothing to support the idea that humanists embraced a Promethean view of humanity, and much to the contrary – *humanitas* not being opposed to *divinitas* – Luther and the Council of Trent are agreed in finding an Erasmus or a Sadoleto deficient in their reading of sin and salvation. Perhaps, as Dresden argues, *humanitas* is less a metaphysical ideal than 'an obstinate determination to do all that is humanly poss-

---

40. 'Utopia and Geneva', in T. K. Robb and J. E. Siegel (ed.), *Action and Conviction in Early Modern Europe: Essays in Memory of E. H. Harbison* (Princeton, 1969) pp. 107–17; cf. also Martin Greschat, who points to the gradual shift of humanist self-consciousness from being a loose union of fellow-spirits (Geistesbund) to becoming a quite specific urban corporation or *conjuratio; op. cit.*, p. 384.

41. 'The Course of German Humanism', in *Itinerarium Italicum* . . . (Brill, 1975), p. 414.

42. *Op. cit.*, II, 440.

43. H. Liebing, 'Die Ausgänge des europäischen Humanismus,' in H. Liebing and K. Scholder eds., *Geist und Geschichte der Reformation*, Arbeiten zur Kirchengeschichte, 38 (Berlin, 1966), pp. 367, 376.

44. Though seldom so crudely as in Erwin Iserloh's claim that 'To the end (Erasmus) gave peace, which benefited his own well-being and that of "good letters", the priority over truth'. *Katholische Reform und Gegen-reformation. Handbuch der Kirchengeschichte IV* (Freiburg, 1967), p. 157; the tendency of church historians to concentrate unduly on Erasmus is very noticeable.

ible'.[45] If so, the question of what *is* humanly possible remains!

There does seem to come a point in many of the leading reformers' lives when humanism loses its ultimacy for them. With its rather florid cult of friendship, its concern for glory in the eyes of contemporaries and posterity, its hero-worship (and its ruinous appetite for expensive books) humanism has many of the characteristics of a youth culture. In Contarini and Zwingli and so many others one notes at a certain stage the onset of 'melancholy', a religious crisis, a greater 'seriousness', a turning towards gloomier Augustinian waters, to the issues of guilt and destiny and death. Classical humanism, it seemed, could offer fewer answers here. The weakness of Erasmian exegesis of Pauline themes and of the Old Testament is a pointer in this direction.

On a social, or ecclesiastical level the humanists' hopes of a harmonious, gradualist, consensus-based reform programme also went sour. In particularly favourable conditions such as those in the imperial cities, where the machinery for structured debate and decision existed, something like consensus could be maintained, but only on a local or regional level. Colloquy broke down elsewhere. The powerful emotions released by religious revival, often yoked with social discontent, brooked no delay; no accommodation, however temporary, to a Church now seen as hopelessly corrupt.[46] The cries for 'moderation' became increasingly ineffectual. Humanism would continue to extend its influence, but after the 1540s only within a confessional context and a divided Christendom.

The way in which the concept of reform was influenced by humanism is perhaps best illustrated by reference to three reformers; Gasparo Contarini (1483–1542), the greatest of the Catholic reformers, Martin Luther (1483–1546), the founding father of Lutheranism, and Thomas Müntzer (1488?–1525), the most original theologian of the Radical Reformation.

Gasparo Contarini incorporates so many of the humanist ideals that it is hard to know where to start. He was educated within a humanist context and upon his death he left behind a magnificent library. He was a fine teacher and scholar, not least of Aristotle. Throughout his life he attracted a circle of humanist friends. As the diplomatic represen-

---

45. 'Érasme et la notion de "humanitas",' in *Scrinium Erasmianum, op. cit.*, pp. 540, 529; he quotes also, p. 530, Erasmus' educational principle that people, too, are works of art: '. . . homines, mihi crede, non nascuntur, sed finguntur' from *De pueris . . . instituendis*, ed. J.-C. Margolin (Geneva, 1966), p. 389.

46. For a brief period at the beginning of the 1540s the Strasbourg reformers astonished Bullinger and Calvin by suggesting a temporising policy of this kind; cf. my forthcoming article in the *Archive for Reformation History* (1989), 'Martyrdom or Mission: a Protestant Debate'.

tative of Venice and then, from May 1535 a reforming cardinal, he managed to combine the determined advocacy of often unpopular policies with the values of scholarly detachment and restraint. His world was that of the patrician, the courtier, the activist. J. B. Ross, however, has pointed to another, all-important side to him:[47] he was a member of a highly intelligent and conscientious group of Christian humanists who sought to live out the Aristotelian and apostolic ideal of friendship, to live sacrificially for others, and to share in a common spiritual quest. Despite a serious and prolonged religious crisis, he remained true to the values of civic humanism and refused the persuasions of some of his friends to join the monastic life.[48] He became an early advocate of the *renovatio ecclesiae*, on the eve of the largely abortive Fifth Lateran Council (1512–17). Savonarolan and *Devotio Moderna* traditions appear to have influenced him. His *De officio episcopi* (1517) criticises the ignorance, superstition, non-residence, and pomposity of the episcopacy; this concern for the pastoral revival of the clergy remained with him to the end of his life.

But he saw his lay, civic and civil duties as being as much part of his discipleship as his devotional life, or his Biblical studies. From the mid-1530s he co-operated with rigorists like Carafa on commissions to reform the Curia, and combed the libraries of Venice for materials to prepare for the projected General Council. This would, he hoped, reform and reunite the Church Catholic and pacify Christendom. At the Colloquy of Regensburg he represented the Papacy of Paul III. For all its failures it was an irenic stone of offence in a confessional century.

He was a humanist, however, not only in his ethos but in his theology. Like so many of the Italian humanists, lay and clerical, men and women, he was an 'Evangelical',[49] building on a base of Biblical humanism a very different, certainly much profounder structure than that of Erasmus. The themes of sin and grace and predestination absorbed him, and gave him considerable sympathy for Luther's soteri-

---

47. 'Gasparo Contarini and his Friends', *Studies in the Renaissance* XVII (1970), pp. 192–232; there is a good review of recent scholarship by G. Fragnito, *Dizionario Biografico degli Italiani* 28, pp. 172–92; the standard biography remains that by Franz Dittrich, *Gasparo Contarini, 1483–1542* (Brunswick, 1885); cf. P. Matheson, *Cardinal Contarini at Regensburg* (Oxford, 1972).

48. H. Jedin, 'Das Turmerlebnis des jungen Contarini', *Historisches Jahrbuch* 70, (1951), pp. 115–30.

49. There are a number of excellent studies on individual 'evangelicals' or *spirituali*; cf. D. Fenlon, *Heresy and Obedience in Tridentine Italy: Cardinal Pole and the Counter-Reformation* (Cambridge, 1972); A. Jacobson Schulte, *Pier Paolo Vergerio: The Making of an Italian Reformer* (Geneva, 1977); P. McNair, *op. cit.*; cf. also Ruth Prelowski's helpful introduction to the *Beneficio di Cristo* in *Italian Reformation Studies in Honor of Laelius Socinus*, ed. J. A. Tedeschi (Florence, 1965), pp. 22–102.

ology, though not his ecclesiology. His 'own' doctrine of double justification did not triumph at the Council of Trent, and some recent appreciations of it have been somewhat chilly,[50] but it has its decided interest as one of the few creative contributions by humanists to sixteenth-century theology. Humanism, then, of the Contarini variety, played a formidable part, not only in fostering Catholic reform, encouraging new patterns of lay and clerical piety, and in preparing the way for the Council of Trent, that is, for structural change, but in offering Catholic hospitality to Biblical criticism, and to theological challenge. In the short term, that is, for four centuries, some of the latter work may have been undone.

The synthetic achievement, however, remained impressive: of Platonic and Aristotelian traditions, of personal piety and social responsibility, of a deep personal loyalty to his Church with a passionate belief in moderation, reason, persuasion, dialogue, Contarini's humanism is conservatism at its most open and attractive. He fostered the myth of Venetian harmony and the anachronistic dream of a reunited Christendom. His aristocratic programme of reform envisages an enlightened élite which would spare the majority too much agonised questioning. His Catholicism and his humanism remain, in the end, quite inseparable.

Martin Luther launched a new culture as well as a new theology. It is one which must be sharply differentiated from the neo-Protestantism of the post-Enlightenment period, but its humanist features are nonetheless prominent, indeed unmistakable: the centrality of Scripture and of verbal communication, the priority given to education, shaped in a Classical mould by humanists like Camerarius and Melanchthon, the insistence on a learned ministry and a participatory laity, a work and family and political ethic which affirmed the *saeculum,* and – not least – a *pietas litterata.*

Yet the same Luther who genuinely loved music and history and the Classics, and who was one of the greatest wordsmiths of all time, was also the pitiless scourge of the most humanist form of Protestantism, that of Zwingli and his adherents.[51] The human, rational, 'mathematical' considerations of Zwingli, he believed, diluted and distorted Scripture so fundamentally that his understanding of the Eucharist, of God and Christ and humanity – a fairly comprehensive list – were 'of another Spirit', that is of the Devil.

---

50. Fragnito, *op. cit.*, p. 185, talks of his 'elegant and ingenious doctrinal constructions': but labels them as *'artificiose'*; a more sympathetic assessment by H. Chadwick, 'Justification by Faith: a Perspective,' in *One in Christ* (1984) pp. 191–225.

51. Zwingli was a 'sacramentarian', whose books are the 'prince of hell's poison', *Luther's Works* XXXVII p. 252.

And then there was, of course, his grand confrontation with Erasmus on the servitude of the will in 1525.[52] Luther never forgot his and all Christendom's debt to Erasmus' philological and linguistic skills. The sheer difficulty of the controversy with Erasmus about it has led to much uninformed generalisation. It should be seen in the light of Luther's refutation of the scholastic theologian Latomus, and is not in any sense a condemnation of 'humanism'. It is too seldom observed that both Erasmus and Luther wrote in this controversy in a philosophic mode in which they were both ill at ease.

The nub of the matter is that – in the interests of God's authority and dignity – Luther swept aside those of humanity: 'For of course what is most deeply offensive to our common-sense or rationality is that God deserts or hardens or damns men of his own volition'. "Hoc iniquum, hoc crudele, hoc intolerabile est de Deo sentire".[53] The trickier question is whether this transcendental absolutism is applied in the epistemological as well as the soteriological sphere.[54] At times, in his polemic with Latomus, or Erasmus, or Zwingli, Luther's anti-rationalist stance appears – irony of ironies – so philosophically water-tight that no human capabilities or perceptions whatever seem to be given validity.

Normally, however, Luther argued on two levels: *coram Deo* we can know nothing worth knowing; in *rebus naturalibus*, however, we are a wondrous creation, little lower than the angels.[55] It is in relation to the former that he denounces Erasmus: 'Let him who can abide Satan delight in your songs, O Erasmus'.[56]

Recent research, especially that of Junghans, has shown that his humanism goes far beyond the usually acknowledged debt to humanist linguistic, philological and grammatical tools, substantial though this is.[57] His Biblical humanism rested on the work of Lefevre and Reuchlin

---

52. *Luther and Erasmus: Free Will and Salvation*, Library of Christian Classics, XVII, ed. E. G. Rupp and P. S. Watson (1969).

53. *WA*, 18, 719.

54. Many would deny this; cf. K.-H. zur Mühlen, 'Luthers Kritik der Vernunft im mittelalterlichen und neuzeitlichen Kontext', in *Lutheriana: Zum 500. Geburtstag M. Luthers* . . . ed. G. Hammer and K. H. zur Mühlen (Cologne, Vienna, 1984), esp. pp. 3–5.

55. Luther interprets Genesis 1[26 f], humanity made in God's image, in functional not ontological terms; we are like God in that we control the small world of the body, and 'because the human being, like God, produces words', *WA* 9, 67, ll,[15–18], quoted in Junghans, *op. cit.*, p. 215 f.

56. *WA, Tischreden* I, 446.

57. Helmar Junghans points out that as early as 1509 he was developing his knowledge of Hebrew with the help of Reuchlins', *De rudimentis hebraicis* (1506); *op. cit.*, p. 182; cf. Siegfried Raeder, *Grammatica Theologica: Studien zu Luthers Operationes in Psalmos* (Tübingen, 1977); Junghans' work is essential reading and the following exposition leans heavily on it.

as well as Erasmus; he developed a keen sense for the authenticity of patristic and Scriptural texts; he became aware that the thought world of, say, Paul could only be penetrated if its formal, rhetorical structures were understood. It was by rigorously applying humanist principles to the text that Luther broke through to his new understanding of the Gospel, not through some great 'spiritual' experience,[58] and the Wittenberg university reform, the substitution of Scripture and the Fathers for Aristotle, was 'the common product of the Reformation and of humanism'.[59] Luther's God is a *deus dicens*, a God who speaks. Heinz Otto Burger even talks of Luther's 'affective rhetoricism'.[60]

Thus the humanists who swarmed to Luther's support did so because, quite correctly, they perceived him to be applying their own principles and processes to Scripture. Only gradually did they notice that he went beyond many of them in his critique of the Fathers, and that although he loved the letter of Scripture, its 'outward clarity', its earthy, historical vesture, he also applied his own theological criteria to reveal the 'inner clarity' of Scripture,[61] its coherent witness, as he believed, to a God whose strength was in weakness, whose wisdom folly, whose righteousness the justification of the godless. He was impatient of Erasmus' tendency to flit from philology to allegory, from precision to mystery. Scripture's truth, for Luther, was clear to the inner eye of faith, but it is a truth always under contradiction, always incarnate, never abstract principle or morality.

There are nominalist and apocalyptic currents here as well as humanist, and in practice polemical, pastoral and apologetic motifs also surfaced. Yet as preacher, publicist, educator and catechiser Luther was also the humanist, transporting his contemporaries back into the strange worlds of Israel and the apostles in language so urgent and gentle and drastic that his *via rhetorica* became for them the *via salutis*. Those who can still thrill to the cadences of the Authorised Version will recognise that it was an example that was to be followed. *Es machte Schule.*

Yet Luther was no humanist reformer. Programmes to reform the Church interested him little or not at all. Reform of theology, yes. Even, as the *Appeal to the German Nobility* testifies, the reform of society. But his world was racing towards the Last Day. The unleashing of the Gospel had stirred Satan from his lair; and in the

---

58. Cf. my article, 'Yesterday's Reformation Today', *Theology*, July 1979, pp. 271–9.

59. M. Brecht, *Martin Luther: His Road to Reformation*, tr. J. L. Schaaf (Philadelphia, 1985), p. 282.

60. *Renaissance – Humanismus – Reformation: deutsche Literatur im europäischen Kontext* (Bad Hamburg, Zurich, 1969), pp. 418–24.

61. Cf. *The Bondage of the Will*, in *Luther's Works* XXXIII, 28.

person of the Papal Antichrist, and crazed prophets like Carlstadt and Müntzer, or of blaspheming Jews, he was launching a terrifying final onslaught on the world. So it was a time for confession and defiance, not discussion and dialogue. From his earliest days we can trace this apocalyptic reading of history which dominates so much of his later writings. His hold on reality was further diminished by a life-long institutional conditioning by monastery and university, capitalist bankers and merchants filling him with as much alarm as revolutionary miners or peasants. Fortunately, the reception of his teachings, not least by the humanists, filtered out much of the nonsense. Nowhere is the impact of humanism on reform more evident than in the way in which it modified Luther's message, though not always, of course, for the better!

Thomas Müntzer (1488?–1525) has been variously described as a mystic, an apocalyptic prophet, a revolutionary leader, a Biblicist, a religious reformer.[62] In Gritsch's striking phase he is a 'Reformer without a Church'.[63] After his torture and execution at the end of the Peasants War his followers were scattered, his books suppressed. Yet there is no doubt about his outstanding role in the Radical Reformation as a liturgist, theologian, social activist and reformer.[64] Only of late, however, has attention been drawn to the humanist components in his thought.[65] We still know little about his early life, but his earliest surviving letters, writings and notes suggest strong humanist influence, as is often the case with the Radicals. He knew some Greek and Hebrew, read Plato and Quintilian, taught pupils the elements of Latin grammar and syntax, and above all buried himself in the study of the Church Fathers, especially the historians and the North Africans: Tertullian, Cyprian, Augustine.

He became convinced that in its liturgy and discipline the pure virgin Church of the Apostles had been replaced by a wretched hag, corrupt and corrupting. He translated the Mass into German before Luther, and the *Order and Explanation* of his German Order of Service shows a broad and contextualist understanding of the development and variety of Christian traditions in East and West.

---

62. The most recent bibliography by Tom Scott, *Journal of Ecclesiastical History*, 39, 4 (1988), pp. 557–572; new editions of his work are in preparation in the two Germanies which will supersede G. Franz, *Gesammelte Schriften und Briefe* (Gutersloh, 1968); cf. my *Collected Letters and Writings of Thomas Müntzer* (Edinburgh, 1988).

63. E. W. Gritsch, *Reformer Without a Church: The Life and Thought of Thomas Müntzer* (Philadelphia, 1967).

64. G. Rupp, in *Patterns of Reformation*, (1969), pp. 157–353 has contributed most to establishing his importance for British historiography.

65. Cf. U. Bubenheimer, 'Luther-Karlstadt–Müntzer: soziale Herkunft und humanistische Bildung . . .', *Amtsblatt der Ev. – Luth. Kirche in Thüringen* 40 (1987), pp. 60–68.

Bubenheimer has pointed to his use of Quintilian's concept of the
*ordo rerum*, the disposition of material to provide for a harmonious flow
of argument from beginning to end, of an integration of the parts and
the whole.[66] Müntzer, however, transmutes this into an alternative
cosmology, a divine order of creation. This had been disrupted, he
believed, both within the individual and throughout the whole of
creation. In the elect, who stretched far beyond the boundaries of
Christendom, elements of rationality remained and could still be
appealed to. In fact a great process of *Besserung*, of improvement and
reform, was taking place, of which the Church reforms were only one
aspect. The original order of creation had to be restored in the social
and political realm as well. The typically humanist concept of harmony
has become the legitimation for an apocalyptically conceived transformation of Church and society.

The ability to distort Quintilian's advice on rhetoric into an alternative cosmology is hardly conclusive proof of a humanist orientation.
It certainly reminds us, however, that the Bible was not the only book
to be interpreted in strange ways in the sixteenth century. The avail-
ability of humanist texts on an unprecedented scale often sparked off
conclusions that would have mightily surprised their authors.

For Müntzer, in any case, his humanist period proved to be a passing
phase. It seems to have been during his time as preacher in the bustling
town of Zwickau, in 1520–21, that he broke with humanism, largely
no doubt because of his conflicts with the preacher of St Mary's,
Zwickau, the humanist Egranus. As Müntzer made contact with the
underprivileged groupings in the town, the 'moderate', rational faith
of Egranus appeared to fit all too neatly with his social conservatism,
his love of a 'sweet Christ'.

Increasingly Müntzer found himself questioning those who believed,
with the Wittenbergers, that the Gospel had to be preached by the
learned, by those trained at university. Book-learning was that of the
Scribes and Pharisees, a 'theft' of truth from others, a poor, tired
substitute for personal knowledge. It was used, moreover, by Lutheran
prince and preacher to keep the common people under their control.

When the book, itself a 'creature', is worshipped; and when Scripture
is seen as the exclusive authority, it becomes a tyranny. This analysis
of the social control exercised by education, including humanist
education, is not without its merits; though like all anti-intellectual
intellectuals Müntzer, himself trained in universities, and propagating
his ideas in books, is less than consistent.

His critique of humanist models of reform is complemented by
alternative strategies. His German liturgies proved highly popular and

66. Ibid., pp. 66 f.

40

were consciously designed as a training ground for the elect. Marxist scholars have recognised their importance in this regard.[67] In his discussion groups, and sermons, his circular letters, and dream-interpretations he provided new forms of teaching ordinary people. From mid-1524 he completely abandoned the use of Latin in his letters.

Thus he may have realised that the reform sought by many of the common folk in town and country was not that of the humanist, but rather conscientious pastoral care, earnest preaching of Scripture, services in their own language, a more participatory Church and concern for the common weal.[68] Were the *gelehrten* indeed the *verkehrten*, the learned the perverted?

Thomas Müntzer's radical and optimistic concept of reform[69] raises some of the larger questions about humanism. Insofar as humanists and Reformers were allies was the effect of their work, as Delumeau argues, to Christianise Europe effectively for the first time, freeing rural areas in particular from the grip of ignorance and superstition?[70] Or did they constitute a puritanical élite which in the interest of godliness and good order trampled underfoot the popular culture, the legitimate interests of common folk?[71] Has the whole educational achievement, particularly of Lutheranism, been grossly exaggerated?[72] Did the alliance of humanist and reformer represent a second, repressive stage in the process of reform, closely supervised by the authorities, after the common folk's dream of a genuinely communal reformation had been shattered?[73]

Those who write, of course, within today's disintegrating European culture, have their own peculiar perspectives. Ours is hardly a heroic

---

67. M. Steinmetz, 'Luther, Müntzer und die Bibel . . .', in G. Vogler etc. (ed.) *Martin Luther: Leben – Werk – Wirkung* (Berlin, 1983).

68. Cf. P. Blickle, *Gemeindereformation* . . . (Oldenbourg-Munich, 1985).

69. It is perhaps as close as the sixteenth century comes to the idea of progress: 'From day to day there is a drive for improvement in all man's worldly undertakings . . .' (Franz, *op. cit.*, p. 162[3-5]).

70. 'The New Testament commentaries of the Jesuit Salmeron, the patristic publications of the Benedictines of Saint-Maur, the *Annales Ecclesiastici* of Baronio . . . bear witness to the rapid rise of positive theology'; i.e. a humanist emphasis on Scripture, the Fathers, Church history (J. Delumeau, *Catholicism between Luther and Voltaire: a new view of the Counter-Reformation*, tr. J. Maiser (London-Philadelphia, 1977), p. 42).

71. P. Burke, *Popular Culture in early modern Europe* (1978).

72. G. Strauss, *Luther's house of learning: indoctrination of the young in the German Reformation* (Baltimore, 1978).

73. P. Blickle; *op. cit. passim*; one of the least attractive aspects of humanism: a contempt for the peasant, the artisan, was all too eagerly taken up by the Reformers; Luther had few good words for them; Melanchthon wanted the closest control of teaching and preachers; Pole and Contarini sharply suppressed any sign of popular dissent.

and certainly not a confessional age. Nostalgia for a vanished universe of letters may incline us to cloak sixteenth-century humanists in liberal attire or to deck out the Reformers in all too romantic feathers. Still worse, we may lapse into that revisionism which has ever been the refuge of the knave and the fool. The coincident miracles of Renaissance and Reform deserve a better fate.

Separately, but also together, they opened up, or recovered, a vast Classical and Christian heritage, and launched an impressive onslaught on corruption and complacency. Often in a love–hate relationship, especially in the Calvinist camp,[74] they fed off one another rather than on one another. In the greatest of the Christian humanists – More or Contarini or Johann Sturm or Melanchthon or Cranmer – the blending of humanist and reforming concerns seems the most natural thing in the world. More frequently one senses the tension. But where, as in Spain, one triumphed at the expense of the other both suffered in the end. The Reformation (or the Counter-Reformation) was not the 'fate' of humanism. Even in the simplistic days of confessionalism both continued to modify, or balance one another.[75] Neo-latin literature and the natural sciences continued to flourish. The subversive quality of the great Scriptural and Classical texts was always latently present, waiting for a Milton to emerge. Christian humanism had made its point, and remained a live option for the future.

---

74. Cf. Calvin's virulent attack on Erasmians and Ciceronians, proud minds who stumble over Scripture, in: *Des Scandales qui empêchent aujourdhui beaucoup de gens de venir à la pure doctrine de l'Evangile* . . . (1550), ed. O. Fatio, Librairie Droz (Geneva, 1984); but also John Bossy's comment that Calvin was the greatest of those 'whose humanist instincts or talents enabled them to treat the printed word not simply as a convenience but as an artistic opportunity' (*op. cit.*, p. 102).

75. François Wendel argues that Calvin made the humanist method 'the very basis of his exegesis and in doing so founded the modern science of exegetics'. *Calvin: The Origins and Development of His Public Thought*, tr. P. Mairet (1963), p. 31; the determined rationality, the philological and communication skills of Calvin are commented on by countless scholars.

*Chapter Three*

# Humanism and Political Thought

### RICHARD TUCK

## I

F or fifteen hundred years, from the fourth century to the nineteenth, schoolchildren in Europe were exposed daily to two books. One was the Bible, and the other was the works of Cicero. The co-existence of these two texts in our culture is a remarkable phenomenon, for on a clear-headed reading of each of them they have very little in common (though their readers' heads have seldom been entirely clear). Cicero and the other comparable Roman authors, such as Seneca, Sallust or Quintilian, remained the writers who instructed the young in correct Latin, the role they have always performed; they thus in a sense controlled access to the Bible itself. And yet the moral messages contained in the pagan writers were not merely superficially at variance with the moral message of the Bible, but were fundamentally in conflict with it. Unravelling this conflict and taming the old, pre-Christian culture was the concern of generations of Christians, and different approaches were popular at different times; the Renaissance itself can be seen as yet another move in this prolonged campaign.

The fundamental challenge to Christian values represented by these authors rested on their implicit or explicit endorsement of the themes of late Hellenistic philosophy, and in particular of both Stoicism and Academic scepticism (the Academy of Plato having by the time of Cicero become a centre of scepticism). In general philosophical matters, indeed, Cicero was avowedly a sceptic, providing in his *Academica* one of the central texts of ancient epistemological scepticism: the sceptics argued that there can be no secure knowledge of the physical world, vitiated as our perceptions are by illusion and uncertainty. But equally avowedly, Cicero did not extend this scepticism fully to moral matters: in this area, the common concern of the Roman writers was the pursuit of a *beata vita*, something conventionally translated as a 'happy life'.

In the Stoic tradition which they all more or less followed, man (like all animals) was taken to be fundamentally self-interested: 'Every living creature loves itself, and from the moment of birth strives to secure its own preservation; because the earliest impulse bestowed on it by nature for its life-long protection is the instinct for self preservation and for the maintenance of itself in the best condition possible to it in accordance with its nature', wrote Cicero in his *De Finibus* (V.24), and similar passages could be cited from his *De Officiis* and from Seneca (particularly his *Epistula Moralis* 121).[1] This view immediately set up a tension in the pursuit of *beatitudo* between what was directly beneficial to oneself – described by the Romans as *utile* – and what was conventionally 'moral' – *honestum*. All the Roman moralists worried about the relationship between these concepts, particularly as they had constantly to look over their shoulders at the Epicureans with their message that all that mattered was what was *utile*. They also had to be concerned about the sceptics, represented above all by the second-century B.C. philosopher Carneades, who denied the possibility of any stable universal principles of morality, but were prepared to accept that men are always motivated by the desire of preserving themselves. There was in fact a strand in Stoicism (far more marked in Seneca than in Cicero) which entirely endorsed this, and which stressed the need for a complete intellectual and emotional detachment in order to preserve oneself psychologically – a condition they termed *apatheia*.

The standard Roman answer to these views was given extensive discussion in Cicero's *De Officiis*: it was that what was *honestum* was what was *utile* to human society. Cicero in fact very often identified the requirements of human society with those of one's own state, eloquently defending the idea that 'there is no social relationship more close, none more dear than that which links each one of us with our country' (I.57). Usually, the requirement of one's *respublica* was that one lived a life defined by the cardinal virtues of prudence, justice, temperance and fortitude, and Cicero in general denied that the interests of the state could lie in any other kind of conduct. 'The occasion cannot arise when it would be to the state's interest to have the wise man do anything immoral' (I.15a). But in certain passages he conceded that political interest could override certain orthodox moral rules; thus promises might be broken for political reasons. 'Suppose that a man

---

1. The quotation from *De Finibus*, like all the quotations from Cicero which I shall cite, is from the Loeb edition.

who has entrusted money to you proposes to make war upon your country, should you restore the deposit? I believe you should not, for you would be acting against the state, which ought to be the dearest thing in the world to you,' (III.95, Loeb translation corrected).

Playing one's appropriate role in the service of the *respublica* was the source of glory among one's fellow-citizens, and all these Roman writers stressed the importance of glory as a goal for action: the public esteem attached to one's conduct was a powerful motive to behave in the way the public good required. Cicero wrote a whole treatise *De Gloria* which was still extant at the beginning of the Renaissance, though it has subsequently disappeared, and the term resonates throughout both his works and those of Seneca. The Roman historians explored the implications of this in the history of Rome: it had been a 'glorious' republic by virtue of its imperial expansion, and both Livy and Sallust inquired into the reasons for this greatness (Sallust, particularly, stressing the importance of free republican institutions).

The idea that your state represented the focus of your moral life might be taken to imply that only political action was truly *honestum* or virtuous. Quintilian was fiercest in arguing this (especially 12.2.7), but neither Cicero nor Seneca were single-mindedly in favour of the life of action. In the *De Officiis* Cicero did say (e.g. at I.153) that political action should be ranked higher than any other virtuous activity, and in particular than the life of *contemplatio* or *cognitio* (that is, philosophy); but even in that work he could say that 'earnest and thoughtful men' might be justified in certain circumstances in retiring to a contemplative life of *otium* or leisure (I.69). Seneca wrote extensively on just this topic, with ambiguous results; in one treatise devoted entirely to it, the *De Otio*, he made the compelling point that both the Epicureans and the Stoics 'consigned us to *otium*' though by different routes: 'Epicurus says, "the wise man will not take part in politics, except upon some special occasion"; Zeno [the founder of Stoicism] says, "the wise man will take part in politics, unless prevented by some special circumstances".'[2]

What these special circumstances were, was rather indeterminate: old age or ill health certainly qualified, but so could disgust at the corrupt state of political life – a circumstance which Seneca enlarged on in his *Epistulae Morales*. Philosophical *otium* could be defended as itself in the interests of the *respublica*, and in *De Otio* and his *Epistulae* Seneca argued both that philosophy could be of greater service to some republics than political action, and that there was a wider human community than the

---

2. *Dialogorum* VIII.3.2; trans. A. Stewart, *Seneca. Minor Dialogues* (1900) p. 242. For an excellent discussion of the whole Roman approach to this issue, see M. T. Griffin, *Seneca. A Philosopher of Politics* (Oxford, 1976) chapter 10.

state whose interests were certainly served more by philosophy than by political action. In a lost work entitled *Hortensius* Cicero himself probably argued the same. Apparently (according to Cicero and Quintilian) the question, 'should a wise man take part in public affairs?' was a regular exercise in the rhetoric schools of the late Republic and the Principate, and it is clear that the Roman orators were not tied by their general theory to any particular answer to this question.

The commitment to serving the republic in some form, even through appropriate *otium*, might also be thought to imply a commitment to what we would call republican forms of government, in which such political participation was widely possible. Cicero is famous for just such a deduction, but again there are qualifications to be made: Seneca in his *De Clementia* provided an eloquent defence of virtuous *princely* rule, arguing that such a prince would be the most effective protector of his state: 'Men love their own safety, when they draw up vast legions in battle on behalf of one man . . . he is the bond which fastens the commonwealth together.'[3]

This Roman moral philosophy was of course avowedly pagan – indeed, virtually atheistical, for though *contemplatio* might include thinking about divine matters, it need not. Cicero in his *De Natura Deorum* gave prominence to a number of sceptical arguments about religious belief, though in the very last sentence he rather lukewarmly sided with Stoic theism against scepticism. But the defence of *contemplatio* in the Roman tradition as something which might serve the *respublica* naturally challenged the primacy of religion, making it something which had in some sense to serve the state. The service which Cicero or Seneca had in mind, no doubt, was of a rather high-minded kind; but there was a persistent belief in antiquity (voiced most eloquently by the Greek historian Polybius) that the Roman governing class used religion in the most cynical way to bolster its own power over the masses.

Accordingly, Roman moral philosophy suffered a direct and often bitter and jeering assault from early Christian Latin writers. Themselves often trained up in the rhetoric schools, the Christians did not merely put an alternative view alongside that of the Romans; they directly disputed the meaning of the key terms which the pagan philosophers used, and sought to give a narrowly Christian connotation to each of them. This process was taken to its extreme in Lactantius's *Divine Institutes* (c. 310–20), which methodically changed the meaning of all the principal classical moral terms such as *honestum*, and which also came close to advocating a kind of cultural revolution, in which the

---

3. *De Clementia* I.4, trans. A. Stewart, *op. cit.* p. 385.

pagan texts would be extirpated and replaced by properly Christian ones. 'No one can doubt that false religions will quickly disappear, and philosophy altogether fall, if all shall be persuaded that this alone is religion and the only true wisdom.'[4] This period of attack ended with terms such as *beatitudo* and *contemplatio* having taken on their familiar Christian meaning, and the Roman philosophy having become something which committed Christians found difficult to reproduce sympathetically.

The one element in it which Lactantius at least *could* endorse was the occasional use by the Roman Stoics of the term 'law of nature'. They had used it to refer to the basic natural instincts and capacities of men and animals, though one should not overestimate its centrality within their writings; but Lactantius picked up some passages (now lost) from Book III of Cicero's *De Republica* extolling the importance of the natural law, and remarked 'who that is acquainted with the mystery of God could so significantly relate the law of God, as a man far removed from the knowledge of the truth has set forth that law?'[5] As this illustrates, the *legal* character of the 'law of nature' was crucial to the Christians, for they straightforwardly associated the law of nature with the law of God upon which they relied for their distinctive ethical beliefs.

It is Augustine, above all, whom the Latin West has to thank for preserving the Roman philosophy. If the radical views of men like Lactantius had triumphed, we would no doubt have seen a burning of the books; but Augustine explained to a Christian audience how one might use Roman culture for Christian purposes. He did so in a variety of ways, but the principal one is illustrated by the title of his greatest book, *The City of God*. Within every human *respublica*, he argued, there have been hidden elements of an ancient and much wider *respublica* or *civitas*, the *civitas* of God. This *civitas* is formed of citizens intent on understanding and worshipping God; but once that is allowed for, the standard Roman glorification of the *respublica* can simply be applied to this special *civitas*. It will then be true that our 'state . . . ought to be the dearest thing in the world', though our state will not be the Roman *respublica*. The Roman philosophers can then be read as a kind of general guide to living in cities of all kinds, and the primacy of the Christian religion will be secured by its quasi-political expression in the City of God. (The Greek East, at about the same time, found a different route to the same conclusion: the conversion of Constantine, argued Eusebius of Caesarea, had transformed the Roman Empire itself into

---

4. Lactantius, *Works* trans. A. Roberts and J. Donaldson, *Ante-Nicene Christian Library* (Edinburgh, 1871) p. 302.

5. Ibid., p. 371.

a *civitas Dei*, and all that the Roman writers said in defence of their state could then be applied directly to the defence of a Christian *civitas*.)

There is a poetic elegance to Augustine's vision, but it rested of course on a *metaphor*. It left the Roman writers unassailed as texts in the Latin schools, and if one was unpersuaded by the metaphor it also left one exposed to the fundamental discrepancy between their views and those of conventional Christianity. There was still plenty of scope for a new account of how these texts fitted into a Christian view of the social world. That new account was provided from the twelfth century onwards by the ethical works of Aristotle: it is, I think, seldom recognised how much Aristotle's ideas (in this area) in fact came as a *relief* to Christians troubled by the Roman writers. Historians have tended to concentrate on the orthodox Christian hostility to Aristotle's works of natural philosophy (which were the works banned at Paris in 1210), and to assume that in some way the hostility would also have been directed towards the ethical works; but read straightforwardly, Aristotle's *Ethics* offers a new and persuasive solution to the dilemma I have outlined. Aristotle argued in the *Ethics* that the virtues necessary to maintain a desirable civic life – the 'moral' virtues in the strict sense, products of 'practical wisdom' – are intrinsically worthwhile, and need no defence in terms of any values beyond themselves; this was an argument very close in spirit to the Roman authors'. But he went on to argue (notably in Books VI and X) that there are other virtues, the 'intellectual' ones, which are also intrinsically worthwhile, and which include above all scientific inquiry and contemplation. Moreover these virtues are *superior* to the moral virtues, in the sense that a life lived in pursuit of philosophic contemplation will be better than one lived in accordance with the needs of one's city, though both ways of life would be intrinsically good. The *Ethics* thus did the Christians' job for them admirably, for it provided an argument which entirely respected, and indeed endorsed, the views of the Romans about civic virtue, but which justified the theologian in believing that the pursuit of religious truth was nevertheless the finest goal of humanity (for religion could effort-lessly be placed into Book X as the highest form of contemplation).

It is, incidentally, interesting that the first bits of the *Ethics* to be translated into Latin (probably early in the twelfth century), the *Ethica vetus*, were Books II and III, which expound the theory of moral virtue – Aristotle seems first to have been treated as an adjunct to the Roman writers, and only at the beginning of the thirteenth century with the appearance of the comprehensive *Ethica nova* did his alternative view become clear.[6] In a sense, the *Ethica vetus* belongs to the so-called

---

6. B. G. Dod, 'Aristoteles latinus' in *The Cambridge History of Later Medieval Philosophy* ed. N. Kretzmann, A. Kenny and J. Pinborg (Cambridge, 1982) pp. 47–9.

twelfth-century Renaissance, the period in which the study of the Roman writers reached heights which it was not to scale again for two hundred years; the coming of the *Ethica nova* symbolises the dominance for a time of an anti-Roman philosophy.

One of the important implications of the Aristotelian theory was that the Roman writers should continue to be used as models for the study of moral virtue, provided that it was continually recognised that they were *merely* that, and provided that Aristotle was treated as their philosophical master. The subordination of the Romans to the Greek was symbolised in the widespread organisation of courses in the new universities which came into being from the twelfth century onwards: the basic Arts course required students first to master the *Trivium*, in which grammar, logic and rhetoric were studied, and for which the Roman texts were basic, and then to proceed to the *Quadrivium*, effectively the study of Aristotle's works. The success and status of the universities was from the beginning posited upon the supremacy of *science* argued for in Aristotle.

But this being acknowledged, the Roman texts could be used as models in many circumstances where rhetorical effects – persuading people to action – were crucial; above all, often, in politics. A striking example of this, and one which is particularly appropriate in a volume dedicated to Denys Hay, comes from Scotland itself. There in 1320 an anonymous author drafted the famous 'Declaration of Arbroath', a letter to the pope in which the independence of Scotland from the English Crown was asserted. Petrarch himself was only sixteen at the time, and one would hardly have expected a Scotsman of this date to have exhibited a Renaissance-like approach to politics; and yet the Declaration consists in part of a network of paraphrases and direct quotations from Sallust praising the ideal of 'liberty' – 'that alone, which no honest man gives up but with life itself.'[7]

What the Declaration of Arbroath illustrates is that in appropriate circumstances anywhere in medieval Europe, the Roman rhetoric of republican liberty might be called upon. Such circumstances, however, arose most often in Northern Italy, for it was there above all that political entities had self-consciously to defend their 'liberty' from external attack. From the beginning of the twelfth century, the Italian cities sought to establish their independence from the jurisdiction of the emperor, and though at first writers on their behalf exploited the interpretative possibilities of the Roman Law, they also turned automatically to Cicero or Sallust as models. The best example of this, as Quentin

---

7. G. W. S. Barrow, 'The Idea of Freedom in Late Medieval Scotland', *The Innes Review*, 30 (1979) p. 28.

Skinner has pointed out[8], is Brunetto Latini who composed his *Li livres dou trésor* in the early 1260s, drawing on a number of earlier works such as the *Oculus pastoralis* of *c.* 1220 and John of Viterbo's *De regimine civitatum* (*c.* 1250). These writers' primary concern was with the methods used by the rulers of the cities to maintain peace and good order within them; they display very little acquaintance with Aristotle, and use the Roman moralists almost exclusively in order to make their point. The *Oculus pastoralis* even asserted that successful rulers will bring *glory* to their city by safeguarding its tranquillity, a clear case of a Roman theme re-appearing in an Italian context, and a noteworthy contrast with the later Christian Aristotelian suspicion towards the ideal of worldly glory.

But writers much more openly conscious of the force of Aristotelian arguments could also utilise the Roman writers in just this way; a notable example of this is Marsiglio of Padua, writing at about the same time as the Declaration of Arbroath was penned, who began his *Defensor pacis* by stating (with a number of direct quotations from both Sallust and Cicero) the evils of discord and the importance of *pax*, before launching off into his examination of the new source of discord unknown in antiquity, the pretensions of the Church. The bulk of the *Defensor pacis* is thoroughly Aristotelian; but the terms in which its theme is first broached are equally thoroughly Roman. Moreover, Marsiglio's conclusion was that, *inter alia*, the peace of the *civitas* will best be secured under a regime where the rulers are *elected* by the people, for such a regime will both secure the common good and will leave the citizen body *free*. Such an argument is of course highly Ciceronian; it is not particularly Aristotelian, though Marsiglio strained every possible passage of Aristotle to try to show that it was.

Because of this conjunction of Aristotle and Rome, it has always proved difficult for historians of political thought satisfactorily to isolate specifically 'humanist' themes. For example, the idea that only what we would call 'republics', of the kind Marsiglio had in mind, could secure a proper and secure life for their citizens – an idea often associated with Quattrocento humanists – was present in many fourteenth-century Italian Aristotelians other than Marsiglio (Ptolemy of Lucca is an obvious example); while a degree of pessimism about republican politics and a stress on the need for a single ruler to master the lawless mob is found in both thirteenth-century Aristotelians and in Petrarch. Nevertheless, the repudiation of Aristotle, or at least of the Aristotelian placing of the Roman writers in a subordinate context,

---

8. Q. R. D. Skinner, 'Ambrogio Lorenzetti: The Artist as Political Philosopher', British Academy Raleigh Lecture on History, forthcoming in *Proceedings of the British Academy*.

which gathered pace during the fifteenth century, did have some marked effects on political discourse.

## II

The emancipation of the Romans from their Greek tutelage is conventionally ascribed to early Quattrocento Florence, and there still seems little reason to deny this (once due allowance has been made to Petrarch as a forerunner of the movement). The crucial symbolic move was made by Leonardo Bruni, who embarked on a daring programme of translating Aristotle into classical or Ciceronian Latin. Such a programme carried a clear ideological message: this was because the existing medieval translations of Aristotle had in many cases quite deliberately left Aristotle's Greek technical terms in what amounted to the original. A fine example is the word 'politics' itself, which was of course by classical Latin standards a peculiar term, supplanting the study of the *civitas* by the study of the *polis*; but it had the inestimable advantage of being (for a Latin audience) unconnected with the specifically *civic* themes of the Romans, and therefore applicable to the concerns of barbarous Northern monarchies. In general, Aristotelianism appeared in the medieval translations as a different and higher *science* of ethics and politics, ruling the Romans through greater technical virtuosity.

Bruni disputed this in his new translations, of which the most famous were the *Ethics* (1416–19) and the *Politics* (1437). As a preface to his *Ethics* he added an essay explaining what he was doing, and making explicit his desire to render Aristotle in *Ciceronian* Latin.

> What is commoner among those who write about morals than the word *honestum*? For instance the Stoics, of whom Seneca is the most important to us, thought that the point of having goods was to lead a life of *honestas*; moreover there is frequent debate about the difference between what is *utile* and what is *honestum*, while we say that the whole life of virtue is contained in *honestum*. But for this *honestum* in Greek, the Latin translation of Aristotle always has *bonum*, absolutely absurdly . . .[9]

Contemporary Aristotelians were fully aware of what Bruni was up to: one of them, the Castilian Alonso García de Santa María or Alfonso de Cartagena (the son of the converted ex-rabbi Solomon ha-Levi)

---

9. A. Birkenmajer, 'Der Streit des Alonzo von Cartagena mit Leonardo Bruni Aretino' in his *Vermischte Untersuchungen zur Geschichte der Mittelalterlichen Philosophie, Beiträge zur Geschichte der Philosophie des Mittelalters*, 20 (1922) p. 159.

engaged in a prolonged debate with Bruni over this translation. He pointed out that while Cicero and Seneca were pre-eminent in rhetoric, 'I have never read that they had such a pre-eminence in the scientific distinction of virtues and the subtle investigation of moral instances.'[10]

The debate between García and Bruni is one of the key documents of the Renaissance, for it shows exactly what was at stake in the move by humanists into territory traditionally patrolled by medieval Aristotelians. Bruni's translation made Aristotle a participant in a conversation whose general form was determined by the Roman moralists, and very quickly Aristotle's arguments about, in particular, the superiority of intellectual to practical virtue were assimilated to the Senecan or (partially) Ciceronian arguments for the superiority of philosophical *otium*. The importantly different grounds upon which Aristotle based his case tended to be disregarded. A good example of this, coming from an absolutely representative fifteenth-century Italian humanist, is provided by the Neapolitan Giovanni Pontano's remarks in his *De prudentia* (1499) about the superiority of *contemplatio*. He used both Senecan and Aristotelian phrases, but the overall thrust of his argument was undoubtedly Senecan. (The growth of a kind of humanist Platonism can also be seen in this light – the Platonists used the Roman arguments in support of their own programme of meditative retirement.)

Now the tables had been turned: Aristotelian science was justified as serving the republic, rather than politics being justified according to the principles of Aristotelian science. Once the relationship was put this way round, the humanists were not necessarily opposed to the study even of Aristotle's most technical writings, provided that they were put into an intelligible Roman form; thus Alamanno Rinuccini, the pupil of one of the great humanist translators of Aristotle, Johannes Argyropulos, remarked 'as we are taught by Cicero, the eloquent man we seek cannot be formed without philosophy', and urged his readers to seek a true understanding of Aristotle.[11] One of the greatest Renaissance Aristotelians, Agostino Nifo (1473–1546) ('alter Aristoteles' as he was termed by contemporaries) believed the same: he too produced modern, humanist translations of Aristotle's scientific works, and he defended his scientific activity in the Roman terms of social utility – thus when he wrote a treatise entitled *De iis qui apte posse in solitudine vivere*, the arguments he used in favour of the solitary, contemplative life were far more Senecan than Aristotelian – for example, that the life

---

10. Ibid., p. 173.

11. J. E. Seigel, 'The Teaching of Argyropulos and the Rhetoric of the First Humanists' in *Action and Conviction in Early Modern Europe* ed. T. K. Rabb and J. E. Seigel (Princeton, 1969) p. 252.

of philosophy developed the cardinal virtues in a man just as much as a life of political action.[12]

The lead given by these earlier writers was followed enthusiastically by some humanists in the later sixteenth century, such that a Roman defence of the necessity of philosophical *otium* and even of religion itself came to be a widespread and influential phenomenon. The movement in part took the familiar form of translating Greek philosophy into appropriate Latin: thus in 1535 Mario Nizzoli of Brescia published his *Observationes in Ciceronem* with an appendix listing the chief technical philosophical terms which were un-Ciceronian and suggesting alternatives, while in 1540 Joachim Péron of the university of Paris began a programme of translating the central works of Greek philosophy into absolutely pure Ciceronian Latin. Plato's *Timaeus* appeared in 1540, and two years later Péron started a series of translations of Aristotle which eventually covered all the major texts. He added to his translation an essay, *De optimo genere interpretandi*, which set out the guiding principles of this ultra-Ciceronian school. A few years later the great Cicero scholar Denys Lambin published improved versions of Péron's translation of the *Ethics* and *Politics*.

Such writers and translators sought to allow themselves to be Aristotelians by putting Aristotle into a Ciceronian style, and despite the frequent oddity of their approach others did the same with their Christianity. Two early examples of this were a couple of papal secretaries, Pietro Bembo and Jacopo Sadoleto (both of whom ended as cardinals), about whose devotion to Cicero many anecdotes circulated. It was said that Bembo advised Sadoleto not to read St Paul's letters, as they would corrupt his prose style. Certainly Bembo's history of his native Venice contained many strained examples of Ciceronian diction – the Turks became the Thracians, and the nunneries, temples of vestal virgins. Even in his official correspondence, Bembo referred to the Virgin Mary as *Dea ipsa*. Nevertheless, though Bembo's locutions look pagan to us, and were (as we shall see presently) fiercely attacked by some contemporaries, there is no doubt about his piety, nor about that of Sadoleto (who despite Bembo's alleged advice wrote commentaries on St Paul). Sadoleto was the more philosophically inclined of the pair, writing Ciceronian dialogues *De gloria* and *De laudibus philosophiae* – the latter an attempt to reconstruct the argument of Cicero's *Hortensius* in defence of philosophical *otium* and religious contemplation as a means of serving the republic.[13] Péron is a particularly good example of the same phenomenon from a slightly later period, for alongside his Ciceronianising of Aristotle he published in 1549 a Ciceronian volume entitled

---

12. The treatise is to be found most accessibly in his *Opuscula* (Paris, 1645).
13. *De laudibus philosophiae libri duo* (Lyons, 1538) pp. 201 ff.

*Topicorum theologicorum libri duo, quorum in posteriore de iis omnibus agitur, quas hodie ab haereticis defenduntur.*

Péron's pressing Cicero into the service of the Roman Catholic Church against the 'modern heretics' was to be prophetic, for as the Jesuit Order organised itself with precisely this intention, it too based itself upon Cicero. At the Roman College of the Society, from its foundation in 1551 onwards, Jesuits worked on a universal plan of education in the schools and colleges which the Society was founding, a programme which culminated in the famous *Ratio Studiorum* of 1599. In all the early drafts of the *Ratio* as well as in the final definitive version, the imitation of Cicero is the principal exercise in the study of the humanities. This corresponded to a widespread adherence among the early Jesuits to the principles of Italian Ciceronianism; so that as early as 1548 one of the first Jesuits, Peter Canisius, could congratulate his fellow Jesuit Adrian Adriani on coming into the Ciceronian camp – 'I am glad to see you have changed your style, brother Adrian, and I hope to see you pre-eminent among the Ciceronians'. Peter John Perpinian, author of a treatise on education in 1565 which was very influential among his fellows, also proclaimed his former error in not being a dedicated Ciceronian.

The imitation of Cicero in the sixteenth-century Society reached its climax, perhaps, in the work of Julius Negrone of Genoa, a teacher in some of the Jesuit colleges of Italy, who published a collection of his lectures in 1608. In them he praised Cicero, 'whom our nascent Society embraced as its own and proposed to us as a model, tacitly warning all not to depart from this master of the spoken and written word.' He even proposed to erect at Padua a votive tablet inscribed M. T. CICERONI M. F. HUMANAE FACUNDIAE PRINCIPI QUAEST. AEDI. PRAET. COS. PROCOS. IMPERATORI P. P. STUDIOSI ELOQ.[14] The fact that Péron and the others had made Aristotle legible for a Ciceronian was a great service to these Jesuits, for it was a combination of Cicero and Aristotle upon which they founded their intellectual machine, and the compatibility between the two authors was a crucial postulate.

Not only Catholics adhered in this way to the insights of the 'pure' Ciceronians. Among Lutherans, there also grew up a tradition of studying Cicero and Aristotle together in this way. This was something which they inherited from the man who pre-eminently inspired the first generation of Lutheran educators, Philip Melanchthon. Melanchthon was the first true humanist to become a Lutheran, and his writings are full of praise for both Cicero and Aristotle, and attempts to reconcile them, not with Catholic, but with Evangelical Christianity. The fore-

---

14. A. P. Farrell, *The Jesuit Code of Liberal Education* (Milwaukee, 1938) pp. 177–80.

word to his edition of Cicero's *De Officiis* (1534) contains the essentials of his view:

> as it is right for Christians to develop and foster a civil society, so this doctrine of civic morals and duties must be studied. For it is not godly to live like the Cyclops, without a legal order or an ethical doctrine, or the other frameworks to our life which classical literature provides. Those who abuse philosophy, are at war not only with human nature, but also and more importantly with the glory of the Gospel; for it teaches that men should be constrained by civic discipline . . .[15]

The *De Officiis*, according to Melanchthon, contained the 'definitions of virtue' and many suggestions about the moral life, all expressed in a 'popular' oratorical form which men of common sense could follow; Aristotle, on the other hand, should only be studied by educated men, though what he put forward (Melanchthon stressed) was 'not an illiberal doctrine', that is, it was compatible with Cicero.

We must be clear about the implications of this position for all these writers' Christianity. In effect, they were claiming two things. The first was that Christianity was *speculatively true* – that is, that philosophical enquiry could establish the truth of the Christian religion (as earlier Aristotelians had also believed). But the second was that this philosophical and religious enquiry should only be undertaken for *practical* reasons: knowledge of these truths, and the pursuit of this mode of life, was to be justified by their utility to the *respublica*. Faith in Christianity brought social peace and a rightly-ordered way of living. (This was to be precisely the argument which Jesuit writers such as Possevino were to use against Machiavelli.) The problem about holding these two beliefs is of course that they are inconsistent: for if Christianity is true, then it will also be true that religion is not to be justified by its social utility. These Christian Ciceronians were unwilling to abandon either claim; but their position represented precisely the problem which the Christian Fathers had been troubled by.

## III

It was made doubly difficult by the fact that, throughout the period, other Ciceronians were quite prepared to assert absolutely plainly, for the first time since antiquity, the straightforward superiority of *action* over contemplation, and in particular the superiority of a life of political activity devoted to the common good of a city. The very first statement

15. P. Melanchthon, *Werke* III (Gütersloh, 1961) p. 86.

of this case may have been by Pier Paolo Vergerio in a letter purporting to be from Cicero to Petrarch, composed in 1394, but it was put most clearly and influentially by Bruni himself in his famous *Laudatio Florentinae Urbis* of 1403–4. It was there associated with praise for the republican regime of Florence (especially its wide popular base – *governo largo* as it was termed in the vernacular), praise which fourteenth-century proto-humanists had been reluctant to lavish (preferring the rule of virtuous princes), but which as we have seen did have familiar precedents among Italian writers. The distinctiveness of the *Laudatio* lay not so much in its specific constitutional or political views, as in the role which it unequivocally allocated to politics – the role of, in effect, the master-activity of mankind, displacing scientific or religious contemplation from that position.[16]

But a thousand years of effort had gone into taming the Roman moralists on behalf of Christianity, and any suggestion that their cage should now be opened was met with immediate suspicion and hostility. For example, Cino Rinuccini's *Invettiva* against alleged slanderers of Dante, Petrarch and Boccaccio (*c.* 1400) included an attack on contemporary humanists for their paganising tendencies – 'as to the philosophy of things divine, they say that Varro wrote many books on the worship of the pagan gods in a very elegant style, and they praise him most excessively, preferring him in secret to the doctors of our faith . . .'[17] Similar accusations were made (as we shall see presently) against Bembo and his contemporaries: Ciceronianism of the Quattrocento kind always walked along a knife-edge, and might at any moment become an object of suspicion.

That this was entirely justified, is illustrated by the purest and most extreme Ciceronian of them all: Machiavelli. Machiavelli was deeply committed to exploring the Roman ideas on politics, and it can be said that he saw more clearly than any other Renaissance writer the real implications of Cicero's central belief: that the survival and advancement of one's republic had to take precedence over all things, and that the conventional virtues might not in fact always be adequately instrumental to that end. But as Quentin Skinner has stressed, Machiavelli continued to work with many of the same values of the more conventional Ciceronian humanists (for example *glory* was as important to him as it was to any other Italian humanist), and even some of the standard virtues are allowed a place in his writings.[18]

This has always been recognised as basically true for Machiavelli's

---

16. For Vergerio and Bruni, see H. Baron, *The Crisis of the Early Italian Renaissance* (Princeton, 1966) pp. 128, 191–212.

17. Ibid., p. 294.

18. See particularly his *Machiavelli*, Pastmasters (Oxford, 1981).

*Discourses* on the first ten books of Livy, which he wrote (probably) between 1515 and 1519, and in which he extolled the merit of republican institutions and civic feeling as guarantors of a city's liberty. It is true that even in that work, there are elements which are very different from the compromised Ciceronianism of the Quattrocento; in particular, Machiavelli argues that the two means whereby republican *virtù* can best be sustained in a citizenry are, first, a constitution which encourages competition and conflict between the social groups within a city and, second, the appropriate use of religion to foster civic *virtù*. The first of these arguments has some claim to be Machiavelli's most original idea, for it was very unlike any earlier humanist theory (earlier writers, back to the proto-humanists of the thirteenth century, had stressed the need for civic *concord*). But in a way it was a logical extension of the fundamental ideas of the Roman moralists: they had seen the ideal citizen as one who fought for his own freedom and the freedom of his city, and Machiavelli realised that a political structure which obliged citizens to stand up for their own concerns as well as those of their city could foster just this sort of fighting spirit.

The second of the two arguments was what horrified contemporaries most (though the first did disturb other humanists). And yet Machiavelli here was very plainly speaking the Roman language in an untroubled fashion; his originality lay in being prepared to say clearly what the Roman texts implied, but no earlier humanists had dared to articulate so clearly. Seen in this light, Machiavelli's remarks on religion were precisely the kind of threat which Ciceronianism had always posed, and which the Augustinian or Aristotelian strategies had been designed to counter; its re-emergence in the second decade of the sixteenth century drew attention to the need for a new strategy (though percipient contemporaries had divined this need long before they read the *Discourses*, which were not published until 1531).

Superficially, Machiavelli's *Prince* (which he probably wrote in 1513) seems much more of a challenge to Roman moralism. Seneca, who defended the government of princes, did so on the grounds that a *virtuous* prince would secure the liberty of the *respublica*, but the virtues such a prince should exhibit were such things as clemency and liberality (in addition to the more familiar cardinal virtues appropriate to all men). Cicero was not impressed by princely government, and in his works we can find in general only a defence of true republicanism. But Machiavelli in the *Prince* apparently argued for the merits of princely rule while simultaneously denying that the virtues such a prince should exhibit were the conventional ones – instead, he should if necessary be both devious and cruel. But again, there are qualifications to be made to this view. As we saw earlier, Cicero himself in the *De Officiis* did countenance (for example) breaking one's promise in the interests of one's country, though he also asserted that immoral conduct would in practice never further the interests of the *respublica*. If one's *fundamental* value is the survival of one's city, and of one's life as a free citizen within it (which was undoubtedly the fundamental Roman value), and if as a matter of contingent fact a single ruler can secure those goals more effectively in some circumstances than a free republic, and can secure them by conventionally immoral conduct, then the natural implication of the Roman view is that the prince is to be applauded.

The important qualification here is, 'one's life as a free citizen': there is no point (on the Roman view) in one's city being free from outside domination, if the citizens are made the slaves of a single ruler from within the city. A striking aspect of the *Prince* is that Machiavelli effectively endorses this view: he does so in a famous and difficult chapter of the *Prince*, 'Of those who have attained the position of prince by villainy' (Chapter VIII). Two 'villains' are condemned for their brutality in seizing power – Agathocles, tyrant of Syracuse, and Oliverotto Prince of Fermo. The puzzle about this chapter (on some readings of the *Prince*) is that Agathocles at least was spectacularly successful in establishing the independence and indeed the imperial dominance of Syracuse within Sicily, and retained power until his natural death. Why is he a 'villainous' prince, without *virtù*, as Machiavelli expressly says, when other princes such as Cesare Borgia are praised for their effective brutality? The answer seems to be that the route which both Agathocles and Oliverotto took to power was the mass slaughter of the senatorial class in their respective cities – in other words, they in effect closed down politics within their cities, and removed the vital public and political dimension from the lives of their citizens. Machiavelli clearly disapproved of this, holding that even under a prince there must be genuine *citizenship* (a belief manifested also in his insistence that a *virtuoso* prince would rule through a citizen army and not through mercenaries).

In some ways (surprisingly, from our point of view), *The Prince* may have been seen as somewhat less shocking than the *Discourses* by contemporaries, largely because Machiavelli did not spell out in the earlier work his instrumental view of religion. It is interesting in this context that Agostino Nifo in 1523 unblushingly printed in a work entitled *De regnandi peritia* (and dedicated to Charles V) large chunks of the *Prince*, without apparently thinking that they were anything other than a reasonable example of Ciceronian argument. This was in fact the first appearance of the *Prince* in print – it did not appear in full and under Machiavelli's name until 1532.

## IV

Nevertheless, Machiavelli can stand for our purposes as an example of the dangers (from a Christian standpoint) of over-faithful Ciceronianism. The most effective strategy from within humanism to counter these dangers came from the North, in the form of a simple but profoundly influential idea by Desiderius Erasmus – who fully deserved on this account his astonishing reputation among the humanists of Northern Europe. In 1528 Erasmus published a dialogue entitled *Ciceronianus*, in which he launched an explicit attack on the Italian Ciceronians and on one of their recent French followers, accusing them of endangering Christianity itself by their use of purely Ciceronian concepts. 'If ever you have visited the libraries of the Ciceronians at Rome, recall, I pray, whether you saw an image of the crucifix or of the sacred Trinity or of the apostles. You will find them all full of the monuments of heathenism . . . We do not dare to profess paganism. We plead as an excuse Ciceronianism.'[19]

But the important feature of Erasmus's argument was that he did not attack Cicero himself, and that he remained loyal to the essential values of the 'old' humanism. Cicero was to remain as the key exemplar whose ideas were to be followed accurately and fully; but as Erasmus repeatedly said, Cicero was himself a man of his own time and the modern Ciceronian must also be a man of *his* own time.

> What effrontery then would he have who should insist that we speak, on all occasions, as Cicero did? Let him bring back to us first that Rome which was; let him give us the Senate and the senate house, the Conscript Fathers, the Knights, the people in tribes and centuries; . . . Wherever I turn I see things changed, I stand on another stage, I see another theatre, yes, another world. What shall I do? I, a Christian, must speak to Christians about the Christian religion. In order that I may speak fittingly, shall I imagine that I am living in the age of Cicero and speaking in a crowded senate in the presence of the senators on the Tarpeian Rock?[20]

But the general approach of Cicero was still possible. The true modern Ciceronian is

---

19. I. Scott, *Controversies over the Imitation of Cicero* (New York, 1910) p. 75. I prefer this translation to the more recent one in Erasmus, *Collected Works* VI ed. A. H. T. Levi (Toronto, 1986) p. 396, though the ancillary scholarship of the later translation is of course much more up-to-date.

20. Ibid., (Scott) p. 61, (Levi) p. 383.

he who busies himself with the same zeal in the field of the Christian religion as Cicero did in that of secular things; who drinks in the psalms and prophets with that feeling which Cicero drank in the books of the poets; who desires to find out the decrees of the apostles, the rites of the church, the rise, progress and decline of the Christian Republic with such vigilance as Cicero laboured to learn thoroughly the rights and laws of the provinces, towns, and allies of the Roman City . . .[21]

This was the heart of Erasmus's case, and it was (as he repeatedly insisted) an appeal for a more radical and authentic Ciceronianism than that of the apparently radical Italians. A proper attention had to be paid to the governing ideas of Cicero, rather than merely to his language; and in particular, the fact had to be stressed that Cicero's commitment had been to understanding and working within and for the norms of his own society. In our quite different society, the same approach would lead to different results; above all, a fundamental feature of our society is its *Christianity*. Anyone who lived in this way in the modern world was to be praised, and Erasmus even argued that Aquinas and Scotus, 'though they boast themselves neither eloquent nor Ciceronians, are more Ciceronian than those who demand to be considered not only Ciceronians but even Ciceros.'[22] The scholastics had after all been wholly involved in the religion and law of their own time. The Italian Ciceronians' enterprise of expressing in Ciceronian Latin the central themes of ancient philosophy thus became a pointless or misleading enterprise, for a modern Ciceronian might well want to *distance* himself from (say) Aristotle (as indeed the historic Cicero had done), rather than assimilate him.

Again, we have to be clear about the implications of *this* strategy. Whereas the earlier Ciceronians had treated religion as a branch of philosophic contemplation, and had then utilised the only Roman argument which was available for engaging in such a practice, the Erasmian Ciceronians treated religion as an aspect of their practical, political life: Christianity was part of the public life of modern states, and the Bible was a governing text for man's actual life, comparable (as Erasmus said) to the law-books of the Romans. Clearly, this strategy put much less weight on the *truth* of the Christian religion than the earlier one had done, and Erasmus and his followers, when pressed, would concede their closeness to ancient scepticism – the wise man will follow the laws and customs of his country without enquiring into their objective

---

21. Ibid., (Scott) p. 79, (Levi) p. 400.
22. Ibid., (Scott) p. 65, (Levi) p. 387.

truth.[23] It also opened up the possibility that the sceptical critique of Aristotle and the other dogmatic ancient philosophers might be repeated in the modern world.

Erasmus's followers in the battles of the 1530s and 1540s against the contemporary Ciceronians perceived this implication very clearly, and in the name of Cicero or of true eloquence they proclaimed the need for a modern and open-minded approach to ancient philosophy. In particular, an open and extensively-argued anti-Aristotelianism became a central feature of their work, going well beyond the stray barbs which many earlier humanists had launched at Aristotle. One of the clearest examples of this process is provided by Erasmus's close associate in the 1520s and 1530s, Juan Luis Vives, the Spanish humanist who (through his long period of residence in England and the Netherlands) became very influential on northern humanism. In 1532 Vives published his major work, *De disciplinis*, in which the maleficent influence of Aristotle in every branch of human knowledge is systematically exposed; he followed it up five years later with an equally explicit *Censura de Aristotelis operibus*. But the most important figure in this tradition was the Frenchman Pierre de la Ramée (Peter Ramus), who worked away at Paris during the 1540s and 1550s to counter the influence of the humanist Ciceronians and Aristotelians there, and whose name later became a byword for aggressive Anti-Aristotelianism. Ramus proudly proclaimed himself an heir to Erasmus, and wrote a *Ciceronianus* of his own; he was also attacked by contemporaries as a new kind of sceptic.[24]

It is against the background of this Erasmian idea that we must read the only work of Renaissance political theory which rivals Machiavelli's works in importance – Thomas More's *Utopia* of 1516. More had been a supporter of Erasmus in his various ideological struggles since 1499, and like his mentor he had also been a close student of Augustine – no doubt because Augustine provided the most plausible non-Aristotelian strategy for coping with the disconcerting implications of the Roman moralists. Much (though, it must be acknowledged, not all) of *Utopia* makes sense in the context of Erasmus's 'modern' reading of Cicero. The book begins with a dialogue set against the background of agrarian crisis and a demand for land reform in contemporary England (a background identical in many ways to the background of Cicero's political career in the twilight of the Roman republic, a republic brought low, Cicero believed, by the socially disruptive demagoguery of men like the Gracchi). The dialogue is focused on the question of *counsel* – should

---

23. See R. H. Popkin, *The History of Scepticism from Erasmus to Spinoza* (Berkeley, 1979) pp. 5–6.
24. Ibid., p. 29. Ramus's *Ciceronianus* was published at Paris in 1557; for a discussion of it, see I. Scott, *op. cit.* pp. 100ff.

a wise man enter politics, and in particular the service of a Northern monarch with its necessary compromises and subterfuges? One of the participants in the dialogue, the imaginary character Raphael Hythloday, argues that he should not, unless the institution of private property which had led to the agrarian crisis is dismantled and replaced by a new social order. More, speaking in his own person as a young man, responds that this is misguided: it is important to keep the present show on the road. 'Don't spoil the entire play just because you happen to think of another one that you'd enjoy rather more.'[25]

More's sentiments here clearly echo those of Cicero, whose primary moral commitment had been to doing just that, and who had criticised Cato for behaving 'as if he lived in the Republic of Plato, rather than in the dregs of the state of Romulus' (Letters to Atticus II.1, Loeb pp. 108/9). Cicero had also condemned what he took to be the Platonic notion of communism, remarking about one of the schemes for land reform in the late republic that 'it favoured an equal distribution of property; and what more ruinous policy than that could be conceived? For the chief purpose in the establishment of constitutional state and municipal governments was that individual property rights might be secured' (De Officiis II.73). Hythloday is depicted as responding to this Ciceronianism by describing the state of the Utopians in which private property had been abolished, and all worked well. That the Utopians are obtrusively anti-Ciceronian is indeed characteristically hinted at in a passage where Hythloday lists the books he took with him to Utopia – all were in Greek, as 'I didn't think there was anything in Latin that they'd like very much'.[26]

Not only are the Utopians anti-Ciceronian, they are also in effect anti-Christian. Though Hythloday told them about Christ, and though they responded enthusiastically to his account, More goes to some pains to deprive Hythloday of the two things which contemporary Christians (including most definitely More himself) took to be vital for true Christianity – the Bible and the apostolic succession of the priesthood. Hythloday's list of books does not include the Bible, and no priest accompanied him on his voyage.[27] That Utopia is fundamentally at variance with More's idea of religion and the Church is revealed by a

---

25. *Utopia* trans. P. Turner (Harmondsworth, 1965) p. 63. For the most recent study of *Utopia*, which also stresses the Ciceronian aspect, and to which I am greatly indebted (though differing from it in some respects), see Q. Skinner, 'Sir Thomas More's *Utopia* and the language of Renaissance humanism' in A. Pagden ed., *The Languages of Political Theory in Early-Modern Europe* (Cambridge, 1987) pp. 123–58.

26. Ibid., p. 99.

27. Ibid., pp. 100, 118.

marginal note in one of his later works, his polemic against Luther.[28]

So *Utopia* depicts an ideal anti-Ciceronian republic, as Erasmus at least understood Ciceronianism – one in which there are no difficult practical choices to be made, and in which the reality of the modern world (including pre-eminently its Christianity) is kept firmly at bay. The interpretative problem about the book is that *imaginatively* the weight of the work is on the Utopians' side – the minute and concrete description of their state is what has always fascinated readers. Yet how can this be squared with the known position of the Northern humanists on these issues, and with the position which More himself espouses in the dialogue on counsel earlier in the book? We can either suppose that More's imagination here outran himself, or we can conclude that the covert message of *Utopia* is a conservative one – we should not introduce measures such as land reform piecemeal, for we would need a wholly restructured society for them to work at all, and such a radical reconstruction is out of the question in the real world which as true Ciceronians we must inhabit. Which route we take is a question which has occupied all readers of More, and it would, I think, be folly to suppose that it is possible to resolve the question in any wholly persuasive way.

By the middle of the sixteenth century, Ciceronianism (whether of the Italian or the Northern sort) had become the generally accepted language of moral and political discourse, at least outside the circles of technically-minded theologians. The Spanish Empire in particular rested its claims to European domination on the rhetoric of Cicero – either in its more conventional form, as when Sebastian Fox Morcillo portrayed the King of Spain as a Senecan prince in his *De regni, regisque institutione* of 1556, or in a more Machiavellian form, as in the case of Stephen Gardiner's advice to the government of Philip and Mary in England.[29] But by the end of the century the dominance of Cicero was over, and he had been replaced so comprehensively that one is entitled, I think, to talk of a wholly new kind of humanism which differed almost as much from the humanism of the earlier Renaissance as that humanism had differed from Aristotelianism.

## V

The central role in this development was played by *Tacitus*. Though a Roman, Tacitus had never been included in the group of writers

---

28. *Responsio ad Lutherum* in More, *Collected Works* V ed. J. M. Headley (New Haven, 1969) pp. 118–19.

29. P. S. Donaldson, *A Machiavellian Treatise by Stephen Gardiner* (Cambridge, 1975).

studied continuously throughout the Middle Ages; his style was utterly unCiceronian, and his sentiments equally alien to the earlier writers, for he viewed politics and ethics with a sceptical detachment, and treated the struggle for liberty as doomed. Princes, on his account, were wholly untrustworthy tyrants, and republican activists noble but foolish. It is thus not surprising that Ciceronian humanists were repelled by him, and it is noteworthy that even Machiavelli was uninterested in his views. One writer in Machiavelli's Florence did express admiration for Tacitus; this was Guicciardini, whose own vision of Italian politics came close to Tacitus's. But Guicciardini's lead was not to be followed until the 1560s, when a group of Italian exiles at the court of Catherine de' Medici in France began to study Tacitus closely, and to link him with Guicciardini and (to an extent) with Machiavelli as key writers for the modern world, who would have no truck with illusory moralities.[30] An associate of this group even attempted the unpromising task of defending the 1572 St Bartholomew's Day Massacre from moral condemnation, employing a clipped Tacitean prose to do so.[31] By the 1590s the study of Tacitus had virtually replaced that of Cicero as the central activity of the humanist moralist, trying to make sense of European politics in an age of confessional war and imperial aggrandisement. Beleagured Ciceronians (particularly among the Jesuits or their sympathisers) bewailed this development; as one of them, an English Catholic exile named Edward Weston, wrote in 1602, the Tacitist 'neoterici'

> entirely despise the graces of Cicero: like heavily-armoured soldiers (as they themselves say), they set no store by the fragrant scents or sweetly flowing smoothness of cultivated language. They would rather march forward with mail and shield, covered from head to foot with steel, and shattering men's ears with their terrifying expressions: in fact they glory in what they acknowledge is an *armoured* style[32].

Weston saw exactly the moral significance of Tacitism as a prose-style: it was the language of the battle-field, carrying military values with it. When he turned to the substance of his attack on the movement, he argued exactly what one would have expected, attacking Machiavelli (and, interestingly, quoting Sallust against him) and remarking that if

---

30. See G. Cardascia, 'Un Lecteur de Machiavel à la Cour de France: Jacopo Corbinelli', *Humanisme et Renaissance* 5 (1938) pp. 446–52; A. Momigliano, 'The First Political Commentary on Tacitus', *Journal of Roman Studies*, 37 (1949) pp. 91–101.
31. [Guy de Pibrac], *Ornatissimi cuisdam viri, De rebus Gallicis* (Paris, 1573).
32. *De triplici hominis officio* (Antwerp, 1602) II sig.d1.

the *politici* were to be accepted, 'then the consequence would be that these politicians could not properly institute a commonwealth, unless they were to set a cunning prince over a pack of fools.'[33] This defence both of orthodox moral values *and* of a more widespread participation by the populace in political and moral life is absolutely characteristic of the liberal Ciceronian humanist's response to Tacitism.

But Tacitism was not to be stopped by such criticisms, and its influence (interwoven with that of scepticism and of a new kind of Stoicism) was pervasive in the late sixteenth and early seventeenth centuries. It is partly against its background, moreover, that we can best read the great seventeenth-century works of political theory such as Grotius's *De Iure Belli ac Pacis* or even Hobbes's *Leviathan*. Tracing its influence is not part of my present purpose; the conventional view that these seventeenth-century writers lie outside the Renaissance proper has, I think, a common-sense justification precisely in the shift from Cicero to Tacitus as the great ancient moralist. What we intuitively think of as Renaissance humanism is not Tacitism, but an exploration of the implications for modern moral and political thought of the true philosophy of the Golden Age of Rome.

---

33. Ibid., II p. 182.

*Chapter Four*

# Humanism and the Court Arts

SYDNEY ANGLO

## I

In the Thyssen-Bornemisza Collection a painting by Hans Cranach depicts three young women teasing an unhappy bearded gentleman who is obliged to help them spin yarn. The ladies are dressed in contemporary robes; while the man wears a lace collar, a pair of slashed black breeches, and a handsome codpiece. Without an explanatory Ovidian quatrain it would be impossible to know that the picture represents the humiliation of Hercules at the court of Omphale.[1] Has the artist blundered and perpetrated a simple, unthinking anachronism? Is the classical allusion designed to give point to a wholly modern satire on the domination of a powerful man by beautiful women? Does the allusion to Hercules and Lydia in the verse mean that Cranach relied on the viewer's classical knowledge to supply everything which is absent from the picture – both form and content? And how would one set about measuring the humanist component of the scene?

On the face of it, assessing the impact of humanism on the court arts might seem an uncomplicated procedure. Choose the courts; decide on the arts; measure their humanistic content at the beginning of the fifteenth century; measure it again in the middle decades of the sixteenth century: and, hey presto, the job is done!

There are, unfortunately, several obstructive factors, one of which

---

1. D. Ekserdjian and M. A. Stevens, *Old Master Paintings from the Thyssen-Bornemisza Collection* (Catalogue of the Exhibition at the Royal Academy of Arts, London, March–June 1988), pp. 48–9.

is that many aspects of court life derived from traditions other than the purely classical. Art and science, mind and body, image and ritual, arms and letters: all had long been shaped by Christianity and chivalry with their own iconography, artistic monuments, and literary heritage; their own codes of loyalty, service, honour, and courage; and their own accumulated erudition. Moreover, much of the classical tradition had itself been assimilated by these rivals.[2] It is not always easy to isolate an unalloyed humanist impulse or – when traditions intermingled – to determine precisely what they meant to contemporaries.

The riddle of Hercules's codpiece remains insoluble. Nor can we be certain that, when Apollo appears as a pope in the choir of the Eremitani, or Jupiter turns up as a monk in the Campanile at Florence, the donning of Christian attributes is merely the accidental end of a long period of metamorphosis.[3] What were the mental processes underlying the habitual representation of scenes from ancient history where knightly Scipios and Hannibals jousted against each other; where Roman warriors fought in medieval armour with medieval weaponry; where everybody wore modern dress; and where famous deeds were enacted within familiar contemporary towns and banquet halls?[4]

Conversely, the habit of classicizing Christian or chivalric forms is just as problematic. When Capodiferro addressed Julius II as 'Apollo', it may only have been a straightforward metaphor echoing Caesar Augustus's enthusiasm for the Sun God, and suggesting the Pope's role as guardian of Rome's new imperial destiny.[5] But what level of assimilation by one tradition of another is indicated when Christ appeared as a Roman emperor; when scenes from the Scriptures were depicted as though they were episodes from Roman history; or when fifty 'Normands' marched into Rouen dressed as Roman soldiers?[6] What intellectual complexities underlay Cortesi's blending of classical

---

2. On aspects of this immense problem, see E. R. Curtius, *European Literature and the Latin Middle Ages* (New York, 1953); J. Seznec, *The Survival of the Pagan Gods* (New York, 1953); E. Panofsky, *Renaissance and Renascences in Western Art* (Stockholm, 1960); R. M. Ruggieri, *L'umanesimo cavalleresco da Dante al Pulci* (Rome, 1962).

3. Seznec, *op. cit.*, p. 161.

4. These habits were too common, and have been too often illustrated, to require references here. But the thinking which underlay these transpositions is certainly not always to be explained away as mere anachronism or indifference. Why, for example, did Galeotto dal Caretto, in his *Timone*, transform the Olympic games into 'una gran giostra' at Paris? See A. Tissoni Benvenuti and M. P. Mussini Sacchi, *Teatro del Quattrocento. Le corte padane* (Turin, 1983), p. 24.

5. C. L. Stinger, *The Renaissance in Rome* (Bloomington, 1985), p. 274.

6. Seznec *op. cit.*, p. 213; A. Chastel, 'The Arts during the Renaissance' in *The Renaissance: Essays in Interpretation*, (1982), p. 245; Stinger *op. cit.*, p. 269; P. Partner, *Renaissance Rome* (Berkeley, 1976), p. 127; *L'Entrée de Henri II à Rouen 1550*, facsimile with introduction by M. M. McGowan (Amsterdam–New York, n.d.), sig. D.ii^v.

language and Christian meaning, transforming the Church into *senatus*; the Immaculate Conception into *absolutissimus conciliandi actus*; the opinions of saints into *sententiae heroum*; Aquinas into *Apollo Christianorum*; and Adam into *Phaëton humani generis*?[7]

The intellectual and emotional ambiguities which result when different traditions meet, interact, or clash – with ancients modernized and moderns classicized – are especially apparent in the Renaissance taste for triumphal forms. There was no more potent and evocative symbol of ancient grandeur than the Roman triumph, with its processions, cars, trophies, prisoners, and celebratory arches.[8] The whole institution was the object of much fifteenth-century erudition: yet even the enthusiastic Flavio Biondo was uneasy and felt obliged to stress the superiority of Christian Rome over its pagan forebear. He hoped that Christian princes might emulate the deeds of Roman generals, and argued for a resumption of the triumph with the proviso that its symbolism be christianized.[9] The triumph became a focus for the pretensions, both political and cultural, of many Renaissance princes; and scholarly reconstruction was soon succeeded by artistic re-enactment.[10] But the Roman tradition was not unique. There was also the confused literary and pictorial tradition of the Petrarchan *Trionfi*; there was the Christian tradition, itself by no means unadulterated, of Christ's triumphant entry into Jerusalem; and, often alluding to this, there was the late medieval ritual of the joyous entry – when princes were received into their cities to be greeted by pageants and *tableaux vivants*. Classical imagery, architecture and triumphal forms first began to affect civic pageantry in Italy, in the middle decades of the fifteenth century. North of the Alps, this development did not become significant until a century later: though everywhere there were ambiguities and inconsistencies.[11] Sometimes there might be a fundamental inde-

---

7. J. F. D'Amico, *Renaissance Humanism in Papal Rome* (Baltimore, 1983), pp. 154–63.

8. On the triumph in general, see F. Noack, 'Triumph und Triumphbogen', *Vorträge der Bibliothek Warburg: 1925–1926* (Leipzig-Berlin, 1928), pp. 147–201. R. Payne, *The Roman Triumph* (1962) is light-weight but very useful.

9. C. L. Stinger, 'Roma Triumphans: Triumphs in the Thought and Ceremonies of Renaissance Rome', *Medievalia et Humanistica*, new series, X (1981), pp. 194–5; Stinger, *Renaissance in Rome*, pp. 241–3, where he points out that before the end of the fifteenth century the imagery of triumph was being applied not only to the popes but also to Christ himself.

10. W. Weisbach, *Trionfi* (Berlin, 1919); G. Carandente, *I trionfi nel primo Rinascimento* (Edizioni Rai Radiotelevisione Italiana, 1963). For more extended artistic and literary implications, see M. M. McGowan, *Ideal Forms in the Age of Ronsard* (Berkeley, 1985), especially pp. 120–58; A. Pinelli, 'Feste e trionfi: continuità e metamorfosi di un tema', in S. Settis, ed., *Memoria dell'antico nell'arte italiana* (Turin, 1984–86), II, pp. 279–350.

11. In England classical themes made a superficial appearance in the London entry of Anne Boleyn in 1533 but then vanished for another 70 years. See S. Anglo, *Spectacle*

corousness such as Julius II's celebration of Mass on Palm Sunday 1507 as the prelude to his pagan triumph at Rome; or sometimes it would be a detail, as at Paris in 1549, when the greatest authorities on classical architecture in contemporary France, Jean Martin and Jean Goujon, deliberately armed the figure of Hercules (who stood on top of an arch combining the Doric and Tuscan orders) with a chivalric lance.[12]

Most perplexing of all Renaissance triumphs are the series of illustrations prepared for Maximilian I. The emperor, ever indigent, balked at the cost of a triumphal arch in stone, but conceived the brainwave of creating an arch in paper which, by means of the woodcut technique, might be erected in many places simultaneously or could even be read as a book. The text of the *Ehrenpforte* was prepared by the humanist, Johannes Stabius; another humanist, Pirckheimer, concocted its iconological conundrums; Kölderer, the architect, planned the structure; and a team of artists, led by Dürer, executed the blocks. There was no lack of expertise. Yet the immense and indigestible heap of Christian and pagan symbols, allegories and hieroglyphs; the multiplicity of scenes lauding Maximilian's chivalric and military gifts; and the hideous deformity of proportion, and bizarre assemblage of towers, domes and pinnacles – all combine to convey the very antithesis of a Roman triumphal arch.[13]

The *Ehrenpforte* is a Gothic nightmare. The associated series of woodcuts, the *Triumphzug*, is more subtly equivocal: though, once again, the activities represented are those dearest to the Emperor. There is falconry; hunting the ibex, chamois, deer, boar and bear; fencing and tourneying. Maximilian's favourite jester, Conrad von der Rosen, appears with the car of fools; Peter von Altenhaus leads a group of masquers; Hans Hollywars, the fencing master, leads troops of warriors armed with flails, quarterstaves, lances, halberds, battle-axes, swords and bucklers; and distinguished practitioners of the various chivalric

---

*Pageantry and Early Tudor Policy* (Oxford, 1969), pp. 248–58. For the increasing influence of classical tradition on French royal entries, see J. Chartrou, *Les entrées solennelles et triomphales à la Renaissance* (Paris, 1928); McGowan, *Ideal Forms*, pp. 143–8; *The Entry of Henri II into Paris 16 June 1549*, facsimile with introduction by I. D. McFarlane (Binghampton-New York, 1982), intro., pp. 38–44.

12. On 1507, see B. Mitchell, *Italian Civic Pageantry in the High Renaissance* (Florence, 1979), pp. 114–15, where the occasion is described as a 'celebration remarkable for the High Renaissance promiscuity of Christian and classical pagan themes'. See also Stinger, 'Roma Triumphans', pp. 189–90. For the detail of 1549, see the facsimile reproduced in McFarlane, *ed. cit.*, sig. 3ʳ–4ʳ.

13. E. Chmelarz, 'Die Ehrenpforte des Kaisers Maximilian I', *Jahrbuch der Kunsthistorischen Sammlungen des Allerhöchsten Kaiserhauses* (Vienna), IV (1886), pp. 289–319. For a convenient description, see C. Dodgson, *Catalogue of Early German and Flemish Woodcuts preserved in the Department of Prints and Drawings, B. M. London* (1903–11), I, pp. 311–21.

combats popular at the Imperial court accompany knights appropriately armed. The emperor's journey to his Burgundian wedding is shown; his territories are symbolized; and his military campaigns and battles are represented along with prisoners and trophy cars filled with armour and weapons. The courtiers, soldiers, servants, musicians and knights are in no sense *all'antica*. They wear contemporary clothes and armour; they carry contemporary weapons; and they play contemporary instruments. This is an Imperial triumph: but it is emphatically of a German, not a Roman, emperor.[14] Yet, in a way, the very contemporaneity of the *Triumphzug* – where old forms are used to express the triumphator's personality, deeds, and power – make it more genuinely antique than any straightforward reconstruction of a particular Roman triumph could ever be. Creativity and novelty were essential, for mere slavish adherence to ancient forms was not true to the spirit of the ancients. As Lodovico Canossa argues in *Il Cortegiano*, 'se noi vorremo imitar gli antichi, non gl'imitaremo'.[15] The paradox is well observed; and it further compounds the difficulty of assessing the influence of humanism on the court arts.

In any case, what were the court arts? Historians of culture have charted the accumulation of increasingly exact knowledge of the institutions, customs, artefacts and ideas of the ancient world. They have demonstrated the impact of this knowledge on the development of classical forms, themes and techniques in the work of a host of individual artists and writers, and more generally in architecture, sculpture, painting, and every branch of literature. There are libraries-full of relevant books, monographs and articles; and to attempt to summarize them all here would be tedious and pointless. Even if such an attempt were possible, it would not get to grips with the central issue. No one can dispute that humanism profoundly affected what we know as the fine arts. The question is, are these identical with the court arts?

Long ago, Kristeller raised the difficulties concerning the evolution of the modern system of the arts, and he alluded to an amateur tradition of the Renaissance as most elaborately expressed in *Il Cortegiano*. He deemed this account of the pursuits proper to the courtier unsatisfactory as a true systematization, because Castiglione recommended not only the appreciation of poetry, music and painting, but also stressed the

---

14. F. Schestag, 'Kaiser Maximilian I. Triumph', *Jahrbuch* (Vienna), I (1883), pp. 154–81. The plates were published in a supplement to this volume. There is also a useful edition with an English translation of the descriptive text by S. Applebaum, *The Triumph of Maximilian I* (New York, 1964).

15. Baldassare Castiglione, *Il Cortegiano*, I.xxxii. For suggestive observations on this topic, see E. H. Gombrich, 'The Style all'antica: Imitation and Assimilation', in his *Norm and Form. Studies in the Art of the Renaissance* (1966), pp. 122–8.

value of classical learning and eloquence, along with fencing, hunting, riding, dancing, jousting, and other physical and recreational skills.[16] In fact, this heterogeneity is the very heart of the matter. The fine arts were appreciated at court; they were encouraged there; they were used and exploited there; they were sometimes even glorified there. None the less, they did not of themselves constitute the court arts. Recreational and cultural pursuits at court were wide-ranging and eclectic; and they were rarely regarded by contemporaries from the elevated vantage point assumed by the modern critic. It is sobering to reflect that the Palazzo del Te started out as a 'monumentalized stable'; and that even so noted a connoisseur of fine painting and architecture as Federico Gonzaga of Mantua thought more of his dogs, horses and hawks.[17]

For many of the most absorbing courtly interests, classical sources were meagre. Xenophon's observations on the horse and hunting, for example, were well known but rudimentary; and Renaissance equestrianism and venery owed little to ancient authority.[18] The same is true of the handling of weapons – a favourite courtly art and one in which rulers were well versed. Maximilian I had himself depicted participating in every kind of tournament, and was also shown practising the two-handed sword with his fencing master.[19] Henry VIII, Francis I, Henry II, and Charles V were all keen on chivalric activities which they practised assiduously; but the greater part of their training, and of the relevant literature which developed in the fifteenth and sixteenth centuries, was empirical not academic. It owed nothing to the painstaking reconstructions of Greek and Roman military organization which absorbed the attention of classical scholars.[20]

It was, in fact, not until 1553 that Camillo Agrippa (distinguished mathematician, engineer, friend of Michelangelo, and brawler) published the first systematic attempt to apply scientific principles of

---

16. P. O. Kristeller, 'The Modern System of the Arts', *Journal of the History of Ideas*, XII (1951), pp. 496–527, and XIII (1952), pp. 17–46; reprinted in his *Renaissance Thought II. Papers on Humanism and the Arts* (New York, 1965), pp. 163–227.

17. E. H. Gombrich, '"That rare Italian Master . . . " Giulio Romano, Court Architect, Painter and Impresario', in *Splendours of the Gonzaga* (Catalogue of the Exhibition at the Victoria and Albert Museum, London, November 1981–January 1982), p. 79. See also Catalogue Nos. 72–6 and the literature cited therein.

18. For a chronological list, see J. H. Huth, *Works on Horses and Equitation. A bibliographical record of Hippology* (1887).

19. Quirin von Leitner, ed., *Freydal des Kaisers Maximilian I. Turniere und Mummerein* (Vienna, 1880–82).

20. No general survey of personal combat techniques has yet replaced E. Castle, *Schools and Masters of Fence from the Middle Ages to the Eighteenth Century* (1885; repr. 1969). A. Wise, *The Art and History of Personal Combat* (1971) is useful for its illustrations; and there is much valuable material in C. Bascetta, *Sport e Giuochi. Trattati e scritti dal XV al XVIII secolo* (Milan, 1978).

measure, leverage, and timing to the art of fencing.[21] His treatise was dedicated to Cosimo de' Medici whose ancestors are hailed as the true restorers of good letters, sciences, and the honoured languages, and who is himself praised as the support of both arms and letters – a combination which, while much extolled by humanist educators, had also frequently assumed a chivalric guise; particularly from the thirteenth century when Llull wrote his *Book of the Order of Chivalry* to provide a literary basis for knightly skills, analogous to the books which instructed clerks. The union of arms and letters had been highly prized at the Provençal courts where elegant lyrics and formalized eroticism went hand in hand with chivalric activities. In the fifteenth century it may also be seen in Diaz de Gamez's description of the festivities at Serifontaine; at the court of the dukes of Burgundy; and, perhaps most strikingly, in the career of René d'Anjou who composed literary works, illuminated manuscripts with his own hand, wrote on tournament ceremonial, and was an active participant and organizer of chivalric combats, as well as a man of enormous political pretension – if scant achievement.[22]

The relationship between learning and physical exercise was not a specifically humanistic preoccupation. We may see it expressed in La Sale's *Petit Jehan de Saintré* where the hero not only acquires proficiency at riding, singing, dancing, running, leaping, and in arms, but is also given lengthy moral instruction and a crash course in the classics – Livy and Orosius to learn about the Romans' feats of arms; Suetonius on the twelve Caesars; Sallust on Catiline and conspiracies; Lucan for the conflict between Caesar and Pompey; Mathastrius on the kings of Egypt; Dares the Phrygian on the Trojans; Polybius on Ptolemy; Josephus on the Jews; and Victor on the history of Africa. 'You cannot better employ your time', Jehan is told, than by reading these ancient histories 'to instruct your mind in all noble and illustrious acts'.[23] Yet La Sale was scarcely touched by humanism; and his hero is a purely chivalric fiction.

Though the juxtaposition – both by La Sale and Castiglione – of aesthetics, athletics, classical learning and chivalric exercise, may seem wilful, it was not the result of an imperfect conception of the arts. Rather, it resulted from a keen perception of the activities and interests

21. Camillo Agrippa, *Trattato di Scientia d'Arme, con un dialogo di filosofia* (Rome, 1553). On Agrippa, see Castle, *op. cit.*, pp. 45–9; Bascetta, *op. cit.*, pp. 186–207.

22. S. Anglo, 'The Courtier. The Renaissance and changing ideals', in A. G. Dickens, ed., *The Courts of Europe*, (1977), pp. 38–41.

23. Antoine de la Sale, *Little John of Saintré*, trans. I. Gray (1931), pp. 103–4. For a less courtly view and a clear distinction between arms and letters, see Christine de Pisan, *The Book of Fayttes of Armes and of Chyvalrye*, ed. A. T. P. Byles (E. E. T. S., 1932), pp. 6–7.

deemed important at court where their interrelationship was social, not aesthetic. Moreover, they were important not only to courtiers but also, and more significantly, to the princes who set standards and established fashions. Castiglione's courtier was nothing but a scaled-down version of the omnicompetent Renaissance prince best exemplified, perhaps, by the Emperor Maximilian I who died in January 1519. In the following year the Imperial Historiographer, Stabius, presented Charles V with an account of his predecessor's literary legacy. Maximilian had often declared that he intended to have 130 books prepared, recording his deeds, accomplishments and ideas for posterity. Only a few works from this massive programme were ever completed: but these, together with those projected, constitute by far the fullest statement of the interests considered apposite to the Renaissance prince.[24] Life and death; the past, present and future – Maximilian's imagination was all-encompassing. He was concerned with planning his tomb, to be adorned with an army of life-sized statues of ancestors and heroes; with the preparation of lavishly-illustrated celebrations of his genealogy and of the saints whom he especially venerated; and with the design of the great triumphal series already alluded to. History, genealogy, heraldry, magic, the art of war, artillery, music, masquing, dancing, hunting, fishing, fencing, tourneying, and jousting – all engaged the Emperor's intellectual and physical energies; and all were commemorated, or proposed for inclusion, in the books he planned.

Yet Maximilian working in his armourer's workshop, discussing technical matters with his gunfounders, or displaying expertise and daring while hunting in the forest or fighting within the lists, are all depicted as activities on exactly the same level as Maximilian conversing with his scholars, advising his builders, watching his artists at work, or visiting his musicians.[25] Artists, writers and humanist scholars were involved both in Maximilian's courtly activities and in the task of recording them: but their skills were never regarded as autonomous or important for their own sake. They were merely tools to serve their prince's purposes: recreation, pleasure and solace; the

24. The literature on these works is considerable, but for general guidance see the following. *Maximilian I. 1459–1519. Ausstellung* (Vienna, 1959); *Ausstellung Maximilian I. Innsbruck. Katalog* (Innsbruck, 1969); L. Baldass, *Der Künstlerkreis Kaiser Maximilians* (Vienna, 1923); G. E. Waas, *The Legendary Character of Kaiser Maximilian* (New York, 1941; repr. 1966); Pierre du Colombier, 'Les Triomphes en Images de l'Empereur Maximilian I<sup>er</sup>', in Jean Jacquot, ed., *Fêtes et cérémonies au temps de Charles Quint* (Paris, 1960) (this is the second of three volumes on Renaissance fêtes ed. by Jacquot. See below n. 45); G. Scholz-Williams, *The Literary World of Maximilian I: an Annotated Bibliography* (St. Louis, Center for Reformation Research, 1982).

25. For these and other illustrations of Maximilian's interests, see *Der Weisskunig*, ed. A. Schultz, *Jahrbuch* (Vienna), VI (1888).

glorification of the House of Habsburg; the enhancement of Maximilian's court during his life-time; and the assurance that his tastes and achievements might endure after his death.[26]

These multiform interests, and the way in which the arts were exploited, typified the Renaissance court. Castiglione's *sprezzatura*, the art which conceals art – whatever its appeal to individuals – was not characteristic of the essential courtly art. This was, rather, an art which displayed art; proclaimed wealth and brilliance; drew attention to itself by ostentation and prodigality. Princes and their satellites played out roles as stereotyped as those of the *Commedia dell'arte*: and the theatre in which they performed was the court. As Budé remarked of Francis I, his court was a 'perpetuel spectacle d'honneur' and 'le vray theatre des choses vertueuses, et de grande recommandation'. The court was itself the most courtly of art forms.[27]

## II

Changes in court culture did not proceed in a uniform manner and from some fixed and common starting point. Humanistic influence was not some race with all the courts lined up awaiting the starting pistol: and if it were then clearly some entrants enjoyed the advantage of a considerable start, for there were discrepancies between courts north and south of the Alps, and glaring differences between humanism in Italy and elsewhere in Europe. It was one thing to play at Roman empire in medieval Rouen or Paris; quite another to perform the same

---

26. In *Der Weisskunig*, Maximilian replies to one who criticized his expenditure on such memorials: 'He who during his lifetime provides no remembrance for himself, has no remembrance after his death, and the same person is forgotten with the tolling of the bell, and therefore the money which I spend on remembrance is not lost; but the money which is spared on my remembrance, that is a suppression of my future remembrance, and what I do not accomplish during my life for my memory will not be made up for after my death, neither by thee nor by others'. See Waas, *op. cit.*, pp. 97–8. There is an immense specialist literature on dynastic exploitation of the arts. For some recent examples, see A. Chastel, *Art et humanisme à Florence au temps de Laurent le Magnifique* (new edn, Paris, 1981); J. Cox-Rearick, *Dynasty and Destiny in Medici Art. Pontormo, Leo X, and the two Cosimos* (Princeton, 1984); G. Chittolini, G. Cerboni Baiardi, P. Floriani, eds, *Federico di Montefeltro. Lo stato, la cultura, le arti* (Rome, 1986); A-M. Lecoq, *François Ier imaginaire. Symbolique et politique à l'aube de la Renaissance française* (Paris, 1987).

27. Guillaume Budé, *De l'institution du prince*, cited in McGowan, *Ideal Forms*, pp. 14–15. Within the last decade, literature on the courts of Europe has been flooding from the press. The volume ed. A. G. Dickens, *The Courts of Europe*, contains essays on individual courts and has helpful bibliographies. An especially noteworthy series is the *Europa delle Corti* which is being published by Bulzoni of Rome. The first volume of *Le corti farnesiane di Parma e Piacenza 1545–1622*, which is *Potere e società nella stato farnesiano*, ed. Marzio A. Romani, (Rome, 1978), includes a series of brief introductory essays relating to the whole project.

role in the shadow of the Palatine or Colosseum. There were, moreover, many kinds of court. There were big courts and little courts; an imperial court and a papal court; royal courts and ducal courts; and there were myriad minor courts gathered about various dignitaries, both lay and spiritual. Even a court located in one place might vary according to the personality and tastes of its rulers. There could, for instance, scarcely be greater contrasts than between Henry VII and Henry VIII, Louis XII and Francis I, or Borso and Ercole d'Este. But wherever the court, and whatever its style, its denizens were acutely conscious of the need to be effective; and just as courtiers struggled to catch their prince's eye, so princes were themselves under unremitting scrutiny.

The public enactment of ceremonies great and small was essential. The whole point of the coronation of Christian kings was, as Elyot wrote, that 'by reason of the honourable circumstances then used would be impressed on the hearts of the beholders perpetual reverence, which is the fountain of obedience'. If this were not so, he added, then a king might more conveniently be anointed, and receive his crown and regalities, in a private place. It is important to remember that 'we be men and not angels, wherefor we know nothing but by outward significations'.[28] This was just as true when the ruler expired. He could not slip out of the world quietly. State funerals were intensely dramatic spectacles with their solemn cortèges, protracted lying-in-state, and mighty catafalques. In England and France another paradoxical dimension was added by the use of effigies taken from the death mask; and it became the custom in France to give the effigy open eyes so that the departed might appear to be participating actively in his own obsequies – an effect heightened by continuing the service of meals throughout the period of public mourning, as though the corpse could still eat them. Everybody was thus drawn into the bizarre show.[29]

Coronations and funerals, ceremonies of birth and baptism, weddings, royal entries, diplomatic receptions – the great rituals of court life defined the form of the courtly drama. There was, too, a regular daily round: from the morning levée, washing and use of the privy, eating and drinking, and transaction of routine business, to the ceremonial bed-warming and final retiring for the night. There were regular pastimes of hunting, hawking and jousting; religious observ-

---

28. Thomas Elyot, *The boke named the governour*, ed. H. H. S. Croft (1883), II, pp. 197–201; ed. S. E. Lehmberg (1962), p. 163.

29. R. E. Giesey, *The Royal Funeral Ceremony in Renaissance France* (Geneva, 1960; repr. 1983); W. H. St. John Hope, 'On the Funeral Effigies of the Kings and Queens of England with special reference to those in the Abbey Church of Westminster', *Archaeologia*, LX (1906–07), pp. 517–70.

ances; polite and impolite conversations; and always a constant changing of apparel as considered appropriate for each activity. The courtly art comprised the totality of what the court did and, as is the case with every art, it was subject to rules and conventions. However, as far as classical precedents were concerned, there were few which might have enabled the humanists to make a major contribution in this area.

The courts of the Roman emperors and other ancient rulers were well known from histories: but nothing survived in the way of a precise formulary. The only real precedent was the account of ecclesiastical and secular rituals collected together in the ceremonial book of Constantine Porphyrogennetos during the tenth century.[30] 'By beautiful ceremonial', wrote Constantine, 'the imperial power appears more resplendent and surrounded with greater glory; and thereby it inspires alike foreigners and subjects of the Empire with admiration'.[31] This is a perfect expression of the idea of magnificence which was to inform the court life of Renaissance princes: but there is no evidence of any link between Byzantine theory and practice on the one hand and, on the other, the process of systematizing court ceremonial which took place in Western Europe during the fifteenth and sixteenth centuries. The evolution of ceremony and ceremonial records was an essentially pragmatic, *ad hoc* process responding to the needs of polities striving for the prestige conferred by a distinctive and imposing ritual.

The King of England, it is said in the *Black Book of the Household* of Edward IV, compiled early in the 1470s, 'wull have his goodes dispended but not wasted', and the philosophy of the court is well expressed in the prolegomena to this meticulous survey of the functioning of the English royal household, where a number of precedents are set forth.[32] Foremost among these is no less a monarch than King Solomon, the 'exemplar of householding', who astounded the Queen of Sheba less by his magnificence than by the order within which it was manifested. The Queen was impressed by his officers 'fourmed in astate and degrees, all thing executing after theyr occupacions and chargez to the high excellence of the king'. She was amazed at the way in which every member of the household steadfastly obeyed the rules 'to kepe the ministres thereof from any breche, outrage, reproche, or nicetie,

---

30. *De ceremoniis aulae byzantinae*, ed. J. J. Reiske (Bonn, 1829); ed. A. Vogt (Paris, 1935–39). See also J. B. Bury, 'The Ceremonial Book of Constantine Porphyrogennetos', *English Historical Review*, LXXXVI (1907), pp. 209–227; LXXXVII (1907), pp. 417–39.

31. This is cited by C. Diehl in *The Cambridge Medieval History*, (Cambridge, 1911–36), IV, p. 727.

32. A. R. Myers, *The Household of Edward IV. The Black Book and the Ordinance of 1478* (Manchester, 1959), p. 87.

making ordynat reverentz aftyr the distinccions of every high or low degre, and as pepull to straungers cherefull, so many under obedyence in one house'. Here, in Solomon's ordered magnificence, we can see the Renaissance ideal; and the purpose of this English compilation – undertaken by a committee of the most powerful in the land – is succinctly stated in a reference to another, less remote, courtly prototype. The household of Edward III, it says, was the 'house of very polycye and flowre of Inglond, the furst setter of sertayntez among his domestycall meyne, uppon a grounded rule'.[33] This was the art of court life: fixed routine; specified duties; clear demarcations; a place for everybody; and everybody in his place.

The Yorkist attempt to regulate public and household ceremony was repeated by the Tudors.[34] The same impulse – and certainly the inspiration for these English essays – had been evident at the court of the dukes of Burgundy where it was recorded by Olivier de la Marche and Aliénor of Poitiers. The laws relating to precedence, the rigorous ceremonial at state occasions, the rituals of religious observance, council meetings, public audiences, the duties of each member of the household, and every minute detail relating to the preparation and service of meals, are set forth with an earnestness worthy of 'officers of state debating the most delicate of political problems'.[35] Indeed, these were ticklish matters of state. The significance of protocol is equally apparent in the ceremonial book of Francesco Filarete who was constantly battling to ensure that public ceremony followed well-defined rules. ·Predictability was the desideratum: partly because it was necessary, as one historian has put it, 'to minimize dynamic interaction between the principals, and thus control the flow of ritual meanings';[36] and, more prosaically, because it is much easier to organize and budget for an event when you know exactly what is going to happen. The ritualistic framework had a more than symbolic import, for even the slightest departure from prescribed form could be interpreted as a deliberate mark of disrespect. Thus the Florentine citizens worried terribly about whether their representatives climbed more than the proper number of steps to receive visitors. Thus Charles the Bold and the Emperor Frederick III – meeting outside Trier in 1473 – stood for an hour in the

33. Ibid., pp. 81, 84.
34. *A Collection of Ordinances and Regulations for the Government of the Royal Household made in divers reigns from King Edward III to King William and Queen Mary* (1790).
35. O. Cartellieri, *The Court of Burgundy*, trans. M. Letts (1929; repr. 1972). pp. 65–72; W. Prevenier and W. Blockmans, *The Burgundian Netherlands* (Cambridge, 1986), pp. 223–5.
36. R. C. Trexler, *The 'Libro Cerimoniale' of the Florentine Republic by Francesco Filarete and Angelo Manfidi. Introduction and Text.* (Geneva, 1978), p. 66.

pouring rain, arguing about whether the duke should ride behind the emperor or whether they should enter side by side. The two rulers were soaked to the skin, and even this led to difficulties because the emperor very sensibly donned his cloak, whereas Charles would not cover his jewels and decorations.[37] Nearly fifty years later similar punctilios constantly disturbed the meeting between Francis I and Henry VIII at the Field of Cloth of Gold.[38]

In the tricky business of ordering precedence, precedent was all-important. When the Florentine Signoria commanded Filarete to compile a record of all the entries of ecclesiastical and temporal princes who had visited their city 'at least from 1456', they required him to note the ceremonies and the costs involved. He was further required to add each new occasion as it occurred, and to confer with the officials of the Palace in order that 'true records are made so that when comparable cases occur, one can proceed with the correct order'.[39] Such records had long been kept by papal officials, not only for the regulation of the chapel but also for public processions; and this process was formally enunciated when, in 1487, Agostino Patrizi, papal Master of Ceremonies, and his assistant Johan Burckhard, were presented with eight old ceremonial books and requested to compile a new one. Also at this time Burckhard began to keep the ceremonial diaries which have become an important source for historians, but which were primarily intended as an aid for the diarist himself.[40] And much the same may be said of another related genre which developed during the fifteenth century – that is the heraldic miscellany. Heralds had grown in importance as diplomats and emissaries; as official repositories of ceremonial wisdom; as arbiters of etiquette; and as organisers of (and prompters at) state occasions, tournaments, duels and pageantry. The development of these duties had been accompanied by a responsibility for providing written narratives of the events at which they officiated, together with the habit of compiling collections of such descriptions which might serve both as memorial and model.[41] It has been well said of the middle decades of the fifteenth century that it is as though 'Europe had made an irrevocable commitment to a static social order expressed in

---

37. Cartellieri, op. cit., pp. 63–4.
38. S. Anglo, Spectacle, pp. 145–7, 149, 151, 154.
39. Trexler, op. cit., p. 53.
40. E. Celani, ed., Johanni Burckardi Liber Notarum ab anno MCCCCLXXXIII usque ad annum MDVI (Città di Castello, 1906).
41. See G. A. Lester, Sir John Paston's 'Grete Boke'. A descriptive Catalogue with an Introduction, of British Library MS Lansdowne 285 (Cambridge, 1984), pp. 48–58; A. R. Wagner, Heralds and Heraldry in the Middle Ages (1939), pp. 25–55; S. Anglo, 'Financial and Heraldic Records of the English Tournament', Journal of the Society of Archivists, II (1962), pp. 183–95.

prescriptive ceremonial forms; secular heralds and papal clerks would attempt to realize their masters' dreams'.[42]

There is, however, more to the matter. The fact is that there was a prodigious inertia about state rituals. The most important of these had evolved over centuries; and their essential quality was precisely that they were traditional and largely unchanging. They formed a visible bond between past and present. It was this which gave them their immense evocative power. And the combination of ritual inertia and the desire for continuity, regularity, order and predictability meant that humanism was more able to effect change in matters of style and presentation than in the central drama of court life.

Popes and princes could have their palaces built and decorated *all'antica*; they could flatter themselves in simulations of Roman triumphs; and they could wallow in eulogies dense with classical allusion and analogy. But all the scholarship and artistic skill in the world could make them no more Roman emperors or classical heroes than their medieval forebears had been. Michel de l'Hôpital declared that kings had a duty to display their power and deeds, 'comme s'ilz estoient à la veue de tous sur un theatre representez'.[43] Within that theatrical context, the roles of architects, painters and writers are not best understood by regarding them as the culture heroes with whom we are all too familiar. Their mighty buildings, wonderful paintings, and literary masterpieces were simply the scenography, décor, and texts for the courtly performance. This is a less lofty view: but it corresponds more closely to the way in which princes tended to regard those whom they patronized.[44]

### III

Artists of every kind worked for princes – helping to adorn their courts, project their magnificence, and glorify their reputations. Considered individually, however, not one of these fine arts which flourished under princely patronage was itself a courtly invention. The principal art-form specifically created by the political and social needs of rulers and their acolytes was the court festival: a spectacular amalgam characterized by the way in which the various arts, so often rivals with

---

42. Trexler *op. cit.*, p. 25.

43. McGowan, *Ideal Forms*, pp. 15–17.

44. Patronage has become a very modish subject: but it needs to be kept in perspective. Princes disbursed money to please themselves, not for the good of their artists. For some pertinent remarks on the limits and realities of Renaissance patronage, see E. H. Gombrich, 'The Early Medici as Patrons of Art', in E. F. Jacob, ed., *Italian Renaissance Studies: a Tribute to the late Cecilia M. Ady* (1960), pp. 279–311; repr. in *Norm and Form*, pp. 35–57.

competing claims to superiority, were obliged to come together at the behest of princes. Architects, painters, sculptors, carvers, composers, instrumentalists, singers, poets, choreographers and dancers, together with an army of craftsmen, artisans, and labourers, all combined to add lustre to some ritual event. Politically, the value of the fête lay in its demonstration of wealth, taste, and the ability to employ great creative and executive talent. Aesthetically, its quality resided in the virtuosity with which vastly disparate materials were manipulated and success-fully fused. Such a composite art could only flourish at court. The logistical problems of gathering these immense teams, keeping them together to fulfil some spectacular enterprise, and supplying their artistic requirements and creature comforts, could generally only be solved by the resources available to kings and princes.[45]

Important political events had always been marked by celebrations, entertainments and spectacle but, in the closing decades of the four-teenth century, these began to take on a special character and to become increasingly complex, costly and fantastic. The pace – and, to some extent, the pattern – was set by the magnificences presented at the court of the French kings, Charles V and Charles VI: though that initiative petered out with the latter monarch's insanity and with English military ascendancy. More resonant, and better documented, are René d'Anjou's series of allegorical tournaments where dramatic and romance elements were developed to such a point that the combats became the central feature of a multiform and partially rehearsed festival such as the *Chasteau de la Joyeuse Garde* (1448). This was a richly decorated temporary structure, named after Lancelot's castle, where René and his court lived for forty days – enjoying feasting, dancing, and an exotically costumed tournament.[46] This mode was taken up by the dukes of Burgundy in numerous festivals which similarly focused on the tournament. The most frequently discussed was the Feast of the Pheasant (1454), organ-ized as the climax to a series of banquets and feats of arms intended

---

45. The obvious starting point for work on Renaissance court festivals is the volumes edited by the late J. Jacquot, *Les Fêtes de la Renaissance*, 3 vols. (Paris, 1956, 1960, 1975); *Le Lieu théâtral à la Renaissance* (Paris, 1964); *La Vie théâtrale au temps de la Renaissance* (Catalogue of the exhibition at the Institut Pédagogique, Paris, March-May 1963). A useful synthesis of much festival research is in R. Strong, *Art and Power. Renaissance Festivals 1450–1650* (Woodbridge, Suffolk, 1984), which includes extensive bibliographical notes. Useful bibliographies are also provided in the catalogue, *Il potere e lo spazio. La scena del principe* (Florence, 1980); and there is much material in F. Marotti, *Storia documentaria del teatro italiano. Lo spettacolo dall'Umanesimo al Manierismo. Teoria e. technica* (Milan, 1974).

46. On René, see R. A. Lecoy de la Marche, *Le Roi René: sa vie, son administration, ses travaux artistiques et littéraires* (Paris, 1875); Comte de Quatrebarbes, *OEuvres complètes du roi René* (Angers, 1845–46).

to inaugurate a crusade;[47] but the most coherent (or rather the least incoherent) Burgundian festival was prepared for the marriage of Charles the Bold and Margaret of York. This was the *Pas de l'Arbre d'Or* at Bruges in June 1468.[48] The wedding ceremony was followed by the state entry of the new duchess into the city where she was greeted by a pageant series, primarily of biblical inspiration. Then, for the rest of the week, the court participated in a tournament based on a literary fiction set out in an allegorical letter and developed both as the theme for the combats and as a decorative motif. The market place was enhanced by a simple *mise-en-scène*; the jousts were regulated by a herald Arbre d'Or, accompanied by a giant and a dwarf; and there were ceremonial pageant cars, semi-dramatic speeches, poetry and music. Each evening, after the fighting was over, a prodigious feast was served in a specially constructed wooden building, some 140 feet long, 70 feet wide, and 62 feet high. Its ceiling was covered with blue and white woollen material; its walls were hung with tapestries celebrating the story of Jason and the Golden Fleece; and the lighting was supplied by men, hidden in huge castles, working machinery and mirrors which made it seem as though the hall was filled with 10,000 people. The service of the banquet was spectacular. One evening, for example, the meat dishes arrived in thirty ships each bearing the name of one of the ducal dominions. All the arms were in silk, the cordage in fine gold, and men-at-arms and sailors swarmed over the ship, 'tout au plus-pres du vif qu'on pouvoit faire la semblance d'une caraque ou d'un grand navire'. Also on the groaning tables were thirty great pies formed like castles, painted gold and blue, each with the arms and name of one of the duke's cities. Entremets were presented on most evenings and included a griffon from whose beak issued forth live birds; a unicorn and a leopard bearing the arms of England; a singing lion; and a dromedary mounted by a wild man. There were also three shawm-playing goats who, with a buck blowing a 'trompette saquebutte', executed a motet; four wolves performing a flute quartet; and asses singing a four-part chanson, *Faictes vous l'asne, ma maitresse*.

During the week of the tournament there were presented the twelve labours of Hercules, spread over three evenings. These were performed on a stage at one end of the hall: each labour revealed by the drawing

---

47. Cartellieri, *op. cit.*, pp. 139–53; A. Lafortune-Martel, *Fête noble en Bourgogne au XV⁰ siècle. Le banquet du Faisan (1454): Aspects politiques, sociaux et culturels* (Montreal and Paris, 1984).

48. Cartellieri, *op. cit.*, pp. 124–34, 157–63. The principal descriptions of this festival are: Olivier de la Marche, *Mémoires*, ed. H. Beaune and J. d'Arbaumont (Paris, 1883–88), III, pp. 101–201; and the same author's *Traictié des Nopces*, Beaune and d'Arbaumont, IV, pp. 95–144; an English herald's account, printed in S. Bentley, *Excerpta Historica* (1833), pp. 227–39. See also Lester, *op. cit.*, pp. 118–22.

of a curtain ('fut la courtine retirée'), and its significance indicated by a ten-line verse attached to the scene. On the final evening, the entremet was a pageant built like a whale, some sixty feet long, and so high that two mounted men – one at each side – would not have been able to see each other. Its eyes were two enormous mirrors, and its whole body seemed alive as it swam into the hall, preceded by two giants. When it opened its mouth out came two sirens singing a strange song, followed by knights of the sea who began to dance a moresque, but soon fell to blows until parted by the giants. It was, said Olivier de la Marche, a very fine entremet for there were more than forty people inside the whale; and John Paston, who was present with the English entourage, was deeply impressed by Burgundian hospitality and entertainment. He wrote home to his mother, 'I herd never of none lyeke to it save Kyng Artourys cort'.[49]

The Pas de l'Arbre d'Or was the most sumptuous and extravagant spectacle presented by the most sumptuous and extravagant court of the fifteenth century. Organized by a committee headed by the duke's Master of Ceremonies, Olivier de la Marche, it employed every kind of artistic skill to prepare the special banquet hall and theatre for the indoor entertainments, and to adapt the town square as a theatre for the tournament; to decorate them; and to rehearse and dress the shows which were spread over several days. Especially striking is the heterogeneity of the display; but, though it is easy to mock the naivety and lack of decorum, an exactly similar appetite for artistic hotch-potch may be encountered in the Italian courts of the late fifteenth and early sixteenth centuries – where, for instance, a drama by Plautus might be interrupted by totally unrelated moresche, mock combats, and exhibitions of juggling. One of the most famous theatrical performances of the Renaissance, Bibbiena's La Calandria produced by Castiglione at Urbino in 1513, was punctuated by intermezzi including a morescha in which Jason sowed dragon's teeth and fought the warriors who sprang therefrom; moresche of Venus, Amorini, and nine gallants; Neptune and a sword-dance with monsters; and Juno with peacocks, ostriches, sea birds, and parrots, all performing another sword-dance. When the comedy was finished, one of the Amorini appeared, to explain what the intermezzi were all about – because they were a 'separate thing from the comedy itself'.[50] This lack of decorum persisted not only in the spectacles organized by the Spanish and imperial heirs to the Burgundian tradition but also in Italy despite the work of generations of

49. Paston Letters and Papers of the Fifteenth Century, ed. N. Davies (Oxford, 1971), I, pp. 538-9.
50. Castiglione's own account is translated in J. Cartwright, The Perfect Courtier. Baldassare Castiglione, His Life and Letters, 1478-1529 (1908), I, pp. 335-41.

humanists expounding the classical unities, and a considerable literature on artistic, literary, rhetorical and dramatic proprieties.

Copiousness and prodigality were still blatant in some of the most famous Florentine festivals a century after the *Pas de l'Arbre d'Or*. To celebrate the marriage of Francesco de' Medici and Joanna of Austria in 1565, there were two groups of spectacle – the first cluster in December, and the next group in the following February. The bride entered Florence on 16 December and proceeded through the city which was adorned with triumphal arches. Two days later the marriage ceremony took place and, in the following week, there was a performance of Francesco d'Ambra's comedy *La Cofanaria* in the Palazzo Vecchio, where the Salone dei Cinquecento had been transformed into a theatre with a raked auditorium facing a raised stage decorated with an illusionistic Florentine street scene and separated from the audience by a painted curtain.[51] The five acts of the play were preceded, punctuated and followed by six intermezzi based on the story of Cupid and Psyche, spiced with descents from the heavens, and with 'piccoli monticelli' and demons hurtling up through trapdoors in the stage. The next group of festivals began on 2 February 1566 with a nocturnal procession of dreams through the city. There were sirens blowing trumpets; the four humours; standard bearers; Cupid and a host of lovers accompanied by Hope and Fear; Narcissus with those besotted by Beauty; Fame, Glory and Prize of War with emperors, kings and dukes; Plutus with Greed and Rapacity; Bellona with Terror, Courage and the brave; and finally Pazzia with Folly and the fools. There were also forty-eight witches and priestesses and a final pageant car depicting the cave of Somnus Prince of Sleep. A fortnight later there was a two-day bombardment and assault on a mock fortress built in the Piazza Santa Maria Novella. And finally, after a two-day respite, there came a procession, the *Genealogia degli Dei*, with twenty-one pageant cars and 329 mythological and allegorical characters, all visiting Florence to join in the marriage celebration.

The themes for these triumphal entries and processions were devised by a committee of savants led by Vincenzo Borghini, and executed by a team of distinguished artists including Vasari, Bronzino, Giovanni da Bologna, and Zuccaro. These are great names, and their mighty display of knowledge is seemingly far removed from the naive medieval view of classical mythology displayed in the Burgundian festivals. But there are different kinds of naivety. Mere heaping up of images – largely culled from iconological encyclopaedias, and mingling 'all the mongrel and barbaric divinities which in these texts, as in the manuals, supplant

---

51. For a summary of the sources, see A. M. Nagler, *Theatre Festivals of the Medici 1539–1637* (New Haven, 1964), pp. 13–35.

the classical gods'[52] – is evidence neither of sophistication nor artistic taste. It also had the disadvantage that few people could understand what was going on.[53] Nor did matters improve at Florence over the next quarter of a century. Even so renowned a spectacle as the performance of Bargagli's *La Pellegrina* (1589) had the acts of the comedy interspersed with intermezzi – devised by a different author, Giovanni Bardi – of such erudition that only an expert philologist could have comprehended them. Stupendous classical scholarship and a coherent scheme underlay all six intermezzi which were presented with a scenographical virtuosity far beyond anything dreamt of at the court of Burgundy. But they still had nothing to do with the play.[54]

Another feature of the Bruges *Pas de l'Arbre d'Or* which was to remain characteristic of court festivals was the extent to which the greater part of the enterprise was necessarily ephemeral. The contributions of the huge teams of artists generally survive only vicariously in written descriptions, or in drawings, sketches and engravings of structures, décor, and costumes which were never meant to remain behind once they had served their passing purpose, however brilliantly they had been executed. As Vasari writes of three large canvases painted by Bronzino for the Florentine magnificences of 1565, they were done 'in so beautiful a fashion that they did not seem like things for a festival, but rather worthy to be displayed for ever in some honoured place, so finished were they and executed with such diligence'.[55] Music, too – instrumental, choral and song – filled these festivals. Yet only a tiny fraction of it survives.[56] Literary texts, by their very nature, have fared better: and this has had a distorting effect on subsequent interpretations and evaluations of these shows. The poets' words have, inevitably, triumphed. In the Renaissance itself the spectator's scale of values was different. It was the spectacular mode which was at a premium; and this was rarely built to make the arduous journey through posterity.

Once performed, the festival's scenery, effects, and décor would be dismantled. Some of the properties might be preserved for use on another occasion: but sooner or later they were broken up and lost for ever.[57] This was the case with the Bruges banquet hall of 1468, just as

52. Seznec, *op. cit.*, p. 285.
53. Nagler, *op. cit.*, p. 34, and n. 74.
54. Ibid., pp. 70–92.
55. Giorgio Vasari, *Vite de' piu eccellenti pittori scultori e architetti* (Milan, 1807–11), XV, pp. 189–90.
56. See the comments by D. P. Walker, 'La musique des intermèdes Florentins de 1589 et l'humanisme', in Jacquot, *Fêtes*, I, pp. 133–44.
57. It is interesting in this connection to note the dismantling and reassembling of the seating in the Salone dei Cinquecento in the Palazzo Vecchio at Florence. See Nagler, *op. cit.*, p. 3; *Il potere e lo spazio*, pp. 323–6.

it had been half a century earlier in the same city where the special 'grande salle', built for the entertainment of Isabel of Portugal, was designed for destruction: 'ce fut faicte neufve, pour abattre'.[58] It was the case with the temporary wooden theatre at Ferrara where Plautus's *Menaechmi* was performed in 1486;[59] and with the theatre built for Ludovico Sforza's castle at Milan about 1490, which has cost us décor and machinery by Leonardo da Vinci;[60] with the theatre built within the Castello at Mantua in 1501, considered a model for 'all who wish to erect appropriate theatres for the performance of ancient and modern plays'; and with the enormous theatre built on the Campidoglio at Rome in 1513.[61] It was the case with the mighty English temporary palace and theatre at the Field of Cloth of Gold at Calais. Yet these were the masterpieces of obscure English artists whose sole surviving works now consist of a few scraps of heraldic painting and some moth-eaten funeral effigies leaking horse-hair. This was the case with the theatre built for Henry VIII at Greenwich in 1527: the dismantling of which has cost posterity two large canvases by Holbein, an astrological ceiling by the same artist, and antique busts by Giovanni da Maiano.[62] And it was true of the theatre built in Mantua for the wedding festivities of Guglielmo Gonzaga in 1561. This last structure was used only for a tournament. Yet it was architecturally magnificent, richly embellished and, according to Leone di Somi, might have outshone the ancients if only it had been fashioned of some durable substance rather than lath and plaster: 'but all the greater was Duke Guglielmo's magnanimity in spending so many thousands of ducats on that marvellous set and then destroying it when it had served its immediate purpose'.[63]

---

58. *Chronique de Jean le Fèvre Seigneur de Saint-Remy*, ed. F. Morand (Paris, 1876–81), II, p. 160. Compare earlier examples in 1389, *Chronique du religieux de Saint-Denys*, ed. Bellaguet and De Barante (Paris, 1839–52), I, pp. 586–9.

59. Marotti, *op. cit.*, p. 29; Benvenuti and Sacchi, *op. cit.*, pp. 17–18; W. L. Gundersheimer, *Ferrara. The Style of a Renaissance Despotism* (Princeton, 1973), pp. 210–11.

60. K. Steinitz, 'Le dessin de Léonard da Vinci pour la représentation de la Danae de Baldassare Taccone', in Jacquot, *Lieu théâtral*, pp. 35–40.

61. The quotation on 1501 is from a description by Sigismondo Cantelmo, trans. in J. Cartwright, *Isabella d'Este, Marchioness of Mantua 1474–1539* (1903), I, pp. 183–5. On 1513, see F. Cruciani, *Il teatro del Campidoglio e le feste Romane del 1513 con la riconstruzione architettonica del teatro di Arnaldo Bruschi* (Milan, 1968).

62. On these buildings, see Anglo, *Spectacle*, pp. 139–44, 159–68, 211–34. For a very interesting reconstruction of the Calais theatre, see R. Hosley, 'The Theatre and the Tradition of Playhouse Design', in H. Berry, ed., *The First Public Playhouse. The Theatre in Shoreditch 1576–1598* (Montreal, 1979), pp. 47–79.

63. An English translation of Leone di Somi's *Dialogues* is published as an appendix in A. Nicoll, *The Development of the Theatre* (1927), pp. 237–62. The above quotation is at p. 258.

The problem of ephemerality was seen in its most acute form at the banquet given in the Palais Episcopal of Paris where the French court celebrated the entry of Charles IX's new queen, Elizabeth of Austria. Part of the decoration was a series of six allegorical tableaux depicting the history of Minerva. The sculptures were learned and their imagery complex; and they culminated in a representation of the city of Athens and of a debate between Neptune and the goddess. The series had been devised by the poet Jean Dorat, the greatest classical scholar in France; and the work was directed by Germain Pilon, the foremost French sculptor of the day. However, nothing has survived, for the classical scheme was brilliantly executed in sugar. It was all designed to be eaten.[64] This may seem a *reductio ad absurdum* of the evanescent nature of court festivals and the theory of conspicuous consumption. But it reminds us that the most distinguished scholars and artists could be involved in the most transient spectacles; and that their efforts in wood and on canvas, in mime, song and movement, were generally no more enduring than the classical 'sucreries' of 1571.[65]

Throw-away theatres remained a normal feature of festivals throughout the Renaissance and beyond: though an appeal for a permanent theatre at Rome had been made by Sulpizio di Veroli in the dedication of his edition of Vitruvius in 1486. The relationship between humanism and theatre design remains ambiguous, uneven and sometimes vexed. Certainly scholars were interested in discovering as much as they could about the physical presentation of classical drama: but, as with so many other aspects of the reconstruction of ancient institutions, it was a difficult and slow labour based first on the inadequate descriptions in Vitruvius and on the intelligent speculations of Alberti, and subsequently on the analysis and measurement of enigmatic ruins. There were, moreover, conflicting and almost incompatible interests involved in theatre design and décor. Scholars and scholarly architects may have wished to build on the basis of their research into classical forms. Their patrons, on the other hand, were more concerned with spectacular effects and effective spectacle than with archaeological accuracy.[66] The same artists who pondered the structure, dimensions

---

64. *La ioyeuse Entree de Charles IX Roy de France en Paris*, facsimile with introduction by F. A. Yates (Amsterdam and New York, n.d), sigs. F.iv^v-G.ii^v; V. E. Graham and W. McAllister Johnson, *The Paris Entries of Charles IX and Elisabeth of Austria 1571* (Toronto and Buffalo, 1974), pp. 393–4.

65. The problem of artistic ephemerality in the Renaissance has been little studied, though there has been some very interesting work on later material. See especially M. Faggiolo d'Arco and S. Carandini, *L'effimero barocco* (Rome, 1977); A-C. Gruber, 'Les décors de table éphémères aux XVIᵉ et XVIIIᵉ siècles', *Gazette des Beaux-Arts* (1974), pp. 285–300.

66. On this crucial problem, see R. Klein and H. Zerner, 'Vitruve et le théâtre de la Renaissance Italienne', in Jacquot, *Lieu théâtral*, pp. 49–60.

and conventions of the Roman theatre were kept busy devising increasingly illusionist stage sets; while the multiple needs of courtly revels were often more satisfactorily met by temporary structures, or by the adaptation of existing space.

Nevertheless, the impact of classical scholarship on theatre design and scenography in Italy, and the ways in which archaeological knowledge was creatively, if often mistakenly, deployed for new purposes, can be documented from the late fifteenth century onwards – though it was not until the closing decades of the sixteenth century that permanent court theatres based upon classical models were built at Vicenza, Sabbionetta and Florence; and temporary theatres erected in court-yard, banquet hall, or city square remained a striking feature of Medici festivals in the seventeenth century. Elsewhere, humanist learning exerted a slower and less powerful pressure. In England, for example, disguisings, masks, and other entertainments were sometimes presented in temporary buildings planned and executed on a grandiose scale. The greatest of these, at the Field of Cloth of Gold, was regarded by one Italian observer as exceeding anything that even Leonardo himself might have devised. Yet it was wholly medieval in character. Neither the round-house built for masks at Calais in 1520, nor the 'long-hows' built for entertainments at Greenwich in 1527 – despite superficially antique features – owed anything to theoretical reconstructions of ancient theatres; and the scanty evidence concerning temporary English banquet halls *cum* theatres later in the sixteenth century suggests no greater humanist influence. It was not until the reign of James I that Inigo Jones adapted Palladian theory to the needs of the court masque.

France did not have to wait for an Inigo Jones to bring back ideas from Italy. Instead it had Sebastiano Serlio himself who had been invited by Francis I to become his court architect. Indeed, the second Italian edition of Book Three of the *Architettura* – which includes reconstructions of Roman theatres – was dedicated to the king of France.[67] Serlio's misfortunes after the death of his patron, when he was frozen out by his French counterparts, did not lessen his impact on architecture in general; but, as far as we can tell, his presence made little difference to French festivals where the first important court theatre had been prepared for an ambassadorial reception in Paris in 1518. The court of the Bastille was roofed over and transformed into a great *salle des fetes*, fitted with galleries along the sides for spectators, and tables in the *cavea* for the diners. It was provided with an apposite zodiacal decorative scheme; and completed at one end with a raised and lavishly appointed stage divided into four parts by five 'colomnes esquarres'. As in any

67. McGowan, *Ideal Forms*, pp. 121–8.

theatrical performance, this stage was the focal point for all onlookers. But the drama was provided simply by the king taking his place there upon the throne. Troops of masquers did enter and dance, and there was a general ball; but these took place in the main body of the hall. One commentator remarked that the festival was 'a la mode et magnificence Rommaine', regretted that his own descriptive powers lacked the 'propriété exquise' of Vitruvius, but believed that the banquet surpassed Plato, Augustus Caesar and Lucullus. None the less, neither the proportions nor disposition of the theatre owe anything to classical precedent or to specifically humanist scholarship.[68] And a similar lack of debt is suggested by the surviving scraps of information concerning the banquet and masquing houses built for Francis I at Ardres in 1520 – even though Fleuranges described one of these as being in the fashion 'comme de temps passé les Romains faisoient leur théâtre, tout en rond'.[69] We know just as little about the adaptation by Philibert Delorme of the court-yard of the Château-Neuf at Saint Germain for theatrical performances.[70] And even when we arrive at the sophisticated union of words, music and dance devised for the *Balet comique de la Reine* in 1581, we find that the theatre and décor have less relationship to contemporary Italian developments than to the combination of fixed scenes and mobile pageant car entries which had characterised Burgundian entertainments and tournament scenography over a century earlier.[71]

In 1468 at Bruges, the duke of Burgundy and his courtiers had enjoyed the story of Jason adorning the walls of the banquet house, and watched Hercules performing his labours in mime and dance upon the stage. Fourteen years earlier at Lille, Hercules's exploits had been hung about the walls, while the story of Jason was enacted in choreographic combat.[72] The Burgundian dukes were fond of antique heroes. Versions

---

68. A. Bonnardot, ed., *Les rues & églises de Paris, vers 1500. Un fête à la Bastille etc.* (Paris, 1876), pp. 77–107; *Calendar of State Papers Venetian*, II, 1128; Edward Hall, *Chronicle*, ed. H. Ellis (1809), p. 596.

69. Fleuranges, *Mémoires*, ed. Michaud and Poujoulat (Paris, 1838), p. 69; *Calendar of State Papers Venetian*, III, 60, 80, 94; Hall, *Chronicle*, p. 607.

70. A. Chastel, 'Cortile et théâtre', in Jacquot, *Lieu théâtrale*, pp. 46–7.

71. *Le Balet Comique by Balthazar de Beaujoyeulx 1581*, facsimile with introduction by M. M. McGowan (Binghampton–New York, 1982).

72. Olivier de la Marche contradicts himself on the tapestries of 1468. In his *Mémoires*, ed. Beaune and d'Arbaumount, III, p. 118, he says that they represented 'l'Ystoire de Jason'. In the *Traictié des Nopcès*, IV, p. 107, he says that there was a tapestry of 'Gedeon'. The English account also thought that Gideon was shown on this occasion (*Excerpta Historica*, pp. 234–5). Clearly there were problems with these two golden-fleece heroes. According to Olivier de la Marche, in his *Epistre pour tenir et celebrer la noble feste du Thoisin d'Or*, the Order of the Golden Fleece was originally based on 'la poeterie de Jason', but had been changed by Jehan Germain, bishop of Chalon and 'chancellier en

of the Trojan legends figured prominently in their libraries; Jason's deeds were constantly evoked in the ceremonies of the Order of the Golden Fleece; and Hercules was regarded as founder of the Burgundian dynasty.[73] Yet, as Panofsky observed, educated Northerners were familiar with the 'topical content' of the classical tradition without realizing its 'estrangement from classical forms'.[74] In the tapestries which decorated their palaces, and in the miniatures which enhanced their manuscripts, the Burgundians would see Alexander the Great or the Trojan warriors fighting their campaigns in the manner and garb of contemporary chivalry.[75] The adventures of Jason and Hercules, as performed at their court festivals, were no more accurate in historical detail or sympathy. These were not classical plays. They were simply shows about knights sporting classical names.

A taste for the real thing was, however, rapidly developing in Italy where humanists had long been concerned not only with the reconstruction of ancient theatres but also with the plays which might have been staged there. They had commented upon these texts, translated them, and even performed them: but it was the production of Plautus's *Menaechmi*, sponsored at enormous cost by Ercole d'Este in 1486, which inaugurated a new era of collaboration between scholarship, drama, and princely desire for prestige.[76] The rest of Ercole's reign witnessed presentations of most of Plautus's major plays, and some by Terence. During the same period, similar performances became a regular feature of Roman festivals; and other Italian courts soon followed suit. At the same time, humanists were active writing new comedies in a classical manner – relying on erudite commentaries upon ancient authors for their stylistic proprieties, and ransacking non-theatrical classical sources, history, and mythology for their themes.[77] The inclusion of a classical or neo-classical play as part of a princely entertainment became very modish. But the fashion was never popular outside Italy; and, even there, classical plays were more important for pedagogical than for courtly purposes.[78] They only occasionally consti-

---

l'ordre', and based instead upon 'le fort Gedeon, qui est histoire de la Bible et approuvée' (Beaune and d'Arbaumount, IV, pp. 163–6).

73. Seznec, *op. cit.*, pp. 25–6; Cartellieri, *op. cit.*, pp. 172–6; Prevenier and Blockmans, *op. cit.*, pp. 220–21.

74. Panofsky, *op. cit.*, pp. 201–8.

75. W. G. Thomson, *A History of Tapestry from the Earliest Times until the Present Day* (1906), pp. 101–32; Prevenier and Blockmans *op. cit.*, pp. 310, 318.

76. Gundersheimer, *op. cit.*, pp. 209–12.

77. Benvenuti and Sacchi, *op. cit.*, pp. 19–26.

78. Classical drama made only a fitful and insignificant appearance at the early Tudor court and – apart from a few vernacular adaptations in the latter half of the sixteenth century – not at all under the Valois.

tuted the most significant part of a festival; and, when they did, they were not an unqualified success. When, for instance, Ercole d'Este presented five Plautine comedies in 1502 as part of the festivities for the marriage of his son Alfonso to Lucrezia Borgia, the audience was considerably more amused by the wholly irrelevant intermezzi of *moresche* and other dances than by the revival of ancient drama. In fact, when at the performance of the *Bacchidae* only two dances were introduced into the play, the audience were dismayed: 'and at the end we heard nothing but groans and complaints from the spectators, who had already sat there more than four and a half hours'.[79] This preference for the spectacular, balletic and mimetic garnish rather than for the dramatic meat itself persisted throughout the Renaissance and well beyond.[80]

The future of court festivals, and of the theatrical forms which evolved within them, was as deeply rooted in the recent medieval as in the remote classical past. Princes may have been delighted to have their ancestry traced back to the Trojans: but even those most anxious to prove their ancient lineage saw themselves, simultaneously, as heirs to a chivalric tradition which was more solid to them than the web of historical fantasies spun by their official pedants and propagandists. Thus while scholarly forms and themes, such as the triumph and imperial destiny, enjoyed a vogue throughout the Renaissance, so, too, did the chivalric romances – however much they may have been despised by humanists. There was no lack of neo-Latin historical epics lauding the dynasties of the Renaissance: yet it was Amadis who captured courtly as well as popular imagination; while the deeds of Charlemagne's knights, Godefroy of Bouillon, and other Christian warriors gained a new lease of life when transformed by the literary sophistication of Boiardo, Ariosto and Tasso. And these mutated chivalric epics, in their turn, provided a rich repertoire of themes and characters for festivals, masques, ballets and operas for centuries to come.

Similarly, despite the theatrical researches of antiquaries and the sometimes brilliant creativity of playwrights working in classical forms, court festivals continued to be dominated by the tournament – that is

---

79. The sources for these Ferrarese entertainments are set out in B. Mitchell, *Italian Civic Pageantry*, pp. 28–30. My quotation is from the English translation of Isabella d'Este's descriptive letters in J. Cartwright, *Isabella d'Este*, I, p. 208.

80. Thus the choleric James I, seemingly indifferent to the literary splendours and arcane subtleties of Jonson's *Pleasure Reconciled to Vertue*, roundly cursed the dancers when they flagged: and thus the Venetian ambassador, bored with Jonson's *Time Vindicated to Himself and his Honour*, dismissed it as 'various preliminaries and appearances of no great account' which delayed the dancing. See C. H. Herford and P. and E. Simpson, *Ben Jonson* (Oxford, 1925–52); *Calendar of State Papers Venetian*, XVII, 752.

by the chivalric exercise *par excellence*. The survival of this obsolescent war game into the seventeenth century is both politically and aesthetically significant. For many princes, as for the dukes of Burgundy, lavish entertainment of visiting dignitaries at knightly combats (and equally important, participating in such displays) was an internationally valid symbolic manifestation of real political power. Even the banker's progeny in pseudo-republican Florence were concerned to shine at feats of arms; and there are no more renowned literary monuments to the Renaissance taste for chivalric contests than the sets of verse purporting to celebrate the otherwise unremarkable feats of the Medici in the lists.[81]

At the same period, the rulers of Naples, the Bentivogli of Bologna, the Este of Ferrara, and the Gonzaga of Mantua were all spending profusely on tournaments: partly because they simply enjoyed spectacle and exercise; and partly because they valued the effects these wrought on spectators.[82] The Bolognese chronicler, Ghirardacci, writing late in the sixteenth century, was completely carried away by the splendour of Giovanni Bentivoglio's tournament of 1470, and recorded that this festival was 'the principal reason that Giovanni increased in good will and opinion not only at home with the Bolognese people, but also with all the princes and lords of Italy; and by this means he soared to greatness of glory and was reputed more and more, from that time, the first man not only of Italy but also of the whole of Europe'.[83] This is manifest nonsense: yet the idea, that such activities conferred political stature, endured. Tournaments were at the centre of the artificial court life, and even more artificial chivalric self-portrait, of the Emperor Maximilian I; and monarchs – from the ambitious but necessitous James IV of Scotland to Francis I, Henry II, Charles V and Henry VIII – spent much time and money jousting, tourneying, and battling at the barriers.[84] Even when the steam had gone out of the fighting in the closing years of the sixteenth century, the later Valois still used contests

---

81. R. Truffi, *Giostre e Cantori di Giostre* (Rocca S. Casciano, 1911), pp. 116–37; I. Maier, *Ange Politien. La formation d'un poète humaniste (1469–1480)* (Geneva, 1966).

82. On Italian tournaments, see Truffi; M. Tosi, *Il torneo di Belvedere in Vaticano e i tornei in Italia nel Cinquecento* (Rome, 1946); *La Società in Costume Giostre e Tornei nell'Italia di Antico Regime* (Foligno, 1986); M. Scalini, ed., *Il Saracino e gli spettacoli cavallereschi nella Toscana Granducale* (Florence, 1987).

83. Cherubino Ghirardacci, *Della Historia di Bologna*, ed. A. Sorbelli, (Città di Castello, 1915–16), I, p. 206.

84. S. Anglo, *The Great Tournament Roll of Westminster* (Oxford, 1968), I, pp. 1–18; W. H. Jackson, 'The Tournament and Chivalry in German Tournament Books of the Sixteenth Century and in the Literary Works of the Emperor Maximilian I', in C. Harper-Bill and R. Harvey, eds., *The Ideals and Practice of Medieval Knighthood* (Woodbridge, 1986), pp. 49–73.

derived from the tournament as the basis for their magnificences; and Queen Elizabeth I encouraged her courtier-knights to squander their own resources, tamely tilting to celebrate her Accession Day as a Protestant festival.[85]

The nature of the impact of humanism on all this is problematic. The question may be posed in two different ways: how far could humanism modify chivalric forms? or how far was humanism itself modified by them? Either way, the question – with regard to the court festivals of the dukes of Burgundy – seems meaningless. The fictions, characterizations, and settings of feats of arms in the Burgundian tradition were entirely inspired by romances of chivalry, with their damsels in distress; their pavilion and castle pageant cars; their dwarves, giants, wild men and women; their hermits, captive knights, and gaolers. In Italy, too, until the middle of the fifteenth century, the imagery of that minority of tournaments which included some pageantic and allegorical element, seems to have been no more classical.[86] When, for example, the defenders at Naples in 1423 made their entry, it was on a gigantic elephant carrying a celestial castle with a choir of angels; and their opponents, disguised as devils, entered on two cars ablaze with fireworks. However, thirty years later at Milan, a mock siege of castles was billed as a contest between Coriolanus and the Volschi; and thereafter classical characters and motifs made more frequent appearances in Italian tournaments.[87] At Padua in 1466, for example, the spectacle included a long series of pageantic entries similar in structure to those favoured in contemporary Burgundy: but, instead of scenes and figures from romance, there were knights armed in antique fashion, Saturn, Danaë, Leda, Castor and Pollux, Jupiter on a wooden horse 'maggior di quello di Troja', Venus and the most famous warriors of antiquity, Mount Aeolus, Juno, Neptune, Bellerophon with the 'vasta Chimera vomitante fuoco', Amazons and nymphs, Mount Parnassus, Enceladus and Typhoeus waging war against the heavens, Mars, Minerva, the Argonauts, Cupid, Vulcan, and the Cyclops. In 1475, Fama, Scipio, Alexander and Caesar appeared at a tournament in Pesaro; in 1481 at Treviso the Cyclops, Mount Aeolus, centaurs,

---

85. On the Valois festivals, see F. Yates, *The French Academies* (London, 1947), pp. 236–74; and the same author's *The Valois Tapestries* (1959). On Elizabethan chivalry, see R. Strong, *The Cult of Elizabeth. Elizabethan Portraiture and Pageantry* (1977), pp. 129–62; A. B. Ferguson, *The Chivalric Tradition in Renaissance England* (Washington-London-Toronto, 1986); A. Young, *Tudor and Jacobean Tournaments* (1987).

86. I say 'that minority of tournaments', because most early Italian tournaments were very straightforward: and this tradition continued alongside the allegorical 'torneo a soggetto' until well into the seventeenth century.

87. E. Povoledo, 'Le théâtre de tournoi en Italie pendant la Renaissance', in Jacquot, *Lieu théâtral*, pp. 99–100.

Ganymede, Vulcan, Neptune, Hercules, Mars and Jupiter, rode through the lists on triumphal cars; while at Bologna in 1490, a tournament was preceded by a debate between Wisdom and Fortune who appeared on rival pageant cars – Sapientia accompanied by four men of venerable aspect with long beards and garments *all'antica* (Plato, Marcus Cato, Quintus Fabius, and Scipio Nasica); and Fortuna with Julius Caesar, Augustus, Adrianus, and Metellus.[88]

Yet, as long as the combats themselves remained serious – and knights, whatever the allegory surrounding their challenge, still fought with all their strength and skill, delivering and receiving hard blows and injuries – so classical names and settings were no less cosmetic than the romance fictions which had preceded them and continued in vogue. Ghirardacci might choose to describe the hammering of maces in a tourney as issuing from the 'forge of Vulcan':[89] but neither a mythological simile nor the presence of Greek and Roman celebrities within the lists could transform the tournament into a humanist entertainment. In the end, the spectators were still watching knights in medieval armour battering each other with medieval weapons.

The discrepancy between classical setting and chivalric practice is most striking in Rome itself. Nowhere was imperial history and myth more deliberately and systematically cultivated than under the paganized papacy of Julius II and his successors. In the course of that ambitious programme, Julius called upon Bramante to do something with the enormous area between the Vatican palace and Innocent VIII's Villa Belvedere. The scheme took more than half a century to complete; and it was a combination of garden and architecture, entirely classical in conception, and influenced by the Roman emperors' palaces on the Palatine Hill. Of the series of terrace courts designed by Bramante to rationalize the slope of the terrain, the lowest was bound on its east and west sides by three-storey facades defined by the Doric, Ionic, and Corinthian orders; and the whole creation was intended to function as a setting for great court spectacles. This it did. But the spectacles displayed there did not include classical drama. It is true that, according to a painting of the Cortile executed in the 1530s by Perino Del Vaga, the lower court was an artificial lake where a mock naval battle was taking place; and it has been remarked that, in Perino's

---

88. For Padua (1466), see G. Visco, ed., *Descrizione della giostra seguita in Padova nel giugno 1466* (Padua, 1852); *Ludovico Lazarelli de Patavino Hastiludo Praeclarissima Carmina* (Padua, 1629). For Pesaro (1475), see M. Tabarrini, ed., *Descrizione del convito e delle feste fatte in Pesaro per le nozze di Costanzo Sforza e di Camilla d'Aragona nel maggio del MCCCCLXXV* (Florence, 1870), pp. 56–62. For Treviso (1481), see G. della Torre, *Dialogo della Giostra* (Treviso, 1598), pp. 156–60. For Bologna (1490), see Ghirardacci, *ed. cit.*, pp. 258–9.

89. Ghirardacci, *ed. cit.*, p. 261.

archaizing reconstruction, Bramante's theatre stands as the recreation of Nero's Vatican *naumachia*.[90] This may be so: but more usually it was the setting for bullfights and jousts. And the best-known representation of the Cortile is the engraving by Du Pérac, in Lafreri's *Speculum Romanae Magnificentiae*, of the tournament held by Pius IV in 1565. Furthermore, the vast cortile theatre audience is being treated not to the relatively safe contest of the tilt, but to a joust *a campo aperto*. Two mounted knights wait at opposite corners of the court yard while, in the centre, attendants try to sort out the wreckage of two other knights and their horses strewn about the ground. The scene demonstrates perfectly the impact of humanism on the architectural and theatrical aspects of court art. It also demonstrates its limitations. The classically defined space is the setting for a very primitive chivalric exercise which owes nothing to classical scholarship or taste.[91]

The encounters at Rome were not, as a matter of fact, typical of the evolution of chivalric combat as a court spectacle in the sixteenth century. These exercises, known generically as tournaments, originated as practical military training for the knights who long dominated the battlefields of Europe where the essence of combat had been the heavy lance charge followed by mounted fencing: though it was not uncommon for knights to dismount and wield their swords on foot. The tournament always faithfully mirrored such battles – a mounted charge followed by sword-play both mounted and on foot – and this division remained constant even as the tournament became increasingly stylized, and the general mêlée was largely replaced by individual jousting and tourneying. Safety precautions proliferated. Armour became heavier and more comprehensive; lances and swords were rebated; and, early in the fifteenth century, the tilt was introduced to separate the horses in individual lance combat. This was a decisive change; and the speedy popularity achieved by tilting (and by foot combats at the barrier which mimicked them) marked a new era in the artificialization of the tournament and its divorce from military realities. The tilt was valuable as an exercise in horsemanship and handling the lance – but real wars were not fought across a safety fence. Gradually new military techniques, organization, weaponry, and attitudes rendered chivalric combat itself, for which tournaments had once been a training, of less and less military utility; and the final step in the

90. Stinger, *Renaissance in Rome*, pp. 270–1.
91. There is a good reproduction of this engraving in Domenique de Menil, ed., *Builders and Humanists. The Renaissance Popes as Patrons of the Arts* (Catalogue of exhibition, University of St Thomas, Houston, Texas, March–May 1966), A.9. For an excellent collection of texts with valuable commentaries on earlier Roman festivals, see F. Cruciani, *Teatro nel Rinascimento Roma 1450–1550* (Rome, 1983).

direction of chivalric irrelevance was the increasing popularity of riding with lance not at a live opponent but at a ring or quintain – which themselves only constituted exercises in preparation for the tilt. The stage was reached when a majority of tournaments consisted merely of exercises for an exercise training knights for a kind of warfare which had itself become outmoded.[92]

This evolution inevitably had its effect upon the way in which tournaments were presented. Moreover, the relationship between tournaments and the sequence of magnificences with which they had always been associated – banquets, dances, mimes and masques – was also affected. The difference between the kinds of activity which might go on within the lists and the balletic, predetermined combats which had long been popular indoors steadily diminished, even though the general shape and themes of these festivals did not greatly alter. The issue of allegorical challenges, often first proclaimed at a banquet or ball, remained the norm. So did the staleness of their conception. Captured damsels and knights, love-lorn heroes and wicked gaolers, all continued to thrive, despite the changing military, intellectual and aesthetic climate. Diners, including the Emperor Charles V and his son, Philip of Spain, comfortably settling down to the closing stages of a sumptuous repast, could still be interrupted by a knight errant of dolorous countenance, presenting a cartel and urging them to visit Binche where they would witness strange matters (recounted in his letter) concerning a terrible magician who held knights prisoner in his mist-enshrouded Château Ténébreux (1549).[93] Banqueters at Ferrara fared no better when they were disturbed by a group of oriental musicians from the land of Queen Alfarabia, issuing their defiance to deliver the knight Colocauro held prisoner by an evil magician in the Castello di Gorgoferusa (1561).[94] Imperial revellers at a feast in Munich, about to tuck in to a large mouth-watering pie had their appetites blunted when it burst open to reveal a sword-brandishing dwarf proclaiming a tournament (1568).[95] The dwarf was still active in 1613, popping up with

---

92. S. Anglo, 'Le declin du spectacle chevaleresque', in *Arts du spectacle et histoire des idées. Recueil offert en hommage à Jean Jacquot* (Tours, 1984), pp. 21–35. See also L. Clare, *La quintaine, la course de bague, et le jeu des têtes. Etude historique et ethno-linguistique d'une famille de jeux équestres* (Paris, 1983); M. Scalini, *Il Saracino*.

93. On the sources and festivals at Binche, see D. Devoto, 'Folklore et politique au Château Ténébreux', in Jacquot, *Fêtes*, II, pp. 311–28; D. Heartz, 'Un divertissement de palais pour Charles Quint à Binche', Ibid., pp. 329–42.

94. A. Argenti, *Cavalerie della città di Ferrara. Che contengono il Castello di Gorgoferusa, Il Monte di Feronia et il Tempio d'Amore* (Ferrara, 1566). For a brief account, see Povoledo *art. cit.*, pp. 101–4.

95. G. Schöne, 'Les fêtes de la Renaissance à la cour de Bavière', in Jacquot, *Lieu théâtral*, pp. 171–82.

a herald at a court ball in Florence to let everyone know that two knights, Fidamante and the Cavalier of Immortal Passion, would defend with lance, axe and rapier the thesis that the ways of Cupid were just.[96] Even in Florence, as late as 1628, courtiers could still not get through their supper without having a terrible sorcerer, accompanied by a swarm of Furies, burst in on them to announce a combat between the knights of the Orient and Occident.[97]

The form of the challenges remained largely intact: yet the chivalric kernel of the tournament had completely altered. The distance and the route travelled by the tournament-based court festival may be easily demonstrated. At the *Pas de l'Arbre d'Or*, there was only a rudimentary attempt to establish thematic coherence between the different parts of the entertainment; the *mise en scène* consisted of a decorated tree and scaffolds; and hard fighting constituted the focal point of the whole series of celebrations. A century later, at Ferrara in 1565, the *Tempio d'Amore* had an argument systematically, if inconsistently, developed throughout the festival; and its spectacular effects were prodigal and mechanically sophisticated. A contemporary account summarizes them.

> There were alps, valleys, mountains, woods, plains, countryside, buildings, inscriptions, perspectives, paintings, spires, statues, lights, reflexions, personages, wild beasts, recitations, incantations, clouds, thunder, lightning, thunderbolts, fires, earthquakes, songs, sounds, strange sights, transformations, reconversions, entanglements, disentanglements, triumphs, colossi, imprese, mottoes, liveries, combats, illusions, and other things of the greatest abundance and variety; besides the revolving, descent, raising, opening, closing, swallowing up, death and birth of so many subjects.[98]

The verse was by a team of poets including no less a personage than Torquato Tasso who may even have been responsible for devising the entire programme.[99] The full resources of the Accademia de' Concordi (which included the thirty-two singers and musicians of the ducal Chapel, the best 'dilettanti' of Ferrara, and singers from various convents) were deployed throughout the action. And the show was performed in a cortile transformed into a magnificently appointed theatre – almost exploding with antique statuary – where mechanics

---

96. For a description of this festival, see Nagler, *op. cit.*, pp. 119–25.
97. Ibid., pp. 139–61.
98. Cited in Truffi, *op. cit.*, pp. 163 n.
99. I. Mamczarz, 'Une fête équestre à Ferrare: il Tempio d'Armore' (1565); in Jacquot, *Fêtes*, III, pp. 349–72.

and artists had every resource to provide the amazing range of scene-changes, lighting, and sound effects. The huge army of participating knights entered in a long series of triumphal cars; but the combats themselves had been rehearsed, and the outcome was predetermined. Virtue, despite many setbacks and vicissitudes, had to triumph over vice. The result could not be left to the hazard of a serious lance thrust or sword stroke.

The basic elements of the spectacle – literary exchanges, speeches, music, disguising, processions and fighting – like the fictional challenge, remained the same. What did alter was the proportional importance attached to them: that is the way in which imagination and effort were increasingly devoted to the physical and artistic presentation of the shows; and the way in which combat became so deeply embedded within the allegorical fantasies and lush decorative inventions that it virtually disappeared from view. These developments did not occur simultaneously or evenly all over Europe: but by the middle decades of the sixteenth century, the choreographed mock fighting of the banquet hall intermezzo was moving outside into the lists; while, within doors, chivalric encounters continued to provide dynamic action to enliven the convoluted and image-laden progress of the *ballet de cour*, masque, and torneo-opera.[100]

The artist and architect, musician and choreographer, theatrical machinist and poet, had assumed complete ascendancy. They could rarely agree on the relative significance of their own roles (the famous dispute between Ben Jonson and Inigo Jones is symptomatic of persistent conflict),[101] but whichever art might be dominant, the knights had certainly been demoted. Whereas, at one time, artists had been employed to heighten the effect of chivalric spectacle, now they manipulated chivalry to heighten the spectacular effects of their own shows. But here, once again, it is difficult to assess the part played by humanism in effecting that change. Humanists had always made extravagant claims for their own speciality – that is eloquence, and facility in handling classical language – but they had never been keen to advance the pretensions of rival skills. Indeed, they had generally been scornful of painters, sculptors and others who worked with their hands and got themselves dirty. Nor, despite the inebriate enthusiasm

---

100. The tradition continued well beyond the Renaissance and long after chivalry had become merely the object of academic study. Lully was still exciting opera audiences in late seventeenth-century France with combats at the barriers, and struggles between knights and monsters. *Amadis*, for example, is full of balletic battles; while the whole of the second act of *Alceste* is devoted to a siege.

101. F. J. Gordon, 'Poet and Architect: the Intellectual Setting of the Quarrel between Ben Jonson and Inigo Jones', *Journal of the Warburg and Courtauld Institutes*, XII (1949), pp. 152–78.

of Ficino, had humanists been markedly better disposed toward the ancient liberal art of music. It was only gradually that the usefulness to princes of talents other than the purely literary became apparent and pressing. The arts, which by the middle decades of the sixteenth century had supplanted chivalry, were on the threshold of making exorbitant philosophical claims for composite court festivals: partly, perhaps, as a rationalization of the practical gains which had already been achieved. By 1581, the lofty theories of men such as Balthazar de Beaujoyeulx – asserting that the harmonious combination of all the arts could not only affect the moral well-being of spectators and participants but could also influence political affairs – were being translated into practice. The steadily deteriorating political, moral and religious state of France under Catherine de' Medici and her corrupt offspring may have raised doubts in some minds as to the efficacy of the outrageously expensive programme.[102] Princes and their artists remained undeterred.

That the increasing elaboration of festivals utilized an increasingly encyclopaedic classical erudition is evident. The triumphal cars and arches, antique statuary and architectural orders, ancient gods and heroes, and the whole vast apparatus of classical allusion, without doubt modified the tone not only of court festivals but also of the courts themselves. Yet, in comparison with the altered status of the fine arts, such things were superficialities; and, although humanists had contributed to this development, it is not at all easy to trace and articulate their role. What does remain clear is that, within the courtly context, humanism was itself as much a casualty of the change as was chivalry.

---

102. McGowan, *Le Balet Comique*, pp. 38–42.

*Chapter Five*

# Humanism, Magic and Science

### ANTHONY GRAFTON

## I

Shortly before the crisis of 1493–4 that would destroy the cultural world they had both flourished in – and during which they would both die – Angelo Poliziano wrote to Giovanni Pico della Mirandola. A few days before, he explained, he had been discussing with some 'young Florentines' his poem of 1483, the *Rusticus*, which he had written as the introduction to his course of 1483–4 on Hesiod's *Works and Days* and Virgil's *Georgics*. In lines 461 ff. he had described, as his classical predecessors had before him, the properties of the days of the lunar month. He had drawn his rich information not only from the ancient poets but also from Plutarch and other anonymous ancient and Byzantine scholars.[1] He thus knew, for example, that the sixth day after new moon was suitable for producing male, but not female offspring; that the eleventh day was suitable for sowing seed and planting trees; and that the sixteenth day was inappropriate for marriage 'because the sun is very far from the moon,' as indeed it is at full moon. But while going through his old text and its older sources, Poliziano had been struck by a new question – whether these ancient doctrines had any foundation in fact:

> I began to wonder, most learned Pico, if these ancient obser-
> vations were derived from natural causes or from the credulity
> of the vulgar.

---

1. For the oldest recoverable form of the material Poliziano used, see *Scholia vetera in Hesiodi Opera et Dies.* ed. A. Pertusi (Milan, 1955).

Accordingly, he turned to Pico – himself engaged on a massive work *Against the Astrologers* – for advice, as to the one who could 'prescribe how far one should follow the ancient poet's rules, which we have made our own by imitation.'[2]

The incident was typical both for the two men and for their generation of scholars. In the late 1480s and early 1490s Poliziano and Pico embarked together on physical and intellectual voyages of the greatest novelty and interest. They discussed Poliziano's favourite Alexandrian poetry, Pico's beloved Greek philosophers, and the Hebrew Bible.[3] In 1491 they visited Venetian and other libraries, comparing notes about the manuscripts of Aristotle.[4] And they did research together in Fiesole about the technical terminology used by the scholastics.[5] Their collaboration dramatically enhanced Poliziano's once feeble interest in the dialectic, metaphysics and natural philosophy of the ancients – a change of perspective starkly visible from the incomplete *Secunda Centuria* of his *Miscellanea*.[6] And it is vital for our purposes in a larger sense as well as a characteristic episode of the second half of the fifteenth century, when the literary studies of the humanists had decisive effects on the history of natural philosophy, the theory and practice of magic, and the origins of modern science.

## II

The humanists do not receive a particularly good press in most general accounts in English of Renaissance or early modern science. They win points for their detestation of scholasticism, their appreciation for the beauties of nature and their interest in classical scientific texts. They are damned with faint praise for having 'made available' stimulating and even vital ancient materials: Archimedes for mathematicians, Ptolemy for astronomers, Galen for doctors. But they are usually criticized more pungently than they are praised. Most histories of science dismiss them as obsessed with literary questions, docile towards classical authorities, and unoriginal in their conception of nature. Humanism and philology seem blind alleys next to the royal road of direct study of nature,

2. The relevant portions of Poliziano's letter (*Epistolae* XII.7) are readily available in I. Del Lungo's commentary on the *Rusticus*, in his edition of A. Poliziano, *Prose volgari inedite e poesie latine e greche edite e inedite* (Florence, 1867), pp. 326–8.

3. A. Poliziano, *Miscellanea* I.14, *Opera* (Basel, 1553), p. 238; I.80, ibid., p. 288.

4. G. Pesenti, 'Diario odeporico-bibliografico inedito del Poliziano,' *Memorie del R. Istituto Lombardo di Scienze e Lettere, cl. di lettere, scienze morali e storiche,* ser. III, 14 (1916), pp. 229–39.

5. A. Poliziano, *Miscellaneorum centuria secunda*, ed V. Branca and M. Pastore Stocchi (Florence, 1972), IV, p. 14.

6. Poliziano, *Coronis Miscellaneorum, Opera*, p. 310.

controlled experiment and quantitative natural laws that the great men of the Scientific Revolution would have to travel.[7]

In recent decades, however, these simple beliefs have been subjected to detailed scrutiny and considerable modification, in monographs and articles if not in general surveys. Both in Italy and elsewhere historians have made clear how complex the connections between the new philology of the humanists and the new science really were. These revisions have taken several distinct forms. Eugenio Garin, Paul Oskar Kristeller, Frances Yates, and D. P. Walker have shown that the humanistic revival of the classics did have dramatic effects on received ideas about the cosmos and man's place in it. The Byzantine scholars who brought Greek literary culture back to the West did not offer their pupils the pure dialogues of Plato, but embedded them in a rich and elaborate setting of Neo-Platonic commentary. Thus Western scholars were conditioned to view Plato through the firmly fixed lens of his late, systematic interpreters like Iamblichus and Plotinus. This reduced Plato's difficult dialogues to fixed allegories of a coherent system, and enlarged some later Platonic writers, whose works purported to be the older sources of Plato's, to proportions as divine as his. And it offered the view of Plato's cosmos and man's place in it found in such derivative works as the dialogues of 'Hermes Trismegistus' as an authoritative exposition of profound truths long forgotten.[8]

The humanists thus came to believe, as the Neo-Platonists had, in a visible world which manifested like a great three-dimensional hieroglyph the beneficent intentions of its creator. And they proclaimed, as eloquently as any late-antique writer, that the wise man had the power to rise above the material world in which his physical body was embedded, by drawing down the powers of the stars through study and incantation. He could thus work wonders on earth and save himself from earthly corruption at one and the same time. This vision of power transformed the practice of magic from a marginal and suspect study to a reputable science with a very long pedigree in the ancient world. It made many intellectuals hope that study of nature might offer keys not only to knowledge but to power. And long after the methods of the magi became obsolete, their hopes for bettering the condition of

---

7. For some samples see M. Boas, *The Scientific Renaissance 1450–1630* (New York, 1962); A. R. Hall, *The Scientific Revolution 1500–1800*, 2nd edn (Boston, 1966); E. J. Dijksterhuis, *The Mechanization of the World Picture*, tr. C. Dikshoorn (Oxford, 1961); A. G. Debus, *Man and Nature in the Renaissance* (Cambridge, 1978).

8. See, for example, E. Garin, *Rinascite e rivoluzioni* (Bari, 1976); P. O. Kristeller, *Renaissance Thought* (New York, 1961), ch. iii; F. A. Yates, *Giordano Bruno and the Hermetic Tradition* (Chicago, 1964); D. P. Walker, *Spiritual and Demonic Magic from Ficino to Campanella* (1958).

man continued to inspire such prophets of the New Science as Francis Bacon.[9]

Other scholars of more diverse kinds, usually specialists in the history of a single technical scientific discipline, have shown that the humanist recovery of classical scientific texts amounted to far more than an occasional pursuit or a mechanical exercise. To be sure, the early humanists – from the time of Petrarch to that of Valla – concentrated on literary rather than scientific classics and subjects. They made fun of contemporary natural philosophers, whom they thought obsessed with trivial and irrelevant questions. They ridiculed traditional segments of the classical scientific tradition, like medicine and astrology, as the occupations of quacks who demanded high rewards for treatments and predictions that invariably turned out wrong or ineffective. And they insisted that direct study of moral philosophy, history and eloquence would do more than natural philosophy to fit men for civic duty – to enable them to see the right path and induce their fellow citizens to take it.[10]

From 1450 on, however, the humanists applied their philological skills to a wider and wider range of texts, and these in turn made available skills, methods and ideas that had simply not formed part of medieval scientific culture. The *Epitome* of Ptolemy's *Almagest* produced by Regiomontanus and Peurbach during the 1460s offered the first detailed account in unbarbaric Latin of Ptolemy's actual models and their derivations – as opposed to the tables based on Ptolemy and the elementary, qualitative models that had long been available. This work of recuperation and criticism laid the foundation on which all sixteenth-century astronomers would build, down to the time of Brahe and Kepler. Copernicus himself owed to the *Epitome* the mastery of Ptolemy's theory and methods that enabled him to provide the first full-blown alternative system of the world.[11]

---

9. The most powerful statements of this case – which are by no means identical – are E. Garin, 'Magic and Astrology in the Civilization of the Renaissance,' in his *Science and Civic Life in the Italian Renaisance*, tr. P. Munz (Garden City, N.Y., 1969), pp. 145–65 and F. Yates, 'The Hermetic Tradition in Renaissance Science,' in *Art, Science and History in the Renaissance*, ed. C. Singleton (Baltimore, 1967), pp. 255–74. For contrasting discussions of more recent date see R. Westman and J. McGuire, *Hermeticism and the Scientific Revolution* (Los Angeles, 1977) and C. Webster, *From Paracelsus to Newton* (Cambridge, 1982).

10. For an original discussion of this literature see K. Park, *Doctors and Medicine in Early Renaissance Florence* (Princeton, 1985).

11. The text of the 1496 edition of the *Epitome* is reprinted in Regiomontanus' *Opera Collectanea*, ed. F. Schmeidler (Osnabrück, 1972); for its importance for Copernicus see O. Neugebauer and N. Swerdlow, *Mathematical Astronomy in Copernicus's De Revolutionibus* (Heidelberg, 1984).

Similarly, the editions of Hippocrates and Galen produced by the Aldine press in the 1520s did far more than make available new texts. They exposed for the first time, in their original form, the empirical medical science, based on case histories, of the Hippocratic *Epidemics* and the systematic anatomical research, based on original dissection, of Galen's *On the Use of the Parts of the Body*. And they too provided not just grist for scientists' traditional mills but a forgotten model of medical science, one first applied systematically by Vesalius in the very work that eventually overthrew Galen by applying his own empirical method in a more rigorous and consistent way.[12] In areas where progress depended on correction of textual errors, collation of diverse sources, and the establishment of genealogies of extant texts – areas like botany and natural history – the humanist commentaries on Pliny and other texts again offered the platforms on which a new empirical science could be reared.[13]

A third set of inquiries, finally, has moved down a third road. Italian scholars above all, notably Garin and Paolo Rossi, have emphasized that the humanists reorientated the rhetoric of natural philosophy in fundamental ways, even if they did not produce all the technical tools that scientists needed. The humanists uncovered the wide range of disagreement over means and ends that characterized ancient scientific thought; they recovered ancient suggestions for alternative explanations of important phenomena; and they discovered in classical rhetoric new ways of making scientific results provocative and accessible. It was the humanists who made clear, for example, that Pliny had not always understood his Greek sources, and thus could not be cited as an absolute authority on plants or species. The humanists discovered and printed the passages in Cicero and Plutarch that showed that distinguished ancient thinkers had been willing to contemplate a heliocentric rather than a geocentric cosmos – and thus inspired Copernicus, as the holograph of his great work *De revolutionibus orbium coelestium* clearly shows. And the humanists revived the classical custom of offering profound philosophical arguments in the form not of a technical treatise but of a lively dialogue – thus providing Galileo with one of the most powerful weapons he wielded in his great assault on the Aristotelian picture of the world. The humanists, in short, were the creators not of a new science but of a new culture. Those who shared its values confronted the world of nature as well as that of books with

---

12. See V. Nutton, *John Caius and the Eton Galen* (Cambridge, 1987); *The Medical Renaissance of the Sixteenth Century*, ed. A. Wear et al. (Cambridge, 1985).

13. See C. Nauert, 'C. Plinius Secundus,' in *Catalogus translationum et commentariorum* (Washington. D.C., 1960–), IV, pp. 297–422; K. Reeds, 'Renaissance Humanism and Botany,' *Annals of Science* 33 (1976), pp. 519–42.

a new freshness and independence. They revised received ideas with an enthusiasm and energy previously unknown. And in doing so they made the Scientific Revolution possible.[14]

Naturally, recent research has painted in minute detail as well as in broad strokes. We have come to see that humanism was not the only intellectual force – or always the main one – operating on the highly charged intellectuals of fifteenth – and sixteenth-century Italy. Even in the Florence of the Medici, Marsilio Ficino's formation was essentially scholastic, and he continued throughout his life to use scholastic ideas and techniques: for example, in his account of the operations of natural magic, a subject one might have thought pre-eminently humanistic and novel. We have come to see that some of the most powerful and productive Renaissance speculations about nature, like the physical arguments with which Copernicus tried to prove the 'thinkability' of a heliocentric cosmos in Book 1 of *De revolutionibus*, owed more to medieval debates about force and motion than to the humanist recovery of classical ideas. Nancy Siraisi has traced in meticulous detail the continued use of Avicenna's *Canon*, a basic text of medieval medical learning, in the medical schools of sixteenth-century Italy; she reveals powerful continuities in the method and content of instruction as well as numerous efforts by commentators to introduce specific novelties into their courses. And even the most rebarbative of late medieval approaches to the natural world – like the work of the Oxford *calculatores*, Heytesbury and Swineshead – continued to circulate and stimulate debate along with the newly burnished classics, down to the time of Galileo and beyond.[15]

Yet these minute revisions leave the general outlines firm and sharp. The interaction of science, magic, and humanism was a characteristic feature of the late fifteenth century. It represented in part the humanists' effort to assert their control – and the supremacy of their method – over all fields, philosophical and scientific as well as philological and literary, as Poliziano pointed out more eloquently than most:

> [The grammarian] must inspect not only the schools of philosophers, but also the jurisconsults, and the doctors, and the dialecticians, and all who make up what we call the encyclopedia

14. Garin, *Rinascite*, chs. viii–ix; P. Rossi, *Philosophy, Technology and the Arts in the Early Modern Era*, tr. S. Attanasio, ed. B. Nelson (New York, 1970).

15. See B. P. Copenhaver, 'Scholastic Philosophy and Renaissance Magic in the *De vita* of Marsilio Ficino,' *Renaissance Quarterly*, 37 (1984), pp. 523–54; *A Source Book in Medieval Science*, ed. E. Grant (Cambridge, Mass., 1974), pp. 621–4; N. G. Siraisi, *Avicenna in Renaissance Italy* (Princeton, 1987); C. Lewis, *The Merton Tradition and Kinematics in Late Sixteenth and Early Seventeenth Century Italy* (Padua, 1980).

of learning, and all the philologists – and not just inspect them, but examine them from close up.[16]

It produced powerful works of compilation and scholarship, like Giorgio Valla's encyclopedic treatise *De rebus fugiendis et expetendis* and Pico's *Disputationes adversus astrologiam divinatricem*, to be discussed below. And it brought into accessible form the canon of scientific classics from which the classical sciences of astronomy and anatomy took off, while other sciences at least built on their smaller and less complete classical inheritances. Throughout the sixteenth century, moreover, Italian and Northern scientists alike carried on a recognizably similar enterprise of collation and explication of scientific texts, and debated recognizably similar ideas. What remains, then, is to examine in some concrete instances just how this new combination of disciplines, texts and ideas formed itself into a recognizable Renaissance idea of nature and man's place in it.

### III

Consider, first of all, a powerful exposition of the general world picture that humanists and philosophers built from the rich but disparate ingredients newly available in the late fifteenth century. The Italian Renaissance produced many systematic descriptions of the physical universe, its form, its content, and its laws. But none of them reveals more vividly than Tommaso Campanella's *Città del Sole* the logic, the elegance, the occasionally traditional qualities or the genuinely innovative force of this intellectual construct. The work of a South Italian Dominican who had called into being with his sermons a desperate, doomed rising against Spanish rule and social injustice in the south, the book was written in prison. It describes in dialogue form an ideal society on the other side of the world from Europe, in or near Taprobana (Ceylon). The City of the Sun, unlike Europe, is a society in harmony with the cosmos as a whole, in physical as well as political terms. Its form reproduces not the sprawling confusion of a European city but the logic and coherence found in Renaissance Italy only in fortresses and plans for ideal states. Its seven concentric circular walls reproduce on earth the spheres of the seven planets. Its walls and its temple bear an elaborate sculptural and pictorial programme: a detailed representation of the entire universe. This includes celestial and terrestrial globes, seven temple lamps to represent the seven planets, detailed

---

16. Poliziano, *Opera*, p. 229.

maps of all countries and detailed taxonomies of all plants and animals, executed in gruelling verbal (and presumably pictorial) detail:

> On the outer wall are shown all manner of fish to be found in river, lake or ocean; their particular qualities; the way they live, breed, develop; their use; their correspondence to celestial and earthly things, to the arts and to nature. I was astonished when I saw bishop fish, chain fish, nail fish and starfish exactly resembling such things among us.[17]

The City of the Sun, in other words, incarnates wisdom and power as well as justice and productivity. It amounts to a visual encyclopedia – well supported, Campanella explains, with verbal glosses – that enfolds all natural phenomena and facts in a single interacting whole. And as the last quotation and the layout of the city both suggest, the stars provide the governing heart of this complex, organic system. Passing in their fixed courses through the perfect and superior world of the heavens, they control almost everything that takes place on earth. They both generate and tie together the swarming animals, plants and elements of the terrestrial world below them; for example, they determine by their conjunctions the propitious moment at which a given plant may be of medical use to a given part of the human body. Accordingly, astrology is the one coherent, unifying science that the City knows.

Astrology aids Campanella's Solarians in their ambitious and curious programme of eugenics. After they have selected tall handsome women for each tall handsome man – and fat women for the thin men, to produce offspring of moderate compass – all members of both sexes who have been chosen to breed sleep in adjoining cells until an astrologically propitious moment, determined by the city astrologer and doctor, preferably a moment when the sign of Virgo is rising over the eastern horizon, and definitely one when Mars and Saturn can exert no malefic influence. Astrology also provides the Solarians' explanations for all great changes in history, politics, and culture – from the prevalence of queens in sixteenth-century European royal houses to the prevalence of effeminacy and lechery among modern poets and courtiers. And it governs their own ceremonial calendar, with its festivals at new and full moon and other celestially determined appropriate times.

The beauty and vividness of Campanella's cosmic city are now clear. So, however, are some of its more traditional qualities. It seems to

---

17. T. Campanella, *The City of the Sun*, ed. and tr. D. J. Donno (Berkeley, 1981), pp. 34 (Italian) and 35 (English tr.).

reproduce an orderly, bounded natural world – a cosmos perfect and changeless above the sphere of the moon, imperfect and changeable below it. It explains the relation between the perfect and imperfect, superior and inferior segments of that cosmos with astrological doctrines standard since Hellenistic times. The linear gradation of qualities, from corruptible plants and elements at the centre of the cosmos to perfect stars at its rim, is inherited from Plato and Aristotle. The effort to present all natural knowledge in a single, coherent system of moderate compass is descended from the similar efforts of classical writers like Cicero (in his *Scipio's Dream*), his commentator Macrobius, and encyclopedists and astrological writers like Martianus Capella and Firmicus Maternus in late antiquity. It has many post-classical parallels in the writings of the twelfth-century school of Chartres as well as in Renaissance literary, political and religious texts of the most diverse kinds. English readers will remember – to choose a non-Italian example, but one with an Italian setting – Lorenzo's evocation of the ordered cosmos to Jessica in *The Merchant of Venice*. No wonder, then, that historians have sometimes used such visions of the cosmos as evidence of the tradition-bound and backward-looking character of Renaissance thought – even though they occur in the work of a revolutionary like Campanella, who challenged the social order with his revolt and the intellectual order with his brash and perhaps counter-productive defence of Galileo.[18]

Yet Campanella's cosmos has at least two features that clearly reveal its novelty. The first lies in the character of the natural knowledge that it purveys. For this is not the closed system of the traditional encyclopedia but its opposite – a visibly fluid set of disciplines that mingle with one another and sometimes seem bent on combining only in order to produce an explosion. The Solarians' universe is astrologically controlled but hardly orderly. Its elements are not eternal bodies of matter confined to neatly demarcated spheres, but living by-products of the constant struggle of cosmic forces. The universe has not a precise and inviolable order but a constantly fluctuating metabolism:

> They believe in two physical principles: that of the sun as father and of the earth as mother. The air is impure sky: fire comes from the sun: the sea is the sweat of the earth, liquified by the sun and uniting earth and air, as blood unites the human body and spirit. The earth is a great beast and we live within it as worms live within us.[19]

---

18. For a classic evocation of such continuities, see C. S. Lewis, *The Discarded Image* (Cambridge, 1967).

19. Campanella, *City of the Sun*, pp. 112–13.

Even the Solarians' stars differ from the Europeans'. Not chained to spheres that carry them around, they too are living beings. Their motions result from the effect on them of the attractive power of the sun, which pulls them away from the earth when they are in conjunction with the sun, and towards the earth (and thus also towards the sun) when they are in opposition, with the earth between them and the sun. The Solarians dismantle the whole apparatus of spheres and epicycles and reject Ptolemaic and Copernican models of the universe with equal brusqueness, as mechanical falsifications of an organic reality. Like any organism, finally, the cosmos as a whole undergoes momentous changes as it passes through the stages of growth, maturation and decay. And the great conjunctions of Jupiter and Saturn that take place every twenty years, the new star of 1572 and the associated changes on earth – the invention of printing and of gunpowder, the discovery of the New World – all betoken something unheard-of in more traditional cosmologies: 'the world will be uprooted and cleansed, and then it will be replanted and rebuilt.'[20] At that point, presumably, even the Solarians' encyclopedia will become as obsolete as the rest.

Campanella's cosmos tries to combine traditional assumptions about the order and nature of the cosmos with new visions of physical force, astronomical law and the world of the elements. The combination is both illogical and unstable; incongruities appear at every point. Why should planets not tied to spheres, or bound to a perfectly predictable future course, reveal the immutable laws of human history, especially when the heavens and the earth are soon to be transformed? How can one combine human freedom, the rule of the stars, and the potential of a totally new order? One cannot – as the Solarians themselves confess when they admit that the stars do not in fact dominate all men in the same way, that 'the constellation that drew infectious vapours from Luther's cadaver drew fragrant exhalations of virtue from the Jesuits of that period and from Hernando Cortés, who established Christianity in Mexico at that same time.'[21] The Solarians' city is orderly to a fault, but the universe it tries to mirror is in fact in flux, and any representation of it can be at best partial and temporary.

Campanella's cosmos, in other words, is not a compound but a suspension – and one made up of elements that cannot be brought into contact without danger. It tries to fuse materialist and animistic ways of understanding the whole universe, derived through earlier Renaissance thinkers like Telesio from ancient sources, above all Lucretius, with mathematical and metaphysical assumptions of an entirely contrary order, derived through Patrizi and Ficino from other, equally

20. Ibid., pp. 120–3.
21. Ibid., pp. 126–7.

authoritative sources, above all Plato and his interpreters.[22] It has much
in common with the terrifying infinite cosmos of Campanella's older
and still more radical contemporary Giordano Bruno. And similarly
baffling visions, similar self-destroying models of the world, can be
found in a great many famous Renaissance works of natural philosophy: for example, in the contemporary efforts of Johann Kepler, who
tried in 1596 to combine his own Copernican astronomy, Platonic
metaphysics and the empirical evidence in the equally unstable and far
more productive compound of his *Mysterium Cosmographicum*. This
heady vision of a cosmos and a curriculum in flux – this vividly
portrayed collision of irreconcilable doctrines and assumptions – is as
subversive in its way as Campanella's political plans for the Italian
South. And its central organizing quality – the unquenched desire to
find harmony, order and a providential order in facts that seemed to
deny the existence of all three – would remain one of the deepest
motivations of scientific work through the sixteenth and seventeenth
centuries. In the end it stimulated Galileo, Kepler and Descartes to
destroy the traditional order of the world to which Campanella
remained attached.

Campanella's vision is civic in motivation as well as transitional in
character; and here too it is characteristic of its period. The point of
knowledge of nature, for the Solarians, is that its owners can transform
nature for the better, lengthening the human life span, improving the
quality of human offspring, and so on. Perfect science creates a perfect
society. This ideal too has no place in the classical or medieval encyclopedic tradition, which offered at best a therapeutic understanding of
the world. But Campanella drew on a tradition of thought developed
by such humanists as Vives and Rabelais, who had urged that practical
knowledge could improve the social order and the human condition,
and such Utopian writers as More and Patrizi, who had insisted that
ideal societies would manipulate the physical as well as the social
world.[23] And in arguing that science can and must contribute to the
community that nourishes it, Campanella enunciates another powerful
ideal – one that the very different prophets of the New Science,
Descartes and Bacon, would make their own as a justification for their
still more radical redistribution of the intellectual landscape.

---

22. For the sources and evolution of Campanella's thought see the rich monographs
of N. Badaloni, *Tommaso Campanella* (Milan, 1965) and G. Bock, *Thomas .Campanella*
(Tübingen, 1974).
23. See, for example, Garin, 'The Ideal City,' in *Science and Civic Life*, pp. 21–48;
L. Firpo, 'Political Philosophy: Renaissance Utopianism,' in *The Late Italian Renaissance*,
ed. E. Cochrane (New York, 1970), pp. 149–67.

# IV

At least as problematic as the nature of the cosmos Renaissance intellectuals envisioned is that of the role they allotted to man within it. Recent historiography has emphasized their considerable faith in the possibility of active human intervention. In rediscovering the late antique magical texts of Iamblichus and Porphyry – so Garin and Yates have argued – the humanists gave the magician a new respectability as the man who could not only understand but manipulate the laws of nature. The ancient magician had been able – so the Hermetic Corpus claimed – to make statues speak. The modern classicizing magician, drawing on Arabic and other Eastern traditions as well as strictly classical ones, could carve amulets and devise incantations that would draw down to a given point the beneficent power of the sun and Jupiter and avert the malevolence of Mars and Saturn. He could thus compensate in part for the perilous effects of a lunar or solar eclipse, as Campanella tried to do for his papal patron Urban VIII in 1628, when the two of them lit candles and performed apotropaic rites together.[24] He could prescribe effective drugs, offer advice on important decisions, and assign auspicious times for major enterprises. And he could claim in providing all these services to be the professional descendant not of the disreputable medieval sorcerer but of the Chaldean and Egyptian priests whose revelations had so dazzled Solon and Plato.

These practices unquestionably flourished in late medieval and Renaissance society. Many Italian rulers would not start a building, sleep with their wives, or plan a campaign without astrological advice. Magical remedies formed a prominent part of the Renaissance medicine canonized and practised by Ficino, and adapted in northern Europe by Paracelsus and his many followers. And the walls and ceilings of churches and palaces blossomed during the fifteenth and sixteenth centuries with splendid horoscopes in pictorial form of the buildings or their builders – the most concrete evidence imaginable of the widespread belief that the new-style magician had real power over nature.[25]

Moreover, a good many Renaissance texts do reveal the confident notions Yates and Garin attributed to the period about the powers and status of the *magus*. Pico, for example, gave magic a very prominent place in the magnificent *Oratio* with which he had meant to begin the disputation – never in fact held – over his famous 900 theses in Rome

---

24. See above all Walker's *Spiritual and Demonic Magic*.

25. J. Seznec, *The Survival of the Pagan Gods*, tr. B. F. Sessions (New York, 1953) offers a fine survey of these practices and beliefs. See also J. Cox-Rearick, *Dynasty and Destiny in Medici Art* (Princeton, 1984) and S. J. Tester, *A History of Western Astrology* (Wolfeboro, N.H., 1987) (the latter is stronger on classical texts than on the Renaissance, but offers the best survey of the whole subject now available).

in early 1487. Here he admits that magic can be either evil or good. *Goeteia* – the magic that relies on demons to do its work – was 'a thing to be abhorred, so help me the god of truth, and a monstrous thing.' But *mageia* – the magic that evokes the hidden powers of nature without demonic intervention – was 'a perfect and most high wisdom' and 'a higher and more holy philosophy.'[26]

The practitioners of *mageia* included all great philosophers, from the ancients Pythagoras, Empedocles, Democritus and Plato – as well as the more esoteric sages Zamolxis and Zoroaster – down to the Arab Alkindi and the scholastics Roger Bacon and William of Auvergne. *Mageia* gave such men the insight they needed to trace the hidden web of sympathies that linked all beings and objects to one another and to the stars, and then to exploit them with rituals properly performed. The magician's craft

> brings forth into the open the miracles concealed in the recesses of the world, in the depths of nature, and in the storehouses and mysteries of God, just as if she herself were their maker; and as the farmer weds his elms to vines, even so does the *magus* wed earth to heaven, that is, he weds lower things to the endowments and powers of higher things.[27]

No wonder, then, that Pico argued both in his *Oration* and in many of his theses that true *mageia* could both improve the condition of men and lead to a vastly enhanced knowledge of God. No wonder, either, that modern historians, struck by his vision of man's power and by its consistency with his attack on the astrologers, have seen in Pico's confident assertion of the virtues of magic the origin of the modern scientist's assertion of the power of his studies to alter nature itself for the better. Whatever the difficulties and contradictions of the Renaissance vision of the cosmos, man's place in its centre seems a powerful and distinguished one, and Campanella's case, discussed above, seems to bear out the analysis of Pico.

Yet these arguments do not do justice to the full range of evidence. The Italian Renaissance saw many theorists of magic at work whose sense of their place in the cosmos differed radically from Pico's. His friend Ficino, for example, believed in a magical and semi-animate world, with rays of influence connecting stars to elements, planets to parts of the body; but he saw himself less as the master than the servant of the cosmic forces that constantly irradiated him, and sometimes felt

---

26. G. Pico della Mirandola, 'Oration on the Dignity of Man,' tr. E. L. Forbes, in *The Renaissance Philosophy of Man*, ed. E. Cassirer *et al.* (Chicago, 1948), pp. 246–7.
27. Ibid., p. 249.

that Saturn was persecuting him – as he had persecuted other gifted men – deliberately.[28] Girolamo Cardano, the sixteenth-century north Italian mathematician now remembered for his pioneering theory of probability and his unfortunate prediction of long life for Edward VI, left a detailed autobiography in which he vividly revealed the texture of a life felt to be the prey of occult forces. He recounted at length the astrological influences that had almost left him monstrous and impotent. He detailed the portents – including strong smells of wax, the sound of feet marching where there were no walkers, and even the shapes of clouds – that announced in advance the many disasters he would suffer, notably his son's execution for murdering his wife. And he even recorded in rich detail his dream life, which included terrifying sleep-experiences, as when, in 1534, Cardano dreamed that he was running with a crowd of men, women, and children, asked 'whither we were all running, and one of the throng replied, "To Death."' Cardano saved himself by climbing a steep hill, only to be confronted by a sickeningly deep abyss before him.[29] And he drew the moral of his experiences so crisply that no historian could improve on it: these anxieties were to be expected in a cosmos like ours, given the greatness of the heavenly bodies and beings that controlled us and the minuteness of 'these slender shadows in which miserably and anxiously we are enveloped.'[30]

The *magus*, in other words, could feel himself either the hunter or the quarry, either the slayer or the slain; and no evidence yet produced shows that Pico's aggressive optimism was the majority position. Many intellectuals, like Campanella's Solarians, tried to cure their anxieties about causality by hatching some sort of compromise between freedom and necessity. They repeated like a mantra the traditional axiom that *Sapiens dominabitur astris*: 'the wise man will rule the stars.' They tried to retain a partial autonomy for man and to set moderate (or immoderate) limits on the effects of the stars. But others, like the Aristotelian Pietro Pomponazzi, rejoiced in the neat logic of a system that explained every conceivable event on earth as the foreordained result of a single omnicompetent causal law. He explained prophecies and portents as the operations of laws as natural as those that governed the seasons; he insisted that all human institutions, even religions, obeyed the same set of celestial commands; and he thus found reason for confidence and joy in the determinist analysis of the magical world that Pico rejected and that filled Cardano with despair.[31]

---

28. Seznec, *Survival of the Pagan Gods*, pp. 60–61.
29. G. Cardano, *The Book of my Life*, tr. J. Stoner (New York, 1930), p. 156; for the original see Cardano, *Opera* (Lyons, 1663; repr. Stuttgart, 1966), I, p. 29.
30. Cardano, *The Book of My Life*, tr. Stoner, p. 214; *Opera*, I, p. 39.
31. E. Garin, *Lo zodiaco della vita* (Bari, 1982).

No formula will do justice to this plethora of contradictions. But one general point is worth making. The late antique dialogues and manuals that offered all Renaissance magicians a speculative basis and an ancient pedigree for their practices were themselves the products of a culture more and more alienated from and apprehensive about the physical world – a culture that produced dreamers of terrifying anxiety dreams like the martyr Perpetua and masters of self-mortification like the Cynic Peregrinus.[32] And the assertions of human power that resound through the Hermetic Corpus are a special case even within the general late antique age of anxiety. The Greek-speaking Egyptians who wrote the revelations of Hermes had been stripped of political autonomy and national culture by centuries of invasion and occupation. Their claim to offer ancient Egyptian wisdom about the secrets of nature was in part the characteristic voice of the vanquished in any premodern society, trying to avenge political defeat in the realm of religion and the spirit.[33] It seems only reasonable that during the Italian Renaissance, with its attacks of collective panic over the Turkish threat in the 1470s and the universal deluge the astrologer predicted in February 1524, many sought out the ancient *magi* because they too could find the power they needed only in the realm of incantation and ritual.[34] It seems equally likely that they often found their fears not diminished but increased when they did so. The fearful *magus* makes a more likely companion-figure to Savonarola and Luther, to Dürer's *Melencolia I* and Cardano's melancholy, than the optimistic one.

## V

Humanists read their texts historically as well as systematically. They tried to explicate difficult terms and passages in the light of historically germane facts and texts (thus Leonardo Bruni distinguished, as scholastic interpreters of Aristotle had not, the *tragoedia* that he analysed from straight satirical poetry).[35] They used facts from writers' lives and contexts to explain obscure allusions and unusual traits of style (thus

---

32. E. R. Dodds, *Pagan and Christian in an Age of Anxiety* (Cambridge, 1968).

33. G. Fowden, *The Egyptian Hermes* (Cambridge, 1986).

34. A. Warburg, 'Heidnisch-antike Weissagung in Wort und Bild zu Luthers Zeiten (1920),' in his *Ausgewählte Schriften und Würdigungen*, ed. D. Wuttke (Baden-Baden, 1980), pp. 199–304; E. Cantimori, *Eretici italiani del Cinquecento* (Florence, 1967), ch. ii; M. Reeves, *The Influence of Prophecy in the Later Middle Ages* (Oxford, 1969); D. Weinstein, *Savonarola and Florence* (Princeton, 1970); 'Astrologi hallucinati': Stars and the End of the World in Luther's Times, ed. P. Zambelli (Berlin, 1986).

35. H. Goldbrunner, 'Leonardo Brunis Kommentar zu seiner Übersetzung der pseudo-Aristotelischen Oekonomik: ein humanistischer Kommentar,' in *Der Kommentar in der Renaissance*, ed. A. Buck (Boppard, 1975), pp. 99–118.

Poliziano explained Statius' excessive adulation of the emperor Domitian as the natural practice of a court poet whose patron considered himself divine).[36] And they liked to collect and arrange in chronological or systematic order the names, views and relations of the ancient masters who had founded and developed each intellectual discipline and their achievements.

What the humanists had to say about the early history of astronomy or medicine was not always profound. At their most banal – a level often found in their introductory lectures to university courses – the humanists offered little more than a list of the various earlier authorities for a field of learning. At their most rhetorical, they churned out an undifferentiated celebration of every worthy who had ever practised, read about or even shown interest in the subject. Thus the German humanist Regiomontanus compressed the history of astronomy (and much more) into a single brief introductory oration at the university of Padua. His account began with legendary sages about whose scientific work nothing could be known – Abraham, Moses, and Hercules. True, it distinguished between these gentlemen and the true fathers of astronomy, Hipparchus in the second century B.C. and Ptolemy in the second century A.D. But even about the latter Regiomontanus said only that Hipparchus had suspected the existence of precession of the equinoxes, and Ptolemy had provided a precise value for it in the *Almagest* (7.3). Of the origins of Greek planetary theory, the paths by which Chaldean observations became available to Greek scientists, the specific nature of Ptolemy's debt to Hipparchus, he said nothing – though he was in fact, as the *Epitome* of the *Almagest* shows, as qualified as anyone in Europe to raise and answer these questions. The conventions of the genre and his own practical interest in stimulating more translations and attracting more students dictated an approach verbally florid but analytically austere.[37] And even those humanists who, like Polydore Vergil, dedicated themselves to collecting all the facts about the origins of classical arts and sciences did not always offer richer descriptions or deeper explanations than Regiomontanus.[38]

On occasion, however, humanist historical method interacted directly and powerfully with the classical sciences. None of these was more popular, more contentious or more stimulating than astrology. It had the best of pedigrees; both its practitioners and its enemies thought that it had been devised by the wise priests of ancient Egypt

---

36. A. Poliziano, *Commento inedito alle Selve di Stazio*, ed. L. Cesarini Martinelli (Florence, 1978).

37. J. Regiomontanus, *Oratio habita Patavii in praelectione Alfragani, Opera Collectanea*, pp. 43–53; see the analysis by N. Jardine, *The Birth of History and Philosophy of Science* (Cambridge, 1984), ch. viii.

38. D. Hay, *Polydore Vergil* (Oxford, 1952), ch. iii.

and Chaldea, and transmitted and perfected by the most proficient of Greek astronomers, Hipparchus and Ptolemy. True, many critics denied that the astrologers' assumptions could be reconciled with Christian theology. Others attacked specific doctrines, such as the popular one that the great conjunctions dictated the course of history, or piled up what they took to be decisive negative instances, such as the standard one that twins born under identical celestial conditions could have entirely different fates. And still others ridiculed the astrologers' specific failures – as Luther did, after the fact, when they predicted a universal flood that did not happen in 1524 and did not predict the Peasants' War of 1525.[39]

Late in the fifteenth century one scholar produced a critique that cut far deeper than the traditional ones; and humanist method gave his weapon its sharp cutting edge. In his last years, Pico was profoundly attracted to the religious reformer and prophet Savonarola and profoundly disturbed by the anti-Christian implications of astrology and many forms of magic.[40] As we have seen, he worked closely with one of the most proficient humanist scholars of the time, Poliziano, and exchanged ideas with him about ancient sources that prescribed rules for the interaction of celestial bodies and human affairs. Though he did not live to produce his full attack on all the enemies of the Church, he did turn out a brilliant set of *Disputationes contra astrologiam divinatricem* – a work that won the deep respect, though not the full assent, of Kepler a century later.

Pico's critique of astrology touches many of the traditional stops. But it also raises historical questions that no previous attacker, ancient or modern, had considered. Pico examined the historical evidence in detail. Where widely accepted legends held that classical astronomy and astrology had developed over thousands and thousands of years (470,000 years in one particularly exaggerated case), Pico found no trace of this long-term history in the surviving works of ancient philosophers and astronomers. The only account he could find of the transmission of Chaldean data to the Greeks – a passage in the late antique commentary by Simplicius on Aristotle *On the Heavens* – said that Aristotle's pupil Callisthenes had sent back the Chaldeans' observations when Alexander conquered Babylon, and that these covered only 1903 years before the fall of Babylon.[41] The technical evidence of Ptolemy suggested an even shorter evolution, for the earliest astronomical

---

39. Garin, *Lo zodiaco della vita; 'Astrolóoi hallucinati'*, ed. Zambelli.
40. Weinstein, *Savonarola and Florence*, ch. vi.
41. Simplicius on *De Caelo* II.12, 293 a 4; ed. J. L. Heiberg (Berlin, 1894), p. 506. The reading 1903 is attested not in the Greek tradition but in the Latin translation by Moerbeke.

observations he or anyone else recorded were dated from the accession of Nabonassar to the Babylonian throne in 747 B.C, only six hundred years before Hipparchus. Moreover, as Pico pointed out, Hipparchus himself did not 'arrive at complete certainty' about the motion of the closest of the planets, the moon; 'therefore he was corrected by Ptolemy, who, surpassing Hipparchus, approached but did not quite attain the truth.'[42] The claims of ancient and modern admirers of astrology were 'false and mendacious'.

Astronomy and astrology, in Pico's analysis, lost their shadowy millennial past and became, like the rest of classical culture, a creation of the first millennium B.C. This momentous historical revision challenged the whole notion of an ancient revelation, so prominent in Pico's own early thought; and it offered a sketch of the evolution of ancient science strikingly similar to that produced by modern historians using cuneiform as well as Greek sources. But Pico went further still. He argued not only that astronomy was relatively recent but that astrology, its sister art, was a still later – and deplorable – deformation of it. In Aristotle's *Metaphysics* Pico turned up a brilliant critique of the followers of Pythagoras, who had mistakenly held 'the elements of numbers to be the elements of all things' in the universe. Aristotle explained the error with a pioneering bit of sociology of science. The Pythagoreans had been proficient mathematicians; they then made the mistake, natural in those who have mastered a difficult discipline, of thinking that it offered the key to the secrets of nature as a whole: 'being trained in [mathematics] they thought that its principles were the principles of all things.'[43] Pico applied this explanation to the first astrologers in Chaldea. They too had been expert mathematicians; they too had committed the error that afflicts 'all who are totally absorbed in a single discipline: they want to see everything in its terms.' '*Omnia illis erant stellae*' – so ran Pico's lapidary summary.[44]

Humanism, science and magic thus came together in a novel and powerful thesis – one that burst the bounds of normal humanist inquiry into the past and transformed the accepted account of how the classical sciences came into being. Pico's arguments certainly did not win universal assent. But for a century and more they stimulated debate, provoked powerful counter-arguments from energetic readers like Ramus, and won the respect of such great experts as Joseph Scaliger.[45] And Pico was by no means the only scholar whose inquiry into the

---

42. Pico, *Disputationes* XI.2; *Opera omnia* (Basel, 1572), p. 715.
43. *Metaphysics* 985 b 23 ff., tr. W. D. Ross; quoted and discussed by G. E. R. Lloyd, *Early Greek Science: Thales to Aristotle* (1970), pp. 25–7.
44. Pico, *Disputationes* XII.3, *Opera omnia*, p. 721.
45. A. Grafton, *Joseph Scaliger*, I (Oxford, 1983), ch. vii.

natural world included a substantial textual and historical component. The Galenic scholars of the later sixteenth century, like John Caius, recently studied to brilliant effect by Vivian Nutton, carried on a very similar tradition of 'medical philology' in which science and scholarship intersected to their mutual benefit, and in the course of which scientists sometimes did philological work of a sophistication that the humanists could not always match.[46] And as late as the mid-seventeenth century Pierre Gassendi, Ismaël Boulliau and other scientists pursued a set of linked historical and philosophical studies recognizably descended from the encyclopedism of the fifteenth-century humanists.[47]

## Conclusion

The humanists, in sum, had no single approach to nature or attitude towards magic and science. But they did retrieve ingredients and forge attitudes that proved vital to the development of sixteenth-century thought about nature. They did enable sixteenth-century intellectuals to draw stunning – though unstable – maps of a constantly shifting cosmic and intellectual order. They had a substantial hand in the development of the notion, widely held by the seventeenth century, that science has profound social impact and responsibility. They provided much of the new rhetoric that seventeenth-century science would deploy in its own defence – sometimes against later defenders of the humanist tradition. And they developed a new model of inquiry, at once philological and philosophical, textual and empirical, historical and scientific, that found widespread employment in the sixteenth century even if it has often been ignored in modern historiography. The contemptuous dismissals of humanism that we know from Descartes' *Discourse on Method* are no safe or helpful guide to the strenuous and successful odysseys of the mind completed by men like Poliziano and Pico.

---

46. See Nutton, *John Caius,* and the essays by Nutton and I. Lonie in *The Medical Renaissance of the Sixteenth Century* (Cambridge, 1985), ed. Wear *et al.*

47. L. S. Joy, *Gassendi the Atomist* (Cambridge, 1987) traces the afterlife of humanist scholarship in the age of Descartes with much instructive detail and comment.

*Chapter Six*

# Humanism in Italy

## George Holmes

### I

Humanism means an interest in Latin and Greek literature which sets a high value on the lessons to be drawn from it.[1] A definition more precise than this would be misleading. Such a general inclination obviously leaves room for vast differences. The attachments of humanists to particular classical authors can lead to diverse results: passions for Plato, Cicero or Tacitus imply very varied interests. Equally the way the classical enthusiasm fits into the more general way of life of the humanist leads to its having a very different significance. Bruni and Valla, Erasmus and Machiavelli were all great humanists but they lived in different circumstances with varied professional concerns which led to contrasting structures of thought. An observer might wonder whether there was any justification for including them in the same category. The defence of this classification depends on the fact that the flowering of interests in history, politics, religion and philosophy as well as literature in the period 1400–1550 was inseparable from writers' devotion to classical authors in a manner much more intense and scholarly than had been the case in the medieval centuries, although such writers as Aristotle and Virgil had come high on the list of venerated authorities. The phase of thought with which this book is concerned begins in fact rather suddenly with a change in style of

---

1. For a general consideration of humanism see P. O. Kristeller, *Renaissance Thought* (New York, 1955) and *Renaissance Thought II* (New York, 1965); E. Garin, *Italian Humanism: Philosophy and Civic Life in the Renaissance*, trans. P Munz (Oxford, 1965)

thought and depth of understanding which takes place principally in Florence in the early years of the fifteenth century.

Before the fifteenth century there is one writer whose name cannot be omitted. Petrarch (1304–74)[2] had carried out a long and lonely campaign to elevate and improve his understanding of the classical authors he valued, particularly Cicero. He had done this with such varied and intense creativity that his work was itself a turning point in the history of thought which established many of the assumptions and literary forms which were to become commonly adopted in the Renaissance world. Petrarch is best known nowadays as the inventor of a type of sonnet. That is not what he would have valued most highly in his career or what had most influence on his successors in the next two centuries. In the first place Petrarch established a new precision in the understanding of classical authors and civilisation: he rediscovered lost letters of Cicero, emended the texts in manuscripts and took an interest in the material remains of the ancient world such as buildings and inscriptions. He was closer than any predecessor to the modern classical scholar. Second, he developed and popularised several of the types of literature which became widely favoured among later humanists, notably the letter and the dialogue in which a great many humanist thoughts were to be expressed. Third, he set up the study of classical culture and the imitation of classical authors as a pursuit which had a central importance for civilisation. He admired the intellectual value of classical literature, he despised the logic-chopping of university scholastics and he ignored the literature of romance legend. He proposed a new collection of intellectual values which a great many people were to accept and follow in the next two centuries. It might be added that his conscience was also obsessed with the conflict between the pagan models which he exhibited and the truths of Christianity which he also accepted. This problem of dualism was to be a central feature of the humanist centuries, sometimes faced fairly squarely, as it was by Valla or Erasmus, much more often largely ignored, as by Machiavelli, but always present.

Petrarch was partly trained as a lawyer before he became a man of letters and was the son of a successful Tuscan notary. The role of the notarial and legal professions in Italian society is an essential part of the background against which humanism developed.[3] These were lay professions which involved an expertise in the writing of Latin documents, sometimes simple legal contracts, sometimes elaborate letters and speeches. They encouraged in their practitioners an acquaintance with Latin literature and an admiration for and wish to imitate the style

---

2. N. Mann, *Petrarch* (Oxford, 1984)
3. L. Martines, *Lawyers and Statecraft in Renaissance Florence* (Princeton, 1968)

of ancient authors. The existence of this lay class of men who knew some of the classics but were not involved in the study of theology or of the philosophical systems of the universities was perhaps the most important predetermining factor which made humanism possible. It was a feature of Italian society which was present in a particularly strong form in Florence. This was a city which, in spite of its great commercial wealth, a large bourgeoisie and a strong tradition of secular literature going back to the time of Dante, did not have a great university. The university of Florence had a rather intermittent existence and was dominated by the city rather than the ecclesiastical authorities. These were circumstances which, looking back to them, we can see made possible the emergence of an independent secular culture much stronger and more original than anything analogous in other European cities. Petrarch had very little to do with Florence and there were culture-loving proto-humanists in other Italian towns before 1400. But Florence provided the ideal circumstances in which a humanist movement could establish itself with a degree of self-sufficiency and independence in the years after 1400.

The group of enthusiasts who carried out the humanist revolution in Florence grew up originally under the leadership of the chancellor of the republic Coluccio Salutati (1331–1406)[4], a disciple of Petrarch and the author of a number of writings concerned in one way and another with classical topics. Salutati was behind the remarkable and important step which the commune of Florence took of inviting the Greek scholar Manuel Chrysoloras to hold a professorship of Greek in the city during the years 1397–1400. Knowledge of Greek was at this time a rarity in northern Italy and Chrysoloras's visit was important for that reason. But he also inspired his hearers with a liking for the material remains of ancient buildings and art from which stemmed the close connection between humanists and artists in the Florentine Renaissance, a connection which was to have such fundamental importance in establishing a humanist-inspired view of the world expressed visually as well as in thought. Another dominant figure in the humanist group was Niccolò Niccoli (1364–1437)[5], a local gentleman who seems to have devoted himself single-mindedly to the pursuit of classical interests. These included not only ancient languages, the copying of manuscripts of Latin authors and italic script but also ancient buildings, sculpture and engraved gems. The scene was thus set for a rather broad approach to the ancient world which aimed at a general appreciation of classical civilisation.

---

4. R. G. Witt, *Hercules at the Crossroads. The Life, Works, and Thought of Coluccio Salutati* (Durham, N. Carolina, 1983)

5. G. Zippel, *Niccolò Niccoli* (Florence, 1890)

The most prominent person in Florentine humanism in the first half of the fifteenth century was Leonardo Bruni (1370–1444)[6], an extensive writer and eventually a dominant figure and austere authority in the Italian intellectual world. Bruni is the archetypal Renaissance humanist because he was both a highly regarded professional writer of state documents – in the early part of the century he was a secretary at the papal court, then from 1427 chancellor of Florence – and a scholar who evolved new ideas based on his classical learning. His largest work, a *History of the Florentine People*, pioneered a new kind of historical writing which, in contrast with the medieval veneration of the Roman Empire, glorified the Roman republic, linking this with a high estimation of the contemporary Florentine republic as against the despotic regimes which were common in the north Italian world. The interest in republicanism and classical literature led Bruni to present historical evolution as essentially a story of civilised culture struggling with barbarism, a transformation of the vision of the past whose implications were to be elaborated for centuries to come. Bruni was also the author of an apologia for Florence produced at the beginning of the century during the wars with Milan. His work contains the genesis of a republican political thought concerned with the city state and owing little to medieval ideas because it was based mainly on reading Latin authors like Cicero and Livy, and was therefore unlike the political thought produced by the university scholastics which had been more heavily dependent on Aristotle.

In spite of his Latin instincts Bruni also made himself a Greek scholar and translated some of the works of Aristotle and Plato. The Florentines were voracious in their dedication to the whole ancient world and it is important to remember this when thinking of the implications of their work. In some ways, however, a more typical Florentine of this generation was Poggio Bracciolini (1380–1459),[7] although he was employed for most of his life at the papal court. Poggio's Greek was poor. His importance rests on two other things which showed the direction and potentialities of humanism. He carried on the interests of Petrarch as a great collector and copier of Latin manuscripts. He also wrote several dialogues on such subjects as avarice and hypocrisy. These are lively and pungent works which show what could be done in the dialogue form. They are also, alas, in Latin. This brings out in a sense the limitations of the humanist position. Their admiration for

---

6. On Bruni and his world see H. Baron, *The Crisis of the Early Italian Renaissance* (Princeton, 1955); L. Martines, *The Social World of the Florentine Humanists 1390–1460* (1963); G. Holmes, *The Florentine Enlightenment 1400–50* (1969)

7. E. Walser, *Poggius Florentinus* (Berlin, 1914)

good Latin and their wish to imitate it put the humanists in touch with classical literature, opened their eyes to pagan culture and gave them a certain freedom from domination by the contemporary Christian world. But it also involved the avoidance of their native tongue as an inferior method of communication. This had a crippling effect on original literature and no doubt explains in part why the Italy of the fifteenth century produced no writer remotely comparable with Dante or Boccaccio. It took some time for Italian to recover from the heavy blows dealt to it by Petrarch and the early fifteenth-century Florentine school.

One major writer of this early period, however, perhaps the greatest of them, did write in Italian. This was Leon Battista Alberti (1404–72),[8] a member of a notable exiled Florentine family who, like Poggio, earned his living at the papal court. Alberti composed three very important treatises: on the family (*Della Famiglia*), on painting (*Della Pittura*), and on architecture (*De Re Aedificatoria*) of which two were in Italian. *Della Famiglia* presents a humanist view of social and political life. It is not a closely argued philosophical work and could not be regarded as important in the history of political thought, but it is a very interesting bourgeois view of society and gives us, in Italian, elaborations of things like the view of life as a struggle between *virtù* and *fortuna* which are important in the humanist vision of the world. *Della Pittura*, however, is, to say the least, a seminal work of the first importance because it is the first dramatic statement in 1436 of the connection between humanism and the visual arts and in a sense the ancestor of all later art criticism. Alberti was himself a practising visual artist, in particular an architect who designed several classical buildings, for example the façade of S. Andrea at Mantua, and knew some of the great artists at Florence, notably Brunelleschi and Donatello. The message of *Della Pittura* is that artists should use perspective realism as developed at Florence to give paintings realistic space, that pictures should contain realistic stories, not symbolism, and that the good artist was an individual genius worthy of the highest estimation. This view of art arises from a combination of observing recent Florentine novelties, themselves produced in part under humanist influence, and reading about art in Pliny and Vitruvius. It is a completely new start in ideas about art.

To understand the environment of Alberti one must look at the art produced in the early fifteenth century by Brunelleschi (1377–1446),[9]

---

8. L. B. Alberti, *On Painting and Sculpture*, ed. and trans. C. Grayson (1972)
9. E. Battisti, *Filippo Brunelleschi* (Milan, 1976)

Masaccio (1401–28)[10] and Donatello (1388–1466).[11] Brunelleschi, the builder of the dome of Florence cathedral, which revived the ancient glories of Mediterranean architecture associated with Constantinople and Venice, was the inventor of Renaissance architecture in the loggia of the Innocenti and the Old Sacristy of S. Lorenzo at Florence, put up in the 1420s. The new round-arched style might be seen as owing more to Romanesque than to Roman art but it was an attempt to revive the antique, produced under the influence of the local humanists of the school of Salutati. Donatello the sculptor was also powerfully influenced by ancient models which he had seen and was no doubt encouraged by humanists around him. One of his most remarkable works, the bronze David in the Bargello, might be taken as a symbol of the secularisation of the visual arts which was made possible by the influence of humanism. This David is a nude youth, ostentatiously swaggering and exquisitely beautiful, who has practically nothing to do with the religious significance of the figure of biblical legend. Most first-class painting and sculpture at this period still had a religious subject-matter but Masaccio and Donatello had a consuming interest in figural and spatial realism which was in some ways carried still further by the painters Uccello (1397–1475) and Piero della Francesca (d. 1492).

From the 1420s to the 1460s the most important patron of humanists and humanistic art in Florence was the rich banker Cosimo de' Medici, who also acquired a dominant political position in the republic. Patronage was important and Cosimo's distinctly humanist tastes should probably be regarded as a major factor influencing the direction of both intellectual and artistic effort at this time. The importance of patronage can also be seen if we look at the geography of emerging humanism outside Florence and observe the way in which humanists were employed by friendly despots at Milan, Ferrara, Urbino, Naples and elsewhere. The most important centre of humanist activity outside Florence, however, was at the papal court, partly because it employed a large number of highly-paid letter writers, partly because of the close social and political links between Rome and Florence.

It is a curious and important fact that, throughout much of the period with which we are concerned, the papal court did not cling to medieval traditions of literature and art or express horror at the paganising tendencies of humanism. On the contrary it was often at the forefront in the employment of literary humanists and their artistic cousins. This was a result partly of the relatively great wealth available

10. L. Berti, *Masaccio* (Milan, 1964)
11. R. W. Lightbown, *Donatello and Michelozzo* (1980); H. W. Janson, *The Sculpture of Donatello* (Princeton, 1957)

at the popes' court, partly of their determination to maintain a high profile among the Italian secular powers by employing the same methods of ostentatious display. In the mid-fifteenth century the papal court became for a time the most lavish centre of patronage for humanism. Pope Nicholas V (1447–55) was perhaps the most ambitious of all the humanist popes of the Renaissance period. He took over completely the ideas which he had seen in action in Florence[12]. His aim was a double one. On the literary side he wished to build up a complete humanist library, making all Greek literature available in Latin translation, and therefore employed both Byzantine exiles and Italian experts such as Valla and Filelfo. On the visual side he had grand plans for rebuilding and decorating Rome to make it a capital city in classical style for which he called on the services of Alberti and the Florentine painter Fra Angelico. Nicholas's pontificate was too short for the fulfilment of his plans but he had the effect of clinching the strong links between the papal court and humanist ideals. Not long after this the papal see was filled for a time by a pope who had been in effect a professional humanist, Pius II (1458–64).[13] Enea Silvio Piccolomini, to give him his real name, had been an active belle-lettrist and was the author of a frank autobiography, an important expression of the penetration of humanist ideals into the highest circles of the Church. He also devoted a great deal of money to building a monument to his family in the town of Pienza, converted into a group of classical buildings which still stand. It is clear that at this period the uneasy combination of Christian and classical worlds was accepted with comparatively little discomfort.

## II

Perhaps the most original and remarkable of the humanists of the mid-century was a man whose career owed more to the courtly patronage of the international world than to either Florence or Rome though his attitudes were derived originally from that matrix, Lorenzo Valla (1407–57).[14] Valla was a Roman who failed to get employment at the papal court and resorted to the circles of the Visconti at Padua and King Alfonso I at Naples. Exclusion combined with his sceptical genius in encouraging him to carry humanist skill forward from the genial indifference to religious questions and scholasticism which had been

---

12. The connections between the papal court and humanism in the period 1400–1550 are best set out in various chapters of L. Pastor, *History of the Popes*, vols I to XII (1899–1912). See also C. L. Stinger, *The Renaissance in Rome* (Bloomington, 1985)

13. R. J. Mitchell, *The Laurels and the Tiara* (1962)

14. S. I. Camporeale, *Lorenzo Valla, umanesimo e teologia* (Florence, 1972)

characteristic of the Florentine and Roman schools into a serious attack on central Christian propositions. *On Pleasure* which he composed in 1431 was the most original of the humanist dialogues of the fifteenth century, a semi-serious defence of the view that epicureanism and the pursuit of pleasure, rather than Bruni's austere stoicism, was the classical philosophical movement most compatible with Christianity. In the service of the anti-papal king of Naples he composed *The Donation of Constantine* which used humanist scholarship to demolish the authenticity of the forged document which popes had used for centuries in defence of their claims to temporal power. His book *On the Elegancies of the Latin Tongue* attacked on linguistic grounds the misuse of the classical languages in the Christian Aristotelianism of the scholastics. Finally his *Adnotationes in Novum Testamentum* began the process of using humanist understanding of Greek for the revision and interpretation of the text of the New Testament. Valla was a rather isolated figure who founded no school, but in the eyes of the historian he can be seen as the first man who grasped the possibility of a critical and potentially destructive confrontation between humanist technique and some of the central documents of the Christian faith. His work on the New Testament was to be an inspiration for Erasmus half a century later, and he is in a sense the originator of the critical movement of ideas which was to be carried forward into the French enlightenment of the seventeenth and eighteenth centuries.

The first phase of Italian humanism, with which we have been concerned so far, though it involved a fair amount of translation of Greek texts by Bruni and Valla for instance, was principally Latin in its inspiration. It was the resurrection of Ciceronian Latin and of Roman art and architecture which chiefly inspired scholars and artists, and no serious approach was made to new sources of inspiration in the Greek world. The second phase in the second half of the fifteenth century is dominated by the revival of Plato and neoplatonism. This move towards interest in the Greek world was much affected by the close contact between Italian and Byzantine scholars which was characteristic of the mid-fifteenth century when the Byzantine empire was finally engulfed by the Ottoman Turks. The Council of Florence in 1439, an attempt to shore up the Byzantine world by means of a reconciliation between the Catholic and Orthodox Churches, brought to Italy a collection of leading Greek scholars with a knowledge of ancient philosophy who made a powerful impression on Italian humanists. The final collapse of the Byzantine empire, completed in 1453, led to a significant diaspora of learned Greek scholars into Italy. Among them were Janos Argyropoulos (1415–87), who lectured in Florence on Aristotle and Plato between 1456 and 1471, and Bessarion (1403–72), who became a cardinal of the Roman Church and helped to introduce

Italians to Greek philosophy and whose books became the nucleus of the library of St. Mark at Venice.

The most important result of the new enthusiasm for Greek was the work of Marsilio Ficino (1433–99)[15] carried on at Florence under the auspices of the two great Medici, Cosimo (1389–1464) and Lorenzo the Magnificent (1449–92). The dying Cosimo, a great patron of earlier humanists inspired by contact with Greeks brought to Italy by the Council of Florence, wanted to open up the secrets of truth which he believed were concealed in the writings of Plato. He therefore commissioned Ficino to translate Plato's writings into Latin and this was done by 1469. While Aristotle's works had been well known to university philosophers since the thirteenth century, Plato had remained a largely obscure and unknown figure. Ficino's translation was an enormous gift to the Latin and Western worlds which made a vast new corpus of ideas readily available. Later in his life Ficino also translated the neoplatonic writings of Plotinus and Proclus, thus making available the true sources of neoplatonist ideas which had long influenced medieval thought but only through derivative and second-hand versions. Ficino's life-work is the most remarkable case of humanist scholarship providing the West with a large body of inspiring classical philosophy which had been hitherto only very imperfectly known.

Ficino became a priest and was devoted to the authenticity and uniqueness of the Christian religion. His work on Plato and Plotinus and the Greek Hermetic texts of the Roman period, however, opened up a new vision of a general history of religious and philosophical doctrine within which Christianity could be placed. Ficino believed in the existence of an original, early theology which contained permanent truths revealed in various ways in the writings of Plato and Plotinus as well as in Christian doctrine. He was the author of a *Platonic Theology*, presenting Platonic ideas of the immortality of the soul in contrast with the Aristotelian philosophy of the scholastics. He adopted the neoplatonic idea of the universe as a hierarchy of being extending from gross matter to the indivisible purity of the Godhead, in which the human soul, with its capacity for pure thought, was placed in a central position. On the basis of his reading of Plato he promoted the idea of the capacity of the soul to move upwards towards God under the impulses of reason and will. Ficino was also interested in magic and astrology. He gave Italy a fascinating assembly of ideas, a thought-world quite different from that of the previous generation of

---

15. R. Marcel, *Marsile Ficin* (Paris, 1958); M. J. B. Allen, *The Platonism of Marsilio Ficino, A Study of the Phaedrus Commentary, its Sources and Genesis* (Berkeley, Los Angeles, London 1984)

humanists, in which myth and symbolism were allowed a large part, allied with a spiritualist belief in the potentialities of the immortal soul.

Ficino was at the centre of the humanist-inspired group which we associate with Laurentian Florence and was indeed patronised by Lorenzo, himself a poet, a collector of ancient objets d'art and the builder of a great library.[16] Lorenzo's ambiguous but certainly dominant role in Florentine politics between 1469 and 1492 gives the regime the appearance of a humanist republic. It is indeed true that an exceptionally wealthy city with a strong tradition of lay patronage of art, a large circle of expert humanists and a leading politician sympathetic with their ideas created an atmosphere of lay cultural refinement which was novel and has seemed to later observers to be the mark of a golden age. The idea of the Platonic Academy, which gives too strong an impression of formality, has been associated with the meetings of Lorenzo's humanist friends. Among them were Cristoforo Landino, a literary neoplatonist who published an imaginary discussion among the humanists in his *Disputationes Camaldulenses* and Angelo Poliziano, who, besides being the author of poems and dramas, was also a considerable classical scholar. A remarkable vagrant from Lombardy who moved temporarily into this world was Giovanni Pico della Mirandola (1463–94).[17] Pico was not a disciple of Ficino but his extraordinary writings did in a sense carry forward Ficino's elevation of the greatness of the human soul and his liking for mythical interpretation. Pico was much influenced not only by Greek but also by Arabic and Jewish philosophy which formed the basis for an advanced religious and philosophical syncretism, advocating the existence of a widely spread understanding of ultimate truth which was difficult to reconcile with Christian orthodoxy. His best-known work is the brief *Oration on the Dignity of Man*, putting forward the idea that man's soul possesses an unlimited capacity for spiritual self-development which can be promoted by the cleansing power of philosophy.

The links between humanism and art in Laurentian Florence led to a new kind of painting, embodied in Botticelli's *Birth of Venus* and *Primavera* which have remained the visual symbols of the epoch. Sandro Botticelli (1445–1510)[18] painted these pictures for rooms in Medici houses under the influence of the valuation of classical myths derived from Ficino. This was the beginning of a new kind of panel-painting of mythical subjects which is in marked contrast to the religious painting which had of course been universal before this period. The

---

16. A. Chastel, *Art et Humanisme a Florence au temps de Laurent le Magnifique* (Paris, 1961)

17. E. Garin, *Giovanni Pico della Mirandola* (Florence, 1937)

18. R. Lightbown, *Sandro Botticelli* (1978)

precise significance of such classical figures as the three Graces in *Primavera* has been much disputed. The intention was probably to use figures from pagan mythology to convey a perfectly acceptable moral lesson. The important thing is that they established classical mythology at the summit of painting of the highest quality where it was to remain throughout the Renaissance period, to some extent replacing Christian subjects. Botticelli's greater contemporary, Leonardo da Vinci (1452–1519) was, as far as subject matter is concerned, a more traditional painter, devoting himself to religious subjects, like the *Adoration of the Magi*, and to portraits, and his astonishing hydraulic and anatomical researches probably owe little to humanism. His zeal for the perfection of naturalistic painting is of course a continuation of the efforts of earlier artists imbued with the humanist liking for realism. But he seems little influenced in a direct sense either by the Latin humanists or by Ficino. Botticelli's subject matter, on the other hand, is a direct expression of the ethos of Lorenzo's 'court' and was to change the direction of art in a more dramatic way.

By the end of the fifteenth century humanist expertise and the admiration for ancient literature and art which it carried with it were widely distributed in the Italian cities and courts outside Florence and Rome. Federico da Montefeltro, duke of Urbino from 1474 to 1482, created a centre of humanist learning and art in a rather poor town whose buildings still convey something of the civilised charm which he promoted. One of the most determined classicists among the painters of the period was Andrea Mantegna (d. 1506),[19] who was employed by the Gonzaga family at Mantua. One of his enterprises is the series of nine paintings of the *Triumphs of Caesar*, now at Hampton Court. The imagined spectacle of a Roman triumph passing through Rome allowed him to present the onlooker with a great assembly of ancient costumes, inscriptions and classical buildings to which he applied a considerable antiquarian expertise in the attempt to recreate the classical world. Mantegna was also a great promoter of figural realism and perspective. His paintings, without the spiritual leanings of the contemporary Florentines, are the ideal case of the fusion of historical romanticism, with a real archaeological basis, and the realistic technique which was also related to classical inspiration. His patron, Lodovico Gonzaga the ruler of Mantua, was a serious student of Latin and collector of books who had been a pupil of Vittorino da Feltre (1378–1446) the most prominent of the creators of the new humanist education, in which the study of the classics was given supreme importance as a source of both intellectual and moral precepts. Apart from

---

19. R. Lightbown, *Mantegna* (Oxford, 1986)

the professional interest of the document-writers, which we have already mentioned, and the serious intellectual and aesthetic enthusiasm of the more prominent rhetoricians, we must include the development of a humanist educational system among the factors which enabled the movement to take root and spread. By the late fifteenth century that was implanting humanist ideals in the minds of a large number of people who could not have had any professional interest in writing or thought, more especially in the upper levels of society.

We must also include among the factors promoting humanism the new technology of printing which appeared in Italy in the 1460s. Most of the classical works printed in the fifteenth century were printed in Italy. The biggest centre of the new industry was Venice which quickly became pre-eminent in Europe. It was there that Aldus established new standards by printing large numbers of Latin and Greek works in elegant small volumes. The Aldine press was a monument to the financial strength of Venice, not the most intellectually interesting of the Italian cities, and it promoted the process by which humanist ideals were transmitted along the lines of commercial and social contact with a speed that would not have been possible with heavy folios or manuscripts.[20]

It was this North Italian world which gave birth to one of the most successful popularisers of humanist ideals. Baldassare Castiglione (1478–1529)[21] came from near Mantua and was employed for most of his life by the courts of Mantua and Urbino which provided him with the setting for his book *The Courtier*. This is intended to describe how gentlemen should behave. Its ideal of good and easy manners is in a sense very far from the republican model presented by the early Florentines, though it arises in part from the personal ideals found by humanists in Cicero and other classical writers with the addition of the platonic idea of the importance of love. The difference arises from the fact that the Courtier is a man living within the aristocratic world of a society ruled by a despot. What Castiglione has done is to adapt the humanist ideas for use with a social model appropriate for princely, courtly and aristocratic societies. This is an important development because, by the time he wrote in the early sixteenth century, the republican city-state world mirrored in the work of the early Florentine humanists, was becoming less important both in Italy and in Europe. Castiglione provided a vehicle for the transfer of humanist ideas outside the sphere in which they had arisen.

20. M. Lowry, *The World of Aldus Manutius: Business and Scholarship in Renaissance Venice* (Oxford, 1979)

21. J. R. Woodhouse, *Baldesar Castiglione: a reassessment of 'The Courtier'* (Edinburgh, 1978)

Further developments, in a sense of an analogous kind, can be found in the careers of two of Castiglione's contemporaries, also northern Italians. Isabella d'Este (1474–1539) was at first brought up at the court of Ferrara and her marriage to a Gonzaga took her to Mantua. Her high intelligence and her leisured life as a member of despotic families enabled her to become one of the most remarkable female humanists of the Italian Renaissance period. Though not a significant writer, her learned taste enabled her to become a constructive patron both of painters and of men of letters, including Castiglione. Again we see humanism moving into courtly society in a way which allowed its general transfer to the European world. Lodovico Ariosto (1474–1533),[22] another Ferrarese, was arguably the most significant imaginative writer in Italian of the Renaissance period. His great poem, *Orlando Furioso*, is an adaptation of Romance legend for the taste of the early sixteenth century. The legends of Charlemagne's retainers, like the Arthurian legends, were central parts of the material out of which the stories of the medieval poets had been constructed since the twelfth century. No subject matter could have been more remote from the thought-world of the early humanists than these tales of knightly chivalry and courtly love. Ariosto was a writer of comic dramas for the Ferrarese court. He then took up the Orlando story which had been used in the *Orlando innamorato*, by an earlier Ferrarese courtier Boiardo, and constructed a great sequel in which a courtly story was told with drama and humour and with the application of humanist material drawn from classical authors. Here we are on the edge of the humanist world but the new confection which entranced Italy and Europe created a novel mixture of medieval and Renaissance taste which could be welcomed in a very wide world.

## III

In the sixteenth century the continued commercial prosperity of Venice made her unquestionably the wealthiest city society in Italy. Her painters pursued their trade with a continuous grandeur and refinement of technique which made this school, as a whole, more impressive than the contemporary schools of Florence and Rome. Here we see a new efflorescence of humanist-inspired techniques and subject matter.[23] The founder of the sixteenth-century school was Giorgione (d. 1510), an obscure figure but certainly the creator of a new advance in landscape and figural realism – in the *Tempesta* and the unfinished *Sleeping Venus* – and also in classically inspired themes in the *Three Philosophers*. Gior-

---

22. C. P. Brand, *Lodovico Ariosto: A Preface to the 'Orlando Furioso'* (Edinburgh, 1974)
23. J. Wilde, *Venetian Art from Bellini to Titian* (Oxford, 1974)

gione's successor Titian (d. 1576),[24] though also of course the author of a vast number of paintings of traditional religious scenes, was the most monumental of all the Italian Renaissance artists in his adaptations of scenes drawn from classical mythology and symbolism. They stretch across the first half of the sixteenth century from the early allegorical *Sacred and Profane Love*, through *Bacchus and Ariadne* to the last great Diana paintings done for Philip II of Spain. They contain a marvellous combination of subjects drawn from antique legend with the glowing perfection of the modern painter's technique. Meanwhile in the middle of the century the architect Palladio (1508–80)[25] was building his villas in the Venetian *terraferma* in which classical motifs drawn from the earlier humanist buildings of Florence and Rome and from the classical writer on architecture, Vitruvius, were applied to the design of the country house to create a new perfection of classical architecture.

While Venice advanced into the sixteenth century with apparently undiminished wealth and with its republican constitution unimpaired, the world of Florence, the original home of serious humanism, was much more troubled and decadent. Florence was not powerful enough to withstand the force of the invasions which beset Italy from 1494. She was also incapable of re-establishing a republican constitution after the flight of the Medici in 1492, and a series of revolutions ended with the return of the Medici and the installation of a duchy in 1537.[26] The combination of repeated political disturbance with economic difficulties and the exceptionally rich intellectual and aesthetic traditions of the city produced a rather mobile and adventurous approach to both thought and art. Florence in the sixteenth-century Italian Renaissance world is like France in the world of nineteenth-century Europe as far as its art is concerned: the centre of aesthetic adventure. It was here that the most sophisticated exaggerations of Mannerism were developed. In intellectual novelties Florence must now yield to the North but it did produce important works of political thought. The Platonic Academy was followed after the departure of the Medici by the meetings of cultivated gentlemen in the garden of the Rucellai family which continued the tradition of gentlemanly discussion.

Two important political thinkers emerged out of the Florentine anguish about the constitution of the city. Francesco Guicciardini (1483–1540)[27] is best remembered for his *History of Italy* which told the story of the country during the Italian Wars. He also wrote treatises

---

24. H. E. Wethey, *Titian* (1969–75)

25. J. S. Ackerman, *Palladio* (Harmondsworth, 1966)

26. J. R. Hale, *Florence and the Medici: The Pattern of Control* (1977)

27. F. Gilbert, *Machiavelli and Guicciardini: Politics and History in Sixteenth-Century Florence* (Princeton, 1965)

on the politics of Florence which advocated control of the city by a fairly narrow oligarchy as the best means of ensuring stability. Of all the historians of the Renaissance period Guicciardini is perhaps the one who was most successful in the task of writing contemporary history with the ideals which humanists had adopted from the classical historians, that is to say of providing a narrative which was not merely annalistic but attempted to explain in a continuous way the operation of causes on events. Guicciardini was mainly concerned with political, diplomatic and military affairs; his work would seem to a modern observer to lack the social and economic dimensions. But he wrote with a strong sense of the interplay of character and fortune in politics with which he had been intimately concerned. Writing history was an important sector of the humanists' interests and the *History of Italy* might be regarded as the summit of the movement which started with Bruni's writing on the history of Florence a century earlier in its combination of realism, genuine analysis and literary grace.

Out of the innumerable treatises on politics written by humanists during the Renaissance period only *The Prince* by Niccolò Machiavelli (1469–1527)[28] has survived to the present time as an acknowledged masterpiece. Machiavelli was not a notable humanist scholar, like some of his predecessors in the Chancery at Florence, but he was undoubtedly a thinker formed by humanist education and inspiration working in the tradition established by Bruni. He made clear that he believed in following the examples of successful and unsuccessful politics provided by history, and the cases which he used were drawn indifferently from contemporary experience and from the reading of ancient historians. The cyclical view of the movement of political systems through a good republic, a corrupt republic and a tyranny, which he presented at the beginning of his other main political work, the *Discourses on the First Ten Books of Livy*, was drawn from a reading of Polybius on the Roman republic. The *Discourses* is in fact a lengthy study of Livy's history of Rome used as the basis for general observations on political life and contemporary examples which is evidently intended to be as much a study of the problems of modern Florence as of its classical ancestor. Machiavelli cannot be said to have made striking advances in appreciating the real transformations of society during the two thousand years of history which fell under his gaze: in this respect there is not much advance on the age of Bruni. But he used his historical examples as the basis for a much richer collection of political and sociological analyses, though these appear to the modern reader to be vitiated by the real differences in social and political struc-

28. J. R. Hale, *Machiavelli and Renaissance Italy* (1961)

ture which he tended to ignore. *The Prince* is famous for its advice to rulers that they should abandon the precepts of morality proper for personal life if they want to keep control of their states. Machiavelli also, incidentally, believed that Christianity's advocacy of meekness was positively harmful in politics and admired the secular state's use of religious cults for political purposes which he thought he saw in the ancient world. Put in its Renaissance context, however, *The Prince* clearly developed the vision of the individual in history struggling with the problems presented to him by external Fortune which had been one of the main strands of humanist thought since Petrarch. Though its moral maxims have a piquancy appealing to all epochs its style of thought and approach to historical problems belong to the humanist age.

While Florence was struggling with the exigencies forced upon it by political misfortune, the papal court at Rome was spreading its wings in the last age of grandeur before the Reformation. The pontificates of two great papal patrons, Julius II (1503–13) and Leo X (1513–21) came in the prosperous and tolerant period before the disasters of Luther and the Sack of Rome in 1527. Their aim was to revive the humanist splendour at Rome, which had first been inaugurated by Nicholas V, by schemes for the patronage of literature and building. The papal court was graced by the presence as a secretary of Pietro Bembo (1470–1547), the most distinguished man of letters of his day. Bembo was from the north of Italy but he was famous for his command of Tuscan Italian and Ciceronian Latin and his formulation of rules for the writers of the vernacular. This Italianism with a humanist accompaniment was appreciated at the pope's court in spite of Bembo's alleged sexual depravity. It was the last age in which the court of Rome was happy to house free-living devotees of pagan literature. At a slightly earlier stage the dominant figure in the architecture of Rome was Donato Bramante (1444–1514) who devised a delightful new style based essentially on the adaptation of classical forms to the building of palaces and centrally planned churches. His best-known work is the charming circular *tempietto* of S. Pietro in Montorio. In the pontificate of Julius II the papacy set to work on its most grandiose scheme, to rebuild St Peter's itself in a classical style. Bramante did not live to see more than the beginning of the work but it was his plan, later much modified, with which it started in 1506.

The most remarkable survivals of the papal rebuilding of this period are paintings rather than buildings. Raphael (1483–1520)[29] was in Rome from 1508 until his death, chiefly occupied with the decoration of apart-

---

29. R. Jones and N. Penny, *Raphael* (New Haven and London, 1983)

ments in the Vatican palace. One of his works was the fresco of the *School of Athens* whose subject matter can be taken as a symbol of the penetration of humanist ideas into the heart of the Church. Within the portrayal of a great classical basilica the painting is dominated by the figures of the philosophers Plato and Aristotle. Around them are grouped a number of masters of classical thought, Diogenes, Socrates, Pythagoras and others. The fresco is accompanied by others which represent Theology, Poetry and the Sacraments, but the *School of Athens* presents a particularly memorable picture of the grandeur and serenity of classical building housing the supreme embodiments of the capacities of human reason, drawn from the ancient world, and shows the importance which Raphael and his masters attributed to the classical inheritance as the source of wisdom. It is interesting that the man who painted the fresco was also concerned at the same time with important advances in portraiture and with an archaeological investigation into the plan of ancient Rome. Only a little before this time, in the year when the foundation stone of the new St Peter's was laid, Rome had been delighted by the archaeological chance of the unearthing of the Laocoon which seemed to add a new dimension to the knowledge of ancient sculpture.

While Raphael was painting the Vatican rooms Michelangelo (1475–1564) was painting the ceiling of the Sistine Chapel. After he left Rome Michelangelo returned to Florence and in the 1520s undertook the building of the New Sacristy of S. Lorenzo which contains the figures of Giuliano and Lorenzo de' Medici with Day, Night, Dawn and Dusk. Michelangelo was less classical and more Christian in his intellectual instincts than Raphael, but his sculpture has seemed understandably to embody the most perfect adaptation of the technique revived from the ancient world, the skill in the accurate representation of the human body, to modern needs, and the later draping of the nude figures in his fresco of the Last Judgement in the Sistine Chapel has been seen as the desecration of classical beauty by ignorant piety when the Renaissance was over. Between 1520 and 1550 Florentine art took off from the earlier works of Michelangelo to move into the phase now commonly known as 'mannerist', the exaggerated postures, elongated forms and obscure symbolisms which we associate with the paintings of Pontormo, Parmigianino and Salviati.

A survey of the impact of humanism may end conveniently with the *Lives of the Painters, Sculptors and Architects* first published by Giorgio Vasari (1511–74)[30] in 1550. Vasari's *Lives* is a consummation of the humanist ideal for two reasons. Firstly because it presents the artists

---

30. T. S. R. Boase, *Giorgio Vasari, the man and the book* (Princeton, 1979)

as great men, the attitude which had first been popularised by Alberti more than a century earlier. But here the lives of the artists who had worked since that time were told with a wealth of detail to represent them as real people. Secondly because Vasari holds in the most extreme fashion to the view that the arts collapsed with the decline of Rome to revive in the Italian Renaissance and eventually to advance towards the new excellence which he had seen in his own day. The Renaissance of art had taken place, triumphantly and under the influence of the imitation of classical models.

What had the impact of humanism achieved? Large areas of the Italian mind were scarcely affected by it. Popular religion and the piety of the mendicant orders continued to dominate most Italians throughout the Renaissance period. Natural science was assisted by the recovery of the works of Ptolemy and Galen translated from the Greek but it is broadly true that humanists, as humanists, were not much interested in science and did not contribute much to it. Humanists were interested in man, society and art, and it is in those areas that we must look for their influence.

The most direct effect of humanism was to establish literary genres which enabled a more realistic view of human nature and society to be adopted: the dialogue, the new history. Out of these the influence spread to other literary forms which allowed for a wider effect on literature in general, like Poliziano's poetry. The influence on social writing – that is history and political thought – was particularly marked. Outside literature humanism had an enormous effect on all the visual arts. We associate humanism with an awakened sense of the concrete: real human bodies, real historical events, rather than the symbolical and the allegorical. This is not, of course, entirely just. We have only to think of the complex problems of interpreting the symbolism of Botticelli's paintings. Nevertheless the figures, however symbolical they may be, are real individualised people, and artists under the influence of humanism were pioneers in painting portraits which capture the character of a single man or woman.

It is curious that the advance towards this kind of realism, so marked in Italy, should have been closely connected with the study of dead languages and a dead civilisation. It is arguable that the admiration for Latin and Greek was a serious hindrance to speakers of Italian who might have done better to follow Boccaccio rather than Petrarch. It is difficult to decide how far the apparent results of humanism were in fact a result of social change which would have brought them about anyway. There was however one great advantage in the study of Latin and Greek writers which must not be forgotten. They presented their readers with a secular world which allowed them to withdraw from the accepted traditions of Christian philosophy and theology and to create an independent world view. There was something unreal about this. With exceptions, humanists lived to some extent in a make-believe world which tended to ignore the real dualist world about them which they could not change. The exaggerated pursuit of a single aspect of the universe can however have dramatic results – modern science is another example of it – and there is no doubt about the humanists' success in enlarging the Italians' consciousness.

## Chapter Seven

# Humanism in the Low Countries

## JAMES K. CAMERON

### I

In a beautiful painting in the Pitti Palace in Florence, entitled 'The Four Philosophers', Peter Paul Rubens conveys in a masterful way something of the essential features of humanism in the Low Countries. Justus Lipsius (1540–1609), one of the most notable scholars of his age, is seated at a table with Jan Vowverius (1576–1635), an alderman of Antwerp, councillor of Brabant, and a diplomat in the service of the Archdukes Albert and Isabella, and friend of Josephus Justus Scaliger (1540–1609), and Philip Rubens (1574–1611) the painter's brother, successor to Jan Boch (1555–1609) as town clerk of Antwerp, who died 'before his full potential as a scholar had been realized'; the artist (a self-portrait) is standing in the background. Lipsius is depicted as expounding a passage in an open book before him, which is almost certainly a work by Seneca whose bust looks down from a niche in the wall. In the background, as through a window, an Italian landscape evokes the country of humanist origins.[1] In the Low Countries, classical and biblical scholars, academics, diplomats, public administrators, men of letters, of the arts, and of commerce, all united in their devotion to antiquity, worked together to establish in their country a golden age of humanist achievement that enriched the western world.

---

1. The painting is reproduced in black and white in *Leiden University in the Seventeenth Century: An Exchange of Learning*, ed. T. H. Lunsingh Scheuleer and G. H. M. Posthumus Meyjes (Leiden 1975), p. 195 (hereafter referred to as *Leiden University*); L. Voet, *The Golden Compasses* (Amsterdam. 1969) I, 388.

It was from Italy that humanism reached this region, initially through personal contacts brought about by diplomatic, ecclesiastical, scholarly and cultural exchange. Its successful development, which extended over several generations, was largely accomplished by the enlightened application by a patriotic people of some of the country's increasing economic and commercial prosperity. This is all the more remarkable in that the political conditions generally supposed to be necessary for nurturing the seeds of a great cultural flowering were in the Netherlands of the fifteenth and early sixteenth centuries at best precariously balanced and at times decidedly lacking.

The nearest universities, Cologne (founded in 1388) and Louvain (founded in 1425), were bastions of scholasticism and were largely to remain so. The centres of learning were the monasteries, and the contemporaries of the poets and literary men of the Italian Trecento were the mystics Ruysbroek (1293–1381) and Groote (1340–84). Further, the future of literature seemed to be in the vernacular.[2] The fortunes for Latin and ultimately for humanism changed only at the end of the fifteenth century with the strengthening of Latin studies at the schools of some of the chief cities, among them Bruges, Ghent, Deventer, Zwolle, 's-Hertogenbosch and Groningen. For this advancement credit has usually been assigned to the Brethren of the Common Life, but it is now generally agreed that their importance as educators has been exaggerated.[3] Although their founder, Gerhard Groote, showed an interest in books and learning, his example was not always followed by his associates and successors. 'The city school, with its Latin and logic, was enough for them! Philosophy was unnecessary, not to mention theology, law, or medicine.'[4] However, as humanism began to make itself felt towards the end of the fifteenth century in the schools of the cities where the Brethren had their houses, and where they maintained hostels for young boys, they began to take an interest in it and in developing closer relations with the rectors and teachers.

---

2. J. IJsewijn, 'The Coming of Humanism in the Low Countries', *Itinerarium Italicum; The Profile of the Italian Renaissance in the Mirror of its European Transformations*, ed. H. A. Oberman and T. A. Brady, Jr (Leiden, 1975), pp. 193–301; see also R. Walsh, 'The Coming of Humanism to the Low Countries: Some Italian Influences at the Court of Charles the Bold', *Humanistica Lovaniensia, Journal of Neo-Latin Studies*, 25 (1976), pp. 146–97.

3. R. R. Post, *The Modern Devotion: Confrontation with Reformation and Humanism* (Leiden, 1968); see also R. Mokrosch 'Devotio moderna II, Verhältnis zu Humanismus und Reformation', *Theologische Realenzyklopädie*, ed. G. Krause and G. Müller, Berlin, 8 (1981), pp. 609–12; W. Lourdaux, 'Dévotion moderne et humanisme chrétien', M. G. Verbeke, J. IJsewijn, *The Late Middle Ages, and the Dawn of Humanism outside Italy* (Louvain and The Hague, 1972), pp. 57–77.

4. Post, *The Modern Devotion*, p. 418.

Humanist influences were not imposed by the Brethren of the Common Life, yet they helped to put into effect what was being advocated by others. In the history of humanist education in the Low Countries, pride of place must be given to the city schools in which the 'new Latin' was fostered by generations of learned rectors, many of whom were or were to become significant humanists.[5] The school at Deventer, for example, where Alexander Hegius (c. 1433–1498) was rector from 1483 to 1498, reached unparalleled fame, and is regarded as the first school north of the Alps to provide for its pupils instruction in Greek.[6] Such schools were for the greater part public institutions in which local civic leaders took considerable interest, and they undoubtedly benefited from the developing economic prosperity, and they in turn served their communities by providing them with well educated merchants and administrators.

The origins of the teaching of the 'new Latin', the solid foundation of Northern humanism, had been prepared in the mid-fifteenth century at Louvain by Antonius Hameron (d.1490), whose aim was 'to teach Latin from the ancient sources and on a level adapted to the capacities of the young students' minds'[7], and by Rudolph Agricola (1444–85) who had 'thoroughly assimilated humanism in its Italian form'.[8] He stressed the study of the Bible and the moral reformation of Christendom as did the group of scholars associated with him and Wessel Gansfort (1419–1484) and known as the Adwerth (Aduard) Academy.[9] Following the practice of John Pupper of Goch and Gansfort of adopting humanist linguistic dress in their religious writings, Agricola attained an unrivalled pre-eminence in the early history of humanism in the Netherlands. Strenuously advocating the study of Greek, he aroused the enthusiasm for that study in Alexander Hegius through whom the torch of learning was passed on to the generation of Erasmus and Vives.[10] The study of Latin was at this time revolutionised by the publication of the famous grammar of Despauterius which 'remained

---

5. Ibid., 554.
6. P. N. M. Bot, *Humanisme en onderwijs in Nederland* (Utrecht and Antwerp, 1955), pp. 182 ff.; Post, *The Modern Devotion*, 577; L. J. Johnson, 'Alexander Hegius, Humanist Pedagogue', *Acta Conventus Neo-Latini Turonensis*, ed. J.-C. Margolin, (Paris 1980), I, pp. 377–88
7. IJsewijn, 'The Coming of Humanism', p. 219; he was professor of Latin in the university of Louvain 1430–37.
8. Ibid., p. 229
9. Ibid., p. 228; Post, *The Modern Devotion*, p. 597; M. van Rhijn, *Studien over Wessel Gansfort en zijn Tijd* (Utrecht, 1933), pp. 127–9; H. de Vocht, *History of the Foundation and Rise of the Collegium Trilingue Lovaniense, 1517–1550*, Part I, *Humanistica Lovaniensia*, 10 (1951; Kraus Reprint, 1976) pp. 139–58.
10. IJsewijn, 'The Coming of Humanism', pp. 230, 239; Post, *The Modern Devotion*, 467–86.

the basis of Latin grammars in the Low Countries until the twentieth century'.[11] A former pupil of Carolus Viruli of the Lilium Paedagogium in Louvain, Despauterius was also the author of the popular *Epistolarum Formulae* which, along with Hameron's *De Epistolis Brevibus Edendis*, was highly significant in encouraging an acquaintance with classical forms.[12] However, these early beginnings in classical studies, which were to become so 'prominent a feature of humanist learning and litera-ture' in the Low Countries in the sixteenth and seventeenth centuries, important as they were, have been authoritatively described as 'modest'.[13] Only later and as part of the harvest of the schools did a Latin-loving and an increasingly economically prosperous patriciate emerge and humanist culture secure 'the indispensable social base for a full flowering'.[14]

## II

The next stage in this development centres on the foundation of the *Collegium Trilingue* in Louvain in 1517. The way had been prepared by the establishment of a lectureship in Latin literature held by Italian scholars in the last quarter of the previous century – with the happy result that the young Erasmus found there 'a busy centre of humanistic studies in full flourish'.[15] The founding of the College was the direct outcome of an intense but locally confined interest created by the two-way intellectual traffic between Italy and the Netherlands that had followed in the wake of trade and diplomatic relations. It was made possible by the generosity of one of those who had taken part in this exchange, Jerome Busleyden (1470–1517),[16] and the untiring efforts of Erasmus.[17] Busleyden's travels in France and Italy provided him with an intimate knowledge of the Renaissance in many of its varied forms and inspired in him the plan, fostered by Erasmus, to set aside from the considerable fortune which he had amassed (largely from ecclesi-astical benefices held subsequent to his ordination) sufficient funds for the founding of the Trilingual College. Shortly before his death in 1517

11. IJsewijn, 'The Coming of Humanism', p. 244.

12. Vocht, *Collegium Trilingue*, Part I, pp.85–98, 120–4, 201–14; see also *Humanistica Lovaniensia*, 24 (1975) 25 (1976) for Hameron's *Opera*.

13. IJsewijn, 'The Coming of Humanism', p. 267.

14. Ibid., p. 269.

15. Vocht, *Collegium Trilingue*, I, p. 61.

16. H. de Vocht, *Jerome de Busleyden, Founder of the Louvain Collegium Trilingue: His Life and Writings, Humanistica Lovaniensia*, 9 (1950). Busleyden had probably received his early education at the Lilium, a pedagogy of the University of Louvain, under Carolus Viruli. *Collegium Trilingue*, pp. 194–200.

17. Vocht, *Collegium Trilingue*, I, pp. 12–20; Vocht, *Busleyden*, pp. 74–80.

he bequeathed much of his wealth, together with the fine collection of classical manuscripts which he had brought together at his Renaissance residence in Mechlin, for establishing in Louvain a college with adequate provision for both professors and students of the great languages and literatures of antiquity: Latin, Greek, and Hebrew.

The initial stages proved difficult despite the fact that the university numbered among its professors some who were more than anxious to further the new cause. Nevertheless such was the determination of the college's promoters that professors were appointed and the nascent institution had entered on its career even before arrangements could be made for housing it. Rapidly, thereafter, and with its recognition as part of the university, it succeeded in becoming not only the chief centre of humanist learning in the Netherlands, but also one of the most effective means of diffusing it throughout Northern Europe. As described by its historian, its aim was to set forward the reform plan of Erasmus, to bring back 'Theology from the muddy marshes of the *Sententiae* and *Summae* to the limpid fountain of Holy Scripture and the teaching of the Fathers'.[18] Much attention was, however, given to Latin literature, particularly to Cicero and to Greek authors, as texts became increasingly more available through the endeavours of Dierk Martens, the father of Greek printing in the Low Countries.[19] The study of Hebrew moved forward at a slower pace.[20] As interest in the new foundation and in the new learning developed, student numbers increased year by year and began to include not only those with a professional interest in scholarship, but also young noblemen, the sons of aristocrats from many countries, and the sons of the merchant classes rising to prominence with the country's economic prosperity.[21] But perhaps for the impact of humanism in the Netherlands the college initially rendered its finest service by providing an ever increasing number of teachers for the city Latin schools in most of which humanism was to secure a dominant place,[22] thereby encouraging in the future members of civic society a love of learning and of classical literature, along with the desire to become proficient in it and to contribute to its propagation.

Among those who studied at Louvain who not only disseminated the new learning but also achieved distinction are to be numbered the Greek scholars of Antwerp, Josse Valerius[23] and John Servilius,[24] and

---

18. *Idem., Collegium Trilingue*, I. p. 297.
19. See further *ibid.*, I. pp. 256–83; II. pp. 109–18 and below note 45.
20. *Ibid.*, I. pp. 253–6; II, pp. 118–122.
21. *Ibid.*, II, pp. 122–35.
22. See further Bot, *Humanisme en onderwijs in Nederland*.
23. *Biographie Nationale de Belgique*, 26, pp. 519–21
24. *Ibid.*, 10, 786–8; Vocht, *Collegium Trilingue*, II, pp. 186–8.

the neo-Latin poets Cornelius Musius (d. 1572) [25] and Cornelius Crocus (d. c. 1555)[26] of Amsterdam. Crocus, apart from writing manuals for his pupils, won for himself a reputation by his drama *Joseph* published in 1535, one of the most notable plays in a literary genre that had been encouraged earlier in Louvain by Martin van Dorp (d. 1525)[27] and Adrian Barlandus (1486–1538)[28] and which was to become very popular among neo-Latin writers. Another student, John Sartorius (d. 1577),[29] became schoolmaster at Amsterdam and later taught the three languages at Noordwijk. Equally distinguished among the *ludigmagistri* was Peter Nannius (1500–57),[30] director of the schools at Gouda and Alkmaar. Subsequently he was appointed Professor of Latin at the *Collegium Trilingue*. The influence of the *Trilingue* extended to those studying in the higher faculties of Theology, Law, and Medicine. The theologian Martin van Dorp exhorted his students to study the scriptural texts *de ipso fonte ut bibant* and upheld the study of Greek for the help it provided in understanding the Vulgate.[31] Others strenuously advocated getting as near as possible to the original meaning of the Bible by using a philological approach.[32] Similarly the jurist Vigilius of Aytta,[33] a student at the Trilingual College from 1523 to 1525, advocated legal studies *ad fontes*; and the physician Hubert Barlandus turned his students away from the prevailing doctrine 'based on pseudo-Avicenna and the Arabian School for that of the Greeks'.[34] Many of those who studied at the Trilingual College did so prior to entering public service and were so imbued with the spirit of humanism that they devoted much of their leisure to literary pursuits. Pre-eminent among them was Joannes Secundus (1511–36)[35] rightly regarded as one of the greatest of neo-Latin poets. Not content with merely imitating

25. Vocht, *Collegium Trilingue*, II, pp. 196–201.
26. Ibid., pp. 202–8.
27. Ibid., I. pp. 214–22, and II, pp. 502–8.
28. Ibid., I, pp. 226–31, pp. 267–71; E. Daxhelet, 'Adrien Barlandus: Humaniste Belge 1486–1538', *Humanistica Lovaniensia*, 6 (1938), pp. 10–16.
29. Vocht, *Collegium Trilingue*, II, pp. 477–82.
30. A. Polet, 'Une gloire de l'humanisme belge Petrus Nannius 1500–1557', *Humanistica Lovaniensia*, 5 (1936), pp. 1–28. He was the author of a highly praised comedy, *Vinctus*, in the style of Plautus and Terence. Polet, pp. 33–42 and Vocht, *Collegium Trilingue* II, pp. 177–9.
31. Ibid., p. 503.
32. Ibid., pp. 505–8.
33. Ibid., II, pp. 145–50.
34. Ibid., II, pp. 519, 522.
35. D. C. Crane, *Johannes Secundus, Life, Work and Influence on English Literature* (Leipzig, 1931); A. M. M. Dekker, *Janus Secundus (1511–1536): De tekstoverlevering van het tijdens zijn leven gepubliceerde werk*, (Nieukoop, 1986).

classical models, he is held to have raised neo-Latin poetry north of the Alps to the level of creative literature. His chief works, the *Basia* and the *Julia*, together with his epigrams, formed a significant contribution to literature and have won for him just praise as 'a magnificent instance of the all vivifying spirit of humanism'.[36] The Low Countries later provided a considerable number of public figures who distinguished themselves in this type of scholarly endeavour, especially at the turn of the century, but 'in a strictly literary sense the major literary influence . . . remains that of Joannes Secundus'.[37]

## III

Humanistic studies could not, however, have flourished without the outstanding efforts and pioneering work of the developing printing industry. Indeed, 'the history of humanism in the Netherlands is inseparably connected'[38] with that of its great printing houses which both shared in and contributed to the region's commercial prosperity. Before 1500 significant presses were in operation at Utrecht, Delft, Gouda, Deventer, Zwolle, Nijmegen, Leiden, Louvain, and Antwerp.[39] The most prolific of the Northern printers, Richard Pafraet and De Breda at Deventer together printed 71 per cent of all Dutch classical editions, some 114 works in all. In addition and indicative of the stress upon Latin in the schools there was an extensive printing of grammars. The presses of Deventer appear to have worked in close association with the schools as they were responsible for nearly half of all Dutch fifteenth-century school grammars. Painter, in his bibliographical study, estimated that the proportion of editions of the classics, grammars, and humanist texts, no less than 48 per cent of all Dutch printing, was probably higher than that in any other country.[40] Printing in the Southern Provinces was, however, no less significant. Between 1477 and 1495 Johannes van Westphalen,[41] along with his associates in Louvain, published translations of Aristotle and Plato as well as editions

---

36. Vocht, *Collegium Trilingue*, 2, p. 440; F. A. Wright, *The Love Poems of Joannes Secundus* (1930).

37. I. D. McFarlane, *Renaissance Latin Poetry*, (Manchester, 1980) p. 9.

38. J. E. Sandys, *A History of Classical Scholarship* (1967), II, p. 213.

39. See further G. D. Painter, *Catalogue of Books printed in the XVth Century now in the British Museum* (1962), p. ix.

40. These included the complete works of Juvenal, Sallust, and Vergil and representative selections from Cicero, Plautus and Terence. Cicero (nineteen editions) and Vergil (seventeen editions) were the most popular authors. See Painter, *Catalogue* pp. ix–xix.

41. Vocht, *Collegium Trilingue*, I, p. 181.

of classical and humanist writers.[42] He has in addition been credited as the first to use Hebrew type in a book in the Netherlands in order to demonstrate the unreliability of the Vulgate.[43] Some of his classical texts were printed to meet the needs of students attending lectures on Latin literature, but others, beautifully executed, were destined for wider circulation, thus giving proof of an ever-increasing interest in the new learning.[44]

The co-operation of printers and humanists is admirably illustrated in the output of Dierik Martens (1446–1534) who was successor to Westphalen. Having imbibed his humanism in Italy, Martens was on the best of scholarly relations with contemporary humanists, especially Erasmus, much of whose work he printed as well as that of his contemporaries. His presses also produced editions of the Church Fathers and were the first in the Low Countries to print texts in Greek.[45] In the opinion of J. E. Sandys his Greek classical texts were 'better printed than any produced in Paris before the establishment of the Royal Press by Francis I in 1538'.[46] His use of Roman type, which he firmly established in the Low Countries, qualifies him along with Aldus and Froben to be regarded as one of 'the three greatest printers of their time'.[47] The printing of Greek texts continued at Louvain after Martens left in 1529 but by the mid-century its place had been taken by Antwerp.

The rise of Antwerp as a humanist centre lagged behind that of Louvain, Deventer, and Zwolle.[48] Its development as an educational centre coincided with its emergence as a city of extraordinary commercial prosperity and was inseparably connected with it, thereby enabling it to play a leading role in the outstanding development of the art of printing that had already taken place throughout the Low Countries.[49] With the aid of the Antwerp printers, scholars were enabled to take

---

42. These included Cicero, Ovid, Quintilian, St Augustine, Petrarch, Boccaccio, Aeneas Sylvius, Lorenzo Valla, and Filelfo. For details see M. L. Polain, Catalogue de Livres Imprimés au Quinzième Siècle des Bibliothèques de Belgique, 4 vols. (Brussels, 1932).

43. A. Offenberg, 'The First use of Hebrew in a book in the Netherlands' Quaerendo, 4, (1974) pp. 44–54.

44. Painter, Catalogue, p. xxxvi.

45. He may have used Greek type as early as 1493 (G. D. Painter, 'The First Greek Printing in Belgium', Gutenberg Jahrbuch 1960, pp. 144–7).

46. Classical Scholarship, II, p. 213.

47. H. D. L. Vervliet, Sixteenth-century Printing Types of the Low Countries (Amsterdam, 1968), p. 56.

48. Painter, Catalogue, p. xxxvi.

49. See further W. Nijhoff and M. E. Kronenberg, Nederlandsche Bibliographie van 1500 to 1540. 2 vols (The Hague, 1923), p. 1940; C. Clair, Christopher Plantin (1960), pp. 9–11.

'an extremely important part in the development of Western thought'.[50] The settlement of Christopher Plantin (1514–89) in Antwerp (by no means the first of its printers) marks the beginning of a new stage in the history of humanism in the Low Countries, one in which 'Plantin became the foremost printer of the humanism of the second half of the sixteenth century. He was not, however, a merely passive instrument; morally and intellectually he could meet the greatest spirits of his age on equal terms'.[51]

Plantin, with an acute business sense, settled in Antwerp as a book binder because, as he wrote to the pope, 'no other place in the world could furnish more convenience for the trade'[52] he wished to practise. Within a few years he became 'the foremost printer in what was then one of the greatest printing centres in the western world'.[53] His patrician residence, which was also his printing house, was to become 'for more than a century . . . one of the important centres of humanism in the Netherlands'.[54] As well as the rising commercial importance of Antwerp and the opportunities for trade which it held out, the nearness of the renowned university of Louvain was an additional incentive. Plantin not only hoped to be of service to the university and its Trilingual College but also hoped to avail himself of the guidance and counsel of its professors 'to the great benefit of the public'.[55] Thus it can be seen that humanism was far from being seen as élitist, rather it was intended to extend into the life of the entire educated populace. Significantly, the first work to leave his printing presses was by the itinerant Venetian humanist Giovanni Michele Bruto, then staying in Antwerp, namely a manual in Italian and French on the education of young ladies of the nobility.[56] Editions of Greek and Latin classics which provided Plantin with his daily bread headed the lists of his educational output. Some of his Greek works were in fact pioneer texts collated from manuscripts and were accompanied by Latin translations.[57] He was, however, no narrow specialist. Among the volumes issuing from his presses he included theological and legal treatises as well as illustrated

---

50. L. Voet, *The Golden Compasses: The History of the House of Plantin – Moretus* (Amsterdam, 1969), I, p. v.

51. *Ibid.*, I, p. 137

52. *Ibid.*, I, p. 13.

53. *Ibid.*, I, p. 31.

54. *Ibid.*, I, p. 362.

55. *Ibid.*, I, p. 13.

56. *Ibid.*, I, pp. 17 f., 33, cf. 33.

57. Among the most popular were editions of Aesop, Aristotle, Ausonius, Caesar, Cicero, Claudian, Demosthenes, Euripides, Horace, Lucan, Ovid, Propertius, Sallust, Seneca, Suetonius, Tacitus, Terence, and Vergil. He published first editions of Hesychius and John of Stobi with translations by Adrian Junius and Guilielmus Canterus (Clair, *Plantin*, p. 115).

parables and allegories and botanical works. Above all he encouraged contemporary humanist scholars, among them Justus Lipsius whose study, *Variarum lectionum libri III*, was published in 1569. That year also saw the publication of Goropius Becanus's famed *Origines Antwerpianae*, which was soon followed by various lavishly illustrated editions of Arias Montanus's *Humanae salutis monumenta*.[58] Even during the turbulent years of the Revolt (1576–82) he continued to publish works that were to establish his fame, among them the splendid Italian and French editions of the *Description of the Netherlands* by Ludovico Guicciardini, editions of the *Theatrum Orbis Terrarum* of Abraham Ortellius, and the 'magnificent' edition of the French Bible in 1578 and that of the Latin Bible in 1583.[59] The outstanding achievement of his career must for ever be the monumental Royal Polyglot Bible.

The printing of editions of the Bible, in the original languages and in the vernacular, forms a significant element in the history of humanism in the Netherlands.[59A] Erasmus, whose epoch-making Greek text of the New Testament was published in Basel in 1516, had imbued in northern humanists a keen desire to study the original languages. However, scholars in the Low Countries initially did not play a leading part in working on the text of the Scriptures, probably because of the association of such study with the rise of heterodoxy. Nevertheless the Low Countries were to benefit from the earlier achievements of biblical humanists and scholar printers, and in particular the city of Antwerp in an outstanding endeavour which has been described as 'a later flowering of the earlier sowing in the Complutensian Polyglot'[60] Antwerp had been in the early days of printing an important centre for the diffusion of the printed Bible; between 1500 and 1540 at least seventy editions of the Scriptures or of Biblical extracts were published in the city.[61] Johannes Hentenius (1500–66), a Dominican of Louvain and biblical scholar of some repute, prepared a highly regarded version of the Vulgate, which was printed by Gravius in 1547. In its preparation he had used earlier printed versions, those of Estienne and of Colines and Kerver, as well as some thirty manuscripts.[62] Published by Plantin in 1559, it proved a resounding success. An edition of the Hebrew bible followed in 1566.[63] The impelling objective of biblical humanists to

---

58. Voet. *Golden Compasses*, p. 69.
59. *Ibid.*, p. 91.
59A. C. Clair, *A History of European Printing* (1976.) pp. 195–200.
60. B. Hall, 'Biblical Scholarship: Editions and Commentaries', *The Cambridge History of the Bible: The West from the Reformation to the Present Day*, ed. S. L. Greenslade (Cambridge, 1963), p. 47.
61. Clair, *Plantin*, p. 60.
62. Cf. *ibid.*, pp. 59 f., 255 n. 4.
63. *Ibid.*, p. 61.

arrive at an authentic text behind that of the Vulgate had, however, to be met, and to that end Plantin, encouraged by his success, proposed to issue a revised version of the Complutensian Polyglot. A project of such colossal dimensions required and was given careful preparation. The entire work was to be officially sponsored by Philip II, king of Spain, and was to be under the expert supervision of the erudite and indefatigable Benedictus Arias Montanus (1527–98) who settled in Antwerp in 1568. The collaboration of the finest scholars was secured, including Joannes Isaac Levita who was given responsibility for revising Sante Pagini's Hebrew Lexicon, and Guy Lefevre de la Boderie, whose expertise in the Syriac version of the New Testament brought this valuable text within the reach of all European scholars.[64] Plantin also enlisted the help of several scholars in collating texts and in the arduous work of correcting proofs, among them the Hellenist Guilielmus Canterus, the Syriac specialist Andreas Masius, and Franciscus Raphelengius, his son-in-law and subsequently Professor of Hebrew at Leiden. No effort was spared in making use of contemporary scholarship, Jewish, Protestant, and Catholic. Begun in August 1568, the entire work in eight magnificent volumes was completed in May 1572. It represents the cumulative endeavours of some of the outstanding humanists of the day, and not just in the Low Countries, and remains a lasting monument to contemporary biblical scholarship that concentrated on the text and its historical understanding. To assist in the study of the text the Polyglot provided much ancillary humanist material. Its *Apparatus Sacer* included Hebrew, Aramaic, Syriac, and Greek dictionaries, and a vast amount of miscellaneous information in a series of treatises on the geography of the Holy Land and the antiquities of the Jewish people.[65]

The publication of the Royal Polyglot marked Antwerp's heyday in the history of humanism in the southern region of the Low Countries. A new phase began after the reconquest in 1585. Thereafter humanism in Antwerp was to take on a different colour. It was still 'the principal cultural centre of the Southern Netherlands', but its scholarship became more narrowly defined, serving primarily the Counter-Reformation.[66]

## IV

The impact of humanism in the Low Countries is only represented in part by its academic institutions and its printing houses. Indispensable as they were as centres of nourishment and transmission, humanism

---

64. See further, *Cambridge History of the Bible*, p. 24.
65. Clair, *Plantin*, pp. 57–86; Voet, *Golden Compasses*, pp. 60–6.
66. *Ibid.*, 390.

could not have flourished without the efforts of individual scholars together with the support and collaboration of an educated and prosperous patriciate. Among the scholars Erasmus towers above all others. His role in the founding and early development of the *Collegium Trilingue* has already been noted but as he was an international rather than a national figure his contribution is not discussed. His emphasis on the rejection of scholasticism and on the reform of the Church by a return to the ethics of the Sermon on the Mount, the so called *philosophia Christi*, is too well known to require elaboration. We begin with his younger contemporary Juan Luis Vives (1492–1540), described as 'the most adequate expression of the great movement which animated the first half of the sixteenth century, the humanist ideal'.[67] Educated in Spain in contemporary scholasticism, he was won over to humanism in Paris, arrived in the Low Countries in 1512 and settled in Louvain to become the friend and disciple of Erasmus, from whom he largely assimilated the principles of humanism that formed the background to his 'grand pedagogical system'.[68] He is thus a genuine son of the humanism of the Low Countries, which he regarded as his *patria*. A prolific writer and editor he proved himself to be on a par with Erasmus and Budé.

In 1531 he published his most remarkable educational treatises, entitled *De Disciplinis*, the fruit of research and experience, and two years later his *Rhetoricae, sive de Dicendi Ratione*, in which he elaborated a complete system of education, beginning with the initial instruction given by the mother right up to that to be provided for the advanced student. Each stage in the child's intellectual and moral development is discussed in detail. His principles, subsequently incorporated throughout Europe, included education in the mother tongue, the intellectual education of women, the active participation of the child in his own education, and the necessity of physical exercises and games. He is a pioneer in acknowledging the role of psychology in education. Grammar, he held, should be treated as part of the study of literature. In studying history he argued that the pupil should be encouraged to re-live the course of events and to think deeply about the events that are recalled. The teaching of geography should be concerned with the way man adapts to his environment. Above all, education should concentrate on the moral and religious development of the pupil, on his 'humanisation'. Nor does he neglect to emphasise the moral character as well as the ability of the teacher. In the humanism of Vives with its concern for education, for proper public assistance of the poor, and the pursuit of peace, there is that blending of the classical and the

---

67. Vocht, *Biographie National de Belgique*, 26, pp. 789–97.
68. Vocht, *Collegium Trilingue*, I, p. 233.

Christian which was the distinctive embodiment of much of the northern revival of learning.[69]

One of the outstanding pupils of the Latin schools, whose significant role in providing the basis for the later flowering of humanism has already been noted, was Petrus Nannius (1500–57).[70] For a time he taught at Gouda before becoming Professor of Latin at Louvain. His Latin drama *Vinctus*, based on classical models and written for the benefit of his pupils, gave a clear indication of his abilities as a humanist. Later he enjoyed friendly relations with members of the circle of humanists at the royal court. A distinctive feature of his scholarship was the combination of his Latin studies with the literature of Greece in order fully to understand and appreciate the classical texts. This approach won for him a considerable reputation as a comparative philologist. Nannius, who was a priest, extended his interests to religious texts. His study of the *Wisdom of Solomon*, based on a comparison of the Vulgate and Greek texts, exemplified the method inaugurated by Erasmus. He thus combined some of the essential features of Northern humanism – an interest in philology, in textual criticism, in the Scriptures and in the Fathers, as well as in the great classical writers, and an emphasis on moral and spiritual values. His erudition, his genius as a philologist, and the extent of his publications won for him not only a wide circle of friends on the Continent but particularly in England, among them Bishop Stephen Gardiner and Roger Ascham.[71]

Among those who greatly advanced humanist studies was Hermannus Torrentinus (d. 1520) for a time headmaster of the famous school at Zwolle; his dictionary of proper and foreign names used in poems acquired widespread popularity well into the eighteenth century.[72] A higher distinction, however, was won by the Greek critic Guilielmus Canterus (1542–75)[73] of Utrecht, as one who showed the way to modern textual criticism. His *Syntagma de Ratione emendandi Graecos Authores* is his 'chief title to glory'. Not surprisingly his skills,

---

69. *Biographie National de Belgique*, 26, pp. 789–800; Sandys *Classical Scholarship*, II, pp. 214–15.

70. Vocht, *Collegium Trilingue*, II, pp. 177–9, Polet, 'Petrus Nannius', *Humanistica Lovaniensia*, 5 (1936).

71. His publications included annotations on Theophilus's *Institutiones* and *Apologia* and translations into Latin of *Demosthenis et Aschenis Epistolae*, and some of the Homilies of St. Basil. His philological approach is also demonstrated in his lectures on Vergil's *Aeneid*. See further Vocht, *Collegium Trilingue*, IV, pp. 88–98, 268–98; Polet, 'Petrus Nannius', pp. 12–15, 127–87. On Nannius as a Neo-Latinist see ibid., pp. 32–90.

72. Vocht, *Collegium Trilingue*, I, p. 198; Sandys, *Classical Scholarship*, 2, p. 216.

73. H. de Vocht, 'Cornelii Valerii ab Auwater Epistola et Carmina', *Humanistica Lovaniensia*, 14 (1957) pp. 53–8; Sandys, *Classical Scholarship*, pp. 216–17; R. Pfeiffer, *History of Classical Scholarship*, (Cambridge, 1976) p. 125.

as has been already noted, were sought out by Plantin for whom he worked on the text of the Septuagint printed in the Royal Antwerp Polyglot Bible. Towards the end of his short life he worked on the texts of the Greek dramatists, Euripides, Aeschylus, and Sophocles, providing editions that were to remain in general use for more than two hundred years. Canterus's method of trying to trace the origins of corrupt readings by paying attention to scribal errors in the transmission of texts has been regarded as one of his finest contributions to scholarship, but for him it was the end result that was important, the revivication of Greek literature.

These three scholars, Vives, Nannius, and Canterus, are, perhaps, the most significant representatives of the large number of humanists and the variety of talents that made the Low Countries in the first half of the sixteenth century one of the leading centres of classical learning north of the Alps. Originating in close political and cultural relations with Italy, this learning was also aided by contacts with Spain and France, and to a lesser extent with England. It benefited enormously from the high concentration of the great new invention of printing presses within its prosperous cities. But most significant of all was the receptiveness of the people. There was a deep rooted and widely accepted recognition of the place of scholarship in public life. Those holding high office had intellectual ability and economic resources at hand, and they were eager to devote much of their time and their wealth to the furthering of *humanitas*. However, it is not surprising that when Erasmus was being condemned, his writings placed on the *Index*, and the country being torn asunder by political and religious strife, humanism should have experienced a measure of decline.[74] By the third quarter of the sixteenth century in the southern region

> the once strong tide of humanism was on the ebb, and editions of the classics and these scientific works so close to the heart of Plantin slowly gave ground to the liturgical and theological books. The change was gradual . . . The triumph of the Counter-Reformation attracted men's minds towards theology, and of the humanistic spirit, open to every initiative of speculation, little remained but the cult of good Latin prose.[75]

In the northern region, however, a new day was dawning; 'an event took place that marks an epoch in the history of scholarship in the Netherlands, the foundation of the University of Leiden in 1575'.[76]

---

74. M. Delcourt, 'L'humanisme aux Pays-Bas au Temps de Plantin', *Gedenkboek der Plantin-Dagen 1555–1955*, pp. 70–80.
75. Clair, *Plantin*, pp. 225–6.
76. Sandys, *Classical Scholarship*, II, pp. 218, 300

# V

This new flowering of humanism owed much to public enthusiasm and support for it. Humanist activity in the second half of the sixteenth century had developed throughout the rising patrician and merchant classes and had expressed itself in a variety of ways, but perhaps most significantly in the literary circles formed by younger scholars. One such circle had gathered round Jan van der Does (1545–99), better known as Janus Dousa, the heroic defender of Leiden. Although a public administrator throughout his life, Dousa, at heart a scholar and a neo-Latin poet of considerable merit, was the most prominent of a distinguished group of public servants who used every opportunity to advance the cause of learning in their day.[77] He had received his early education at Delft – a city that could, like virtually every other city in the Netherlands, boast of a fine Latin school, a humanist town clerk, and two physicians[78] – and then moved to Louvain where he enjoyed the company of Cornelius Valerius and Guilielmus Canterus. From Louvain he moved on via Douai to Paris, where he met Jean Dorat and Daniel Rogers.[79] When he returned to his homeland in 1566 he had already won the friendship of a wide circle of scholars, poets, and printers. Dousa is indeed the embodiment of those public aspirations that led to the founding of the university. True, such an enterprise was in line with academic developments that had been taking place over the past twenty-five years in those parts of the continent which had accepted Reformed Protestantism, and was partly intended to meet the pressing need for well-educated pastors, but the Dutch followers of Calvin, like Calvin himself, were in no doubt about the role of education in the humanities and of scholarship in the upbuilding of a Christian country. As the late Professor J. A. van Dorsten wrote, the guiding principle was 'the introduction of a complete humanistic *Academia* in which no faculty was necessarily superior to another'.[80] Thus, in an increasingly confessional age, Leiden became noted for its religious tolerance, as well as for the breadth of vision which it exer-

---

77. J. A. van Dorsten, 'Janus Dousa, Spokesman of the Dutch Revolt', *Acta Conventus Neo-Latini Amstelodamensis* ed. P. Tuynman, G. C. Kuiper, and E. Kessler (Munich, 1979), pp. 336–7; C. L. Heesakkers, *Janus Dousa en zijn vrienden* (Leiden, 1973).

78. See further, Chris L. Heesakkers, 'Janus Dousa and Victor Giselinus: A correspondence around the Literary début of Janus Dousa', *Lias*, 2 (1975) pp. 5–54, especially 36 n. 18 and 47 n. 11.

79. J. A. van Dorsten, *Poets, Patrons, and Professors: Sir Philip Sidney, Daniel Rogers, and the Leiden Humanists* (Leiden, 1962) pp. 26–32.

80. Ibid., p. 6. See also C. S. M. Rademaker, *Life and Work of Gerardus Joannes Vossius* (1577–1649) (Assen, 1981) who wrote 'The University of Leiden was at root a humanistic school of higher learning in which Theology held an important but never dominant position' (*op. cit.*, p. 41).

cised in the choice of its professors, taking into its service some of the most outstanding intellectual leaders of the late sixteenth and seventeenth centuries. For a time Justus Lipsius (1547–1606)[81] held the chair of Ancient History, and Bonaventura Vulcanius (1538–1614)[82] the chair of Greek. No credal tests were required, although the professors of theology had to adhere to the doctrine of the Reformed Church. The politico-religious conditions in the Netherlands, however, made it difficult to maintain ideals of tolerance. Lipsius in time returned to Louvain and to his Catholic faith. The broad-minded Calvinist and irenically orientated theologian Franciscus Junius (1545–1602),[83] appointed in 1592, was replaced in 1603 by the moderate Jacobus Arminius, but the latter was only to be involved in bitter theological strife with his strict Calvinist colleague Franciscus Gomarus (1563–1641). The aim seems to have been to advocate as far as possible a high level of tolerance, but by the end of the first quarter of the seventeenth century the earlier liberality of spirit was being worn down by doctrinal and confessional interests.[84]

Humanist principles, however, remained very much in evidence, as can be seen in the contributions made to biblical study by Louis de Dieu, 'one of Leiden's outstanding philologically inclined theologians',[85] and Daniel Heinsius (1580–1655), a pupil of Joseph Scaliger, who anonymously saw through the press the Elzevier edition of the New Testament which became the *Textus Receptus* of the Western Churches.[86] In the early decades of the century the governors of the university made valiant efforts against a strong dogmatic tide to ensure that in the theological faculty the central place was given to the study of Scripture. The *Notes* and *Lectiones* on the New Testament of Simon Episcopius, Professor from 1612 to 1619, 'reflect in fact the striving for an unprejudiced exegesis', which he 'in true Erasmian spirit mentioned

---

81. See below note 96.
82. Vulcanius' career typifies much that was characteristic of the humanism of the age. Educated at Bruges and Ghent, and then at Louvain and Cologne, he entered the service of a bishop who interested him in the writings of Cyril of Alexandria. He spent some time as a wandering scholar, returned to the Netherlands in 1571, accepted Calvinism, became 'historiographer' for the States General, was secretary to Marnix, and assisted him on his rhymed version of the Psalms. He became professor in 1581. See further A. Dewitte, 'Bonaventura Vulcanius Burgensis (1538–1614)', *Lias*, 8 (1981), pp. 189–201, and J. H. Waszink, 'Classical Philology', *Leiden University*, pp. 161–75; see also footnote 69.
83. Rademaker, *Vossius*, pp. 44–5.
84. *Leiden University*, pp. 1–5.
85. *Ibid.*, pp. 5, 72–4.
86. *Ibid.*, pp. 66; 87–100; he also published *Exercitationes Sacrae ad Novum Testamentum*, 'a strictly philological commentary'.

in his farewell speech to his Leiden students in 1618'.[87] The way had previously been pointed out by Johannes Drusius, an expert in rabbinical and patristic studies and Professor of Oriental Languages from 1577 to 1585 and at the new university at Franeker from 1585 to 1616. Despite the dogmatic pressures of the day, the impact of humanism remained as the Bible continued to be 'the object of intense scientific interest' in Leiden's Faculty of Arts. Professor De Jonge concludes his illuminating study of this subject with these words: 'Indeed the fact that Leiden in the first half of the seventeenth century won international renown as a centre of New Testament studies and played a role which then and later received international recognition, is almost wholly to be ascribed to the learned contributions of the literary scholars: orientalists, classicists, and historians (and it should be noted that teaching in the Oriental tongues, and later in Greek, was financed not least because of its usefulness in the interpretation of the Bible)'.[88]

The study of Hebrew and Oriental languages formed, as we have seen, an integral part in the development of humanism at Louvain's Trilingual College and at Antwerp. In this area of Semitic studies Leiden was to make a profound contribution and win for itself a reputation for the study and publishing of *orientalia* that continues to the present day. At Leiden the basis for its distinction as a centre for the study of Arabic and the printing of Arabic texts was laid by Franciscus Raphelengius, son-in-law of Christopher Plantin and first Professor of Hebrew who previously had worked at Antwerp on the Polyglot Bible.[89]

The study of the Classics, especially Latin, and the creative art of writing Latin prose and poetry form an illustrious part of the contribution to humanism of the northern Netherlands. Those most active in securing the foundation of Leiden University, Janus Dousa, the governor, and Jan van Hout, the town clerk, both poets of distinction, were from the outset bent on making their new university a success as a centre of classical studies – efforts which resulted in making Leiden the great humanist centre of the seventeenth century which it undoubtedly became. In their choice of Lipsius, the great international Latin scholar,[90] as one of the first professors they indicated that classical studies ranked high in their estimation and in their plans for the future education of their countrymen, and confirmed that intention in their choice of Josephus Justus Scaliger (1540–1609) as his successor. Reck-

87. *Ibid.*, p. 66.
88. Ibid., p. 69.
89. Ibid., pp. 203–15; Voet, *Golden Compasses*, I, pp. 159, 171–6; Clair, *Plantin*, pp. 46–8; 159, 166.
90. On Dousa's friendship with Lipsius see *Lias*, 2 (1975), p. 243 n. 39.

oned the greatest scholar of his age, his primary function in Leiden was that of a research scholar with no obligation to lecture.[91] Thus was initiated 'a golden age of Latin studies'.[92] Lipsius, nurtured in the Erasmian tradition in the *Collegium Trilingue* at Louvain, advanced classical studies by engaging in textual criticism and exegetical commentary. His 'masterpiece in this respect'[93] was his edition of Tacitus's *Annales*, with its notes on the establishment of the text, 'his lasting glory',[94] a work that made him the leading figure in the history of philology in the Netherlands. Lipsius was also distinguished for his knowledge of Roman history and antiquities. His interest in Greek centred on philosophical texts which he used in preparing his best known treatises on Stoicism, in particular his *De Constantia* (Leiden 1584) and *Politicorum sive civilis doctrinae libri VI* (Leiden 1589). The *De Constantia*, his most successful book, was '"a best seller" of its day'; it went through more than eighty editions in the next three centuries and won recognition for its author as the foremost representative of Christian humanism.[95] Lipsius, regarded as 'the restorer of Stoicism to the Renaissance' and 'the founder of Neo-Stoicism', [96] expounded in the *De Constantia* those tenets of Stoicism which he found compatible with his Christian faith. In his later works he sought to demonstrate the relations of the Christian and the Stoic ethic and to bring out the best in the two. It was the practical elements rather than the dogmatic that found favour with him. 'His work leaves no doubt that Lipsius' particular interest was not of a religious but of a moral and political nature'.[97] It is noteworthy that these philological and philosophical works date from his Leiden period, and that it was from Leiden that his influence was extended to Protestant countries. In Leiden he was, however, no isolated academic. He had a wide circle of friends from all sections of the cultural community to whom he was the embodiment of Renaissance humanism. He was also one of the great internationals of the age and ambassador of humanism.[98] Apart from his publications and their wide distribution he carried on a vast correspon-

---

91. *Leiden University*, p. 161.

92. Ibid., p. 167.

93. Sandys, *Classical Scholarship*, 2, p. 303.

94. *Leiden University*, p. 166. See also J. Ruysschaert, 'Juste Lipse et les Annales de Tacite', *Humanistica Lovaniensia*, 8 (1949).

95. Clair, *Pantin*, p. 153.

96. B. Anderton, 'A Stoic of Louvain: Justus Lipsius', *Sketches from a Library Window* (Cambridge, 1922) pp. 10–30; J. L. Saunders, *Justus Lipsius: The Philosophy of Renaissance Stoicism* (New York, 1955); G. Oestreich, 'Justus Lipsius als Universalgelehrter zwischen Renaissance und Barok', *Leiden University*, pp. 177–201.

97. Ibid., p. 178.

98. The *De Constantia* was translated into English and published in 1519, 1653, 1654, and 1670. On Lipsius' influence in England see *Leiden University*, pp. 191–3.

dence with upwards of seven hundred of his contemporaries – a number that includes not just leading intellectuals, but also and often the humble wandering student.[99] In many ways he towered above the political and religious conflicts of his time and sought to replace the developing absolutism and confessionalism with that tolerance and individualism that were essential to humanism and to the education of man as 'homo politicus'.[100] Undoubtedly he bestowed an enduring legacy on the cultural life of the Low Countries.

Josephus Justus Scaliger, Lipsius's successor at Leiden, ranks among the most imposing scholars of his age in virtually the entire field of contemporary learning, literary and scientific. Much of his life (from 1563 to 1593) was spent in Italy, France, and England in scholarly leisure, used to win for himself a considerable reputation as an authority on the Latin language. His interests, however, were not confined to philology; they included chronology – both of which developed in the sixteenth century as disciplines in their own right.[101] And both, as Grafton rightly points out, were matters of considerable interest, concerned as they were with arriving at the best and most authoritative texts and with determining the historical context. In these two areas Scaliger was 'taking part in widespread and heated public debates'[102] and establishing himself as one of the great authorities of his time. He also won for himself a contemporary reputation as a neo-Latin poet. Yet, as Sandys wrote, 'His main strength lay in a clear conception of antiquity as a whole, and in the concentration of vast and varied learning on distinctly important works'.[103] In Leiden he exercised a profound influence on contemporary humanist admirers and especially on the new generation of rising Dutch scholars, among them Daniel Heinsius (1580–1655) and Hugo Grotius (1583–1645).

Lipsius and Scaliger are the initial outstanding representatives of a late yet magnificent flowering of humanism in the Netherlands, particularly in Leiden. Yet they do not stand alone. There were others,

---

99. *Inventaire de la Correspondance de Juste Lipse 1564–1606*, ed. A. Gerlo and H. D. L. Vervliet, (Antwerp, 1968).

100. R. Pfeiffer, *History of Classical Scholarship*, p. 126.

101. A. Grafton, *Julius Scaliger: A Study in the History of Classical Scholarship*, (Oxford, 1983), I, pp. 2–8.

102. Ibid., p. 4. The first fruits of his studies in chronology were set out in *De Emendatione Temporum*, 1583, which led to the publication in 1606 of *Thesaurus Temporum*. His philological studies included editions of Ausonius, Apuleius, Caesar, Catullus, Tibullus, and Propertius. See further Waszink in *Leiden University*, p. 165: 'Scaliger was clearly convinced that the preparation of critical and well commented editions, which were moreover comprehensible, was the greatest service he could render the younger generation'.

103. Sandys, *Classical Scholarship*, II, p. 204; see also Pfeiffer, *Classical Scholarship*, pp. 113–19; and especially A. Grafton, *Joseph Scaliger*, I. pp. 2–8, 101–33.

some of whom we shall mention later, who shared their interests and who, while not reaching the same heights of scholarship, made a profound impact on their fellow countrymen and who led the way in securing from the country's prosperity the essential backing. That support for scholarship undoubtedly secured the brief migration of Christopher Plantin to Leiden and the setting up there in 1583 of the *Officina Plantiniana*. The enterprise was carried on by his son-in-law Franciscus Raphelengius, the orientalist, and his sons until 1619. Apart from acting as the university press, the *Officina Plantiniana* had the distinction of printing some of the most significant works of the Leiden humanists already mentioned, such as Lipsius's *De Constantia* and his edition of Tacitus's *Annales*, and also Bonaventura's pioneering studies of Gothic, Scaliger's *De emendatione temporum* and Raphelengius's own *Lexicon arabicum*. The religious tolerance, so distinctive a feature of Leiden's humanists, is likewise reflected in the wide range of its output.[104] The most celebrated and long-lasting of its printing houses was that of the Elzeviers. Apart from the pocket-sized editions of the New Testament in Greek (the *Textus receptus* mentioned above), they excelled in the printing of texts in the main oriental languages in types brought together by Leiden's great orientalist Thomas Erpenius. But, perhaps, one of their most widely appreciated services to humanism was their publication of editions of the classics and of Erasmus in small format and at moderate cost, the success of which is one of the clearest indications of the widespread impact of humanism upon the life and culture of the people.[105]

## VI

In the first half of the seventeenth century humanism in the northern Netherlands flourished almost as never before at the hands of a large number of scholars from virtually every section of educated society, political and administrative as well as professional. Of the academic scholars who succeeded Lipsius and Scaliger, three deserve special attention: G. L. Vossius (1577–1649), Daniel Heinsius (1581–1655) and Hugo Grotius (1583–1645). Not involving themselves too closely in the dogmatic and confessional controversies that darkened so much of the seventeenth century, they persevered in prosecuting that northern

104. E. van Gulik, 'Drukkers en Gelleerden: *De Leidse Officina Plantiniana* (1583–1619)' *Leiden University*, pp. 367–93; Clair, *Plantin*, pp. 150–60; Voet, *Golden Compasses* pp. 175–8.

105. D. W. Davies, *The World of the Elseviers 1580–1712* (The Hague, 1954); De Jonge, 'The Study of the New Testament', *Leiden University*, pp. 89–93; A. Willems, *Les Elzeviers* (Nieuwkoop, 1962), p. clxvii; L. and R. Fuks, 'Hebrew typography in Leiden 1585–1759', *Quaerendo*, 9 (1979), pp. 3–42.

Christian humanism which had been so distinctive a feature of its early development in the Low Countries. At a time when understanding of the past had deepened enormously, when vast new areas of human activity especially in the empirical sciences were being opened up and ever widening man's horizons, and when confessional attitudes were hardening and relations between Christians were becoming more embittered, humanists in the Low Countries were advocating a tolerance and unity of which Vossius,[106] and to a much greater extent, Grotius, were the leading figures. By their vast erudition and enormous literary output they bring to its culmination humanism in the Netherlands.

In the face of Protestant theological scholasticism which began to dominate the academic and religious scene in Leiden, the humanism that had brought about the foundation of the university still held good. The study of Latin and Greek and of ancient history continued the essential basis of scholarship, and to these subjects Vossius contributed significantly.[107] Particularly noteworthy are his dictionaries of Greek- and Latin-writing historians of both antiquity and the Renaissance. The all pervasive influence of humanism in education, fostered by the humanistically-trained in both government and education, found noteworthy expression in the attempt to consolidate past achievements and to transmit them to posterity by legally requiring a uniform national curriculum cast in the humanist mould with ordered progression based on instruction in prescribed classical texts. In the Holland School Act of 1625 the ideal of the humanists 'was elevated to the level of law'.[108]

Endeavours to further humanist education, which as we have seen had gone hand in hand with commercial and economic prosperity, were given significant expression in Amsterdam. In the seventeenth century Amsterdam was becoming 'more and more the focus of cultural life within the Northern Netherlands',[109] and not surprisingly took steps to provide for its citizens a centre for a broadly based cultural education which led to the foundation of the *Athenaeum Illustre*. Not intended to be a university and not permitted to rival its near neighbour, Leiden, it was nevertheless intended that it should by the lectures of its public professors provide for the cultural needs of any of the citizens who

106. On Vossius see Rademaker, *Vossius*, p. 19: 'He took the torch from them [the representatives of the Louvain school] and became one of the greatest representatives of humanism in the North Netherlands of the seventeenth century'.

107. Details are given in Rademaker, *Vossius*, pp. 167–87.

108. Rademaker, *Vossius*, pp. 191, 188–206; E. J. Kuiper, *De Hollandse 'Schoolordre' van 1625: Een studie over het onderwijs op de Latijnse in Nederland in de 17e en 18e eeuw*, Groningen, 1958, (not seen). Bot, *Humanisme en onderwijs in Nederland*, chapter IV.

109. C. L. Heesakkers, 'Foundation and Early Development of the Athenaeum Illustre at Amsterdam', *Lias*, 9 (1982), pp. 3–18: see also F. F. Blok and C. S. M. Rademaker, *Humanists and Humanism in Amsterdam* (Amsterdam, 1973).

cared to take advantage of them. Ambitious from the outset, Amsterdam succeeded in securing the services of Vossius to head the *Athenaeum*. According to the wishes of the founders, he gave lectures on history which they considered as an essential study. In Amsterdam he completed his works on the art of poetry which 'had great influence on dramatic art in the Netherlands as well as abroad'.[110]

The widespread impact of humanism in the Low Countries is given one of its finest expressions in the contribution of the Netherlands to the contemporary art of neo-Latin poetry. Indeed the composing of Latin verse was one of the significant features of sixteenth- and early seventeenth-century humanism. Why this was so need not detain us here. To that literary corpus the contribution of the Low Countries was not only substantial in quantity, but much of it was of very high quality. Mention has already been made of Joannes Secundus who was the major literary influence. Yet virtually every scholar of any note seems to have felt compelled to express himself in Latin verse. Not surprisingly many in public life, such as Janus Dousa and Jan van Hout, were well practised in the Muses' art. Indeed there developed something of a 'Leiden school' in the years immediately following the foundation of the University. Amongst its galaxy of professors, some of whom have already been mentioned, Daniel Heinsius (1580–1655) is regarded as the one who in his day 'made Leiden a European centre of literary scholarship'.[111]

A product of the Latin School in Flushing and the new Academy at Franeker, Heinsius, within a few years of coming under 'the affectionate tutelage'[112] of Scaliger in Leiden, was editing classical texts. His Latin poems were being published, and his *Auriacus*, a tragedy on the assassination of William the Silent written in the manner of Seneca was given public performance. His reputation thus speedily acquired secured for him the patronage of Dousa, appointment first as Professor Extraordinarius of Poetry and subsequently as Professor of Greek, and widespread recognition as 'one of the chief ornaments'[113] of an already internationally acclaimed university. His edition of Aristotle's *Poetics* (1611) was quickly followed by editions of popular classical authors including Horace, Terence, and Seneca. Of the production of his own Muse special attention must be drawn to the *De Contemptu Mortis* and the *Herodes Infanticida*, 'perhaps his most famous poem'.[114] Like so many neo-Latin poets he wrote much in the vernacular, which had

---

110. Rademaker, *Vossius*, p. 304; for his contribution to grammatical studies see G. A. Pudley, *Grammatical Theory in Western Europe 1500–1700* (1976), pp. 117–32.

111. Van Dorsten, *Poets*, p. 55.

112. P. R. Sellin, *Daniel Heinsius and Stuart England* (Leiden, 1968), p. 14.

113. Ibid., p. 18.

114. Ibid., p. 36; *Leiden University*, p. 170.

considerable impact on the development of vernacular poetry in Germany and Scandinavia.[115] Likewise his neo-Latin plays are held to have 'substantially altered the course of Dutch and ultimately German, and perhaps French drama'.[116] His ideas on drama, set out in his *De Tragoediae Constitutione*, earned for him distinction as 'an Aristotelian literary critic of European reputation'.[117] Of somewhat less significance than Heinsius as a neo-Latin poet was his contemporary and later colleague in Amsterdam, Caspar Barlaeus (1584–1648). His career in many ways demonstrates the extent of the impact of humanism on cultural life. Brought up in a humanist environment at home – his father and two of his uncles were neo-Latin poets – and educated at the Latin schools at Brill and Dordrecht, he became 'the most sought after and most widely appreciated occasional poet in the country'.[118]

## VII

The humanism of the Low Countries, which extended into almost every sphere of activity, and deeply influenced, indeed dominated, the entire cultural life of the people, achieved in one man of the early seventeenth century its most significant embodiment. That man, who stands head and shoulders above his contemporaries, was Hugo Grotius (1583–1645). As lawyer, theologian, historian, poet and philologist, he embodied in his chequered international career virtually all of the elements of northern humanism. Although he may not today be widely ranked as an original thinker, his contribution to humanism through which there runs a clearly discernible note of harmony is such as to secure him a place among the great. That note of harmony which arose out of deep religious conviction is a characteristic feature of Erasmian humanism – a blending of the classical and the biblical understanding of man and of his role in society. But Grotius was unquestionably the product of his age and of his country – one in which humanism penetrated all areas. His father, who was a merchant and administrator, was also, like so many of his fellow countrymen, a writer with strong classical interests. He has been described as 'the typical representative of the Dutch Renaissance man'.[119] At an early age, he encouraged his son in the contemporary practice of writing Latin verse, in which he himself engaged, and may have been largely responsible for cultivating

115. T. Weevers, *Poetry of the Netherlands in its European Context, 1170–1930* (1960), pp. 83–7, 100–1.

116. Sellin, *Heinsius*, p. 67.

117. Ibid., p. 123; Sandys, *Classical Scholarship*, II, p. 314.

118. F. F. Blok, *Caspar Barlaeus* (Amsterdam, 1976), p. 4.

119. A. Eyffinger, 'The Dutch Period in the Life of Hugo Grotius', *Hugo Grotius: A Great European 1583–1645* (Delft, 1983), p. 8.

in him the art of writing Latin in which he was later to excel. The fact that he grew up in a war-torn world, a world also embittered by religious strife, undoubtedly made a deep impression on him, which is reflected in his treatise *De jure belli ac pacis*. He entered the university of Leiden, of which his father was a curator, at the age of eleven, and studied privately under Scaliger. Although encouraged to pursue a career in classical philology, his father, like Luther's father and Calvin's, was probably responsible for planning for him a legal career but unlike them he was to see his son succeed in that career and achieve distinction. By the age of twenty-five Grotius had published his *Mare Librum* (1609). Humanist studies were not, however, abandoned. He developed his interest in Greek and Roman history, which, along with many of his humanist fellow public servants, he saw as justifying and supporting the aspirations of the young republic. Theological studies also occupied much of his time during the bitter Arminian controversy, which had brought again into the foreground the issue of the freedom of the will, the topic over which Erasmus and Luther had so bitterly confronted each other. Conflicts in politics and religion, never far removed from each other in the sixteenth and seventeenth centuries, had in 1619 a disastrous outcome for Grotius – imprisonment in Loevestein Castle, followed by an escape to Paris and exile. It was at this stage that the biblical, spiritual element became dominant and led to the writing of his immensely popular *De Veritate Religionis Christianae* (1627).

In the history of humanism in the Low Countries, philological studies were never far removed from the biblical. Erasmus and his northern, as well as some of his most influential southern forerunners, had been both classical and biblical scholars. They had also been deeply involved in cultivating the Christian ethic, in advocating the purification of the Church, and in maintaining its unity. These ideals dominated the life of some of Grotius's closest contemporaries – Franciscus Junius (1545 – 1602), the irenic theologian with whom he lodged as a student, Justus Lipsius, the close friend of his father, J. J. Scaliger, his private tutor, and Gerardus Vossius, probably his closest friend. They were to become the most absorbing and demanding in his own.

During his exile Grotius was in the world of letters widely regarded as 'a glittering ornament'.[120] The *De jure belli ac pacis* embodies his understanding of the legal relationships between groups and individuals that are essential in the development of society.[121] But it is in his theological works, which formed by far the bulk of his literary output,

---

120. H. J. M. Nellen, 'Grotius' Exile', *Grotius*, p. 33.
121. M. Ahsmann, 'Grotius as Jurist', *Grotius*, pp. 37–49; V. Hanga, 'L'idée de droit naturel dans le *De iure belli ac pacis*', *Grotiana*, 6 (1985), pp. 38–45.

that his humanism is given its most practical expression.[122] For example, in the contemporary debate within Dutch Protestantism on predestination, while siding with the Arminian (or Remonstrant) party, he was not in complete agreement with either side, convinced as Erasmus had been in the conflict between Luther and his Catholic opponents that no one party could claim exclusive possession of the entire truth. Professor Posthumus Meyjes maintains that 'To do him justice we must regard him primarily as a Christian Humanist scholar, whose desire was to uphold and continue the religious programme as interpreted in the 16th century by Erasmus and others, in defiance of the bitter reality of a Christian world split and hardened by confessional differences'.[123] Cast out of his own country, he earned for himself an international reputation, not least as a defender of Christianity against the revival of the ancient Arian heresy by the Polish theologian, Socinus, and as the apologist for the uniqueness of Christianity in the face of a renewed awareness of other forms of religion. It was, however, his plans for the restoration of the peace and unity of the Church that concerned him most. To these ends, which encompassed the reconciliation of Protestants and Roman Catholics, he was totally committed.[124]

For Christian humanists, from Lorenzo Valla to Erasmus and on to Heinsius and Grotius, the study of the New Testament was a fundamental concern. To the considerable collection of works on the New Testament entitled *Annotationes* Grotius made a most significant contribution. Today he still enjoys a 'great reputation' in the history of biblical exegesis.[125] Work on the New Testament text was begun during his imprisonment with the prospect that it might be used in a projected polyglot under the direction of Thomas Erpenius, Professor of Arabic at Leiden. This plan was not realised, but Grotius continued for the rest of his life to work assiduously on his commentary. The section on the Gospels was published in Amsterdam in 1641; the entire study appeared posthumously in Paris in 1646 and again in 1650. In the opinion of Professor De Jonge the philological study of the Bible by humanists 'achieved its culmination in the *Annotationes* of Grotius'. 'He is', he writes, 'the most versatile of all annotators' whose work is distinguished by 'his critical acumen and the independence of his judg-

---

122. G. H. M. Posthumus Meyjes, 'Grotius as Theologian', *Grotius*, pp. 51–8.

123. *Grotius*, pp. 52.

124. G. H. M. Posthumus Meyjes, 'Hugo Grotius as an irenicist', *The World of Hugo Grotius* (1583–1645) (Amsterdam, 1984), pp. 43–63; Posthumus Meyjes, *Hugo Grotius, Meletius sive de iis quae inter Christianos convenient Epistola* (Leiden, 1988) pp. 26–40.

125. H. J. de Jonge, 'Grotius as an Interpreter of the Bible, Particularly the New Testament', *Grotius* 59.

ment'.[126] Grotius was in fact pursuing the *ad fontes* principle by approaching the text of scripture in the same way as contemporary philologists approached classical texts, and not as a quarry from which proof-texts were to be extracted for the theologians. By seeking to study the New Testament in its historical context not only was he seeking to recover it for the Church from the clutches of the dogmatic theologians, but he was also furthering one of his primary concerns, the unity of the Churches.

Throughout his life Grotius engaged in writing history, but his major contributions did not see publication till after his death. Much of his poetry, most of which is in Latin, is typical of the age. For the pre-exilic period his life it is properly classed, as is so much of humanistic verse, as 'occasional' in that it was primarily composed to celebrate some social, national or patriotic occasion. He did write in the vernacular, but mostly on devotional topics. From the tradition of Latin love poetry inspired by Joannes Secundus, as well as the more popular humanist genres, inspired by Horace and Catullus, he distanced himself in preference for the widely popular epigram.[127] This was probably a natural choice as his philological interests had centred on editions of Lucan and Seneca. In the opinion of Sandys, Grotius surpassed his contemporaries such as Badius and Nicholas Heinsius 'in the success with which he reproduces the spirit of classical poetry, and clothes modern thoughts in ancient forms'.[128] To the corpus of neo-Latin drama he contributed at an early stage two biblical tragedies, *Adamus Exul* and *Christus Patiens* which some have regarded as 'absolute literary masterpieces'.[129] His later drama *Sophompaneas*, along with his later neo-Latin verse, illustrates the humanist stress on ethics. Although the form in which he wrote, along with his contemporaries Heinsius and Vossius and many others throughout Europe, had no future as a lasting form of literary expression, it has been pointed out that it lent humanist support to the developing 'theory of German Baroque and French classicism'.[130] Grotius surpassed his contemporaries in the depth as well as in the extent of his erudition. The diversity of his talent does not cease to amaze subsequent generations, yet there is in his somewhat tragic

---

126. See illustrative material in *Grotius*, pp. 59–65. It is of interest to learn from Professor de Jonge, p. 63, that 'Grotius' text-critical observations and judgements were soon excerpted from his *Annotationes* and published in the great scholarly edition of the Bible known as the London Polyglot (in vol. VI, London, 1657)'.

127. A. C. G. M. Eyffinger, 'Poet and Philologist', *Grotius*, pp. 88–9.

128. Sandys, *Classical Scholarship*, II, p. 318; A. C. G. M. Eyffinger, *Grotius Poeta: Aspecten van Hugo Grotius' Dichterschap* (The Hague, 1981).

129. *Grotius*, p. 89.

130. Ibid., p. 91.

life that strong religious conviction of the Christian humanist which is the hallmark of northern humanism throughout the entire period.

## VIII

Humanism in the Netherlands from the days of Gerhard Groote and the Brethren of the Common Life to those of Vossius, Heinsius and Grotius was essentially Christian humanism – an amalgam of the values of classical antiquity, biblical, particularly New Testament, ethics, and patristic theology. From that combined inheritance had come into being the unity and harmony of the ancient Christian world which sixteenth- and especially seventeenth-century northern humanist scholars wished to restore and for which there had been brought into being a *Respublica Litterarium* that transcended national boundaries, that sought both to rise above man-made political and religious barriers, and to unite mankind in respect for human dignity, love of human liberty, and the maintenance of harmony. It was the belief of practically every individual who has briefly figured in this survey, a belief shared by the large number of schoolmasters, scholars, statesmen, churchmen, administrators, printers, and philanthropic citizens of the Netherlands who were its unstinting propagators, that a life of scholarship dedicated to those ideals was not only 'the highest form of humanity',[131] but also the essential expression of their faith for their day. This all-embracing devotion to humanism was expressed paramountly in literary production. Nevertheless its inspiration, its impact, was felt throughout the whole of society. It was, however, given dramatic visual expression in the great triumphal procession of magistrates and scholars which took place in Leiden at the formal opening of its university. In a glorious pageant that passed through the streets and canals were portrayed its essential characteristics. 'Sacra Scriptura' in a chariot drawn by four horses representing the four evangelists was followed by 'Justitia', 'Medicina', and 'Pallas'. In a barge under the command of Neptune was Apollo plucking the strings of his lute in company with the nine Muses, some of whom were playing musical instruments, others singing. When the procession reached its destination Apollo and his Muses addressed a welcome to the four faculties in a series of Latin verses composed by Leiden's leading citizen and administrator Janus Dousa. Professor Van Dorsten drew attention to the significant fact that these verses included one to 'Artes sive Humanitatis Studia'.[132]

---

131. Posthumus Meyjes, *Grotius*, p. 54.

132. Van Dorsten, *Poets*, pp. 2–4; *Leiden University*, p. 2, where a print of an engraving of the 'Inaugural Pageant' is reproduced. The sections on 'Sacra Scripture' and 'Apollo and the Muses' are also reproduced in Van Dorsten, *Poets*, p. 5.

*Chapter Eight*

# Humanism in France

## Jean-Claude Margolin

### I

In some respects, despite controversies, it might be accepted that European humanism, especially in Western Europe, oscillated between an enthusiastic practice of the *studia humanitatis* and a philosophy of man based on an acute awareness of his dignity. However, it must also be recognised that this powerful, intellectual and spiritual movement, which nourished and enlivened European civilisation from the Mediterranean to the Baltic and from the Atlantic seaboard to the Carpathian mountains and the Hungarian plain, stimulated the emergence of a wide variety of forms of thought, art, literature, and mental attitudes, depending on such factors as the countries concerned, the precise historical conjuncture, the different works of learning, and individuals themselves.[1] It is because of this that it is possible to write about French humanism while at the same time fully recognising that Italian humanism, which had emerged earlier, exercised a profound effect on France, as elsewhere, both in terms of the birth of humanism there and the various ways in which it manifested itself.

Despite this Italian influence, however, French humanism, which will be studied here with respect to the period of the approximately two generations between 1480 and 1540, was characterised by two peculiar traits. The first was the existence of a greater degree of continuity

---

1. For a brief synthesis and bibliography relating to European humanism, see J.-C. Margolin, *L'humanisme en Europe au temps de la Renaissance* (Paris, 1981). An English translation is in the press at Duke University, N.C.

between those two periods of European civilisation which are still referred to as the Middle Ages and the Renaissance. The second was a critical and even hostile reaction to certain forms of art, thought, and style emanating from Italy which were sometimes seen as constituting an encroaching, and in some cases a paganising phenomenon. Indeed as far as the relationship between French and Italian humanism is concerned, one could quite happily agree with the findings of art historians, particularly those who, studying stylistic developments in civil architecture, have concentrated on the *châteaux*, and houses of the *haute bourgeoisie* during the period in question, which is one that roughly corresponds to the reigns of Charles VIII, Louis XII, and Francis I. At one time it used to be glibly affirmed that 'the Italian Wars', Charles VIII's expedition to Naples, the expeditions of Louis XII and Francis I to Milan, and the numerous and more or less lengthy sojourns of the king, his entourage, and some of the French nobility in Italy, particularly in the Milan region, had resulted in a direct influence on the style of life and on the architecture of the French at the turn of the century and during the ensuing decades. Yet in fact a closer examination of literary texts, fashions in dress, and in cooking, the art of illuminators, and architectural and decorative forms reveals that the 'national' styles continued to flourish: the poetry was still that of the *Grands Rhétoriqueurs*, and the *ballades* and *rondeaux* of Clément Marot were not in any way profoundly different, at least as far as their composition is concerned, from the poetic art of Molinet or Crétin; men and women continued to wear practical and rather graceless clothes; refined Italian table-manners had still not made an appearance on the banks of the Seine or even the Loire; Fouquet's miniatures followed in the path of Bourdichon; and if timber-framed houses are taken into consideration, such as that on the corner of the *rue du Change* and the *rue du Grand Marché* in Tours, it is clear that there is no evidence of a Renaissance of 'Italianising' style at work round about 1530. The same applies to a *château* like that of Jallanges which, dating from about 1505, was built in brick and stone and without any Renaissance motif, like dozens of other *châteaux* in the Loire valley. But it would be dangerous to pursue this line too far: the originality of the most famous *châteaux* of the period, especially in the Loire valley, lies in the transformation, in some cases progressive, in others brutal, of the medieval French prototype, which itself had emerged from the castle, into a refined residence '*à l'antique*' or '*à l'italienne*' with some exceptionally audacious features – like the great staircase at Chambord, the square pavilions at Villandry, or the gallery at Oiron.[2]

---

2. See J. Guillaume, 'Au centre de la première Renaissance,' in *Centre d'Etudes Supérieures de la Renaissance; Rétrospective et Prospective* (Tours, 1982), pp. 81–97.

There is a final preliminary point. Why limit this consideration of French humanism to the sixty years from 1480 to 1540? After all Ronsard was nourished on Greek and Latin literature from his infancy and his poetry abounds with the echoes of the legends, myths, and heroes of antiquity. Does he not therefore deserve to be called a humanist? In fact did not Pierre de Nolhac write a book entitled *Ronsard et l'humanisme*?[3] What about the teachers at the *Collège Royal*, that typically humanist foundation dating from 1530? In their study and teaching of languages and philosophy, did they suddenly cease to find inspiration for their reflections and conjectures among the Ancients? Moving later into the century, how is it possible not to include Michel de Montaigne among such outstanding humanists as Budé, Melanchthon, Erasmus, Cervantes, and Lipsius when one recalls the large folio volumes of ancient and some contemporary authors in his library, the maxims which he had inscribed on the rafters of his study, and that unique masterpiece, the *Essays*? Such objections could be pressed further by remembering, along with Gilbert Ouy and his team,[4] that the intellectual movement contemporaneous with Petrarch and Charles V, which included such eminent men as Jean Gerson and Nicolas de Clamanges, truly deserves to be included within the label of French humanism. Similarly, moving to the seventeenth century, men like Guez de Balzac or Malherbe at the beginning and Bossuet towards the end certainly deserve to be called humanists.

Yet, compared to other dates that might have been chosen, the period 1480–1540 has its advantages. In his well-known book, *The World of Humanism*, Myron P. Gilmore chose 1453 as a *terminus a quo* and 1517 as a *terminus ad quem*, justifying his choice of dates in terms of two crucial and dramatic events:[5] the capture of Constantinople by the Turks, which marked the culmination of a long history of disunity between the Catholic and Orthodox forms of Christianity, and the nailing up of the ninety-five theses at Wittenberg, which marked Luther's decisive entry onto the stage of German and European history and the consequent irreversible division of the Christian West.[6]

---

3. Pierre de Nolhac, *Ronsard et l'humanisme* (Paris, 1921).

4. See, for example, G. Ouy, 'La recherche sur l'humanisme français des XIVe et XVe siècles. A propos d'un ouvrage récent', *Francia*, Band 5 (1977), pp. 693–707, which discusses A. P. Saccaro, *Französischer Humanismus des 14. und 15. Jahrhunderts* (Munich, 1975); G. Ouy, 'Paris, l'un des principaux foyers de l'humanisme en Europe au début du XVe siècle', in *Bulletin de la Société de l'Histoire de Paris et de l'Ile-de-France*, volume for the years 1967–68 (published in 1970), pp. 71–98.

5. M. P. Gilmore, *The World of Humanism, 1453–1517* (New York, 1952; French trans. Paris, 1955).

6. For a general synthesis, see, for example, J. Delumeau, *Naissance et Affirmation de la Réforme* (2nd revised edn, Paris, 1968).

Historians of German humanism frequently choose this date of 1517 when they want to distinguish between Humanism and the Reformation, but in doing so they efface all the writings of the humanist reformers from Melanchthon or the dramatist Naogeorgus onwards. Such neat chronological divisions are less apparent in *L'Âge de l'Humanisme* by Robert Klein and André Chastel[7] but, like Gilmore, they too did not concentrate exclusively on French humanism.

By limiting this study to the period which could be called the first French Renaissance, the opening date makes it possible both to catch the flow of history at the point when printing began, with all the well-known consequences which this had on the intellectual scene, education, the diffusion of texts and ideas, and on social and economic life generally, and to emphasise the peaceful and warlike contacts between the French and the Italians which resulted from the various expeditions into Italy. On the other hand the date chosen for the end of the period under review makes it possible to take into account the movements of religious dissidence which culminated in the Affair of the Placards in October 1534, and the growing distrust felt by those in the traditional power structures of Church and State towards intellectuals like Rabelais, Des Périers, or even Marguerite of Navarre whose literary works, philological enthusiasm, and use of the classical languages were not devoid of either a critical spirit or a desire for reform.[8] By 1540 also a number of educational strongholds had already been established, the most famous being the *Collège Trilingue* or *Collège Royal*[9], and their inspiration was quite radically opposed to the atmosphere which prevailed in most traditional Faculties – not only and notably in the Faculties of Theology, of which the Sorbonne provided the prototype, but also in most Law Faculties, and in Faculties of Arts and Medicine. It is right to call this spirit 'humanist': there was a marked emphasis on the study of authors and texts, certain historical traditions were called into question, myths were scrutinised, and a critical approach was adopted in all areas of research, including sacred biblical texts. Commentaries were no longer simply informative and impersonal glosses; they were real personal forays into intellectual adventure. All the working educational tools, the institutions, and the pedagogical programmes were already in place when the Jesuits took over the *rationes studiorum*, worked out by Erasmus and his European

---

7. R. Klein and A. Chastel, *L'Age de l'Humanisme* (Paris, 1963).

8. For details and bibliographical information about the authors (and many others), see the manual in the series *Littérature française*, directed by Claude Pichois, vol. 3: Y. Guiraud and M.-R. Jung, *La Renaissance, I, 1480–1548* (Paris, 1972).

9. See A. Lefranc, *Histoire du Collège de France* (Paris, 1893).

disciples, and assumed the responsibility, within Catholicism, of a formidable role in the intellectual, moral, and religious formation of the young.[10] Finally if it is accepted that a recource to a quasi-exclusive use of Latin in all areas of research and teaching was one of the characteristics of European humanism, and not simply just in France, then with scholars like Louis Le Roy, Pierre de La Ramée, Henri Estienne II and Charles Estienne, Estienne Pasquier, Palissy and many others, the years around 1540 or 1550 mark the progressively strong entry of philosophy, rhetoric, grammar, geography, anatomy and technics into those *'studia humanitatis'* which would no longer be ashamed to express themselves in a French fashion.

## II

It has long been known – and here the importance of the studies by Lucien Febvre, Henri-Jean Martin, Elizabeth Eisenstein, and others should be emphasised[11] – that the rise and influence of humanism was closely linked to that of printing. This link was all the stronger inasmuch as many printers did not simply publish authors' manuscripts and guarantee them a wide diffusion of their books by reason of the economic networks and branches which they had created in several towns and indeed in other countries, but because they also wrote prefaces for the books they printed, edited texts, and were themselves authors. This was true of, among others, Aldus Manutius in Venice, Jean or Jerome Froben at Basel, Josse Bade and Geoffroy Tory in Paris, and Etienne Dolet in Lyon. In the late fifteenth and early sixteenth centuries printing in France was marked by traits similar to those which characterised the beginnings of the French Renaissance. The books which were published emphasised both continuing medieval traditions – Michel le Noir published a large number of chivalrous romances, Simon Vostre concentrated on Books of Hours, and learned and weighty juridical glosses and scholastic treatises still attracted a specialised clientele – and the new demand for an increasing supply of editions of works by the Greek and Latin authors of the classical world (although with some delay compared to Italy as far as Greek works were concerned). Also in demand were humanist grammars like those by Perotti and Lascaris, scientific works such as those by Lefèvre d'Etaples and Bovelles, commentaries on the Bible, editions of the Church Fathers, and works

---

10. For a general account, see J.-C. Margolin, 'L'éducation au temps de la Contre-Réforme', in *Histoire mondiale de l'Education* (Paris, 1981), Part 2, pp. 213–32.

11. L. Febvre and H.-J. Martin, *L'Apparition du livre* (Paris, 1958; English trans. 1976), E. Eisenstein, *The Printing Press as an Agent of Change*, 2 vols (Cambridge, 1979); E. Eisenstein, *The Printing Revolution in Early Modern Europe* (Cambridge, 1984).

of a more personal nature, such as the great books by Gaguin, Lemaire de Belges, Andrelini, Budé, and Rabelais.

The very nature of the origins of printing in France is of symbolic value. In the heart of Venice, on the Rialto, the Manutius press, from its foundation by Aldus the Elder and continuing through Aldus the Younger right down to the descendants of the late sixteenth century, specialised in editions of both ancient and modern 'lay' works, particularly classical ones.[12] In comparison the press which Guillaume Fichet set up at the Sorbonne provides us with a good representative case of the contrasting traits which characterised late fifteenth-century French humanism. For if Fichet paid visits to Italy, possessed a profound classical erudition, and was well acquainted with the French scholars of his day, he also professed a respect, as did the others of his *milieu*, for the doctrines of Duns Scotus and Thomas Aquinas. Another characteristic and paradoxical feature about the origins of French printing was the contribution made by immigrants from Germany or from Germanic countries. Thus the first printing workshop in Paris, that of Fichet, was in reality a press established by Ulrich Gering from Constance, Michael Friburger, who was a graduate of the university of Basel and a native of Colmar, and the German Jean Heynlin, prior at the Sorbonne, with the assistance of a worker, Martin Krantz, who like Heynlin, was originally from Stein. Of course, it should be noted in passing that it was Germans who in practice started up the printing presses both in their own country and abroad, especially in Rome, Florence, and Venice. But the originality of the German contributions was more marked and lasted longer in France, as can be seen by the continuing use of Gothic type during the early decades of the sixteenth century, whereas Italic type, which was typically Italian and more specifically Venetian (inasmuch as the types had been made by Aldus Manutius), had hardly been brought into play in the French presses by 1510 or even 1520.[13] It should be noted that presses were systematically to sort out their letter types by using Italic for classical works and Gothic type for religious or fictional texts, these latter being written in the language of the Church or in the popular vernacular.

Let us take the example of Josse Bade,[14] the celebrated printer of Belgian origin who was a typical representative of the humanist printer and bookseller, being himself an author, a friend of humanists, and

---

12. On the Aldine press, see J. C. Lowry, *The World of Aldus Manutius: Business and Scholarship in Renaissance Italy*, (Oxford, 1979).

13. See L. Febvre and H.-J., Martin, *op. cit.*, ch. 5, 'Le petit monde du livre', pp. 195 ff.

14. In particular, see P. Renouard, *Bibliographie des impressions et des oeuvres de Josse Badius Ascensius, imprimeur et humaniste (1462–1535)*, 3 vols, (Paris, 1908).

enjoying a gratifying social reputation in Paris which extended far outside the *quartier* of the printers. He had been formed by the Brethren of the Common Life and the result was that his intellectual and moral personality was marked by a Christian 'learned piety' which was receptive to the world and to men. But at the same time he had also been influenced by his visit to Italy, the teaching of Beroaldo the Elder, and by his own teaching activities at Valence and then at Lyon. Such a man plunged enthusiastically into the business of printing pedagogical works, editions of classical authors, Latin grammars, and those books by famous contemporary humanists (particularly Erasmus) which had a bearing on grammar, rhetoric, and style. He published Beroaldo's *Orationes*, and then his *Silvae morales*, which was a collection of extracts chosen from the best classical and modern authors. And when he published the famous *Elegantiae Latinae linguae* by Lorenzo Valla, the fifteenth-century humanist venerated by Erasmus who was the veritable 'patron' of western humanism,[15] he did not hesitate to use his own knowledge of grammar and of Latin in order to add commentaries to the *Elegantiae* and even in some few instances to note down reservations about this or that point of syntax or style.

As his business expanded, and as his reputation as a scholarly editor and printer who was devoted to 'studious youth' and moral values grew, so Bade joined forces with the great Parisian printer Jean Petit, just as he had earlier allied himself with printers in Lyon, like Trechsel, at the time when he was still teaching. An idea of the variety and number of works which were printed at the sign of 'Praelum Ascensianum' (which relates to his full humanist name, Jodocus Badius Ascensianus, after his small home-town of Assche) can be obtained by consulting the three volumes plus supplement of Philippe Renouard's *Bibliographie*.[16] Apart from authors who have already been cited, among some 720 titles there are works by the Carmelite Battista Spagnuoli, alias Mantuanus, the Flemish grammarian Despautère (Van Spauteren), the Franco-Italian poet Fausto Andrelini, and even after the break with Erasmus and Luther's appearance on the religious scene some works, like those of Noël Beda, syndic of the Sorbonne, about which the least that can be said is that they were in no way humanist, either in form or in context.

The shops of the great printers of Paris and Lyon were also important as places where authors, customers, teachers, students, and even *collégiens* met and exchanged ideas. Indeed with all due precaution it could be said that they performed a function which was similar to

---

15. On the 'father' or 'patron' of western humanism, see, for example, S.I. Camporeale, *Lorenzo Valla Umanesimo e Teologia* (Florence, 1972).

16. See note 14.

that of some coffee-houses from the eighteenth century onwards – for example, the Procope in the age of Diderot and d'Alembert. Moreover they were almost all located close to each other and within a restricted area – in the *rue Saint-Jacques* in Paris, and in the *rue Mercière* in Lyon. The names of these printing firms, and even more markedly the affirmation of their personalities, were heavily emphasised by 'devices', which appeared on the title page and/or the colophon of their works, and their emblematic, sententious or even enigmatic significance entered into the spirit of that play on allegories and symbols which the humanists of the period were so fond of. In the case of Sebastian Gryphius of Lyon, for example, a gryphon was framed by the device '*Virtute duce, comite Fortuna*'; in Paris the press of Chrétien Wechel used a flying horse (Pegasus) superimposed on the escutcheon of Basel (the parent-house being located in Basel); and in the case of Nicolas Paris at Troyes a quotation from the Gospels, '*ascendam et appraehendam fructus ejus*', was accompanied by an illustration of a child trying to climb up a palm tree. The sign of the Parisian bookseller and printer Guy Marchant was more complicated. This depicted the handshake of two hands emerging from the clouds and, above the handshake, the presence of two musical notes, a 'sol' and a 'la' (the notes G and A respectively), with two Latin words superimposed, the word *Fides* (the faith) being placed above (*au-dessus*) *ficit* (the truncated part of a verb). This enigmatic riddle, greatly in the taste of the *Rhétoriqueurs*, encoded the device '*Sola fides sufficit*', the respective positions of the two words making it possible to interpolate the missing preposition '*sus*'. The sign, therefore, discreetly projected the image of a bookseller who wished to put his business, as well as his books, his clientele, and himself, under the protection of the Christian faith.

The example of the Estienne dynasty (Henri I, Robert I, Henri II, Charles, Robert II, François) spanned the first two-thirds of the century and is in many ways paradigmatic.[17] For the members of this family participated directly or indirectly in all the cultural and religious movements and upheavals of the period, not to mention the technical revolutions in printing such as the Greek types for the royal press which Robert I, Henri I's son, procured from Claude Garamond, the engraver and type-founder. These enabled him to acquire another jewel for his printing art by adding Greek to his Hebrew and Latin types and becoming a truly trilingual printer and humanist who could be on equal terms with the regius professors and lecturers of the *Collège* established by Francis I, after the model of the *Collegium Trilingue* of Louvain

---

17. See A. A. Renouard, *Annales de l'imprimerie des Estienne ou Histoire de la famille des Estienne et de ses éditions* (Paris, 1843: reprinted New York, 1960; Geneva, 1971).

(1517),[18] or with the scholars of the University of Alcalá de Henares,[19] which had been founded and endowed with a humanist programme at the beginning of the century by Cardinal Ximénez, co-promoter with Antonio de Nebrija of the famous polyglot Bible. Indeed if in honouring the Estienne family by citing the sole example of Robert I (1499?–1559), we should recall that the objective of this humanist printer (or, if it is preferred, this printer *and* humanist) was to provide the best possible texts, and that in this spirit he published a great number of bibles, ·which were to be condemned by the Faculty of Theology in 1547, and that in 1550 he had to leave Paris for Geneva, where he converted to Protestantism, then we will have summarised the careers of some of those printers – but not of course the majority of them – who had an elevated sense of their pedagogical and human mission.

After all, was Lyon not at the cross-roads of the escape-routes of those 'wrong-thinking' authors who wanted to leave France and go to Calvin's Switzerland, or to the duchies of Ferrara or Savoy, all of which were more receptive to new ideas? And so, at a time which goes slightly beyond our chosen period, Robert Estienne, from Geneva, turned himself into the spokesman of both Humanism and the Reformation. But his greatest and most enduring glory lay in his production of lexicons and dictionaries of immense learning: his *Thesaurus linguae Latinae*, dating from 1532, was closely followed in 1538 by a *Dictionarium latinogallicum*, because this great 'trilingual' scholar did not consider that French was a fitting language for the people. This was a point which he made in 1540 when he turned his dictionary of 1538 into a *Dictionnaire français latin* which, as he says in the preface, was aimed at the '*soulagement de la jeunesse françoise, qui est sur son commencement et bachelage de littérature*'. This, as will be seen later, was perhaps the mission of the authentic humanists of the 1540s: to use all the appropriate scientific means (etymological research, grammatical and syntactical comparisons, the juxtaposition of several languages, etc) in an attempt to deepen the knowledge of Latin and the vernacular languages, in this case French, by a better awareness of their respective histories and by resorting, in the case of both languages, to the reading of good authors. In compiling his *Dictionnaire*, Estienne for his part delved into the '*romans et bons autheurs françois*' (among them Rabelais), in just the same way as the Lexicographers of the *Trésor de la Langue*

18. On the Collegium Trilingue of Louvain, see H. de Vocht, *History of the Foundation and the Rise of the Collegium Trilingue Lovaniense* (1517–1550), 4 vols (Louvain: Humanistica Lovaniensia, X–XIII, 1951–55).

19. See M. Bataillon, *Erasme et l'Espagne* (Paris, 1937; Spanish trans., 2nd edn, Mexico–BuenosAires, 1965), *passim*.

*Française* were to justify their examples by using nineteenth- and twentieth-century authors.

### III

The significance of the famous letter on education, which Gargantua sent to his son Pantagruel, in Book two chapter 8 of Rabelais, is well known:[20]

> The times were still dark and feeling the effects of those miseries and calamities inflicted by the Goths, who had destroyed all good literature. But thanks to God's kindness, in my age enlightenment and dignity have once again been accorded to letters, and I see such an improvement that I would now hardly be accepted into the lowest class of little schoolboys, I who as a young man was reputed, and not without reason, to be the most learned man of the century . . . Now all the learned disciplines have been restored, and the study of languages established: Greek, without which it is shameful that a man should proclaim himself to be learned, Hebrew, Chaldean, and Latin; the art of printing such elegant and accurate books, now in circulation, which was invented in my time by divine inspiration, just as, by contrast, artillery was inspired by diabolical suggestion. The whole world is full of learned men, very erudite teachers, and well-stocked libraries, and I am of the opinion that neither in the time of Plato, nor of Cicero, nor of Papinian were there ever such facilities for studying as one sees nowadays . . .

In ascribing to the gigantic Gargantua sentiments and reflexions which he would have loved to express on his own account when remembering the 'old-fashioned' schools of his youth, or the scholastic methods of that 'Gothic' age which he contrasts with those features which almost literally defined the Rebirth of scholarship and the arts (the 'restoration' of learned disciplines, and the 'establishment' of the study of languages), Rabelais accurately reflects the reactions of the first two generations of humanists. He shows the same enthusiasm for the new and forthcoming times, and for the youths who are preparing themselves for the exhilarating tasks awaiting them, and the same acute awareness of a break between the obscurantism of the past, which was still present and was still not commonly called 'the Middle Ages', and

---

20. This quotation is a translation from the edition of Rabelais' text by Guy Demerson (Paris, 1973), p. 246.

the enlightenment of the new age. Erasmus displayed the same enthusiasm when he contrasted 'old fashioned' education, caricatured by that stock theme of the donkey in school which was fairly widely disseminated throughout the Low Countries thanks to a print by the elder Brueghel, with the kind of education he extolled in his own pedagogical works. Then again the lapidary exclamation by the Franconian knight Ulrich von Hutten in 1515 was not without its significance: 'What times! We are living in a new age!'

And yet, with the passing of the centuries, we are not today quite as sure about this radical contrast, as depicted by Gargantua–Rabelais, between the past and the present. On the one hand the brilliant vision of an all-conquering humanism was stained and tarnished by the profound religious crisis, started by Luther and carried on by Calvin and all the other 'dissidents', the bloody wars which engulfed Europe, and the phenomenon of misery in all its various forms – poverty, famine, witch trials, plagues and epidemics, disasters, and all those different kinds of fears and apprehensions which have been analysed by Jean Delumeau.[21] And on the other hand a deeper knowledge of the life and thought of these humanists of the first half of the sixteenth century – with Rabelais himself to the fore – allows us to assert that they were far from rejecting the heritage of the past, or even of the recent past, for the simple reason that this same past continued into the present. Does not Rabelais' novel itself, which was written in French, replete with the echoes of chivalrous romances, and garnished with medieval proverbs and 'gothic' folklore, provide the proof *a contrario* of an 'antihumanism', or at the very least of a humanism which easily came to terms with formulae and remembrances of past times which were more popular than learned? If the humanist, nurtured on Greek, Latin, and Hebrew revealed himself in a few Latin writings or in some verses inspired by the ancients, it was the author of the 'gigantic' adventures of Grandgousier, Gargantua, and Pantagruel who made, and continues to make, his reputation. But why should we contrast or oppose these two aspects? Are not both a thirst for knowledge and a 'vastness' of acquired learning paraded on each and every page of Rabelais' work?

The interest of the particular text which we have been commenting on lies in the fact that it makes it possible to achieve a clearer understanding of what is meant by the 'restoration' or the 'rediscovery' of the ancient world. In the not too distant past it used to be claimed, with too much alacrity, that the humanist movement was defined by a return to the literary, archaeological, and philosophical sources of an ancient

---

21. See especially J. Delumeau, *La Peur en Occident* (Paris, 1978); J. Delumeau, *Le Péché et la Peur* (Paris, 1983).

past, which was held up as the most brilliant age in human history –
a return which was facilitated by the discovery of manuscripts, lapidary
inscriptions, monuments, medals, and statues of ancient Rome. But
when Rabelais placed his own century above the age of Plato or Cicero,
the two outstanding models who were held up to humanist authors and
young *savants* for admiration and imitation, he was reacting in the same
way as the best of his contemporaries, men like Vives, More, Erasmus,
and Budé. These men were aware that cumulative progress had been
made on all fronts since the age of Pericles or Cicero, and they were
above all conscious of their responsibilities in dealing with the fresh and
personal tasks of a new world – whether these tasks were administrative, juridical, diplomatic, pedagogical, political, or religious. Such
men did not turn to the past in order to forget a present age which did
not agree with them; rather they imbibed from the best authors of the
distant past those texts, ideas, symbols and motives which they then
prided themselves in trying to apply, in their own way, to the new
conditions of the present and the future. That was the profound
significance of Erasmus' *Ciceronianus*.[22] Erasmus, who did not forget
Guillaume Budé when he awarded those '*satisfecit*' to good French
Ciceronians, transformed the way in which the great Latin orator was
to be imitated; such imitation was not to consist of a servile reproduction of his stylistic traits or of the celebration of his cultural ideas or
beliefs, but was to be a task which was both difficult and exciting. This
was because it would involve choosing and adapting 'words' and
'things' in relation to a new stage of civilisation and to a historical
moment of time when a new style and fresh thinking would meet the
needs and demands of contemporaries.

That humanists, in their detailed researches into the archaeology and
the '*realia*' of the civilisations of Athens and Rome, described, analysed
and reproduced ancient documents with the greatest possible precision,
is one thing; that they forgot the world in which they were living and
for which they were working, is quite a different matter. In this sense
the most typical example is that of the scholar and the statesman who
undoubtedly dominated French humanism, Guillaume Budé.[23] His
death in 1540 ended the period covered by this study. The son of a rich
Parisian magistrate, Jean Budé, who already possessed a fine Latin

---

22. See L.-E. Halkin, *Erasme parmi nous* (Paris, 1987), ch. 19, pp. 305 ff.

23. On Guillaume Budé, see in particular M.-M. de La Garanderie, *Christianisme et
lettres profanes* (Paris–Lille, 1976); M.-M. de La Garanderie, 'Le style figuré de Guillaume
Budé et ses implications logiques et théologiques', in *L'Humanisme français au début de
la Renaissance* (Paris, 1973), pp. 343–59. See also: Guillaume Budé, *L'Etude des lettres*, a
French translation from *De studio literarum recte et commode instituendo* by M.-M. de La
Garanderie, (Paris, 1988).

library, Budé was a philologist and jurist who had performed brilliantly as a student at Orléans and then at Paris, although like many other young men from the *bonne bourgeoisie* he had for a short time been attracted by society life, riding, and hunting. (It is worth noting that most humanists came from this social background.) But soon Budé dedicated himself entirely to scholarly pursuits; so much so, indeed, that on his own admission he only managed to 'sacrifice' a few hours to his studies on the day he got married. Largely self-taught, he was to become the greatest French Hellenist of his day, outstripping even Erasmus as can be seen by the exchange of letters, written in Greek, between these two friendly rivals. His Latin translations of some small works by Plutarch and of one of the letters of St Basil the Great bear witness to the importance of the heritage of the classical world in his work. And one can also see, even in his *Annotationes in quattuor et viginti Pandectarum libros*, that entirely new contribution to the science of jurisprudence which consisted of the application of philological and historical methods to the interpretation of laws and other juridical provisions. Rejecting the old methodology of glosses and of commentaries on other commentaries, Budé, like all other jurists influenced by the grace of humanism (for example, Andrea Alciati, who was of Italian origin but spent a good deal of his life in France and taught at Bourges), adopted an approach which consisted of scrutinising and comparing words and studying the cultural and sociological contexts which would bring customs and rules to life. At the same time, and as a result of his official duties as a *maître des requêtes* and then as a royal councillor, he was reflecting on the gulf of time which separated the classical world from his own age. Nothing illustrates this better than his treatise on ancient coins, published in 1515 and entitled *De Asse et partibus ejus*. In this he displayed a scrupulous scholarly concern for accuracy when studying such technical aspects as the weights, measures, and coins in use among the Greeks and Romans, as well as providing insights into the civilisation of the classical world. But what is above all of interest in terms of the 'here and now' are Budé's digressions, which are sometimes confused and badly linked to his overall plan, concerning the political problems of his own times, such as the contemporaneous accession of the young Francis I in 1515. In its own condensed way this amazing work expresses the problems facing French humanism during its first Renaissance. There is a preoccupation with ethical values, which was an enduring feature of this kind of humanism, a critical attitude towards an Italy whose literary pre-eminence over France was being called into question, a passionate researching of the 'antiquities' of France itself, which Budé combined with his own political ambitions and his desire to serve the monarchy, and certain reservations with respect to the wisdom of the ancients. For Budé without doubt belonged to that movement which would later be called Christian Humanism and which can be traced back to Erasmus, who clearly defined its sense of direction.

There should by all means be a restoration of the works of classical authors, and the elevated thinking of Plato, Aristotle, Plutarch, Cicero, and Seneca was certainly worthy of admiration. But there should also be the establishment of an order or hierarchy of values which would turn the most sublime pages of the *Phaedo* and of the *Tusculan Disputations* into steps or passage-ways leading to Christian meditations inspired by God. That was the significance of Erasmus' famous formula in his *Enchiridion militis christiani* (*The Manual of a Christian Soldier*) of 1504: 'Do you like *belles-lettres*? You are right to do so, providing it is in the service of Christ.' It was for this essential subordination of pagan literature and 'truths', however profound, that Budé argued, above all in his *De Transitu hellenismi ad Christianismum* (*The Transition from Hellenism to Christianity*), published in 1535. In this he showed that philology led to theology, that theology was the jewel in the crown of all those collective disciplines which he labelled *encyclopaideia*, and that these disciplines were not any the less incommensurable as far as he was concerned. But this 'transition' was not to be achieved without a crisis of conscience. Between his humanistic love of classical literature and philology (he published his *De studio literarum recte et commode instituendo, De philologia*, and *Commentarii linguae Graecae* in 1527, 1530, and 1529 respectively) and his adhesion to the truth of Christ, the reconciliations were not always easy or indeed possible. More than one French humanist would undergo the same crisis of conscience. And it was also an underlying aspect of the war waged in the *Ciceronianus*, a war undertaken at great cost by Erasmus, who made himself the public accuser of those numerous Italians whose love of the ancient world, and especially of Latin and Roman civilisation, had transformed them, so Erasmus thought, into pagans unaware of their paganism or at least into Christians who only retained the empty shell of the gospel message.

However exemplary Budé's case might be with respect to attitudes to classical culture, national culture, and Christianity, we could not apply its lessons to all those French authors, printers, teachers, jurists, and other intellectuals who deserve to be called humanists without making more or less important adaptations. Nevertheless, as Franco Simone[24] has so clearly demonstrated in his studies on the *translatio studii* between the Italian and French varieties of humanism, conflicting sentiments of admiration–resentment and love–jealousy were kept alive by a ceaseless dialogue, which even military invasions did not succeed

---

24. See especially F. Simone, *Il Rinascimento francese: Studi e Ricerche* (Turin, 1965).

in interrupting, at least as far as educated men were concerned. It was these sentiments which essentially characterised the relationship between these two types of humanism – the one looking back in its national heritage to Dante and Petrarch, and the other forced to create a mythical national past because the *Chanson de Roland*, the *Mystère de la Passion*, the *Roman de la Rose*, Rutebeuf, Eustache Deschamps, and François Villon had still not been integrated into a heritage which French humanists were proud enough to claim as their own.

Thus it was that, about half a generation before Budé, Robert Gaguin[25], who is generally considered to have been one of the leading lights of Parisian humanism at the turn of the century, not only documented his *Compendium de origine et gestis Francorum* from a vast collection of medieval and contemporary sources (he did not neglect information supplied by Italian humanists like Bruni and Biondo, and Erasmus acknowledged that he had *fides et eruditio*), but he also echoed the legends which tended to demonstrate the illustrious antiquity of Gaul.

But for our present purpose it is Lemaire de Belges above all to whom we should turn.[26] It might well be asked why this particular author is being summoned up to the humanist cause, for although he certainly knew Latin and went to Italy to partake of those cultural nourishments he considered necessary for his intellectual and moral development, he wrote in French, as is notably witnessed by his *Illustrations de Gaule et singularités de Troie* published in 1511. The answer is that if Latin was effectively then the most common 'medium', authentic humanist inspiration was nevertheless a matter of style and of the development of ideas: a jurist or theologian who used barbarous Latin and was not acquainted with Virgil or Cicero would be far less worthy of the title of 'humanist' than Lemaire. In fact Lemaire demonstrated a vast erudition with respect to antiquity, and his arguments concerning the origins of Gaul were derived from a Dominican who was not French – namely, Giovanni Nanni (or Annius) of Viterbo, who had published a whole series of supposedly ancient texts by Bérose, Manéthon, and others, which have long been known to be apocryphal if not purely and simply fabricated. Using these texts and following the medieval 'topos' of the ages of mankind or of history, it was poss-

---

25. See above all Simone, *op. cit.*, pp. 50 ff.; J. W. Thompson, *A History of Historical Writing* (New York, 1942) I, pp. 514–17; R. Gaguin, *Epistolae et orationes*, ed. L. Thuasne (Paris, 1903); A. Renaudet, *Préréforme et Humanisme à Paris* (Paris 1916; re-ed. 1953).

26. See in particular G. Doutrepont, *Jean Lemaire de Belges et la Renaissance* (Brussels, 1934; re-ed. Geneva, 1974); J. Frappier, 'L'humanisme de Jean Lemaire de Belges', in J. Frappier, *Du Moyen Age à la Renaissance: Etudes d'histoire et de critique littéraire* (Paris, 1976), pp. 341–59; P. Jodogne, *Jean Lemaire de Belges, écrivain franco-bourguignon* (Brussels, 1971).

ible to establish a chronology of primitive times, a parallelism between
biblical chronology and Egyptian and Greek mythologies, and above
all a concordance between those historico-mythical chronologies and
certain 'ancestors' of the European peoples. It was not just France but
the whole of Europe which reacted in this way to the *Commentarii* of
Annius of Viterbo: it provided the opportunity of reacting against the
superiority of Greece – *Graecia mendax* – and also of filling in the gaps
between the Flood and the fall of Troy.

Curiously enough this same 'perfidious' Greece was to be pressed
into service by many humanists – not just Budé but Henri Estienne,
and later on Joachim Périon and Estienne Pasquier – to act as a kind
of dragoman or alternative in the face of an Italian encroachment which
boasted its Latin inheritance. Indeed the study of the etymology of
French words was at times to take on an ideological and even nation-
alistic significance. Some of these etymologies were correct but others
– and the French etymologists were probably not aware of the fact –
were the product of pure fantasy. Thus the word *harpe* was said to be
derived from the Greek *harpè* (signifying the curve of a scythe), *gambe*
('which the Franks pronounced Iambè') from the Greek *kampè* (which
referred to the bending action peculiar to the legs) and *chère* (used by
the French to refer to a smiling face) from the Greek *Chairé* meaning
'Hello'. This idea of a direct transmission from Greek to French (or to
*Francique*) which by-passed Latin was not unconnected with the myth of the
Gallic Hercules,[27] which was linked to the national past and so perfectly
adapted to the personality of the king of France, Henry II, who assimilated the accumulated wisdom and prudence of this God-like figure as
well as his energies and victories (against monsters or against the
enemies of France). Above all it marked a retreat from, or a wariness
of, the Italian–Latin tradition and consciously or unconsciously
expressed a wish to forget or efface the ancient conquest of Gaul by
Caesar's legions. Charles de Bovelles, the Picard who was fond of
French proverbs and also prided himself on his linguistic geography[28],
had recourse to such etymologies, without manifesting for all that any
aversion whatsoever towards the 'Latinizers'.

27. The birth of this myth was due to the publication of a text by Lucian, at the
beginning of the sixteenth century, which enjoyed an immense success, and which also
inspired many artists. It related to a cult, in Gaul, of the god Hercules, who was supposed
to be the god of eloquence and whose words, on leaving his mouth, were relayed to the
ears of his listeners by means of a golden thread or chain. On this subject, see the
monograph by M.-R. Jung, *Hercule dans la littérature française du XVIe siècle* (Geneva,
1966).

28. See his two collections of Proverbs, *Proverbiorum vulgarium libri tres* (Paris, Galliot
du Pré, 1531); *Les proverbes et dicts sententieux . . .* (Paris, S. Nyvelle, 1557); and his *Liber
de differentia vulgarium linguarum et Gallici sermonis varietate* (Paris, R. Estienne, 1533).

During the second half of the century the scholarly Guillaume Postel[29], who commanded several languages and who would never have dreamt of placing the ancient and modern languages in any hierarchical order, nevertheless steered his linguistic researches in such a direction as a result of a monarchist ideology which tended to accord to both the king and his people illustrious historical origins which had never been dominated by Latin culture. But in 1527 a certain Jean Bouchet[30], alluding to the Gauls and the French, regretted that they had 'almost lost their glory because of the suppressions practised by Italian and Roman historiographers, who were ancient emulators as well as being envious of the prosperity of the Gauls and the French'. Thus it was the Romans who, in his view, had acted as borrowers. From a scientific point of view, the more scholarly studies dated from the second half of the century as the study of language became progressively more rigorous. Nevertheless many authors, and some prominent public figures (like Guillaume du Bellay, who worked on a treatise on the *Antiquité des Gaules et de France*), used their knowledge and imagination to create, alongside classical antiquities and biblical culture, '*antiquités francoyses*' which they ended up believing in: for example, Jean Lefèvre de Dreux and his *Fleurs et Antiquitez des Gaules* (1532), Guillaume Corrozet and his *Antiques Erections des Gaules* (1535), and Guillaume Le Rouillé and his *Recueil de l'Antique preexcellence de Gaule et des Gauloys* (1546).

## IV

If, as has been seen, Guillaume Budé invented or reinvented the term *encyclopaedia*, and if his treatise *De Philologia* symbolised the overwhelming importance of philology as the basic discipline of a militant and educational humanism, the general view regarding the relationship between philology and all the other fields of scholarly endeavour was nevertheless much the same throughout the learned circles of most of Europe. Erasmus in particular demonstrated, both in theory and in practice, that the '*grammaticus*' and '*orator*', which were terms that applied to one and the same person, was the key figure of this new world which he wanted the young to have access to in his programme of studies.[31] For it was not simply a matter of grammar, in the limited

---

29. On what follows, see C.-G. Dubois, *Celtes et Gaulois au XVIe siècle* (Paris, 1972); C.-G. Dubois, 'La mythologie nationaliste de Guillaume Postel', in the Actes du colloque international Guillaume Postel, *Guillaume Postel 1581–1981* (Paris, 1985), pp. 257–64.

30. See A. Hamon, *Jean Bouchet* (Paris, 1901).

31. See J. Chomarat, *Grammaire et Rhétorique chez Erasme* (Paris, 1980), Vol. I, part 3, ch. 1, pp. 153–82: 'L'enseignement du grammaticus'.

and technical sense of the word, but of the study of letters generally, the term 'letters' being a happily ambivalent one which could mean both the letters of the alphabet, and their combinations into syllables, words, or syntagms, as well as the *belles-lettres, bonae litterae,* or *humaniores litterae* which, when practised in an accomplished way, perfected a man to the highest degree. Indeed in this latter sense the term 'humanities' was also used, and this included literature and, in addition, some indefinable moral and social attributes inasmuch as the lettered man (these two words being almost synonymous in the humanist conception of man) was destined to live in society, and it was not possible to conceive of a cultivated man – and that was what *litteratus* meant – who was not also a right-thinking man. This was exactly the Ciceronian or Quintilian conception of the orator: '*vir· bonus dicendique peritus*'. It was in this way that the humanists of the first Renaissance fused the ideal of the *orator* with that of the *grammaticus,* with the qualification that a special emphasis was accorded to the spoken word or oral communication. Human relationships certainly owed a lot to the written word, and indeed writing letters was one of the characteristic activities of the humanists, some of whom, like Vives and especially Erasmus, had studied the genre in treatises on the epistolary art[32]. But the kind of man whom the masters of *bonae litterae* wanted to form had above all to know how to use the spoken word with art and efficacy, whether he was a *parlementaire,* an advocate, a teacher, an ambassador, or a preacher. The terms *philologia* and *philologus,* which were so dear to Budé, were also the practical equivalents of the *ars oratoria* (and of the *orator*), the *ars grammatica* (and the *grammaticus*).

Staying with the large number of French scholars and humanists of the period under study (a restricted period which does not therefore include men like Dorat and Muret, despite their erudition and teaching, the Hellenists Turnèbe and Casaubon, Joseph-Justus Scaliger, who surpassed his father in terms of universal knowledge and the linguistic sciences, or Denis Lambin and Jacques Amyot), let us quickly follow a trajectory taking us from Lefevre d'Etaples to Etienne Dolet. As we do so we meet scholars like Champier, Bovelles, Rabelais, and others, as well as members of the first and second generations of the Estienne family, whom we have already encountered but who deserve renewed consideration because of the important contributions which they made in more than one area of the 'encyclopaedia' of human knowledge.

Philology, as has been pointed out, was the fundamental basis of the *studia humanitatis.* Does this mean that it was the rough equivalent of

---

32. See especially Erasmus' *De conscribendis epistolis,* ed. J.-C. Margolin, in *Opera omnia Erasmi* (Amsterdam, 1971), Vol. 1, part 2, pp. 153–579.

the three disciplines of the medieval *Trivium* – grammar, rhetoric and dialectic – which constituted a basis for the ensuing four disciplines of the *Quadrivium*, that is arithmetic, geometry, astronomy, and music? Since this question could be answered in both an affirmative and negative way, it would be as well to pose the problem of the relationships between the human sciences and those which can be provisionally termed the 'exact sciences' within the context of humanists' researches and teaching. What is certain is that philology was essential to all the various disciplines, regardless of whether the treatises in question related to history, geography, mathematics, astronomy and astrology, or medicine. The reason for this is that when a humanist, who was capable of the task, translated this or that Greek text, he invariably added a Latin commentary. This of course was not a characteristic which was peculiar to the French humanists, although it was more pronounced in their case than it was, for example, in that of the Italians. Thus before it actually became a mathematical work Euclid's *Elements* [*of Geometry*] was a text which had to be edited and translated with the greatest of care (and it is worth recalling that, after the Bible, the *Elements* enjoyed the greatest number of editions of all scientific treatises during the sixteenth century).[33] Similarly a medical work by Galen or Hippocrates was, to begin with, an imposing bundle of folios printed in Greek which the scholarly editor, aided by the printer, reproduced, translated, or organised according to the best philological principles. Indeed it was not unusual to see in the margins of such weighty treatises commentaries which dealt with difficult or out of the way expressions by citing not only recognised scientific authorities but also any Greek and Latin authors, including even poets, who had happened to use them. In short even if they had received their basic educational formation in other disciplines, such as the law in the case of Budé or medicine in the case of Champier, a large number of these humanist authors had such an encyclopaedic thirst for knowledge and such a capacity for work that they covered a lot of ground in a wide variety of scholarly endeavours, even if their many different writings and their polymathic learning did not necessarily imply fathoming these disciplines.

33. See P. L. Rose, *The Italian Renaissance of Mathematics: Studies on Humanists and Mathematicians from Petrarch to Galileo* (*Travaux d'Humanisme et Renaissance*, hereafter T. H. R., vol. 145: Geneva, 1975), especially Part II, ch. 8 ('Maurolico and the Renaissance of Greek Mathematics') and Part I, ch. 2 ('Humanist Origins of the Mathematical Renaissance'). Even though this book deals with Italy and the Italians, it is a pity that Bovelles is not even mentioned among the French mathematicians of the first half of the sixteenth century – he did, after all, produce the first treatise on geometry in French!

How, for example, should we consider the Picard Jacques Lefèvre d'Etaples?[34] The beginnings of his career had been marked by some small works on formal logic, as well as studies of a mathematical nature which represented a personal synthesis of fifteenth-century treatises inspired by Pythagoras and Aristotle. In this he had been helped by the collaboration of Josse Clichtove and Charles de Bovelles, who were his friends, pupils, and colleagues at the *Collège du Cardinal Lemoine*. But he was also known for his ingenious *Grammatographia*,[35] which was a grammar made up of arresting, lucid and exemplary scenes, and for his highly original commentaries on Aristotle. Mathematician, grammarian, and philosopher, Lefèvre could also quite justifiably be regarded as a theologian inasmuch as a whole series of his works focused on the Bible, which he interpreted and translated into French, thus bringing upon himself trouble with the religious establishment. But before making much progress in the study of mystical hermeneutics, for which he was prepared by his researches into the thought of Pseudo-Dionysius the Areopagite, whose authenticity as a disciple of St Paul and as the author of the mystical treatises known as the *Dionysiaca* he did not deny, Lefèvre was above all famous for inspiring the circle of Parisian humanists (many of whom were not Parisian in origin) who opposed the traditional teaching of the scholastics, whether in terms of grammar or in theology. Although rather too laconically, Reuchlin, the German Hebraist and humanist, gave a good summation of Lefèvre's eminent role in the development of French humanism: 'Marsilio Ficino', he wrote in his *De arte cabalistica*, 'gave Plato to Italy; Lefèvre d'Etaples has given Aristotle back to France.' Another German humanist, Heinrich Stromer, proclaimed his delight in living at a time when 'a scholar of divine inspiration, and master in all branches of learning', dedicated himself to freeing philosophy from the barbarism which had disfigured it for so long. Here we have the key word: barbarism! This accusatory term was levelled both at the bad Latin used during 'the barbaric age' (or 'the Gothic age', as Rabelais would have it) and at the routine commentaries which were repetitive, completely unoriginal, and devoid of any creative imagination.

As a final contemporary example we may cite the words of the great Italian humanist Mario Equicola, who in 1504 wrote to Cardinal Francesco Soderini more or less as follows: 'Mother Nature continues to produce prolifically, and each day she bestows on us works of genius

---

34. On what follows, see in particular E. F. Rice, Jr., *The Prefatory Epistles of Jacques Lefèvre d'Etaples* (New York and London, 1972); Guy Bedouelle, *Lefèvre d'Etaples et l'intelligence des Ecritures* (Geneva, 1976) (T. H. R. 152).

35. Jacques Lefèvre d'Etaples, *Grammatographia* (Paris, Simon de Colines, 1529).

which are more splendid than ever before.' Then, after praising the outstanding excellence of Giovanni Pontano and Baptista Mantuanus in poetry, Lascaris and Barbaro in encyclopaedic knowledge, and Pico and Ficino in esoterism, he comes to Lefèvre:

> Who after all would not admire Lefèvre for discovering the arcane recesses of philosophy? . . . If we venerate Aristotle, we should also venerate him. If we wish to understand Aristotle, let us read Lefèvre: he defines, analyses, explains, paraphrases, refutes, organises, clarifies, teaches, and, just like the rising sun, he dispels the clouds of obscurity surrounding each of Aristotle's works. Let those who wish to do so consult the ancient commentaries of Aristotle, Alexander, Themistius or Simplicius. As far as I am concerned, Lefèvre is sufficient.[36]

After a lapse of almost five centuries a twentieth-century historian of the Aristotelian tradition has to admit that he agrees entirely with the views of these contemporaries of Lefèvre concerning the introduction into France of radical innovations in the interpretation of Aristotle, beginning with a fundamental correction of the errors in translations which were the result of the quite inadequate knowledge of Greek, and often of Latin as well, which had characterised the Middle Ages. Lefèvre's success lay in the fact that, compared to the Arabic and Paduan traditions, a mastery of Greek and a concern for elegance were for him the necessary precondition for his own philosophical interpretations. A desire for clarity, which prompted him to modify the canonically-sanctioned translations, such as those of Boethius or Moerbecke, even as far as details were concerned, was always his golden rule, and he knew how to pass on his methodological principles to his students. Of these, we will limit mention to Gérard Roussel, who was to become Marguerite of Navarre's chaplain and bishop of Oloron, and François Vatable, who became one of the most famous regius professors of Hebrew.

Another pupil, who has already been mentioned and who collaborated with Lefèvre at the *Collège du Cardinal Lemoine*, was Charles

---

36. According to E. F. Rice, Jr., 'Humanist Aristotelianism in France: Jacques Lefèvre d'Etaples and his circle', in *Humanism in France at the End of the Middle Ages and in the Early Renaissance*, ed. A. H. T. Levi (Manchester and New York, 1970), p. 144, this letter of 11 Dec. 1504 was added *in extremis* to the last page of Lefèvre's book, . . . *totius philosophiae naturalis paraphrases*, which Henri Estienne was at that point just finishing to print – the date on the title page is 2 December, and the letter is on the verso of the last printed folio (fol. 348v.).

de Bovelles (Bovillus in Latin).[37] His was an attractive and very original personality, although for long little was known about him because not only was so much of his life shrouded in secrecy (information about him was meagre for several reasons), but his works, which with the passage of time became ever scarcer, were neglected for more than three centuries. Bovelles can be included among the French humanists for several reasons: he frequented Lefèvre's circle of friends, and was well acquainted with the Parisian humanists and printers Henri Estienne, Josse Bade, and later, Simon de Colines and others; he travelled extensively across Europe and met some of the great intellects of the age, such as Cardinal Ximénez de Cisneros, the astronomer and mathematician Bonet de Latès, the chancellor Jean de Ganay, and his brother, Germain; and his independence of mind frequently involved him in clashes with the theologians of the Sorbonne. Yet his Latin style lacked elegance, his syntax, when tested by the 'rules' of the Ciceronians or of Valla, was incorrect, and the sources for his inspiration were the Bible, Dionysius the Areopagite, the ecclesiastical writers of the late Roman period, and certain medieval commentators, rather than the good classical authors used by Vives, Erasmus, or even Budé. Moreover, after breaking with Lefèvre round about 1520 for reasons which are not very clear, but in which religious factors must have been decisive (inasmuch as the break coincided with the period when Lefèvre joined the group at Meaux and allied his destiny to that of Guillaume Briçonnet), he withdrew to Noyon where he became a canon of the cathedral (in addition to being a canon in his home town of Saint-Quentin). But above all most of his works fall within a philosophical, theological and mystical perspective which brings them closer to treatises of a metaphysical nature or to works of religious meditation than to the *studia humanitatis*. Hence neither his style, nor the authorities he cites, nor even his intentions can make it possible to consider his *Conclusions Théologiques*, his treatise entitled *Le Livre du Néant*, his *Comput des sept âges du monde*, his *Livre des sept péchés*, his letter on St Paul's rapture (*De raptu divi Pauli*), or his four books on Christ's Passion (*Agonologia Jesu Christi*) as being humanist texts. But for our purposes this fact is not an obstacle.

The continuity between the Middle Ages and the new age, the withdrawn and wary attitude towards Italy and her spectacular

---

37. On Bovelles, see for example the volume of the Actes du colloque international de Noyon, *Charles de Bovelles en son cinquième centenaire, 1479–1979*, ed. J.-C. Margolin (Paris, 1982), and the chapter on Bovelles in the *Anthologie des prosateurs français néo-latins* (Paris, 1987). See also the monograph of J. Victor, *Charles de Bovelles, 1479–1553: An Intellectual Biography* (Geneva, 1978) (T. H. R. 161) (which erroneously dates his death to 1553 instead of 1565).

achievements, the emphasis he placed on morality and religion, and the sense of a French and even Picard patriotism which at times prompted Bovelles to write in the vernacular (in his collections of proverbs,[38] in some of his poems, such as the one on the life of St Catherine,[39] and even, it should be emphasised, in his treatise on geometry published in French at the beginning of the century) – all these varied elements have to be laid to the account of French humanism, even if the glory of this particular humanism lies in its very peculiarity. After all, if we accept that the humanist movement insisted on man's pre-eminence over all other earthly creatures, or that the view relating to the correspondence between the microcosm and the macrocosm was largely used by those whom we unhesitatingly call humanists, then Bovelles' views on the relationship between man and the world fit into an intellectual perspective shared by Nicholas of Cusa, Pico della Mirandola, and Marsilio Ficino. For, in terms of the world, Bovelles held that man was its mirror, that it was his duty to bring together the intuitive and the intelligible, that man himself created a new world (that of memory), and that the relationship between man and the world was one of total solidarity. In addition he believed that before the Creation the world had been nothing more than the thought of God and that its future was linked to the fate of man. Even though Bovelles may have been far removed from 'the philosophy of Christ', as it had been conceived of by Vives, More, Budé, and Erasmus, nevertheless his works displayed a constant desire to bring theology and philosophy together, or at least *his* form of philosophy nurtured on neo-Platonic mysticism. This marked him off, if not from the great tradition of scholastic thought as exemplified by someone like Aquinas, then at least from its narrow-minded, decadent, and imitative practitioners who had transformed philosophy into the humble handmaiden of theology, to such an extent that they had reduced it to an arid and bloodless formulary in which human intelligence no longer had a place.

In his correspondence with Budé, Jean de Ganay, and Clichtove, as well as in his friendly dealings with the great astronomer and mathematician Oronce Fine, Bovelles demonstrated that his own mathematical works – on numbers, the problem of squaring the circle, and geometry (this last derived from Euclid) – were the fruit of uninterrupted thought. This observation prompts the question as to whether mathematical researches and treatises can be included in that humanist movement which we are attempting to define and, if so, under what

---

38. See above, note 28.

39. I have prepared an edition of this manuscript (Ms. 1134 of the Bibliothèque de la Sorbonne, fols., 73a–93a), which is now in press and will be published by Droz in Geneva.

conditions.[40] A first reaction might well be negative. We only need to recall what Erasmus said about the school programme which he drew up for boys and young men who were to obtain their 'certificate' in humanism: 'As far as arithmetic is concerned, it is enough that they should have a taste of it.' In fact in a civilisation where the liberal arts were clearly separated from technology and craftsmanship (it was up to the medical doctors to expound on the causes and treatment of disease just as it was up to the surgeons to busy themselves with dead bodies and dissect them), it might well be asked whether reckoning, surveying, and all the other practical skills relating to weighing and measuring had any relationship to humanism at all, even if Latin was used in the process (which was not generally the case anyway). But the mathematical speculations which the humanists treated and discussed with one another were carried out at precisely the level of intellectual contemplation and reflection to which they had been raised by Pythagoras, Plato and Euclid. It should not be forgotten that mathematics constituted part of the *Quadrivium* and that its relevance went beyond the necessary demonstrations and the openness to practical application (a constant preoccupation for someone like Bovelles, who was closely interested, for example, in the circular movement of cart-wheels, as well as in the movement of their different points) and reached upwards to philosophy and religion. There was much mathematical speculation which no longer had anything in common with mere technology – speculation on perfect numbers, the monad and the dyad, numerological and neo-Pythagorean reflections on the number corresponding to man, and metaphysical and religious meditations on the relationship between the triad and the Trinity or on the horizontality of analogical relationships and the verticality of 'assurrectional' ones (to use Bovelles' term). Even the ruler and the compass, which were both symbols and practical tools, were idealised, as were the straight line and circle. Mathematics had become a 'human' discipline thanks to humanist erudition, a return to the classical sources, and philosophy. The authors of the period bear witness to this point, as did later Peletier du Mans, Forcadel, and Oronce Fine, *lecteur royal* at the *Collège* of the same name.

It would be easy to make analogous points with respect to all the other scholarly disciplines, such as history, geography, law, and medicine. The case of Symphorien Champier[41] may perhaps be taken as an example of some of them, although it will be the difficult path which he followed which will above all hold our attention. Indeed if Lefèvre gave Aristotle back to France, it is also true to say that Cham-

40. This is understood by Rose, *op. cit., supra*, note 33.
41. On what follows, see B. P. Copenhaver, *Symphorien Champier and the Reception of the Occultist Tradition in Renaissance France* (The Hague–Paris–New York, 1978).

pier introduced the occult tradition in France. He was one of that group of scholars who made up the first generation of humanists in Lyon, among whom we could include Guillaume and Maurice Scève, although they were younger than Champier, Rabelais (because of his frequent contacts with Lyon), Etienne Dolet, the poet Visagier, and in the following generation the poet Claude de Taillemont or the grammarian Claude Mermet whose research speciality was orthography. The unity of this group is to be explained in terms of their love of Lyon, an independence of spirit which benefited from the absence of a Faculty of Theology and, when circumstances required it, from the proximity of Geneva, Savoy, and the duchy of Ferrara, and meetings in bookshops, rather than any identical views which they held concerning man and the world.[42]

A voracious reader and of unbounded curiosity, Champier, who as well as being a physician was twice an *échevin* of Lyon, had more or less thoroughly digested two contemporary works – the *Margarita philosophica* (1503), which was a vast encyclopaedia with a pronounced emphasis on astrology and the occult sciences, and the *Vita Marsilii Ficini* (1506) by the Italian Giovanni Corsi, which concentrated on those works by Ficino dealing with physiognomy, astrology, and natural magic. It could, it is true, be argued that Champier's *De quadruplici vita* (1507) was nothing more than an extension of Ficino's *De triplici vita*, if not a pillaging of it. But this does not alter the fact that it was thanks to Champier that the idea of man's ascent by means of four degrees, from physiological or animal life, via astrology, to the Christian sphere of a spiritual *vita supercoelestis*, became known first in the region round Lyon and then later in France generally (a mere glance at the list of the editions of his work establishes the point). As for Ficino's treatise, it was largely based on the *corpus* of the magical and hermetical tradition, which established a parallel relationship both between medicine and theology and the body and the soul, and which also sought to attain man's equilibrium by the proper use of the *spiritus*, governed and nourished by scents dispersed throughout the air, music and song. One merely needs to look at the title page of the *De quadruplici vita* to see the kinds of ideas and authors which Champier's eclectic and syncretic mind prompted him to include in this one work: a pharmacological treatise, an oration by Isocrates, the *Enchiridion* of Sextus the Pythagorean, extracts from Pliny the Younger, and some '*silvae medicinales*'. According to Champier and the hermetical tradition, natural magic was a form of wisdom as well as a secret science, and these in turn derived

---

42. See the *Actes du colloque de Lyon* (mai 1972), *L'Humanisme lyonnais au XVIe siècle* (Grenoble, 1974). A second volume on *L'humanisme lyonnais* (Actes du colloque de Macerata, 1985) has been published in 1988.

their power from a superior knowledge – but a knowledge which could not be rationally acquired or explained – of the hidden forces of nature. Moreover, in answer to the accusations which some Christians (and even some humanists) often levelled against such kinds of speculation, which seemed to turn man into a magician who dispensed with the all-powerfulness of God and divine providence, Champier could defend himself by claiming that natural magic, like other varieties of natural divination, astrological predictions, and medical diagnoses, etc., had nothing in common with the demoniacal or diabolical practices in which contemporaries believed. After all, was not this occult medical philosophy based on a profound study, as well as an intuitive under-standing, of the workings of God with respect to the natural world?

Although Champier wrote in Latin, he also produced a fair number of works in French (and this, as we have already seen, was not an absolute criterion debarring someone from belonging to the humanist movement). He wrote several medical works in Latin, such as the *Rosa gallica* (1514) which contained precepts culled from a whole library of Greek and Arabic physicians, the Platonically inspired *Periarchon* (1515?), the *Mirabilia* (1517), the *Pronosticon* (1518), which dealt with the three categories of prediction (those of the prophets, astrologers, and physicians), and many other treatises. But it should be remembered that Champier became the champion of both the nation's glory and the French language by writing his *Recueil ou croniques des hystoires des royaulmes d'Austrasie ou France orientale dite a present Lorrayne, de Hierusalem, de Cicile* (Lyon, 1510), and then the *Grans croniques des gestes et vertueux faicts des tresexcellens catholicques illustres et victorieux ducz et princes des pays de Savoye e Piemont* (Paris, 1516). Moreover, he commented on and discussed the great social problems of the age, contributing most notably to the question of the role and place of women in civil society. Following the example of Sebastian Brant, while at the same time being critical of the spirit which informed his *Narrenschiff* as well as Badius' *Nef des Folles*, he wrote *La nef des dames vertueuses* which, first published in 1503 (?) and then again in 1515, was made up of four books: 'the first is entitled the flower of women, the second concerns marriage; the third is about the Sibylline prophecies. And the fourth is the book of true love. . . .'. If one excludes the third book, which deals with a very precise subject relating to Champier's interest in divination and the occult, then this *Nef des dames vertueuses* steered a course in the wake of which many other 'ships' would follow: those of Vives, More, Budé, Marguerite of Navarre, and all those champions of women's rights, of the liberty of the two sexes in choosing a partner, and of the education of girls, who enlisted them-selves and with good cause, into the humanist movement. We only need to cite the case of the *sénéchal* of Toulouse and *seigneur* of Drusac,

Gratian du Pont, whose outrageous and scabrous misogyny, absolute
conservatism, and profound hostility towards the humanists were
rewarded with the wickedly-tipped barbs which were aimed at him
during his stay in the capital of Languedoc by the young Etienne Dolet,
spokesman for the French nation and fresh both from his studies at the
University of Padua and from decisive encounters in Italy, such as those
with the 'Ciceronians' Longueil and Simon de Villeneuve.

Despite the fact that his judgement may have been affected by the
violence of his passions, his ambitions, and his tenacious hates (which
some, like Scaliger, more than fully reciprocated), it is precisely to
Dolet[43] that we will now turn because, even more brilliantly than
Champier, he provides us with an almost perfect paradigm of French
humanism as well as being an example of the expansion of philology
and all its many 'side-effects'. For if it is true that Dolet, like many
other gifted young men of his day, received a legal education, we will
be concerned above all with Dolet as a philologist, while paying some
attention to him as a poet, translator, editor, and printer. In fact during
the five years or so which he spent in Italy, mainly in Padua and
Venice, he passed the time studying in Faculties of Arts and learning
about Ciceronian eloquence and classical culture.

If it is difficult to pass over Dolet's stance in the quarrel over the
*Ciceronianus*[44] apropos of the problems concerning imitation, the *translatio studii* from Italy to neighbouring countries, including France, and
above all the chronological and ideological divide between the civilisation of the age of Caesar and that of the European Renaissance, we
will certainly not dwell on these matters for long. Indeed humanism
was not a unilateral doctrine to which all its disciples had necessarily
to conform. On the other hand, by violently and contemptuously
standing up to the elderly Erasmus, who was famous throughout
Europe and admired by even his religious enemies, and by falsely
pretending that he was an opponent of Cicero, and hence a kind of
'barbarian', the young and hot-tempered Dolet wanted above all to pay
homage both to the Italy where he had spent the best years of his youth
and to his recently deceased young teacher, Simon de Villeneuve. But
at the same time he was trying to attract the esteem – or at least the
curiosity – of intellectuals by his very violence and lack of conformity.
We will not therefore stop to consider his *Dialogus de Imitatione Cicero-
niana, adversus Desiderium Erasmum Roterodamum pro Christophoro*

43. See M. Chassaigne, *Etienne Dolet* (Paris, 1930); R. C. Christie, *Etienne Dolet*
(Paris, 1886; repr. Geneva, 1969).

44. The complete title of Erasmus' work is *Dialogus cui titulus Ciceronianus sive de
optimo dicendi genere* (Basel, Froben, 1528). See the edition, with an Italian translation, by
A. Gambaro, *Il Ciceroniano* (Brescia, 1965).

*Longolio* (1535),[45] (Longueil had been the butt of Erasmus' irony in the *Ciceronianus*), but will turn instead to that remarkable and celebrated philological treatise, Dolet's *Commentaires de la langue latine (Commentarii linguae Latinae)*, which was first published in 1536 and hailed in all humanist circles as a masterpiece of precision and erudition. The articles, which were arranged in alphabetical order, were far from corresponding to a purely scientific undertaking – 'scientific', that is, in the sense of being ideologically neutral. Indeed they fully reveal Dolet's personality, as was generally the case with this peculiarly humanist genre of commentaries,[46] as has been already noted in the case of Budé's digressions, and as can be seen on almost every page of Erasmus' *Adnotationes* to the New Testament.

A few examples will suffice. Thus the word *Acrimonia* provided Dolet with the opportunity to rake over his past history in order to denounce his enemies or '*obtrectatores*', whom he actually names (for example, Menapius), because they had reproached him for speaking ill of Erasmus. In fact he adds that he had excellent reasons for attacking Erasmus and that he will return to the fray if necessary. As another example of an article in which he refers to Erasmus, or rather with all due respect to the '*scriptator Batavus*' ('the Dutch scribbler!'), let us consider an expression which is apparently devoid of any ideological connotation: '*pro rata*'. This is of course the abbreviated form of '*pro rata parte*'. Dolet, therefore takes the opportunity of confessing that his own Ciceronianism does not extend to condemning the first form of the expression, and he adds that, on this point, he does not differ from the person whom he has so unjustly and cavalierly referred to as 'the Dutch scribbler'. He also grasps the chance to reject all that is vulgar, dirty, sordid, and proverbial, by implying that his selected opponent does not disdain to use a 'low' style (at least as far as his references are concerned). Other articles, like *religio, libertas*, etc, are shot through with Dolet's personal views. And in still other cases, such as the articles *fatum, divinatio, miraculum*, etc., it is possible to question his interpretation and even to ask whether or not there has been a personal intervention by the Latinist lexicologist – which is what Jean Céard[47] has done in his critique of Busson's 'rationalist' interpretation.[48]

---

45. See the *facsimile* of the original edition published with a long study and extensive notes, by E. V. Telle, *L'Erasmianus sive Ciceronianus d'Etienne Dolet (1535)* (Geneva, 1974) (T. H. R. 134).

46. See J. Céard, 'Les transformations du genre du commentaire', in *L'Automne de la Renaissance 1580–1630* (Paris, 1981), pp. 101–15.

47. J. Céard, *La Nature et les Prodiges* (Geneva, 1977) (T. H. R. 158), pp. 106–11.

48. H. Busson, *Le Rationalisme dans la littérature française de la Renaissance* (2nd edn, Paris, 1957).

The career and work of Dolet constitute a good example of the way in which philology penetrated into other disciplines. His Latin poems can be passed over quickly. Writing such poems was a traditional pastime for all French or foreign humanists, and they are more often characterised by a judicious application of the metres of classical authors, biographical indications, dithyrambic eulogies of friends or patrons, and peevish remarks about opponents, rather than by any genuine personal inspiration. But he was also preoccupied by the problems posed by translation (*La Manière de bien traduire d'une langue en autre*)[49] and in the technical art of punctuation, and if these interests undoubtedly always corresponded to a programme of philological research, they were also concerned above all with the defence and illustration of the vernacular language as well as the culture of his own times. As for his editions of books in French, such as Marot's *Enfer* and *Psaumes*, Rabelais' *Gargantua*, and the Genevan French Bible, they point more to an ideological commitment, which at times bordered on provocation, rather than to any real desire to expand the frontiers of knowledge.

The great Rabelais has just been mentioned.[50] He occupies a quite exceptional place both in French literature and in the humanist movement. Despite the contradictory judgements about his famous novel, made both at the time and during the ensuing centuries, and even despite continuing uncertainties as to his true purpose, which have not been dispelled by close examination of his prefaces, *Gargantua* and *Pantagruel* can with good reason be considered as a vast humanist enterprise. Here we have a '*jocoserium*' à *la francaise*, where paradoxes are pushed to the extreme limits of probability, but where, behind the fiction about giants, the excesses of language, and the obscenities – and perhaps because of them – the gravest problems of the age and of the human condition are paraded before our eyes: the problems of war and peace (in the war waged by King Picrochole), of marriage, education, and religion, etc. If the humanists were more preoccupied with the social, political, and cultural problems of their own age rather than with an improbable or even a purely illusory return to the customs of a vanished past (whether of Pericles or of Cicero), then Rabelais fully participated in this movement. It would be a mistake to attempt to

---

49. Etienne Dolet, *La Manière de bien traduire d'une langue en autre* (Lyon, Etienne Dolet, 1540).

50. It is hardly possible to cite the two or three fundamental studies of Rabelais without being arbitrary. However, the series of *Etudes rabelaisiennes*, published in Geneva by Droz (T. H. R. series), can be recommended. See also the chapter on Rabelais in Giraud and Jung, *op. cit.*, I, pp. 243–59; Guy Demerson, *Rabelais* (Paris, 1986); *Etudes Rabelaisiennes XXI* (Colloque de Tours, 1984), ed. J. Céard and J.-C. Margolin (Genève, 1988) (T. H. R. 225).

differentiate too neatly between Rabelais' Latin works – at least those which have survived – and his two-in-one classic of French fiction. Of course the Latin or Latino-Greek letters which he sent to his contemporaries – Guillaume Budé, the jurist Tiraqueau, the poet Jean Bouchet, the *officer* Amaury Bouchard, and Geoffroy d'Estissac, bishop of Maillerais, not to mention Bernard Salignac through whom he addressed Erasmus himself, as has long been known[51] – are different in style from the chapters of *Gargantua* or *Pantagruel*. But in them one finds the same erudition, the same appetite for life, the same concern about social problems, such as the role of medicine in the contemporary world, and the same desire to bring the texts of Hippocrates or of Pliny back to life within the context of progress.

If there was one area of scholarship on which philology had a resounding success, it was indeed on that of medicine, which is so omnipresent in the thought and work of Rabelais – but it was a medicine which witnessed the breaching of the barrier which separated theory from practice. This can be clearly seen in the letter which he sent from Lyon, on 3 June 1532, to André Tiraqueau:

> Among those of our times who have devoted all their efforts to resurrect the ancient and authentic medicine in all its glory is the famous Manardi, whom you did not fail to mention and rightly praise when I was staying with you: this Ferraran doctor combines practical and theoretical excellence, and you value his first letters just as much as those which Paean or Aesculapius might have dictated . . .[52]

This eulogy of an Italian physician, whose second volume of the *Medical Epistles*[53] Rabelais was to edit for publication by Sebastian Gryphius at Lyon (it would be his first scholarly publication), bears eloquent testimony to the open-mindedness of the future doctor of the Faculty of Medicine at Montpellier. In the case of this Poitevin, who made several trips to Italy, staying at Rome and Turin, there was no feeling of jealousy towards an ultramontane colleague. Whether he was editing Hippocrates and Galen, or publishing his *Pantagrueline Prognostication* or drawing up his '*Grande et vraye Pronostication nouvelle pour l'an 1544*' under the pseudonym of Seraphino Calbarsy (an anagram of 'Phrançoys Rabelais'), the 'benevolent readers' to whom he addressed

---

51. See the texts and the translations (by Geneviève Demerson) of these letters in *Rabelais (Oeuvres complètes)* ed. Guy Demerson (Paris, 1973), pp. 933 ff.

52. *Ibid*, p. 944.

53. *Epistolarum medicinalium tomus secundus*.

himself were not different in nature from those for whom he wrote his novel.

A final remark about Rabelais has its symbolic value. In one and the same publication Rabelais in 1549 combined his *Sciomachie*,[54] which is an account in French of a Roman *fête* given by his protector, Cardinal Jean du Bellay, with a Latin ode by the same cardinal in honour of the duke of Orléans. He was displaying a whole series of humanist accomplishments: the use of classical erudition in order to glorify a princely protector, the new king, Henry II; the associating of Latin poetry with French prose; the mixture of serious with funny matters; and the emphasising of the bonds between the royal house of France and the capital of Italy (without any of that animosity which we have occasionally emphasised). Rabelais, according to Chateaubriand, was the founder of French literature. Jean-Louis Barrault for his part compared him to a tree whose roots 'absorbed the loam and manure', whose trunk was 'stiff like a phallus', whose foliage was 'encyclopaedic', and whose flowering was 'united with God'.[55] He was certainly a wonderful and accomplished product of that period of French humanism which we have had no hesitation in extending down to the date of Rabelais' death in 1553.

Without wishing to apply at any cost the adjectival label of 'humanist' to each and every manifestation of the intellect which we might be able to detect during this period, even if the humanist movement was important in the formation of men and had its 'ambassadors' among the printers, in numerous colleges, at the royal court, in the royal administration, and in the episcopal and archiepiscopal sees, yet we must still admit that the spirit of humanism profoundly affected the various scientific, artistic, and literary disciplines. French poetry, as represented by the works of a Clément Marot,[56] doubtless responded to all kinds of demands, and the personal genius of Marot owed nothing to Horace, Virgil, or Pindar. And yet since he constantly had recourse to the mythology and other cultural aspects of antiquity, and because he translated two Latin Colloquies by Erasmus, the first two books of Ovid's *Metamorphoses*, and works by Virgil, Martial, Lucian, Musaeus and, from Italian, Petrarch and Beroaldo, as well as plunging into the great genre of religious lyric poetry and making his personal commitment evident by his translation of the Psalms, Marot was indeed a humanist.

---

54. See the text in the edition by Demerson, pp. 979–86.
55. The quotation is from J.-L. Barrault, *Rabelais* (Paris, 1968), p. 12.
56. On Marot, see the bibliographical summary on him and on Marot studies in Giraud and Jung, I, pp. 335–6.

If we now turn to the treatise on anatomy by Charles Estienne,[57] who was also a humanist printer, translator of Italian works, editor of Ortensio Landi's *Paradossi* (1543), author of the first French travellers' guide to France, the author and editor of works on botany and agriculture, and the editor and adapter of the archaeological treatises of Lazare de Baif, we must surely recognise that its presentation and illustrations reveal the same universal and anthropological spirit. For his *De dissectione partium corporis humani* (1545), which was published in a French edition in 1546, a fact which in itself constitutes a deliberate programme of scholarship, contained among its plates, albeit with the inevitable adaptations required by such a process, a series like *The Loves of the Gods*, which had been drawn by the artist Perino del Vaga in 1527 and then engraved by Jacopo Caraglio of Verona. And when one also remembers that the *Narcissus* by the Mannerist painter Rosso, which is suffused with mythology, appears in this same treatise, but with the bony cap of his skull removed by Estienne (and the artist who helped him) in order to reveal features of the brain, or when one notes that certain biblical scenes are transformed in this same treatise into landscapes peopled with anatomical demonstration-figures, then one cannot help but be struck by this feeling of continuity between art and nature, between life and death, and between aesthetics and science, as well as by the presence of an invisible '*Memento mori*', a sword of Damocles permanently suspended above our heads.

The same points could be made with respect to the anatomical or surgical iconography of Vesalius, in his *Fabrica* (1543),[58] or of the Italian physician Vidius (alias Guido Guidi),[59] who was a *lecteur royal* at Paris. As for Robert Estienne, Henri (I)'s son and Charles' brother, some reference has already been made to his greatness as a lexicographer and humanist. His specialised dictionaries, such as those on agriculture and on arboriculture, certainly cater for the humanist concern over education, but they also respond – and this is true even of his apparently fastidious lists of the different varieties of apples or pears – to a desire to have as participants in a feast of language and tasting both the tongue which talks and the tongue which feels and tastes, the eyes which read and the eyes which see the bunches of fruit on the trees. Erasmus had already made this human joy well up in his literary and festive *Banquets*.

57. See E. Lau, *Charles Estienne* (Wertheim, 1930); P Huard and M. D. Grmek, *L'Oeuvre de Charles Estienne et l'Ecole anatomique parisienne* (Paris, 1965); C. E. Kellett, *Medical Illustrations and the School of Fontainebleau* (Durham, 1957).

58. Andreas Vesalius, *De humani corporis fabrica*, (Basel, Oporin, 1543).

59. See M. D. Grmek, *La fondation de la première chaire de médecine au Collège de France et la personnalité de Vidus Vidius* (Paris, 1968).

## V

Even if the humanist movement – and perhaps the plural form would be more appropriate for the various forms or manifestations of humanism – only directly concerned an intellectual elite of authors, magistrates, *parlementaires*, teachers, and prelates, leaving the vast majority of French men and women of the period to live and die without feeling its effects, it nevertheless progressively and profoundly exercised a considerable historical influence, which we are able to appreciate only because of the distance which separates us from the Renaissance. Doubtless, as happens with most new ideas or audacious reforms, the sheer weight of the political and religious establishment structures, as well as of economic and administrative routines, the inertia of aged institutions, the general fear of novelty, and the illiteracy or scanty education of the majority of people were among the factors which delayed the assimilation of these effects into the very heart and substance of French life.

The problem of the interconnections between humanism and the Reformation in France will not be examined here because we do not subscribe to the thesis – a thesis which for long enjoyed a wide success and which still has its supporters – that the humanist movement contained within itself some powerful 'fermenting agents' of the Reformation. As we have already demonstrated elsewhere, if the phenomenon of humanism cannot be tackled independently of the religious problem,[60] and doubtless also of the problem of reforms in general, such as the various kinds of reform taking place in society, education, moral habits, and religion, nevertheless the reaction of the individual representatives of this vast cultural movement were different and, at times, contradictory. When faced with a radical change and its associated impact on life-styles and belief-systems, we should not simply ignore the varying factors and biographical circumstances of individual people. But we may note in passing that, with few exceptions, those of the French humanists whose sensibilities or even beliefs were, or became, 'reformed' during this period, did not break with the past in the same marked manner as the German humanists did at the time when Luther's break with Rome was consummated. The fact is that the religious history of France was very different to that of Germany, that Francis I favoured a good number of daring ideas, and that if in this respect the Affair of the Placards marked a reaction, it nevertheless did not stop or even slow down the developing emancipation of thought.

---

60. See J.-C. Margolin, *L'humanisme en Europe* (op. cit.), ch. 3 ('L'humanisme et la problématique religieuse'), pp. 63–80.

If humanism was the bearer of reforms, then its foremost impact was on the fields of intellectual and educational endeavour. It was at a veritable 'moral and intellectual reform of France', to use the well-known expression of Renan on the morrow of the war of 1870, that most of the men under study aimed. We have also noted the interest which the king attached to the foundation of the most advanced learned institution conceivable at that time, the *Collège Royal*, and the efforts which he expected from the great intellectuals, the humanists with Budé to the fore, in support of his ambition. The growing centralisation of the state made the king of France the recognised protector of the arts and *belles lettres*, and, with Renaissance allegory and symbolism doing the rest, turned him into a veritable mythical hero. Louis XII was not simply 'the Father of the People'; he was Hector, the brave and unfortunate warrior whose moral virtues were more highly valued than his warlike courage. As for Francis I, a recent book has depicted him, both textually and iconographically, in the different roles and guises which he assumed at varying times – as the Knight of the Cross, a new Constantine, 'the son of Dame Prudence', the second Caesar, or the 'patron and restorer' *par excellence* of the *studia humanitatis*.[61] Among the many tasks conferred on him by Charles VIII and Louis XII, Gaguin was several times rector of the University of Paris, and in this capacity he worked hard to achieve a better balance in the programmes of study of those Faculties which were within his jurisdiction, notably by introducing a much higher percentage of classical authors.

If France did not produce an Erasmus in pedagogical matters, there were a great many teachers in Paris and in the provinces, not all of whose names have survived to posterity, who followed the methodology and the deontological ethics which Erasmus had inculcated into them through his theoretical treatises, such as the *De ratione studii* (or Programme of Studies) and his *De pueris instituendis* (or The Education of Boys). They followed his fundamental conviction, as expressed in the latter work just cited: 'Man is not born a man, he becomes one' (that is, he becomes one by study and by the fruitful collaboration between teacher and pupil). As Chartier, Compère, and Julia have shown in their book,[62] towns were in relative terms massively privileged as far as the cultural infrastructure was concerned, the village school being still in its infancy and hardly influenced by reforming humanism. The economically important towns, those in which printing flourished, such as Paris, Lyon, and Rouen, were also those in which teaching was carried out with most constancy. The administrative,

---

61. See A.-M. Lecoq, *François Ier imaginaire* (Paris, 1987).
62. R. Chartier, M. M. Compère, and D. Julia, *L'éducation en France du XVIe au XVIIIe siècle* (Paris, 1976).

ecclesiastical, and commercial functions of the towns largely contributed to this end. An indication of this intellectual and educational effervescence can be detected in the many school *Colloques*, notably those of Mathurin Cordier, the great pedagogue and school-teacher who spent most of his very long life teaching young boys in Paris, Nevers, Bordeaux, Geneva, Neuchâtel, and Lausanne.[63] He originally conceived his dialogues after the fashion of those by Erasmus and Vives, that is as Latin exercises for the use of schoolboys, but his personal disposition and the evolution of his career prompted him to convert to Calvinism and to introduce more and more religious material into his writing. In fact, shortly before his death in 1559, he did not shrink from writing a highly edifying *Miroir de la Jeunesse* in French, and he even translated his own *Colloquia scholastica* into French.[64]

In effect at a time, during the 1530s, when humanist teachers prohibited their young schoolboys from talking in their own language, even during periods of relaxation or recreation, Cordier thought that it was better to make available a good translation from the Latin rather than to put up with the macaronic Latin jargon used by his pupils. During the course of the century several generations of pupils were to be educated in this fashion, nurtured on good letters and good manners, even if the nature of the moral education they received seems to us today to be old-fashioned and touchingly 'simplistic':

> Le bon enfant craint le Seigneur
> En reverence et tout honneur;
> L'enfant pervers n'a de Dieu crainte
> Et ne fait bien que par contrainte . . .
>
> Le bon enfant aime l'école,
> Vertu et Dieu, et sa parolle;
> Au desbauché est desplaisant
> Tout ce qui est à Dieu plaisant . . .

But of course it is also true that the 134 quatrains of the *Miroir de la jeunesse* were aimed at very young schoolboys, and that we could still point to nineteenth-century catechisms or lay moral books which adopted the same tone and were based on a similarly naive duality.

Even in humanist schools proper, that is in the 'Latin' schools where the programmes of study were essentially based on classical authors,

---

63. See J. Le Coultre, *Mathurin Cordier et les origines de la pédagogie protestante* (Neuchâtel, 1926).

64. Written about 1559, when Cordier was already eighty years old, these *Colloquia scholastica* were not published until a few weeks before his death, by Robert Estienne at Geneva in 1564.

the life of the schoolboys and discipline in general remained ecclesiastical in spirit. It would be wrong and absurdly anachronistic to think
in terms of municipal schools which were lay (in the modern sense of
the word) as opposed to capitular or parish schools – all schools were
Christian in inspiration, and this was as true of Lutheran and Calvinist
regions as it was of the Catholic-controlled provinces. Christian and
humanist principles, in alliance together, contributed to the schooling
of a growing number of children – boys, of course, because concepts
of liberty and of personal and social responsibility were hardly applied
to girls since the socio-historic status of women and anti-feminist prejudices, from which even the humanists did not escape, would not have
permitted otherwise. The female imagination, irritability, and all the
other handicaps which reputedly stemmed from the physiological
nature of women, as well as both the civil and religious traditions, were
further factors which restricted the education of girls. Yet at the same
time those women who did manage to attain to the cultural level and
energetic qualities of men were admired. These were the 'viragos' so
dear to Erasmus. Indeed in one of his colloquies one of these women,
Magdalena, holds her own against an abbot who, because of his old-
fashioned prejudices, is both ignorant and stupid.[65] This may seem to
be a contradiction, but it also shows that there was a consciousness
about this particular social problem.

Which children benefited from education? Were the poor included
in this programme of intellectual and moral reform? If not all teachers
came up with a solution to this problem, which was both a human and
an economic one, in 1539 the charitable *Police de l'Aumône* of Lyon
reviewed the plight of the 'poor orphans', boys and girls alike, and
decided to put the girls into the *hôpital Sainte-Catherine* and the boys
into the *hôpital de la Chanal* in order to 'teach them to read and write,
and to learn all the other good habits which can and should be taught
to young children'. Although this was far from being a unique case,
it must nevertheless be admitted that the educational ideal outlined by
Gargantua in his letter to Pantagruel, and enshrined in the Abbey of
Thélème, undeniably involved social and economic selectivity. Moreover, as has been seen, education was generally directed more to the
art of speaking than to dialectic or argumentation, and this meant that
rhetoric was the most important discipline, along with all its
accompanying images, figures, and symbols, which contributed to the
creation of successive levels or disparate or contrasting terrains of
discourse and to achieving a growing adaptation to the demands of a

---

65. See the French translation of his *colloque* by L.-E. Halkin in *Les Colloques d'Erasme*
(Brussels, 1971), pp. 89–96 ('Le Père Abbé et la Femme instruite').

society which was more subject to law and order, and more worldly and diversified.

In the realms of education and the transmission of culture,[66] French humanism, if we can put it this way, represented an equilibrium between Italian humanism, which was brilliant, more extrovert, and immersed in civil society, and the humanism of the Netherlands, which was more introverted, concerned with the ethico-religious formation of the individual, and anxious to turn the process of educating the young into a veritable apostolate. It should also be noted that, for reasons which were not simply geographical ones, a large number of the schoolmasters of Paris were from the Low Countries: men like Petrus de Ponte from Bruges who published Latin poems and manuals and who, apart from his blindness, led an otherwise unremarkable professional and personal life, or Gilles de Delft, who was born in the diocese of Utrecht but became *lector ethicorum* in the Faculty of Arts of Paris towards the end of the fifteenth century. He also played an important role in the Faculty of Theology and intervened in the *affaire* Reuchlin in a way which did not apparently please all the humanists. Doubtless this kind of influence was counterbalanced by someone like Fausto Andrelini[67] who, in the Paris of Charles VIII, Louis XII, and the early years of Francis I's reign, represented the kind of ultramontane poet, humanist and teacher who, by his colourful nature and facetious humour, was capable of livening up the drabness of a *Quartier Latin* which was still so 'scholastic' and dominated by the austere Sorbonne.

Similar points could be made about other social problems, such as those relating to poverty, the role of women (which we have already encountered), and the 'vertical' relationships within French society: in different ways and with differing degrees of intensity, the preoccupation with such problems appears like a watermark at the very heart of the writings of the humanists. But what should be emphasised here is the historical consciousness of socio-cultural change. As Franco Simone has pointed out,[68] men like Robert Gaguin, Lefèvre d'Etaples and Guillaume Budé experienced and expressed a real enthusiasm for the age in which they lived and which they helped to build. But at the same time this awareness of a new historical age was reinforced, in the case

---

66. See E. Garin, *L'Educazione in Europa, 1400–1600: Problemi e programmi* (Bari, 1957; trans. into French as *L'Education de l'homme moderne*, Paris, 1968).

67. On Fausto Andrelini and his work, see the monograph by G. Tournoy-Thoen, *Publi Fausti Andrelini 'Amores' sive 'Livia', met een biobibliografie van de auteur* (Brussels, 1982).

68. F. Simone, 'Une entreprise oubliée des humanistes français. De la prise de conscience historique du renouveau culturel à la naissance de la première histoire littéraire', in *Humanism in France* (*op. cit.*, supra, note 36), pp. 106–31.

of many such men, by a veritable re-elaboration and re-evaluation of an entire concept of history. With the exception of the Italians, the French humanists possessed a historical sensibility which was more refined than that of humanists in the other countries of Europe. The historical awareness of the Renaissance was reinforced by a reorganisation of the medieval conception of the ages of world history: the ancient world, the Middle Ages, and the modern age made up the three stages of this historiographical trajectory. Nothing could be clearer with respect to the first aspect than Budé's stance in his *De philologia*, which derived from Petrarch but which also aimed to take on the appearance of a manifesto: the new age was separated from antiquity by a period of one thousand years.[69] And this stance was all the more remarkable because it was perfectly combined with an enthusiastic researching of the nation's historical and even mythical antiquities.[70]

An evolutionary conception of history, as well as the idea of progress, was opposed to the view that history was cyclical. Simone has pointed out that at a time when Italian humanism, following Petrarch, was proclaiming itself the only and unique heir of Rome, the French humanists of the fourteenth century already felt that they were the heirs of a direct tradition. This was a continuity which would be emphasised again by Gaguin and Champier. Among the French humanists there existed both a feeling of admiration for the image of culture, as incarnated by Petrarch, and the desire to free themselves from the Italian model. It is interesting to note, for example, that Champier reprinted an *Epistola contra Franciscum Petrarcam* by the fourteenth-century French humanist Jean de Hesdin in his *Duellum epistolare* with Girolamo da Pavia.[71] It was in this way that the Petrarchan schema of ten centuries of darkness, which Budé too hastily adopted, would be modified by historians, during the reigns of Louis XII, Francis I, and Henry II – from Longueil and Claude de Seyssel and, via Jean Bouchet, down to Papire Masson, Bodin, and Fauchet. Paris would be proclaimed the new Athens, and it would be a man of Ronsard's generation, Guy de Brués, who would roundly and emphatically declare that 'foreign nations of the present age are invited to come to France in order to acquire learning, just as in ancient times men went to the famous city of Athens'.[72]

---

69. Guillaume Budé, *De philologia* (Basel, *apud* Ioan, Uvalderum, 1533), p. 155.

70. In fact, as we have already seen the mythical dimension loomed much larger in the work of someone like Lemaire de Belges.

71. The text was printed at the end of a collection of historical studies which Champier published in Lyon in 1507, following his *Liber de quadruplici vita*.

72. See *Les Dialogues contre les nouveaux académiciens*, ed. P. P. Morphos (Baltimore, 1953), p. 87.

## Chapter Nine

# Humanism in Germany

## LEWIS W. SPITZ

### I

In his sparkling and splendid book *The Italian Renaissance in its Historical Background*, Denys Hay wrote:

> To start with, I accept as a fact that there was a Renaissance in the period (to beg a few questions at any rate for the time being) between about 1350 and about 1700. I accept that this Renaissance occurred first in Italy in the fourteenth and fifteenth centuries and that it later affected to a greater or lesser degree the rest of Europe. I say this, because to my mind the evidence is overwhelming.[1]

It seems also to me, after four decades of reading, research, and writing, the 'three R's' of the historian, that the evidence is quite convincing. The impact of the Italian Renaissance upon both the Renaissance and the Reformation in Germany is clear and indisputable. This essay is designed in part as a *mea culpa* (even St Augustine wrote *Retractiones*) and in part to underline the fact that Denys Hay was right and that other unrepentant and intellectually limited scholarly journalists have often been wrong, but can still be rehabilitated. The Reformation, for example, was not a 'miscarriage' of late scholasticism, but it was a rebirth in the same sense as was the Renaissance. The German Renaissance and German humanism, very much dependent upon Italian

---

1. D. Hay, *The Italian Renaissance in its Historical Background.* (Cambridge, 1961), p. 1.

humanism and the great Italian awakening, naturally fused with cultural elements already present in the North.

As to the origins of the northern Renaissance, an earlier theory proposed an indigenous northern phenomenon blossoming under Emperor Charles IV in Prague, founder in 1348 of the university of Prague. His chancellor, Johannes von Neumarkt, authorized a new book of forms for epistolary and chancery documents which was said to have introduced a 'new style' into German and Latin public documents. The notary Johann von Tepl, author of the *Ackermann aus Böhmen*, a discussion between Death and a simple ploughman about the regrettable demise of his wife, is said to have been influenced by Petrarch, but the cultural passages with their references to Plato, Seneca, and Boethius basically reflect medieval sources. This formal type of 'humanism' was transmitted by Albert of Austria, the son-in-law of Sigismund, the last of the Luxembourg rulers. Scholars such as Conrad Burdach and Karl Brandi decades ago argued that the influence of Cola di Rienzo in Prague, who had declared himself a tribune of a new Roman Republic, and barely escaped with his life, was of humanistic inspirational significance in the Holy Roman Empire. Occasionally what great scholars dig up, they should promptly immediately rebury!

Moreover, the 'northern indigenous theory' urged that because of the revival of the scholastic *via antiqua* in the Germanies around the middle of the fifteenth century, a climate favourable to a classical revival was created.[2] Further, it was argued that in one way or another nearly all of the septentrional humanists were birthed or directed by the Brethren of the Common Life, founded by Gerard Groote, who died in 1384. In the year of our Lord 1988 we are treated to academic sessions in celebration of the six hundredth anniversary of the *Devotio Moderna*, a pale reflection of those in 1983 dedicated to the memory of Luther and Marx (Luther's birth and Marx's death!), following those for Goethe! A bit more research should be devoted to the continued influence and the reasons for the eventual decline and end of the Brethren in the late sixteenth century, despite the fact that the reformer Martin Luther was consistently a defender and protector of the Brethren. Luther argued that they, like all nuns in a convent, should be left in peace to live out their lives in service and tranquillity so long

---

2. Of recent articles, two are the most commendable: N. L. Brann, 'Humanism in Germany,' in A. Rabil, Jr, ed., *Renaissance Humanism: Foundations, Forms, and Legacy*, II: *Humanism Beyond Italy* (Philadelphia, 1988), pp. 123–55; E. Meuthen, 'Charakter und Tendenzen des deutschen Humanismus', in H. Angermeier and R. Seyboth, eds., *Säkulare Aspekte der Reformationszeit* (Munich and Vienna, 1983) pp. 216–66.

as they acknowledged Jesus Christ as their all-sufficient Saviour.[3] The Brethren, whether they taught schools, supported students in schools and at the universities, or published many works of piety, were a major influence in the development of German humanism, which was the foremost expression of the German Renaissance. Of course, there were Albrecht Dürer, Hans Holbein, Lucas Cranach and Catholic Renaissance artists, *creatores* of the baroque which blossomed out in the later beauty that all adore in Würzburg, Munich, and in many lesser localities, centres of baroque and then rococco art. But Professor Miriam Chrisman is correct in referring to the 'academic humanism' of the later sixteenth century, a point to be taken up in this essay. Hans Holbein moved to England, Martin Bucer moved from Strasbourg to England, western Atlantic trade and industry moved to Holland and England, and Germany lost out in these cultural and material things, but not in all. There was a shift to the west in Europe, God's playground, and there is no doubt that Central Europe, Italy, and Germany paid a heavy price for the dislocation.

Some of those who have urged a northern origin of the Renaissance have skated on ice thinner than that of the Dutch canals, arguing that northern humanism and then the Reformation were bred in the festering ferment of German mysticism. This mysticism placed man directly in the presence of the ineffable God and reflected an over-whelming inward religious experience. People as intelligent as Hegel have written about the 'basic inwardness' of the German people. This form of mysticism strove for perfection through an infusion of divine grace which would lead to a life modelled on that of Christ.[4] The three leading German mystics of the fifteenth century were Johann Wesel, Puper von Goch, and Wessel Gansfort, who is purported to have had a determinative influence on Luther, a doubtful proposition. Via the French humanist Lefèvre d'Étaples, who edited the works of Nicholas Cusanus (d. 1464), that Dionysian Neoplatonic philosopher and mystic did influence Luther at a critical juncture in his exegetical work on the

---

3. See the detailed account of the Brethren by R. R. Post, *The Modern Devotion. Confrontation with Reformation and Humanism, Studies in Medieval and Reformation Thought,* III (Leiden, 1968), in which he attacked Renaudet, Hyma and Spitz for their assessment of the Brethren's activities and influence. For some of what could be said in response, see the excellent review of the book by Helmar Junghans, *Luther-Jahrbuch,* 37 (1970), pp. 120–27.

4. For a representative recent book on mysticism, humanism and the Reformation, see Steven E. Ozment, *Mysticism and Dissent: Religious Ideology and Social Protest in the Sixteenth Century* (New Haven, 1973).

Psalms and the Epistles of St Paul.[5] The powerful influence of the Italian Renaissance ideas and style in the arts and letters necessarily fused with northern intellectual streams and formed a unique amalgam.

The main transmitters for this transfusion of Renaissance culture were the monasteries, the ecclesiastical and the secular courts, the urban centres, and in due course the universities.

That monasteries were important centres for the new learning is so surprising that scholars all too often have not taken the fact into account, despite the evidence. Late medieval monasticism has, of course, had a bad press with modern secular scholars, who to a regrettable degree are ignorant of patristic and medieval history. Despite the contributions of the monastic establishments, from the days of Flavius Cassiodorus (*c.* 485–583), who developed the Scriptorium, of the Benedictines down to the Schottenkloster in contemporary Vienna, and the contributions of the Dominicans and Franciscans to the medieval universities, scholars of the Renaissance have neglected the importance of monks, friars, and other religious to the culture of the Renaissance. Paul Oskar Kristeller is an outstanding exception, for he has published brilliant pieces on this very subject. Thus in the fifteenth century the Cistercian cloister of Adwert, outside Gröningen, was a lively intellectual centre, where Alexander Hegius, famous as an educator at Deventer, Rudolf Agricola, the 'father of German humanism' and a 'second Petrarch', and Johann Wessel, who spent much time in Greece and Italy, came for study and visits with the learned abbot, Henry of Rees. Similarly the Benedictine cloister of Sponheim in south-west Germany became under Abbot Johannes Trithemius (1462–1516) a centre of humanist learning and a hospice for the legendary Dr Faustus.[6] An intense admirer of Petrarch, Trithemius befriended German humanists whom he knew from his Heidelberg days, such as Rudolf Agricola, Jacob Wimpfeling, Johannes von Dalberg, and Conrad Celtis, who has been dubbed the 'German Arch-humanist'. He was the first German poet laureate of the Empire, crowned by Emperor Frederick III on the hill outside the castle in Nuremberg in 1487. He was

---

5. The excellent work of P. M. Watts, *Nicholaus Cusanus: A Fifteenth Century Vision of Man* (Leiden, 1982) carries the understanding of this difficult thinker well beyond the older authorities. The great work on Italian humanist thought is that of C. Trinkaus, *In Our Image and Likeness: Humanity and Divinity in Italian Humanist Thought*, 2 vols. (Chicago, 1970), with supplementary essays in his *The Scope of Renaissance Humanism* (Ann Arbor, MI., 1983).

6. N. L. Brann, *The Abbot Trithemius (1462–1516): The Renaissance of Monastic Humanism* (Leiden, 1981), an admirable work.

the founder of the Rhenish and Danubian sodalities, loose associations of humanists, largely in the imperial cities.[7]

A second avenue by which Italian humanist influence reached the 'septentrionals' was via the imperial, princely and ecclesiastical courts. One must start at the top, the court of the Holy Roman Emperors, Frederick III and Maximilian I (1493–1519), in Vienna and three other locales for the distribution of justice. Frederick III was fairly lethargic, but Maximilian was, by way of contrast, fairly manic. He was said to have wrestled with bears, climbed mountains, married twice with vigour, and patronized many Renaissance humanists and artists. He through ghost writers, some allege, composed two epic narratives entirely related to his own life, the *Teuerdank* and the *Weiskünig*. But, as is the case with most rulers and aristocrats, their major contribution to culture is through patronage. Maximilian established a chair for poetry and rhetoric at the University of Vienna, recrowned Conrad Celtis, who founded the 'College of Poets and Mathematicians' next to the old university, and commissioned art by Dürer and others. Celtis urged other princes to equal his generosity, writing to Magnus of Anhalt, for example, to support the good arts, and, in an act filled with historical portent, dedicating his edition of the plays of Roswitha, nun of Gandersheim to Frederick the Wise of Saxony and praising him for bringing poets, artists, teachers of Roman law, and scientists, to his court as well as to his new university of Wittenberg, founded in 1502.

Much has been made of the 'urban reformation,' because for two decades the Lutheran Reformation made progress in the cities, and only then, with sufficient university-trained evangelical preachers, could it expand to the countryside under the aegis of the territorial rulers, the 'princely' reformation. Something more should be said about the 'urban Renaissance'. Nuremberg and Augsburg may serve as case studies of German cities in which humanistic studies were introduced and encouraged by an elite mercantile aristocracy. In Nuremberg the Pirckheimers had a tradition of sending their sons to Italy for legal and humanistic education and of educating their daughters in letters and religion. Their handsome bourgeois house, only yards away from the beautiful fountain in the market-place, served as a hospice for both humanists such as Celtis as well as reformers like Luther. Celtis wrote a topographical-historical description entitled the *Norimberga*, which

---

7. While there are materials available in English on Conrad Celtis, such as L. Forster, *Conrad Celtis 1459–1508: Selections edited with transition and commentary* (Cambridge, 1948), and L. W. Spitz, *Conrad Celtis: The German Arch-Humanist* (Cambridge, MA, 1957), the essential work over the past three decades has been done by Professor Dieter Wuttke of Bamberg University, who has devoted his life to the study of Celtis and has actually succeeded in finding some new and previously unknown odes of the bard.

was to serve as a model for all the humanists who were to contribute to a *Germania illustrata*, modelled on Flavio Biondo's *Italia illustrata*. In Augsburg the Fuggers and other wealthy merchants commissioned works of literature, art and architecture. In many other cities, particularly in the south and west, a partially Italian-educated judiciary and citizenship patronized classical scholars and neo-Latin poets and rhetoricians.

A fourth avenue by which eventually the Italian Renaissance literary, though not artistic, culture reached Germany was the recalcitrant universities.[8] The German universities in which the humanistic discipline made substantial progress in the late fifteenth and sixteenth centuries were, roughly in this order, Vienna, Heidelberg, Basel, Erfurt, Wittenberg, Leipzig, Tübingen, and also Ingolstadt (later to become the university of Munich).[9] The traditional account of a fierce battle in the universities between the scholastics of either the *via antiqua* (Thomists) or the *via moderna* (Occamists) against the humanists has been largely discredited, for many professors were half-scholastic and half-humanistic. Moreover, the great controversy often had more to do with chairs and stipends than with intellectual issues. The humanist lecturers stressed the importance of grammar and rhetoric over logic or dialectic, the essential device of scholastic philosophy. While logic can lead to inevitable conclusions within a given dialectical system, the humanists believed that rhetoric is a superior instrument to be used on behalf of truth, for it leads beyond intellectual conviction to move the will to action (*virtù*: that is, intelligent will in action), a higher form of truth. Poetry stirs emotions and history is philosophy teaching by examples. Moral philosophy is to be preferred to metaphysics, though not divorced from it, for it strengthens the fibre of public as well as of individual life.

There is an interesting generational theory regarding the development of northern humanism that seems to be particularly applicable to German humanism. From a biological-genealogical perspective, it has been argued, mankind's history seems to be a steady and continuous flow of a near infinite number of individual lives upon which no collective periodization can be imposed. But, in contrast, the history of the social production of mankind characteristically moves in stages, in distinctive periods of time. The conceptual model of historical generations leads to the meeting point of these two very different

---

8. See the commendable chapter 'Humanism at the Universities, 1500–1515: The Prelude to Reform,' in J. H. Overfield, *Humanism and Scholasticism in Late Medieval Germany* (Princeton, 1984), pp. 208–46.

9. On Ingolstadt, an interesting insight into conservative reform is offered in the little monograph by E. Iserloh, *Johannes Eck (1486–1543): Scholastiker Humanist Kontroverstheologe* (Aschendorff/Münster, 1981), pp. 14–20, including paragraphs on Eck as humanist.

phenomena. Included in 'social production' must surely be cultural productivity, for men are not merely animals, and once again the humanists have preceded the social scientists with a generational theory.[10] In German humanism pioneers such as Rudolf Agricola, first generation, were followed by the high-tide of German humanism, Mutianus Rufus, Johannes Reuchlin, Conrad Celtis, Willibald Pirckheimer, Jacob Wimpfeling, Desiderius Erasmus, Conrad Peutinger, and many others. If the first generation exhausted its energies acquiring classical learning and absorbing what the Italian humanists could teach them, the second generation of humanists did truly creative intellectual and artistic work in their own right. But the third generation of young humanists was impatient. These young men wished to use their learning to change the world for the better. As Bernd Moeller expressed this thought with epigrammatic force: 'Without the humanists there would have been no Reformation.'[11] Luther led the tortuous way in his own life away from late scholasticism to a biblical faith, but did so by totally rejecting scholastic philosophy (whatever carry-overs remained in his theologizing), and using the tools and much of the substance of Renaissance humanism in the cause of the gospel. His supporting cast, Melanchthon, Bucer, Vadian, Zwingli, Oecolampadius, and John Calvin, had a much easier time of it once Luther had made the great evangelical breakthrough. Some few Anabaptists and evangelical humanists also derived much from the tools and religio-intellectual orientation of humanism, including religious leaders such as Balthasar Hubmaier, Michael Servetus, or Sebastian Franck.[12] Hubmaier once commented that nearly all the learned were Lutherans. In his essay *Of Youth and Age* Francis Bacon observed: 'Young men are fitter to invent than to judge; fitter for execution than for counsel; and fitter for new projects than for settled business.' The progamme of the German humanists may be succinctly characterized as being devoted to a form of cultural nationalism and to a vague and ill-defined kind of religious enlightenment.

Luther once commented that to his astonishment his *Ninety-five Theses* had within fourteen days been carried throughout the length and

---

10. H. Jaeger, 'Generations in History: Reflections on a Controversial Concept,' *History and Theory*, 24 (1985), 273–92. Also, L. W. Spitz, 'The Third Generation of German Renaissance Humanists,' in A. R. Lewis, ed., *Aspects of the Renaissance: A Symposium* (Austin and London, 1967), the symposium at which I first met Denys Hay in person.

11. B. Moeller, *Imperial Cities and the Reformation: Three Essays* (Philadelphia, 1972), recently republished by Labyrinth Press; S. Ozment, *The Reformation in the Cities: The Appeal of Protestantism to Sixteenth-Century Germany and Switzerland* (New Haven, 1975).

12. See P. Hayden-Roy, *The Inner Word and the Outer World: A Biography of Sebastian Franck* (Diss., Stanford, 1988).

breadth of Germany. The young German humanists were the chief agents for their distribution, working out of the urban centres where printing presses were established, well before university presses, in Nuremberg, Augsburg, Leipzig, Basel, Constance, Wittenberg, and cities in which humanist sodalities existed, most loosely related to the Rhenish or Danubian sodalities. In 1520 Luther was the most widely published and read author in Germany, and his suspect backer, Ulrich von Hutten, the second most. Indeed, without the support of the humanists in these urban centres Luther's evangelical revival would, humanly speaking, not have succeeded.

The humanists approved of Luther's uncompromising assault on scholastic philosophy, for, he held, the doctors had accommodated theology to the semi-Pelagian practices of a corrupted Church and left the Scriptural existential understanding of the law–gospel, sin–grace, death–life antinomies for a compromised sapiential metaphysical theology of works, a *theologia gloriae* rather than the *theologia crucis et passionis* This radical assault on the theological establishment excited the young humanists, but, of course, aroused the predictable response from the establishment in Cologne, Louvain, Paris, and Rome! The humanists approved of his drive *ad fontes*, back to the Scriptures, but they did not really grasp the depth of his theology. Had they read *On the Babylonian Captivity of the Church* (1520) with more than Erasmian eyes, they would have understood that they were in turbulent waters much over their heads. That treatise, in fact, did frighten some of the older humanists, who began to turn away, a real watershed. From 1520 on the Reformation began to derail humanism in the Erasmian mould. Or did it? Perhaps the Reformation movement saved German humanism from preciosity, irrelevancy, even foppery. It carried the movement on its broad shoulders forward into the seventeenth century, to a point where the *Aufklärung* (German Enlightenment) was able through the Leibniz (Lutheran), Kant (Lutheran), Hamann (Lutheran), and Herder (Lutheran) connection to take an amalgam into the modern world.

Perhaps after all this it would be fitting to include here in brief scope an account of the course of German humanism. In the year 1507 Nicholas Gerbellius, a young humanist, burbled: 'I congratulate myself often on living in this glorious century in which so many remarkable men have arisen in Germany.' The new culture had come to the Germanies earlier than to the other countries of the North thanks to the medieval political ties between Italy and the Holy Roman Empire, the lively trade between Italian and German cities, the cultural ties established by student migration to the universities of Pavia, Padua, and, above all, Bologna, many for legal education. The transition from the medieval 'Wandervogel' and the migrant student, to the rootless poet (Celtis) and the literary humanist (Erasmus), who declared himself to be a citizen of the world, was easy and natural.

The migratory birds of German humanism, like the medieval trou-badours, spread the classical word. Of course, scholars have done root-stretching back to the Councils of Constance and Basel in the first half of the fifteenth century, and have pointed to the influence of Italian churchmen and diplomats such as Aeneas Silvius Piccolomini (later Pius II) in the North. Aeneas had written a flattering picture of Bohemia and of Germany which had flowered under the aegis of the Roman Catholic Church. But during the second half of the fifteenth century the Germans themselves began to trumpet the cause of classical letters and the new Renaissance culture. A poet such as Peter Luder (c. 1415–74) went to Rome as a cleric, travelled about Italy, and joined the German students in Padua. (Centuries later Dr Johnson once commented that anyone who has not been to Italy is always conscious of an inferiority!) In the year 1444 the elector of the Palatinate made him a lecturer for classical languages and literature at Heidelberg University, where he launched an aggressive campaign for classical rhetoric and poetry. More pedagogical types such as Rudolf von Langen, Johannes Murmellius, scholastic humanists such as Conrad Summenhart and Paul Scriptoris, and moralists such as Heinrich Bebel, author of heavy *facetiae*, and Jacob Wimpfeling, cathedral preacher at Speyer and an Alsatian German patriot, carried the cause of moral philosophy and classical letters forward. Friends of Wimpfeling (1450–1528) included Sebastian Brant (1457–1521), author of *The Ship of Fools*, and Johann Geiler von Kais-ersberg (1445–1510), the renowned reforming penitential pulpiteer.

The most prominent pioneer of this older generation was Rudolf Agricola (1444–85). Erasmus wrote of him: 'It was Rudolf Agricola who first brought with him from Italy some gleam of a better litera-ture.' 'He could have been the first in Italy,' Erasmus opined, 'had he not preferred Germany.' In Heidelberg, supported by Bishop Johannes von Dalberg and the Palatinate Elector, Agricola inspired an entire circle of young humanists. 'I have the brightest hope,' Agricola proclaimed,

> that we one day shall wrest from haughty Italy the reputation for classical expression which it has nearly monopolized, so to speak, and lay claim to it ourselves, and free ourselves from the reproach of ignorance and being called unlearned and inarticulate barbarians; and that our Germany will be so cultured and literate that Latium will not know Latin any better.[13]

---

13. *Rudolphi Agricolae Phrisii De inventione dialectica libri omnes et integri & recogniti, etc. per Alardum Aemstelradamum* (Cologne, 1539), II, p. 178.

The high tide of German humanism rose during the first two decades of the sixteenth century. The best lyric poet was clearly Conrad Celtis (1459–1508), the son of a peasant, who studied at Cologne, Heidelberg, Rostock and Leipzig. Upon his crowning as the first poet-laureate of the Empire, he proclaimed: 'O sacred and mighty work of the poets, you alone free all things from fate and lift up mortal ashes to the stars!' In his *Amores* he celebrated his four loves, each symbolizing one of the four extremities of Germany. In his *Odes*, done in the manner of Horace, he wrote of love, life, and learning. From Horace and Cicero he learned that poetry has a passionate and rousing power. He referred to himself as a *vates*, not merely a *poeta*, for he was a prophet and a sage. He quickly journeyed through Italy, visiting Venice, Padua, Bologna, Florence, Rome, but disliked the 'superior' posturing of the Italians. His travels took him to Cracow, Ingolstadt, and finally to Vienna, where he died of syphilis at the age of forty-nine and still lies buried in the short tower of St Stephen's cathedral, his gravestone bearing the caption VIVO, 'I live,' as indeed he does. He lived on also then as a hero of the younger humanists.

Other humanists of this generation made remarkable contributions to learning. Although Mutianus Rufus published little, his house in Gotha, where he was a canon, with his library which he called his *beata tranquillitas*, was a hospice for many young humanists at the nearby university of Erfurt. In Augsburg prosperous patricians supported local artistic and literary men. There Conrad Peutinger (1465–1547) became a prominent legist and humanist, the owner of the tremendous *Tabula Peutingeriana*, a military map of the Roman Empire, which Celtis had found and given to him. In Ingolstadt, Johann Turmair, (Aventinus: 1477–1534) served as tutor to the scions of the duke of Bavaria. Duke Wilhelm IV urged him to write *The Annals of Bavaria*, finished in 1521.[14] Willibald Pirckheimer in Nuremberg wrote in Greek as well as in Latin, and though a busy merchant-banker and city counsellor, wrote poetry and a history of the Swabian-Swiss war. Among his friends he counted Celtis, Dürer, and for a time Luther, who was a guest in his house. His sister Charitas, abbess of a local convent, was so learned that Erasmus compared her to the daughters of Sir Thomas More.

Two events of those two decades involving humanist impact merit special attention. The first of these was the Reuchlin controversy about Hebrew books and the second was the role of that most militant humanist, the knight Ulrich von Hutten. Johannes Reuchlin (1455–1522) served most of his adult life as the chancellor to the duke

---

14. The best work on Aventinus is that of G. Strauss, *Historian in an Age of Crisis: The Life and Work of Johannes Aventinus 1477–1534* (Cambridge, MA, 1963).

of Württemberg. While educated in German universities, on two trips to Italy Reuchlin visited the Platonic Academy, and the Villa Corregi, and was captivated by Marsiglio Ficino's Neoplatonism. He was also intrigued by Pico della Mirandola's discovery of the Hebrew *Kabbalah* and his assertion expressed in the 900 *Conclusiones* that light came from the East (*ex oriente lux*) long before the time of the Greeks. From Pico he learned that the thought of the Cabalists corresponded to the philosophy of the Pythagoreans. 'Marsiglio (Ficino) produced Plato for Italy,' he proclaimed, 'Lefèvre d'Etaples restored Aristotle to France. I shall complete the number and . . . show to the Germans Pythagoras reborn through me.'[15] He wrote a manual of Hebrew grammar, the *Rudimenta hebraica*, and two important works using the Jewish *Kabbalah* apologetically as a support for the Christian faith: *De Verbo Mirafico* and the *De Arte Cabalistica*.[16] He became the target of a vicious obscurantist attack and was defended by the humanists and given encouragement by none other than Martin Luther.[17] Reuchlin later expressed gratitude that Luther had now attracted the hostility of the monks, taking the heat off him! Reuchlin ended his days as a professor at Ingolstadt and Tübingen, a dedicated foe of the Reformation. But his grandnephew Philipp Melanchthon became Luther's colleague and first lieutenant in Wittenberg, the second most important Protestant reformer until the emergence of John Calvin.

Ulrich von Hutten, a knight, was a fighter! When Luther was summoned to appear before the Emperor Charles V and the Diet in Worms, Hutten called to him: 'Long live liberty!'[18] Born in the fortress of Steckelberg on the border of Franconia and Hesse, he was sent at the age of eleven to the ancient monastery of Fulda to lead the life of

---

15. Reuchlin, *On the Cabalistic Art*, dedication to Pope Leo X, in *Renaissance Philosophy*, II: *The Transalpine Thinkers*, ed. H. Shapiro and A. B. Fallico (New York, 1969), p. 28, cited in Brann. 'Humanism in Germany,' p. 155, n. 74.

16. The latest quite felicitous translation of this very difficult book is that of M. and S. Goodman, *Johann Reuchlin: On the Art of the Kabbalah – De Arte Cabalistica* (New York, 1983).

17. The Warburg and Courtauld Institutes seem possibly under the benignant influence of Frances Yates to have turned into a coven. See the interpretation of Reuchlin by C. Zika, 'Reuchlin's *De Verbo Mirifico* and the Magic Debate of the Late Fifteenth Century,' *Journal of the Warburg and Courtauld Institutes*, 39 (1976), pp. 104–38. This reading of Reuchlin is out of character with his basic religious, legal, and philosophical character as revealed in his many other writings and letters. Noel Brann is mistaken to settle for some safe 'middle ground,' 'Humanism in Germany,' p. 146–7.

18. The most recent and very excellent book on Ulrich von Hutten is that of E. Bernstein, *Ulrich von Hutten mit Selbstzeugnissen und Bilddokumenten* (Reinbeck bei Hamburg, 1988). Bernstein is also the author of a valuable monograph, *Die Literatur des deutschen Frühhumanismus* (Stuttgart, 1978). See Helmar Junghans, 'Der nationale Humanismus bei Ulrich von Hutten und Martin Luther,' *Ebernburg-Hefte*, 22. Folge, (1988), *Blätter für Pfälzische Kirchengeschichte und Ic religiöse Volkskunde* (Vol. 55, 1988), pp. 147–70.

a religious. At seventeen he fled from the monastery just a few weeks before Luther entered one in Erfurt. He studied at six different German universities and during the course of his peregrinations he became a fervent anti-scholastic and a humanist given to poetics and polemics. 'Behold, posterity,' he penned, 'the songs of the poet Hutten, whom you are rightly able to call your own!' He aimed to free the Fatherland of ignorance, of the shackles of Rome, and to elevate culture above that of Italy. This angry young man poured out many polemical tracts, like unloading a barrel of grapeshot, all the more devastating for being fired at close range. In one of his dialogues he wrote: 'Even if it cannot be achieved, there is merit in having tried!' He attacked the papacy, following Valla he exposed the False Donation of Constantine, he assaulted the trade in indulgences, and he rallied behind Luther, who, however, kept a safe distance from this firebrand ready to use the sword. Hutten died in 1523 of syphilis and lies buried on the island of Ufenau near Zurich, where he had gone to seek refuge, but was turned away. Many of the younger humanists, such as Beatus Rhenanus, were of a milder more Erasmian disposition. John Sleidan proved to be the best historian of the earlier sixteenth century.[19]

It would outrun the limits of a mere essay to discuss lesser humanists in detail, but the impact of these phalanxes of the hoplites and of the light-armed soldiers, wielding feather pens, upon German literary, artistic, and religious culture would be difficult to overestimate. After this brief survey of the course of German humanism, it is necessary to turn to a problem of much greater complexity, the impact of humanism upon the Lutheran Reformation.

## II

Friedrich Nietzsche was not entirely mistaken when he depicted Luther as a 'vengeful, unlucky priest who brought to shame the one cleverly refined beautiful brilliant possibility – Caesar Borgia as pope.' (*Der Anti-Christ*, aph. 61) Not literally, of course, since Caesar Borgia, duke of Valentinois and Romagna and son of Pope Alexander V perished in 1507 under very difficult circumstances, ten years before Luther published his *Ninety-five Theses*. Contemporary Catholic schol-

---

19. On Beatus Rhenanus, see the superlative book by the late J. F. D'Amico, *Theory and Practice in Renaissance Textual Criticism: Beatus Rhenanus between Manuscript and Conjecture* (Berkeley and Los Angeles, 1988). See also the excellent brief characterization of John Sleidan as a historian in A. G. Dickens and J. Tonkin, *The Reformation in Historical Thought* (Cambridge, MA, 1985), pp. 10–19. See Ingeborg Berlin Vogelstein, *Johann Sleidan's Commentaries: Vantage Point of a Second-Generation Lutheran* (Lanham, MD: University Press of America, 1986). Ms. Vogelstein is currently doing an annotated reduced version of the *Commentaries*.

arship grants the point, and the pioneer of ecumenical Catholic Reformation historical scholarship, Joseph Lortz, declared that some day Luther would be declared a saint. (He would, of course, not acccept, not believing in sainthood, but in a community of forgiven sinners.) For, Lortz reasoned, he gave a decadent Church the shock treatment needed to bring it out of the Italian family – princely concerns back to the true spiritual vocation of the Church.

Nietzsche's idea does point up the fact that one historiographical tradition from the time of Jakob Burkhardt's *The Civilization of the Renaissance in Italy* (1860) to the present has seen Renaissance and Reformation, humanism and Protestantism, as having been antithetical. A second interpretation has been to view them as twin sources of modernity.[20] 'We are at the dawn of a new era!' Luther exclaimed. Erasmus' *alter ego* Beatus Rhenanus responded to the Reformation by declaring: 'I see the whole world reviving!' In the nineteenth century the historian James Froude referred to the Reformation as 'the hinge on which all modern history turns.' By the fateful year 1517, when Luther nailed his theses to the side doors of the Castle Church in Wittenberg, used as a matter of course as a bulletin board since larger university lectures were given in the nave of the church, humanism was well established at Wittenberg University. It was also a cultural force in many universities, though not in some, as events were to reveal. Humanism had also made its impress upon Luther's mind and spirit.

The Lutheran and 'magisterial' Reformation, the Catholic Reformation and to a more limited extent the radical sectarian Reformation owed much to Renaissance humanism and to the classical revival for many reasons. First of all, the humanist emphasis on the importance of classical languages and scholarship, the drive *ad fontes*, was basic to the reformers' return to the Scriptures and to the ancient fathers. Secondly the stress of the humanists upon the importance of education was essential to the whole Reformation programme for change. Thirdly, the shift of the humanists away from dialectic to grammar and rhetoric, the other two major divisions of the *trivium*, and the attendant increased appreciation of history and poetry, marked a major intellectual shift, a culturally paratactic event. Obviously the Protestant emphasis on preaching, the spoken word of the gospel (Luther: *Verbum evangelii vocale*), owed much to the rhetorical emphasis of the humanists. Poetry was related to the rhetorical appreciation of *affectus*, feeling, along with music, a major force touching emotion and thereby the will.

---

20. For an English translation of the archetypical expressions of the Reformation as progenitor of modernity or the Reformation as essentially medieval, as articulated by Wilhelm Dilthey and Ernst Troeltsch, see L. W. Spitz, ed., *The Reformation: Basic Interpretations* (Lexington, MA, 1972), pp. 11–43.

The reformers became increasingly fascinated with history both sacred and secular. The Scriptures came to be viewed as an account of the existential religious experiences of individual believers as well as the history of salvation (*Heilsgeschichte*) of the Old and the New Israel. Sacred history provided case studies of the way in which God deals with man. Secular history provided pragmatic moral lessons, but also retrospectively describes the *locutia*, the words that God has spoken and acted out in history, as he has done and continues to do in nature.

The evangelical Reformation diverged radically from the religious assumptions of the Renaissance classical world, of the Renaissance Catholic world, and of the Christian humanist world of the North. In both anthropology (sin as the root condition of man) and soteriology (Christology, not merely Christocentrism), Luther and the German reformers moved along what proved to be more history-making lines. For Luther Christ was not merely an *exemplum*, a model to be imitated, but an *exemplar*, an example of the way in which God deals with man, as Luther wrote to Reuchlin in his time of troubles, grinding him down into the dust of death, but then, praise God, raising him up again to life eternal! This shift in emphasis from man's contribution to his own salvation towards dependence upon the divine initiative, grace as a benignity, a gift with which the Giver, the God of love and forgiveness, is always present, did indeed mark a dramatic theological and historical change. It also marked a cultural change that Aristotle would have described as a 'transformation from one dimension to another' (*Metabasis eis allo genos*).

'Nevertheless' (*dennoch*) was the word that Luther substituted for Thomas Aquinas' smooth 'therefore' (*ergo*), existential for sapiential. The magisterial reformers provided for the continuity of humanist culture and learning down to the turbulent seventeenth century, a century of crisis, with remnants of their views on culture remaining into the late twentieth century. The reformers were themselves savants. Luther used many more classical references without citation in his famous exchange with Erasmus than did the 'prince of humanists' with his great display of learning. The reformers extended the influence of classical and humanist learning to a much broader spectrum of the European and, in due course, of the American population. They provided for the continuance of the humanist disciplines through their advocacy of universal compulsory education for boys and girls, through their establishment of many classical gymnasia and through humanist curricular changes both on the arts level of the universities as well as through a new approach to theological education. There developed, for example, a greater stress on exegesis based on the biblical language texts, a new approach to homiletics based on humanist rhetorical principles, and a renewed interest in Church history, poetry, drama, and music. The first professor of history was Eobanus Hessus, the most outstanding Protestant poet, appointed at Philipp of Hesse's new university of Marburg in 1524.

St Augustine in his best-known treatise on education reminded the students that to accept what the teacher says uncritically is mistaken, to reject it out of hand is wrong, but to test whatever the teacher tells one, to see in how far it is true, is the right way for the student. Similarly Plutarch wrote that the auditor should not only criticize a lecture, but should be able to improve upon it, as Plato did upon the Greek orator Lysias (who did endlessly boring orations on vineyard property rights). Auditors should not be like the Lacedaemonians, for when they heard that Philip of Macedon had razed Olynthus to the ground they commented: 'Yes, but to create a city as good is beyond the man's power.' Nearly all Protestant reformers were critical of the schooling they had received both on the elementary and on the university level. What could they do by way of improving the educational system?

Luther pounded away on the subject for years! He not only manoeuvred and pioneered curricular changes at the university of Wittenberg along humanist lines, but he effected decisive changes throughout the educational maze. To say system or organization would be saying too much for those times. At the university level he believed that students who came up from the arts faculty with a dialectical mindset were difficult to deal with in the theological school. Those who had taken the revised humanist curriculum with languages, classics, rhetoric, and the like were better prepared for biblical study, and made better evangelical ministers. In his treatise *To the Councilmen of all Cities in Germany that They Establish and Maintain Christian Schools*, he wrote: 'If it is necessary, dear sirs, to expend annually such great sums for firearms, for roads, bridges, dams, and countless similar things, in order that a city may enjoy temporal peace and prosperity, why should not at least as much be devoted to the poor needy youth?'[21] This treatise has been described as a great song of praise for the study of languages. In many of his writings, such as his *Sermon on the Estate of Marriage* (1519) and his *Sermon on Keeping Children in School* (1530), he argued that the civil authorities have the right to compel parents to send their children to school. Luther may well have been the first person in the history of the world to advocate universal compulsory education for boys and girls, for a substantial number of grades. If boys have the ability and nature had not denied them 'sense and wit', they should be urged and financially supported by the State through the university

---

21. Luther, 'To the Councilmen of all Cities in Germany that They Establish and Maintain Christian Schools,' *Luther's Works*, 45, *The Christian in Society*, vol. 2, ed. W. I. Brandt (Philadelphia, 1962), pp. 369–70.

level, so that they could become fully educated to serve Church, State, and Society. In that *Address to the Councilmen* of the Municipalities he wrote: 'The prosperity of a country depends not on the abundance of its revenue, nor on the strength of its fortifications, nor on the beauty of its public building but it consists in the number of cultivated citizens, in its men of education, enlightenment, and character.'[22] Students would eventually serve Church, State, and thereby Society.

If Luther provided the initial thrust, like the first stage of a rocket launching, his learned colleague, Philipp Melanchthon, grandnephew of Reuchlin, known as the *praeceptor germaniae*, provided instruction in method and organization. Certainly the educator who most fully satisfied Melanchthon's ideal was Johann Sturm of Strasbourg, who directed the gymnasium, helped found and organize a good many others, and wrote elaborate treatises on education which gave curricular specifics along the general evangelical humanist philosophy of education. As a friend and correspondent of Roger Ascham, who even named one of his children after Sturm, he influenced advanced education in England, for Ascham was a renowned educator and tutor to Queen Elizabeth I.

German Lutheran education was notable, then, especially for three special emphases. First, it broadened the popular educational base, moving away from the elitism and upper-class orientation of Italian humanism and towards compulsory universal basic education. Second, the curriculum for the secondary schools and at the arts level of the university was to be the humanistic classical curriculum demanding a knowledge of Latin, Greek, and Hebrew, classical literature, grammar, and rhetoric, while not neglecting dialectic, moral philosophy, poetry, history, mathematics and sciences. Third, there was a new emphasis upon teaching as a divine vocation and on the dignity of the teacher, for, Luther asserted, teaching next to preaching is the most useful service a man of God can render to his fellow human beings.

Many aspects of the impact of humanism in Germany remain to be discussed and much research remains to be done, but it is possible here at least to indicate the problematics of the subject. The entire question of the revival of Christian antiquity, along with classical antiquity and patristic study in the sixteenth century, needs to be explored further.[23]

---

22. *Luther's Works*, 45, pp. 355–6.

23. For many years Paul Oskar Kristeller has been advocating rigorous studies of the influence of the patristic writers on humanism and Reformation. A bibliographical guide suggestive for further research to be done is S. Ozment, ed., *Reformation Europe: A Guide to Research* (St Louis, MO.: Center for Reformation Research, 1982). An example of the type of specialized studies needed is Scott H. Hendrix, "Validating the Reformation: The Use of the Church Fathers by Urbanus Rhegius," in Walter Brand Müller, Herbert Immenkötter, and Erwin Iserloh, eds., *Ecclesia Militans: Studien zur Konzilien-und-Reformationsgeschichte*, TT, Paderborn, (1988), 281–305.

The problem of change and continuity is perennial for historians and, when the discussion grows tedious, one thinks of Lord Acton's comment: 'Better one great man of history than a dozen immaculate historians.' The continuity of humanism through the Reformation era and the changes that it underwent as it took on a more academic character and became allied with religious and sectarian interests are worth more intense scrutiny. Certainly a great scholar and savant like Joachim Camerarius (1500–74) was not cut of the same cloth as a frivolous and promiscuous poet like Conrad Celtis. Still, the so-called neoscholastic dogmaticians such as Chemnitz, Calov, or Quenstedt had a knowledge of both classical and Christian antiquity and of the ancient languages, the triple linguistic tiara, far beyond the reach and imagination of the 'high generation' of German humanists as well as of the Italian humanists. Thanks to the magisterial reformers, who not only placed their *imprimatur* upon humanism, but viewed the cultivation of higher culture as a *negotium cum deo*, a business or work carried on with God's blessing and help, humanism made a broader, deeper, and longer-lasting impact upon European and Western culture than might have been the case, had it been confined to the aristocratic elite of the princes and the wealthy. In the final analysis there has been no cultural movement that has enjoyed such a long continuity in its lasting impact, even with its waning intensity.[24] A comparative study of the impact of German humanism with that of other lands would be highly desirable. This could go on, and what used to be known as the 'gentle reader' may by now fear that it will! In the course of time the golden age of German humanism, and the silver age that followed, in the end yielded to the iron age of a technical and industrial society, though

---

24. On the continuity of humanism in German culture, see H. Liebing, 'Perspektivische Verzeichnungen. Uber die Haltbarkeit der *fable convenue* in der Kirchengeschichte,' *Zeitschrift für Kirchengeschichte*, 3 (1968), pp. 289–307; H. Jantz, 'German Renaissance Literature,' *Modern Language Notes*, 81 (1966), pp. 398–463; and L. W. Spitz, ed., *Humanismus und Reformation als kulturelle Kräfte in der deutschen Geschichte* (Berlin and New York, 1981).

25. This essay has deliberately kept documentation to a minimum and has limited references to more recent works. For more complete documentation, the black snow of the scholars, and more replete bibliography, the reader may consult a number of my articles on various aspects of the subject dealt with in this *zusammenfassende Darstellung*. For example: 'The Course of German Humanism,' in H. A. Oberman, ed., *Itinerarium Italicum: The Profile of the Italian Renaissance in the Mirror of its European Transformations* (Leiden, 1975), pp. 371–436; 'Humanism and the Protestant Reformation,' in A. Rabil, ed., *Renaissance Humanism: Foundations, Forms, and Legacy*, 3 (Philadelphia 1988), pp. 380–411; 'Humanismus/Humanismusforschung,' *Theologische Realencyclopedie*, 15 (1987), pp. 639–61; 'Luther and German Humanism,' in M. J. Harran, ed., *Luther and Learning. The Wittenberg University Symposium* (Selinsgrove, PA, 1985), pp. 69–94, and the like.

remnants and sherds remain even today. But for that brief moment in geological and historical time humanism was a brilliant inspiration in Camelot.[25]

Yes, Denys Hay was quite correct in his assessment of the impact of Italian Renaissance humanism and the classical revival, perhaps especially in the case of Germany. Rudolf Agricola expressed this thought in this way:

> We are indebted to Petrarch for the intellectual culture of our century. All ages owe him a debt of gratitude – antiquity for having rescued its treasure from oblivion, and modern times for having with his own strength founded and revived culture, which he has left as a precious legacy to future ages![26]

---

26. *Vita Petrarchae illustrata per eruditissimum virum Rudolphum Agricolam Phrisium ad Antonium Scrofinium Papiensem. Anno salutis 1477 (1473) Papiae*; L. Bertalot, 'Rudolf Agricolas Lobrede auf Petrarcha,' *La Bibliofilia*, 30 (1928), pp. 382–404.

*Chapter Ten*

# Humanism in the Iberian Peninsula

## JEREMY N. H. LAWRANCE

### I

In 1415, Europeans perceived the five independent Crowns of *Hispania* (Portugal, Navarre, Castile, Aragon, and Moorish Granada) as a land of Saracens, bearded Jewish magicians, and uncouth frontiersmen, culturally more akin to Barbary than Latin Christendom. During the course of the ensuing century, Iberia embarked upon a golden century of political unification, expansion, and artistic creativity. By 1563, Habsburg Spain was the dominant European and global power, wielding imperial sway over large parts of the Italian peninsula, and exporting its languages and art all over the known world. With political ascendancy went cultural ascendancy. The Spaniards and Portuguese who began as outsiders picking crumbs from the rich banquet of Renaissance culture soon came to regard the new-fangled Italian scholarship with peevish rivalry; by 1550 they looked down on it. The pride and confidence of the native tradition was to shape the destiny of humanism in Iberia.

We see the worm turning in a funeral eulogy, *The Marquis's Triumph*, written by his secretary Diego de Burgos on the death of Iñigo López de Mendoza, Marquis of Santillana (1398–1458), the chief patron of letters in the Iberia of his day. Diego portrayed Santillana as the man who 'liberated these Spains of ours from blind ignorance, illuminating them with light', and then went on:

> The orators of Italy, if they had heard him speak, would have echoed Apollonius Rhodius's words to Cicero: 'In times gone by the Greeks flourished above all nations in arms and civil institutions, but the Romans have slowly overtaken us. Now you,

Cicero, have stripped us of our last laurels, Learning and Eloquence.'

If Apollonius pitied the Greeks for losing Eloquence to Cicero, how must the Italians of today lament! Through the enlightened intelligence of my noble lord, Eloquence has abandoned Italy for Castile; here she flourishes with such glory, that the Italians are clearly surpassed.[1]

By a typical twist, Diego de Burgos's anti-Italian anecdote, like his topical references to reawakening, had an Italian source. His allusion to Apollonius Rhodius turned on its head a passage from a key text of Florentine humanism, Leonardo Bruni's *Cicero Anew* (*c.* 1416), which set Cicero up as the model of 'civil life', defender of Republican liberty, and father of 'our (i.e. Italian)' literature.[2] In source, style, and even in its chauvinistic envy, Diego's passage stands as a fitting epigraph to the period, running from 1415 to the 1480s, of the first powerful wave of Italian influence in Castilian literature. He was not the only writer to proclaim Santillana the renewer of Spanish letters. Several other poetic plaints on the marquis's death (including the Latin elegiacs by the Italian humanists Pier Candido Decembrio and Tommaso da Rieti) made similar points. The marquis's nephew Gomez Manrique (1412?–90) described him as 'the first man of our times to conjoin science and chivalry, the breastplate and the toga', thus 'rooting out' from the *patria* all prejudice against letters.[3] For the next two centuries, Santillana and the king's poet-chronicler and secretary of Latin letters Juan de Mena (1411–56) were to be seen as harbingers of a new era. Both were considerable poets in the new Latinate style. The marquis's magnificent library of Florentine MSS epitomized the heavy subservi-

---

1. 'Proemio' to *El triunfo del Marqués* (*c.* 1459), in M. Schiff, *La Bibliothèque du marquis de Santillane*, (Paris, 1905; repr, Amsterdam, 1970), pp. 460–4 (462).

2. On the *Cicero Novus* (a 'correction' of Plutarch's Greek *Life of Cicero*) see H. Baron, 'Cicero and the Roman Civic Spirit in the Middle Ages and Early Renaissance', *Bulletin of the John Rylands Library*, 22 (1938), pp. 72–97. A Tuscan translation, *Vita di Cicerone scritta da messer Lionardo Bruni Aretino*, was commissioned by Santillana's friend Nuño de Guzmán in 1458–9; it may have been Guzmán's MS which brought the *translatio studii* topic to Diego's notice. On Guzmán see the studies cited in footnote 21 below.

3. P. C. Decembrio, *Elogium in Ennicum Hispanum, cognomine Lupum*: 'Tu decus armorum Latiis coniungere Musis / Hesperiae proceres, doctus utrumque, iubes', in Schiff, *Bibliothèque*, pp. 468–9, together with Tommaso's effort; Manrique, 'Epistle-Prologue' to *Planto de las virtudes*, in B. J. Gallardo, *Ensayo de una biblioteca española de libros raros y curiosos*, ed. M. R. Zarco del Valle and J. Sancho Rayón, 4 vols (Madrid, 1863; repr. 1968), I, pp. 601–3. For further notes on Santillana's reputation see P. E. Russell, 'Las armas contra las letras: para una definición del humanismo español del siglo XV', in his *Temas de "La Celestina" y otros estudios del "Cid" al "Quijote"* (Barcelona, 1978), pp. 214–15, 230–1.

ence to Italian influence of a circle of contemporary patrons, writers, and men of letters. The Florentine bookseller and biographer Vespasiano da Bisticci noted in the 1480s that Santillana, though unable to construe Latin, had been a competent reader of Tuscan, and had collected his Italian books for a library 'which he made available to all who were interested'. It was this circle of pioneers which, during the reign of John II of Castile (1406–54), initiated the shift away from French models towards Italian ones in Castilian literary and intellectual life. Santillana's apology for the new poetry balanced admiration for the 'crafty versification' of the French with enchantment at the 'inventive genius' of the Italians.[4]

The period was characterized also by a vast activity in the field of 'vernacular humanism' – that is, the translation and adaptation of classical works for the entertainment and instruction of noble and unprofessional readers. In these works the contributions of Italian humanists often played an important part. The Castilian translations of Greek works by Procopius, Basil, Plato, Lucian, Homer, Aristotle, Plutarch, Hermes Trismegistus, and Appian were made from Latin or Italian intermediary versions, adaptations, and falsifications by the humanists Leonardo Bruni, Cencio de' Rustici, Pier Candido Decembrio, Giovanni Aurispa, Marsilio Ficino, and others. Kristeller has noted the striking propensity of Santillana and other Spanish patrons to commission Tuscan translations of the classics.[5]

For these reasons, and above all because contemporaries such as Diego de Burgos consciously expressed the sense of new direction in metaphors of 'reawakening' or 'dawning', this period marked the start of a literary renaissance in Spain. None of the activities of Mena and Santillana, however – not even the latter's four dozen sonnets *al itálico modo* which are one of the earliest essays in the Petrarchist manner outside Italy – would have been recognized by contemporary Italians as 'dispelling blind ignorance', or 'restoring letters'. The translations ushered in, but were not themselves, the advent of humanist philology; they represented a different facet of the Renaissance, a revival based on

---

4. Vespasiano da Bisticci, *Le vite*, a cura di A. Greco, 2 vols (Florence, 1970–6), I, p. 205 (*Vita* of Santillana's son, Cardinal Mendoza, 1428–95); Marquis of Santillana, *Letter to Don Peter, Constable of Portugal*, ed. A. R. Pastor and E. Prestage (Oxford, 1927). On Santillana's library see Schiff, *Bibliothèque*.

5. P. O. Kristeller, 'The European Diffusion of Italian Humanism', in his *Renaissance Thought and the Arts: Collected Essays* (Princeton, 1980), pp. 69–88 (77, n. 23, and 84–5). On Iberian vernacular humanism see N. G. Round, 'Renaissance Culture and its Opponents in Fifteenth-Century Castile', *Modern Language Review*, 57 (1962), pp. 204–15; P. E. Russell, 'Las armas contra las letras', and his *Traducciones y traductores en la Peninsula Ibérica (1400–1550)* (Barcelona, 1984); J. N. H. Lawrance, 'On Fifteenth-Century Spanish Vernacular Humanism', in *Medieval and Renaissance Studies in Honour of R. B. Tate*, ed. I. Michael & R. Cardwell (Oxford, 1986), pp. 63–79.

an idealized late-medieval vision of antiquity. Vernacular humanism thrived unabated for the next century and a half, unaffected by the rise and fall of the professional Latin humanism which is the chief subject of these pages.

For a first encounter with the real aims of the humanists at the court of John II, we must turn to Alonso García de Santa María, bishop of Burgos (Alfonso de Cartagena; *Alfonsus Garsiae Burgensis*, 1384–1456). Cartagena was a *converso* (descendant of a converted Jew); trained at the university of Salamanca as a lawyer and theologian, he entered the service of the Castilian crown at an early age, and had a distinguished career as civil servant and prelate. Amongst his earliest works were translations of Cicero's *Offices, On Old Age, For Marcellus*, and *On Friendship* (1422–3), and of the *On Invention* (completed 1428). Cicero, declared Cartagena, with his solid and useful maxims 'set like precious stones in a mount of persuasive eloquence', offered a *via media* between the dry logic-chopping of scientific scholasticism and the fatuous swank of pagan rhetoric (*elocuencia sin conclusiones*).[6] In the *Retórica de Tulio* he asserted that rhetoric was not an art 'for twisting words about in fancy order and pretty phrases', but rather, as Cicero and Aristotle taught, a weapon 'for moving men's hearts to anger, or pity, or any other emotion which, like any weapon of steel, can be used either for the good or harm of the *república*.'[7] Such views betray the impact of certain fundamental ideas of contemporary Florentine humanists. During a mission to the Portuguese court in 1427, Cartagena met some jurists and rhetoricians recently returned from the Spanish College in Bologna, one of whom showed him Leonardo Bruni's Latin translations of Aeschines' *Against Ctesiphon* and Demosthenes' *De corona*, and of Basil's *On Reading the Classics*. He duly recorded his delight at Bruni's revival of 'Attic eloquence and Greek scholarship, whose streams so long ago ran dry'.[8]

---

6. 'Paresçióme que era bien tomar el medio, e darvos alguna obra mesclada, en que oviesse artículos de sçiençia engastonados en el gastón de la elocuençia', *Libro de Tulio de los ofiçios* (Madrid, Biblioteca Nacional MS 7815, fol. 34).

7. Alfonso de Cartagena, *La rethorica de M. Tullio Ciceron,* .ed. R. Mascagna (Naples, 1969), pp. 29–34 (32, 34). The passage derives not from Aristotle, whose *Rhetoric* Cartagena may have known only by hearsay, but from the *praefatio* of the *De inventione*, and perhaps *De oratore*, I xii, 52–53.

8. *Declinationes*, in A. Birkenmajer, 'Der Streit des Alonso von Cartagena mit Leonardo Bruni Aretino', *Beiträge zur Geschichte der Philosophie des Mittelalters*, 20 (1917–22), Heft 5 (1922), pp. 128–235 (162–4). The Portuguese admirer of Bruni was probably 'messer Valascho Roderighi, chantore Bragarensi di Portogallo', who purchased 'two translations from the Greek by Leonardo Bruni, and a Terence' from the Florentine *libraio* Piero Betucci on 11 March 1425 (Florence, Archivio di Stato, Conv. Sopp. 78 (Badia), vol. 261, I fol. 31). This fixes the date of Cartagena's first acquaintance with Bruni's work to his fourth and last legation to Portugal, September–December 1427. I should like to thank Dr. A. C. De la Mare for this reference.

223

Cartagena's enthusiasm for Ciceronian and Brunian rhetoric was tempered, however, by his professional desire to harness ancient learning in the service of the establishment. This point emerged three years later, in his *Declinationes*, or *Evening Lectures on a New Translation of Aristotle's Ethics* (1430 or 1431). Their 'publication' at the Council of Basel (1436) caused a furore in Italian humanist circles.[9] The work's dedicatee was Fernán Díaz de Toledo, the *converso* head of the Castilian royal bureaucracy; its occasion, a *tertulia*, or erudite evening chat, between the dons of Salamanca and the civil servants of the king's household, to which Díaz de Toledo's nephew Pero (*c.* 1418–66) brought a copy of Bruni's 'new translation' of Aristotle's *Nicomachean Ethics* (1417). Both addressee and setting were significant. Bruni's lambasting of the medieval *vetus interpres* of Aristotle represented a controversial humanist attack, from within the ranks of the professional secretaries to which both Bruni and Díaz de Toledo belonged, on traditional scholastic method, of which Salamanca was a leading centre. Only philologists and Grecians, Bruni proclaimed, could speak with authority on the interpretation of Aristotelian texts. To this debatable point, Bruni added an indefensible one: that any translation of Aristotle must be couched in pure, sweet Ciceronian Latin, not in the rebarbative jargon of those 'barbarian asses', the scholastic translators and commentators. The discussion between Díaz de Toledo's secretaries and the professors must have been heated, inflamed as it was by these professional rivalries.

Cartagena's response, the first serious brush with humanism in Iberian letters, has been represented as knee-jerk obscurantism. It is true that Cartagena's clinching argument – that a real translation of Aristotle must be based, not on what a humanist scholar supposed Cicero might have done with it, but on what Aristotle was actually trying to say – was vitiated by the unexamined assumption that Aristotle's thought is always rational, and can therefore be reconstructed by reason alone, unaided by philology. Nevertheless, Cartagena's Ciceronian versions had already shown that he was no friend to the hispid technicalities of late-medieval scholastic *sophistae*. In insisting that the basic tool for any translation must be a philosopher's mastery of Aristotelian thought,

---

9. *Declinationes super nova quadam Ethicorum Aristotelis translatione*, in Birkenmajer, 'Der Streit', pp. 162–86. The date of composition is deducible from Cartagena's statement in the prologue that the evening discussions of the title took place 'about four years after' his legation to Portugal in 1427 (Birkenmajer, p. 164), and by the reference to John II's wintering in Salamanca, which means 1430 or 1431. On the *Declinationes* and their repercussions in Italy see J. E. Seigel, *Rhetoric and Philosophy in Renaissance Humanism: The Union of Eloquence and Wisdom, Petrarch to Valla* (Princeton, 1968), pp. 123–33 (on Bruni's *Ethica*, 100–21); and O. Di Camillo, *El humanismo castellano del siglo XV* (Valencia, 1976), pp. 203–26.

Cartagena had put his finger on a real blind spot in the early *quattrocento* humanists' programme: their contempt for technical subjects, and especially logic. 'Let us hack off at the root the error of those who think that philosophical meaning is less important than eloquence,' wrote Cartagena, 'for on the contrary it is the higher of the two. *Cicero himself did not deny this*; he claimed oratory as his by right, but left philosophy to others.'[10] The Italian humanists who leapt to the defence of Bruni in 1436 brushed this point aside; they also failed to notice that Cartagena's apology for his ignorance of Greek, which they gleefully held up as proof of his barbarity and incompetence, contained an explicit recognition of the validity of at least one of Bruni's terms of reference. The *Declinationes* are taken up with discussions on the meaning and usage of particular Latin terms, the province of the humanist *grammaticus*. Cartagena noted, for example, that Cicero himself approved the use of neologisms and Greek loan-words for technical terms, a point met with suspicious evasiveness in Bruni's replies.[11] The *Declinationes* were, therefore, a more sophisticated response to Bruni's humanist challenge than is often supposed. As we shall see, they set the agenda for the whole subsequent history of humanist scholarship in Iberia.

By inclination and by the ideology of his *converso* class, Cartagena was both a king's man and ostentatiously orthodox. In the struggle for power between the Crown and the noble factions which was the chief political issue of John II's reign, it is clear that Cartagena (though he perforce used a more traditional vocabulary) regarded both the education of the nobility and religious orthodoxy as powerful weapons in the centralist and regalist cause. His approach to humanism was thus eclectic. It is a striking fact that, after the dust of the *Declinationes* debate had settled, he corresponded on friendly terms with Bruni, as well as with Pier Candido Decembrio and Poggio, commissioning translations of parts of the *Iliad* and Plato's *Republic*, and trying to secure the humanists' services as panegyrists for the Castilian crown. In an epistle to Santillana on the chivalric code (1444), Cartagena used Bruni's researches into the origins of Roman *militia* to emphasize the knight's obligation to the state – even though he was perfectly well aware (as

---

10. 'Nec ipse etiam fons eloquentie Cicero negat, qui oratoriam artem *iure quodam modo proprio sibi vindicans* philosophiam aliis se *concessisse* fatetur', *Declinationes*, Capitulum v (Birkenmajer, p. 175; Seigel, p. 127). The italicized words show Cartagena was thinking of *De officiis*, I, 2: 'nam philosophandi scientiam *concedens* multis, quod est oratoris proprium . . . si id mihi assumo, *videor id meo iure quodam modo vindicare*'.

11. Capitulum III (Birkenmajer, pp. 167–8) cites the *Academica* [I, 25] and *De finibus* [III, 3–5], quoting the latter verbatim. In the same breath, Cartagena cites Isidore's *Etymologies* and the *Catholicon* of Giovanni Balbi as evidence for Greek loan words in Latin; the former was a respectable enough source (and a Spaniard to boot), but Balbi was inexcusable company for a humanist. The passage thus demonstrates to perfection Cartagena's eclectic and heuristic approach.

Bruni affected not to be) that Latin *miles* did not mean 'knight'. On the other hand, in his *Recapitulation of the Kings of Spain* Cartagena resurrected the old thirteenth-century myth of the Castilian monarchy's unbroken descent from the Gothic kings of *Hispania* – a claim which would have sent a shiver up Bruni's back, as 'Gothic' to him was already synonymous with medieval barbarism[12] – in order to justify Castilian royal doctrines of pan-Hispanic absolutism, and to provide an historic sense of mission in the crusade against the Moorish kingdom of Granada.[13]

Typical of this eclecticism was Cartagena's decision to write many of his works in Castilian, epitomized in his translation of Seneca's *On Providence* (1431). The *Libro primero de la providencia de Dios*, part of John II's project to have the complete works of the Cordovan philosopher done into Castilian, became one of the most widely-read and influential works of the age, surviving in at least thirty MSS and numerous printed editions from 1491 to 1551.[14] Its prologue revealed the motives, overtly political and nationalist, behind the project to reclaim the Roman Stoic philosopher for Hispania. By an agile sleight of hand, Seneca's birth in Cordova was turned to account in two ways: first, to make him 'a native of this kingdom and natural subject of the King' (thus emphasizing the 'Gothic succession' of the kings of Castile);[15] and

---

12. In the prologue to his *De bello Italico adversus Gothos* (*c*. 1441), which was translated into Castilian for Santillana's cousin the Count of Alba *c*. 1445 (Schiff, *Bibliothèque*, pp. 357–9), Bruni gave full rein to the traditional humanist jeremiads about the destruction of Roman culture by the Goths.

13. Cartagena's eclectic programme for the education of the aristocracy is expounded in his Latin *Epistola ad Petrum Fernandi de Velasco*, addressed to the Count of Haro *c*. 1440, edited in J. N. H. Lawrance, *Un tratado de Alonso de Cartagena sobre la educación y los estudios literarios* (Barcelona, 1979). For the epistle to Santillana see M. Penna (ed.), *Prosistas castellanos del siglo XV: 1* (Biblioteca de Autores Españoles CXVI: Madrid, 1959), pp. 235–45; for the 'Neo-Gothic' thesis and the *Anacephaleosis regum Hispanie*, R. B. Tate, *Ensayos sobre la historiografía peninsular del siglo XV* (Madrid, 1970), pp. 13–32, 55–73. On Castilian 'absolutism' and the influence of court politics on humanists see A. MacKay, *Spain in the Middle Ages: From Frontier to Empire, 1000–1500* (1977), pp. 131–42, 206–10.

14. The dating and bibliography of John's Senecan project, and of Cartagena's role in it, has been established by the pioneering work of K. A. Blüher, *Séneca en España*, trans. J. Conde (Madrid, 1983), pp. 132–55 [from *Seneca in Spanien: Untersuchungen zur Geschichte der Seneca-Rezeption in Spanien vom 13. bis 17. Jahrhundert* (Munich, 1969)].

15. 'Séneca fue vuestro natural, e nasçido en vuestros reinos; e tenido sería, si biviesse, de vos hazer omenaje . . . E aunque avés grand familiaridat en la lengua latina, peró quisistes aver algunos de sus notables dichos en vuestro castellano lenguaje, por que en vuestra súbdita lengua se leyere lo que vuestro súbdito en los tiempos antiguos compuso' (*Cinco libros de Seneca*, Seville, 1491, fol. 53ʳ; Blüher, *Séneca en España*, p. 137). On the term *(vasallo) natural*, which defined 'the most important relationship of the Castilian polity' by the fact that a subject was born in the kingdom, see MacKay, *Spain in the Middle Ages*, p. 98. The link which Cartagena makes between monarchical propaganda and use of the national language is highly instructive.

second, to claim him as the grand classical representative of Hispanic culture, on whom an alternative Spanish revival of letters, contrary in spirit to Italian national bias and frivolity, might be founded: 'though the Latins give the palm of eloquence to Cicero, his writings are more worldly, and his style slower and more pompous; whereas Seneca puts down the rules of virtue minutely and pithily, as if he were embroidering a silver filigree on the pretty cloth of eloquence.'[16]

Subsequent writers, many of them Cartagena's own protégés, were content to follow the bishop's lead, devoting themselves to the national and vernacular Renaissance without too nice a regard for Italian humanist philology. Even the anti-Italian bias of Diego de Burgos can be traced back to Cartagena, who admitted Italy's cultural pre-eminence but could not resist a sly swipe at Italian scholars 'who torment the world with heaps of books as soon as they are old enough to hold a pen'.[17] Diego made the point about the Spanish revival crystal clear when, in the course of his eulogy of Santillana as restorer of letters, he remarked:

Our great and ingenious gentleman saw with sorrow that the passage of the centuries since *the great era of Lucan, Seneca, Quintilian, and other ancient sages* had robbed his fatherland of its riches and left it desolate; and so he set about with diligence to raise it once again, by his own studies and skill and famous works, to compete with the glories of Athens, the Academy, and Rome.[18]

By Diego's time, lionization of Seneca and these other Spanish-born classical authors had become the order of the day. In 1439, Juan de Mena announced the discovery, dredged up from a medieval Castilian chronicle, that, along with Seneca, Lucan, Trogus Pompeius, Orosius, Averroes, Quintilian, Avicenna, and 'all the philosophers, or almost all', Aristotle had been born in Cordova.[19] The poet and historian Fernán Pérez de Guzmán (1377?-*c.* 1460), who in his elegy on Cartagena's death referred to him as 'that Seneca to whom I played Lucilius', proudly set the solid worth of Seneca, Lucan, and Quintilian against

---

16. *Cinco libros de Seneca*, fols 52ᵛ-3; Blüher, *Séneca en España*, pp. 136-7.

17. 'Non quod nostros Italicis in scripturis coaequemus, cum profecto aequa proportio non est . . . sed [isti] cum sapere incipiunt calamum sumunt, quo fit ut librorum varietate mundum torqueant' (Birkenmajer, 'Der Streit', p. 163). The insult stung Bruni into making a retort about Spanish provincialism (*ibid.*, pp. 198-9) which, as we shall see (footnote 22 below), had notable repercussions.

18. *Triunfo del Marqués*, in Schiff, *Bibliothèque*, pp. 461-2.

19. F. Rico, '*Aristoteles Hispanus*: en torno a Gil de Zamora, Petrarca y Juan de Mena', *Italia medioevale e umanistica*, 10 (1967), pp. 143-64. This was, admittedly, before Mena went to Florence; we hear no more of it after his return.

the 'fool's gold, vain and useless trifles' of the Italian heroes Virgil, Cicero, and Ovid, capping the comparison with the aphorism, 'Spain never gives flowers, only sound and healthy fruit.'[20]

It is interesting to set against these trends the dedication to the Cordovan traveller and bibliophile Nuño de Guzmán (c. 1405–after 1467) of a Latin apology for Seneca's style and Stoicism against the critiques of Quintilian, Aulus Gellius, and other classical writers. The *Life of Seneca* (1440) was one of a number of humanist works commissioned by Guzmán in Florence from his friend Giannozzo Manetti. Manetti's Senecan biography was a serious effort of scholarship, based on ancient sources and illuminated by a real feeling for ancient thought and history; Guzmán's contribution was to inform Manetti of a local tradition which identified a certain house in Cordova as Seneca's. This is the first indication we have of an active antiquarian interest in the classical sites of Iberia. In another Manettian work, a Latin *laudatio* of Guzmán's mother Doña Inés de Torres (1440), the hand of Nuño is again evident in the long excursus – almost half of the complete work – on the traditional identification (erroneous, as it turns out) of Doña Inés's birthplace Zamora with the famous Celtiberian town of Numantia, sacked by Scipio Africanus in 137 B.C.[21]

Guzmán's openly-stated respect for, and even trust of, an Italian made him a loner, at odds with the chauvinistic bias of his contemporaries. But he was on the friendliest of terms with Cartagena, Santillana, and Alfonso de Palencia, whom we shall encounter shortly. In the 1460s, when the ancient geography and history of *Hispania* became a topic of interest to kingly propaganda, and especially after the Union of the Crowns of Castile and Aragon by the Catholic Monarchs (1479), antiquarian investigations on the sites of Roman *Hispania*, of the kind pioneered by Guzmán, became the object of some of the first endeavours of native Iberian scholars to play the Italians at their own game.

The catalyst for this development was the Congress of Mantua (1459–61), where Pius II's ineffectual plan for an international Crusade in response to the fall of Constantinople brought together a remarkable group of Spanish envoys and inspired them to undertake the study and publicizing of their own country's antiquities. The Castilian embassy

---

20. Blüher, *Séneca en España*, pp. 145, 168–73.

21. Giannozzo Manetti, *Vita Socratis et Senecae*, ed. A. De Petris (Florence, 1979). For Guzmán's relations with Manetti, and his travels and book-collecting, see Vespasiano da Bisticci, *Vite*, I, pp. 435–41; J. N. H. Lawrance, 'Nuño de Guzmán and Early Spanish Humanism: Some Reconsiderations', *Medium Ævum*, 51 (1982), pp. 55–84 and *idem, Tres opúsculos de Nuño de Guzmán y Giannozzo Manetti: un episodio del proto-humanismo español* (Salamanca, 1989). The latter contains an edition of Manetti's *Laudatio Agnetis Numantinae*, and further discussion of Guzmán's antiquarianism.

was headed by Iñigo López de Mendoza, the second son of Santillana and later count of Tendilla (d. 1479), whose family were to become the greatest noble patrons of Renaissance architecture and humanist scholarship in the Iberian peninsula. In his retinue was the Sevillian Alfonso de Palencia, an old protégé of Cartagena; with the Papal chancery came another of Cartagena's friends, Rodrigo Sánchez de Arévalo; and with the representatives of John II of Aragon, Joan Margarit.

Rodrigo Sánchez de Arévalo (*Rodericus Zamorensis* or *Palentinus*, 1404–70), bishop of Palencia and *referendarius* in the Curia of Popes Pius II and Paul II, was the first of the three to publish: his *Compendious Hispanic History* was written in Rome and printed there (the first work of Spanish humanism to appear in print) with a dedication to Henry IV of Castile in 1470. Its purpose was twofold: first, to trumpet to a Europe reeling from the Turkish victories the Neo-Gothic myth of the kings of *Hispania* (that is, Castile) and their crusade against the Moors of Granada; and second, to reply to Italian jibes about Spanish barbarism which he had encountered at the Congress.[22] Arévalo's *Compendious History* derived its whole ideology and arrangement from the *Recapitulation* of his revered mentor Cartagena, with one significant exception: whereas Cartagena had been content to stress the Romano-Gothic heritage of *Hispania*, and only to mention in passing the Pre-Roman legends about Hercules' foundation of the 'Spanish' (Castilian) monarchy, Arévalo's furious anti-Italian bias now induced him to comb humanist texts available to him in Rome of sources such as Pomponius Mela, Justin, Strabo, Polybius, and Herodotus, in search of corroboration for his conviction that *prisca Hispania* was a more ancient, more glorious, and more cultured civilization than Rome – and one which was undergoing a renaissance of its own under those descendants of the pre-Trojan Hispanic kings, the monarchs of Castile. He summed up with a ringing quotation from Jerome: 'Nunc in Occidente sol justitiae oritur'. Arévalo's voluminous controversial works confirm that he was no friend to the Italian humanists, but his history was provoked and shaped by the impact of humanism to a greater extent than any previous Spanish book.[23]

Alfonso de Palencia (*Alfonsus Palentinus*, 1423–90) was not a churchman or lawyer like Cartagena, Arévalo, and Margarit, but a

---

22. Arévalo was particularly inflamed by Leonardo Bruni's description of Spain as a provincial outpost 'at the back of beyond' (*in extremo mundi angulo*: see footnote 17), to which he indignantly replied: 'Nonnulli bonarum artium ac rerum inexperti, quod "in angulo mundi" (ut aiunt) Hispania sita esse videatur, contendunt quod in angulo mundi (ut eorum verbis utar) ab orbis gloria aliena videatur' (Tate, *Ensayos sobre la historiografía peninsular*, p. 81).

23. Tate, *Ensayos sobre la historiografía peninsular*, pp. 74–122.

professional man of letters, like the Italian humanists themselves. Like Arévalo, he served his apprenticeship under Cartagena in the early 1440s, after which he travelled to Florence (1447?–1453), where he met Cardinal Bessarion, George of Trebizond, and other humanists. Later he made several official visits to Rome, leading up to the fateful encounter with Arévalo and Margarit in 1459 at Mantua.[24] Besides the ten lost books of his *Antiquities of Hispania*, and his *Little Compendium of the Ancient Sites of Hispania* (in which he referred to Margarit, and refuted his friend Nuño de Guzmán's identification of Zamora as Numantia),[25] the variety and scope of Palencia's works was wider and more unusual than any of the writers I have so far mentioned, ranging from witty Latin epistles to vernacular translations of Plutarch and Josephus, and from Lucianic satires and allegories in both Spanish and Latin to a Latin-Spanish dictionary dedicated to Isabel I. His greatest work, the *Decades of the Deeds of Hispania*, a merciless history of his own times, was never printed.[26] Palencia's Latin style was idiosyncratic but recognizably classical in inspiration, particularly in its indebtedness to the Latin comedians. A MS of Donatus' scholia on Terence (discovered by Aurispa in 1433) with what appear to be Palencia's handwritten annotations (Salamanca University MS 78) shows his interest in Latin style and diction, and suggests (if the marginalia are his) that he had learnt humanist *littera antiqua* script during his Florentine days.

Like Palencia, our third Mantuan delegate, the Catalan cardinal-bishop of Gerona Joan Margarit (*Johannes Gerundensis, c.* 1421–84), knew Italy well before arriving in Mantua. Educated at the Spanish

24. On the Italian travels of Palencia and their influence on his work see R. B. Tate, 'Political Allegory in Fifteenth-Century Spain: a Study of the *Batalla campal de los perros contra los lobos* by Alfonso de Palencia', *Journal of Hispanic Philology*, 1 (1977), pp. 169–86; idem, 'The Civic Humanism of Alfonso de Palencia', *Nottingham Renaissance and Medieval Studies*, 23 (1979), pp. 25–44; and idem, 'El *Tratado de la perfección del triunfo militar* de Alfonso de Palencia (1459): la Villa de Discreción y la arquitectura humanista', in *Essays on Narrative Fiction in the Iberian Peninsula in honour of Frank Pierce* (Oxford, 1982), pp. 163–76.

25. R. B. Tate and A. Mundó, 'The *Compendiolum* of Alfonso de Palencia: a Humanist Treatise on the Geography of the Iberian Peninsula', *Journal of Medieval and Renaissance Studies*, 5 (1975), pp. 253–78; and R. B. Tate, 'The Lost Ten Books of Alfonso de Palencia's *Antiquitates Hispaniae*', in *The Age of the Catholic Monarchs, 1474–1516: Literary Studies in Memory of Keith Whinnom*, ed. A. D. Deyermond and I. Macpherson (Liverpool, 1989), pp. 193–6.

26. On the *Gestarum Hispaniensium Decades* and their humanist traits see R. B. Tate, 'Alfonso de Palencia y los preceptos de la historiografía', in *Nebrija y la introducción del Renacimiento en España: Actas del la III Academia Literaria Renacentista* (Salamanca, 1983), pp. 37–51. The epistles are now available in Alfonso de Palencia, *Epístolas latinas*, ed. R. B. Tate and R. Alemany (Barcelona, 1982).

College in Bologna (1447–53), he spent many years at the Curia in the service of Alfonso V of Aragon and his successor John II (1458–79). On a trip to his diocese in Spain in 1461, Margarit began research for his *Lost Chronicles of Hispania*, about the pre-Gothic period he called the 'forgotten' age.[27] The work remained unfinished on his final return to Rome (1481–84); he intended at the last to dedicate it to the Catholic Monarchs. Margarit's motives paralleled the publicist aims of Arévalo; like him, Margarit saw in the aboriginal virtues of the *prisci Hispani* a powerful charter-myth for the crusading greatness of a reborn and united Spain; but his outlook was that of Mediterranean-oriented Aragon. As his title declared, he had no interest in the Gothic theory, which had been appropriated by the Castilians, and turned by preference to the Ibero-Roman period. Nevertheless, during the shattering civil war of the Catalan revolt (to which he never refers), Margarit remained free of regionalist bias because he was loyal to the Castilian-born John II of Aragon-Navarre, the enemy of the Catalan oligarchs of Barcelona who declared Margarit a 'traitor' in 1471. Perhaps this was why he approached his subject in a more scholarly and dispassionate way than Arévalo, or Arévalo's Italian successor Giovanni Nanni (*Annius Viterbensis*), whose work on the antiquities of Spain, produced in Rome at the behest of the Spanish cardinal Bernardino Carvajal and dedicated to the Catholic Monarchs in 1498, was to push brazen humanist fabrication in the service of this line of historical propaganda beyond the limits of absurdity.[28] Margarit used the latest Latin translations of Strabo, Ptolemy, Diodorus Siculus, Appian and Plutarch, as well as Pomponius Mela, Solinus, and the Antonine *Itinerary* for his researches into the ancient geography and anthropology of the Peninsula. He also visited the ancient sites and ruins himself, and in the five extant revisions of his work took care constantly to replace less reliable medieval sources by antique ones as they came to his notice. Margarit was aided by Aragon's first Hellenist, his fellow in the Curia Jeroni Pau (*Hieronymus Paulus Barcinonensis*, died 1497), who was already writing to friends in Barcelona for information about the ancient epigraphy of the city in 1475. Pau's own works on ancient Iberian toponymy were written for Italian friends who knew nothing about Spain except what

---

27. In his *Templum Domini* (1464), Margarit referred to the *Paralipomenon Hispanie Libri*, then in their first stages, as 'tractatus rerum *obliteratarum* Hispanie', which shows he understood the derivation of *Paralipomenon* (the title of Chronicles I and II in the Vulgate) from the Septuagint's description of Chronicles as 'the kings of Judah *omitted* in Kings I and II'.

28. On the falsifications of Nanni's *Commentaria super opera auctorum diversorum de antiquitatibus loquentium* (Rome, 1498) see Tate, *Ensayos sobre la historiografía peninsular*, pp. 24–32.

they had read in the classics, and therefore wanted to know about such marvels as the Pillars of Hercules, rock-dissolving springs, and horses impregnated by the wind.[29]

In general, the role played by court interests in promoting the impact of humanism in the Crown of Aragon was no less preponderant than we have seen it to be in Castile. In the chanceries of John I (1387–95) and Martin I (1395–1410), a circle of Catalan bureaucrats, zealous followers of Petrarch and Boccaccio, began to write each other Latin epistles in which they strove for a purer style.[30] The stage seemed set for an efflorescence of humanist endeavour in Catalonia; the classicizing movement enjoyed the emphatic prestige of royal favour, and the support of the religious. But the death of Martin I, last of the line of the house of Barcelona, was a blow to Catalan culture. His Castilian successors for a time continued the tradition of royal support of arts and letters, but in 1432 Alfonso V (1416–58) left Catalonia for Italy, never to set foot in Spain again. Once king of Naples (1442), Alfonso pursued that policy of relentless self-aggrandizement which included his well-known maintenance of a menagerie of Italian humanists.[31] The result of this emigration was a lull in the fortunes of humanism, Latin and vernacular, at the provincial courts of Barcelona, Valencia, and Majorca, for a time overshadowed by the activities of Crown Prince Charles of Viana, patron of Theodore Gaza and Angelo Decembrio, in neighbouring Navarre.[32]

---

29. Tate, *Ensayos sobre la historiografía peninsular*, pp. 123–82, and idem, *Joan Margarit, cardenal i bisbe de Girona* (Barcelona, 1976). The biography of Margarit in Vespasiano da Bisticci, *Vite*, I, 207–21, is interesting. On Jeroni Pau see the edition of his *Obres* by M. Villalonga, 2 vols (Barcelona, 1986).

30. J. Rubió i Balaguer, 'El Renacimiento en las letras catalanas', in *Historia General de las literaturas hispánicas, III: Renacimiento y Barroco*, ed. G. Díaz Plaja (Barcelona, 1953), pp. 730–84; idem, *La cultura catalana del Renaixement a la Decadència* (Barcelona, 1964), pp. 9–25. The term 'humanism' should not be applied to this classicizing movement: L. Badia, 'L' "Humanisme català": formació i crisi d'un concepte historiogràfic', in *Actes del 5è Colloqui Internacional de Llengua i Literatura Catalanes, Andorra, 1–6 d'octubre de 1979* (Montserrat, 1980), pp. 41–70.

31. A. Soria, *Los humanistas de la corte de Alfonso el Magnánimo según los epistolarios* (Granada, 1956); J. H. Bentley, *Politics and Culture in Renaissance Naples* (Princeton, 1987).

32. The inventory of Viana's library in 1461, printed by P. Raymond, 'La Bibliothèque de Don Carlos, Prince de Viane', *Bibliothèque de l'École des Chartes*, 19 (1858), pp. 483–7, lists a remarkable collection of Italian MSS of classical and humanist works (including some in Greek) purchased during his residence in Italy, alongside the French romances and translations of his French-speaking predecessors. Viana, who was for a time the patron of Pier Candido Decembrio's son Angelo, himself made a translation of Bruni's version of Aristotle's *Ethics* into Aragonese: A. R. D. Pagden, 'The Diffusion of Aristotle's Moral Philosophy in Spain, c. 1400–c. 1600', *Traditio*, 31 (1975), pp. 287–313.

Typical of the modest figures concerned was the Majorcan jurist and civil servant Ferran Valentí (*Ferdinandus Valentinus, c.* 1400–76), translator of Cicero's *Paradoxa* (*c.* 1450). In Florence in the early 1440s Valentí came under the tutelage of Bruni, whom he eulogized as 'my father and preceptor, glory and honour of the Tuscan language'; back in Majorca, he baptized his children with such names as Theseus, Hippolyta, Phaedra, Polyxena, and Lucretia, wrote Latin epistles and Horatian odes to his colleagues, and read classical texts with a circle of like-minded friends in the Majorcan *palazzo* of councillor Ramon Gual.[33] After Alfonso V's death and the return of the court to the Spanish mainland, there was a rapid revival of Aragonese participation in the new learning. Before long the new presses of Barcelona and Valencia were printing Joan Esteve's adaptation of Valla's *Elegantiae*, Joan Ramon Ferrer's work on pronouns, Italian humanist grammars such as Perotti's *Rudimenta* (Barcelona, 1475), and even classical texts to compete with the Italian industry.[34] Such books catered for the tastes of circles of humanistically-inclined secretaries in Saragossa and Barcelona, notably the one whose members – Valentí's son Teseu, Jeroni Pau, Joan Peyró (the patron of the edition of Perotti), and the Italian brothers Geraldini (Alexander, 1455–85, and Antonio, 1457–1525) – are brought alive for us in their Latin epigrams and epistles, collected by the inveterate scribbler, antiquary, and bibliophile Pere Miquel Carbonell (*Petrus Michael Barcinonensis*, 1434–1517).[35]

The visit to Barcelona in 1432 of Guiniforte Barzizza, the son of the educationalist Gasparino, offering to celebrate the deeds of the kings of Aragon in humanist Latin, came to nothing because Alfonso left the city a few months later.[36] The task was subsequently entrusted to Italian

33. Ferran Valentí, *Traducció de les "Paradoxa" de Ciceró*, ed. J. M. Morató Thomàs (Barcelona, 1959). Valentí is famous for his defence of the vernacular in the prologue to the *Paradoxes*, but it was surely his Latin verse which led Francesco Malecarni to describe him, in a poem submitted to the Florentine *Certame coronario* of 1441, as 'il cortese Ferrando Valentino, / il cui nome in Italia è tanto chiaro': C. Grayson, 'Four Love Letters attributed to Alberti', in *Collected Essays on Italian Language and Literature presented to Kathleen Speight*, ed. G. Aquilecchia and others (Manchester, 1971), pp. 29–44.

34. Rubió, 'El Renacimiento en las letras catalanas', p. 831; F. Rico, *Nebrija frente a los bárbaros: el canón de gramáticos nefastos en las polémicas del humanismo* (Salamanca, 1978), pp. 22–39. On the editions of classical texts and grammars in Barcelona and Valencia before 1480 see British Museum, *Catalogue of Books Printed in the XVth Century now in the British Museum, Part X: Spain, Portugal*, ed. with introductions by L. A. Sheppard and G. D. Painter (1971), pp. x–xi, xxxviii–xl.

35. Rubió, *La cultura catalana*, pp. 79–89.

36. Soria, *Los humanistas de la corte de Alfonso el Magnánimo*, pp. 51–4 and 154–200. Guiniforte's most important patron in Aragon was the royal chancellor Dalmau de Mur, archbishop of Saragossa, an avid collector of classical and humanist texts who was also courted by the rapacious Poggio (*ibid.*, pp. 209–18).

scholars: Lorenzo              ʳ (1445), while
Antonio Becadelli                                  ɔmeo Fazio (1455)
celebrated the deeds and                          th true Neapolitan
unction. Such works set                           which humanists
were to play in celebrat                           ɔ's successors, his
brother John II (1458–79)                          (1479–1516); their
imperialist and Caesarist                          the mainstream of
Spanish historiography when Ferdinand joined his fortunes to those of
Isabel I of Castile in 1469. The subtlest native fruit of this tradition was
the Sallustian *Life of John II of Aragon* (1514) commissioned in 1501 by
Ferdinand from a distant relative of Cartagena, the Saragossan *converso*
jurist Gonzalo García de Santa María (*Gundisalvus Garsia de Sancta
Maria*, 1447–1521).[37]

Another characteristic product of the Aragonese-Italian connection
were the Latin comedies and poems celebrating important events such
as the capture of Granada from the Moors in 1492. The poems were
imitations of classical epics, panegyrical odes, and epithalamia, such as
Baptista Mantuanus's *Alfonsus* and Zuppardi's *Alfonseidos*. The comedies were humanist adaptations of the Italian *farse* and allegorical
masques performed at the Aragonese court in Naples during the royal
entries and pageants so beloved of Alfonso and his heirs, whose most
enduring monument is the Triumphal Arch constructed on Roman
models for Alfonso's entry into Naples in 1443, commemorated in
Porcellio de' Pandoni's Latin *Triumph of Alfonso of Aragon on the Fall
of Naples*. Sannazaro's Italian *Trionfo della fama* (on the fall of Granada)
and Girolamo Morlini's curious pastoral *Parthenopea* (on the French
expedition against Naples), were thus paralleled by the more strictly
humanistic Latin comedies of Carlo and Marcellino Verardi, *Ferdinand
Preserved* (in verse, on the attempted assassination of Ferdinand in
Barcelona, 1492) and *Andalusian Story* (in prose, set against the capture
of Granada), performed in Cardinal Carvajal's household in Rome in
1493 and printed there, in Salamanca, and in Basel a number of times
before 1500. However, it was the pageant element, rather than the
humanistic one, which was uppermost in Iberian imitations, which
continued the masques (*momos*) and revels (*entremeses*) which had characterized Iberian courts since the early fifteenth century. There was,
nevertheless, one aspect of these mummeries which lent itself to specifically humanist treatment. It was customary for the court revels to
include scenes played by the shepherd-buffoons of Nativity plays; these
rustic yokels were transmogrified, by humanist poets, into the swains
and shepherdesses of classical pastoral, giving rise on one side to

37. Tate, *Ensayos sobre la historiografía peninsular*, pp. 212–62.

234

humanist *contrafacta* such as Antonio Geraldini's religious *Bucolica sacra*, written in Saragossa in 1484, and on the other to the hybrid vernacular *Eclogues* of the musician Juan del Encina (1468–1529), a pupil of Nebrija at Salamanca who later visited Italy where some of his plays were written and performed, and the *farsas*, *autos*, and *comédias* of the Portuguese court playwright Gil Vicente (1465?–1536?). The plays of Bartolomé de Torres Naharro (*c.* 1485–1520?), performed in the Roman household of Cardinal Carvajal and published there in 1517, introduced still further humanist elements such as the five-act structure into the eclogue-pageant tradition.[38]

Turning to the far west of the Peninsula we find a similar tale to the one we have traced for Castile and Aragon. When Alfonso de Cartagena visited the Portuguese court in the 1420s, the contacts of Lusitanian bureaucrats and lawyers with Florentine and Bolognese scholarship and booksellers were not far behind those of Castilians at the same date.[39] But there was no nobleman of the stature of Santillana willing to indulge a dilettante taste for Italian books, and the products of Portuguese vernacular humanism were shadows of the work going forward in neighbouring Castile.[40] The whole responsibility for fostering the new scholarship thus devolved upon the monarchs and secretaries of the house of Avis. The court maintained good contacts with Italian scholarship through its diplomats and prelates, as we see from the biographies of Portuguese clients in the *Vite* of Vespasiano

---

38. On the Neo-Latin panegyric in Spain see Alcina's essay in *L'Humanisme dans les lettres espagnoles*, ed. A. Redondo (Paris, 1979), pp. 133–49; D. Briesemeister, 'Episch-dramatische Humanistendichtung zur Eroberung von Granada (1492)', in *Texte–Kontexte–Strukturen: Festschrift K. A. Blüher*, ed. A. de Toro (Tübingen, 1987), pp. 249–63. For Sannazaro and Morlini see M. T. Herrick, *Italian Comedy in the Renaissance* (Urbana, 1966), pp. 24–9; for Spanish pageant plays, N. D. Shergold, *A History of the Spanish Stage from Medieval Times until the End of the Seventeenth Century* (Oxford, 1967), pp. 113–42, 145–50, 167–8; for the humanist influence on the dramatic eclogues, M. J. Bayo, *Virgilio y la pastoral española del Renacimiento* (Madrid, 1959), pp. 1–63. On the separate tradition of humanist school-comedy, see below, footnotes 67–8.

39. See footnote 8 above.

40. The translations of Cicero's *De officiis*, *De amicitia*, and *De senectute*, of Vegetius, and of Pliny's *Panegyricus*, produced in most cases by the Castilian Vasco Fernández de Lucena for Duke Pedro of Coimbra and his nephew Alfonso V, probably derive from Castilian versions (though this is disputed by J. M. Piel, in his edition of 'Infante Dom Pedro de Coimbra', *Livro dos Ofícios de Marco Tullio Ciceram* [Coimbra, 1948], pp. v–lxxvi). In contrast, the 'Memória dos livros do uso (1438)' of their predecessor Edward I (1433–38) – for whom Cartagena translated Cicero's *De inventione* – reveals a medieval taste, even in the few classical authors mentioned: Seneca, Valerius Maximus, Cicero: A. Caetano de Sousa, *Provas da Historia Genealogica da Casa Real Portugueza*, 6 vols (Lisbon, 1739–48; repr. in 11 vols. ed. M. Lopes de Almeida and César Pegado, Coimbra, 1946–54), i ii, pp. 257–9.

da Bisticci.[41] The most intriguing of these is 'messer Velasco di Portogallo' – student madcap, devotee of Petrarch, and avid bibliophile, he
must be the *Velascus Portugalensis*, 'orator of the King', addressed in
three epistles of the indefatigable leech Poggio, one of them (1436) on
the importance of ancient rhetoric; and it was probably he who
arranged Poggio's panegyric of Prince Henry the Navigator, discussed
below. Poggio's accusation that Velascus's niggardliness in providing
emolument for services rendered was due to crypto-Judaism ('neither
Jew nor Christian, you care not a fig for either faith') proves that this
Velascus was Vasco Fernández de Lucena (1410?–95), a Castilian
*converso* jurist who served as Portuguese spokesman at the Councils of
Basel and Florence, and later as translator, chronicler, and secretary
under three Portuguese kings. His name crops up in connection with
almost every humanist initiative in fifteenth-century Portugal.[42]

   There was one respect in which Portugal outpaced her easterly
neighbours. Dom Pedro of Coimbra (Regent, 1439–47), who visited
Florence in the late 1420s,[43] and his ward Alfonso V (1438–81) realized
the important role which humanism and the revival of letters might
play, not merely in giving the sheen of elegance to princely life, but
more particularly in broadcasting the overseas explorations of Portuguese navigators, which began to astound Europe in the 1430s. This
was one Iberian interest which was eagerly reciprocated by the Italian
humanists themselves. We have noted that Poggio wrote to Henry the
Navigator on his exploits (*c.* 1439), angling for an invitation to become
official chronicler. He was not employed – to employ Poggio was to
risk extortion and blackmail – but his *India Revealed*, in a version

---

41. Vespasiano da Bisticci, *Vite*, I, 193–9 (Cardinal James of Avis, 1433–59); I, 349–51
(Alvaro Afonso, Bishop of Evora); II, 83–9 ('Velasco di Portogallo'). Bishop Afonso was
the recipient of a most interesting letter (1441) from Poggio concerning the rumour of
a complete MS of Aulus Gellius at the monastery of Alcobaça: see Poggio Bracciolini,
*Lettere, II: Epistularum familiarium libri*, ed. H. Harth (Florence, 1984), pp. 373–4. *Velascus*
is mentioned in this letter as intermediary; the addressee is wrongly identified as Alfonso
de Cartagena by R. Sabbadini, *Le scoperte dei codici latini e greci*, I, 92, and by subsequent
scholars (Poggio's first letter to Cartagena is dated 1443).
   42. The letters to 'Velascus' are in Poggio, *Lettere, II*, pp. 213–14, 220, 245; for the
identification with Lucena see N. Espinosa Gomes da Silva, *Humanismo e Direito em
Portugal no século XVI* (Lisbon, 1964), pp. 114–16. For Vasco's role in propagandizing
the Discoveries see below.
   43. Coimbra's bookish interests were rewarded in Florence by the dedication of
Ambrogio Traversari's Latin translation of a Greek text by John Chrysostom: G. Battelli,
'Una dedica inedita di Ambrogio Traversari all'Infante Don Pedro di Portogallo, Duca
di Coimbra', *La Rinascita*, 2 (1939), pp. 613–16. During this voyage Dom Pedro may
also have made contact with Pier Paolo Vergerio, whose *De moribus ingenuis et liberalibus
studiis* he had translated into Portuguese by Vasco Fernández de Lucena on his return to
Portugal: Pedro de Coimbra, *Livro dos Ofícios de Marco Tullio Ciceram*, pp. xlvi–vii.

adapted by Pius II, is supposed to have influenced Columbus. The significance of the letter for us is that Poggio for the first time applied the concept of 'discovery' to the Portuguese explorations. The notion was a humanist one; what Poggio meant was not that the newly-charted lands and seas were uninhabited, but that they had been *terra incognita* to classical geographers. Comparing Henry to Alexander the Great (a comparison taken up by Gomes Eanes de Zurara in his *Chronicle of the Affairs of Guinea*, and by many subsequent writers), Poggio stated that, whereas the ancient hero had only conquered the known world, the Portuguese prince had ventured into the unknown.[44]

The celebrated Bull *Romanus Pontifex*, issued in 1455 by Nicholas V in recognition of Portuguese rights to discoveries in Africa (the Portuguese orator in these negotiations was the ubiquitous Vasco Fernández de Lucena), initiated a series of politico-legal debates on the conquests – debates which were to become acute with the Spanish conquest of the New World. From the first, humanist scholars had a vital role to play in these debates, as propagandists and later (as we shall see) as participants. It was an important moment, therefore, when in 1460 Alfonso V commanded his tutor and secretary, the Italian Matteo Pisano (d. 1466), to translate the *Chronicle of the Siege of Ceuta* (1450) of Gomes Eanes de Zurara (*c.* 1420–73/4) into Latin: the capture of the North African stronghold in 1415 had marked the beginning of Portuguese overseas expansion.[45] Bigger fish soon began to bite: in 1461, Flavio Biondo wrote to the monarch, probably as an official representative of the Pope, offering his services as historian of the Moroccan conquests.[46] Alfonso declined, giving the job instead to the recently-appointed Italian bishop of Ceuta, Fra Giusto Baldino, who was carried off by beri-beri before putting pen to paper.

In 1489, a similar offer was made to Alfonso's successor John II (1481–95) by Politian, who by that time counted amongst his distinguished Portuguese pupils in Florence the sons of John's chan-

---

44. Poggio Bracciolini, *Epistolae*, ed. T. Tonelli, 3 vols (Turin, 1832–61; repr. in 1 vol. 1963), II, pp. 379–82 (also in *Monumenta Henricina* [Coimbra, 1960–], IX, no. 186, pp. 297–302). On the letter's significance see W. G. L. Randles, 'Sur l'idée de la Découverte et sa diffusion', in *Les Aspects internationaux de la découverte océanique aux XV^e et XVI^e siècles: V^e Colloque International d'Histoire Maritime, Lisbonne 14–16 septembre 1960*, ed. M. Mollat and P. Adam (Paris, 1966), pp. 17–21; and P. Chaunu, *European Expansion in the Later Middle Ages*, trans. K. Bertram (Amsterdam–New York–Oxford, 1979), pp. 201–4.

45. *De bello Septensi*, in J. Correia da Serra *et al.*, *Collecção de livros ineditos de historia portugueza* (Lisbon, 1790), I, pp. 1–57; F. de Figueiredo, *A Epica Portuguesa no Seculo XVI* (São Paulo, 1950), pp. 69–74.

46. Figueiredo, *A Epica Portuguesa*, p. 89, records the destruction of the Dresden MS of Biondo's letter by Allied bombing during the Second World War.

cellor João Teixeira. Politian once again rehearsed the notion of 'discoveries of new lands, new seas, new worlds, and even new stars'. The humanist perspective implied in this statement was made even clearer when Politian described the explorations, in a metaphor familiar from other contexts, as 'bringing forth the new from the shadows of ancient Chaos'. This time the king accepted the offer, in a letter which makes it quite clear that what he wanted from the Florentine scholar was the epic grandeur conferred by the polish of his humanist Latin; but Politian, too, died before beginning his task (1494).[47] By that time the king was looking to native Latinists such as Vasco Fernández de Lucena, Fernando de Almeida, and Diogo Pacheco to publicize the glories of Portuguese overseas expansion in the speeches of fealty to the Roman pontiff which were used to announce the pretensions of the Portuguese Crown.[48] Meanwhile the *Arcitinge* (*c.* 1490), a Latin poem on the capture of Arzila and Tangier (1471) by a resident Sicilian humanist, Cataldo Parisio, took the first step towards raising the Portuguese exploits to the level of epic, a path which was continued in the humanist chronicles of Damião de Góis and João de Barros, and ended in the greatest literary triumph of the Portuguese Renaissance, Camoens's *Lusiads*.

## II

Humanist orators of the 1480s were fond of proclaiming themselves the torchbearers of a 'new epoch'. What lay behind this bombastic claim, apart from the advent of printing, was the migration of the humanists from the courts and chanceries of princes to stipendiary posts in the universities – summed up in the 1490s by the coining in Italian academic circles of the opprobrious term *umanista* to describe the new class of professional classicists (the word was a witty cross-formation of the term *studia humanitatis* and the titles of the humanists' arch-rivals, the canonists, jurists, and legists). Modern historians consequently treat the years 1480–1530 as the heyday of humanist activity. But we must beware of applying the neat periodization too crudely. Confidently to date 'the beginning of the Renaissance' in Portugal to the year 1485 and the arrival in Lisbon of Cataldo (*Cataldus Parisius Siculus, c.* 1453–after

---

47. Figueiredo, *A Epica Portuguesa*, pp. 90–108 (with texts of the letters).

48. On the *orationes obedientiae* pronounced by Lucena (1485, printed in Rome the same year), Almeida (1493), and Pacheco (1505 and 1514) see Figueiredo, *A Epica Portuguesa*, pp. 75–85, and L. de Matos, 'L'Expansion portugaise dans la littérature latine de la Renaissance', in *L'Humanisme protugais et l'Europe: Actes du XXIᵉ Colloque International d'Études Humanistes, Tours 3–13 juillet 1978* (Paris, 1984), pp. 397–417.

1516?) is an unconvincing ploy. It is less absurd to make an epoch of the publication, at Salamanca in 1481, of Antonio de Nebrija's *Latin Introductions*; but even in Iberia, as I have tried to show in the preceding section, Renaissance humanism was not invented overnight by a couple of enlightened individuals. Cataldo, for example, made all the expected noises, describing himself as the Hercules who wrestled single-handed with the many-headed Hydra of Portuguese barbarism;[49] in reality he was a wandering scrounger who accepted a lucrative invitation to the Portuguese court as tutor to John II's bastard, and thereafter devoted himself to grooming the sons of various noble houses. That he should have found employment and an enthusiastic welcome for his indecent epigrams and well-turned compliments at the dinner-tables of the mighty implies that a taste for humanism had wormed its way into Portuguese society before he arrived.

Meanwhile many of the native Portuguese who were to effect the business of expelling barbarism during the reigns of Manuel I (1495–1521) and John III (1521–57) were in Italy, studying at the Spanish College at Bologna, at Padua, or in Florence under Politian himself.[50] In the 1490s Lisbon grammarians were still teaching Latin with the *arte velha* ('old grammar') of the fifteenth-century Castilian barbarian Juan de Pastrana, albeit in their own updated versions (*artes novas*). Before long, however, a convert to the school of Nebrija, Estêvão Cavaleiro (*Stephanus Eques Lusitanus*), proposed a wholesale reform, in the spirited prologue to his *New Art of Grammar* (1493, revised 1516), which he dedicated 'to expelling pertinacious barbarism from Lusitania, and also to the honour and glory of God and the Virgin Mary'. He attacked Pastrana and all previous tinkerings with Pastrana as muddy cesspools of corruption and fields of wild oats. Cavaleiro's spite was directed at the older readers at Lisbon university, who preferred their own methods to his. As examples of civilized Latinists, Cavaleiro listed his friends Diogo Pacheco, Luís Teixeira, Francisco Cardoso, and Cataldo Parisio. The latter crucified Pedro Rombo, the last professor who favoured Pastrana's *arte* (in an edition published by himself in 1497), as 'that long-earned donkey with his ugly tonsure and

---

49. 'Conquaestio ad Iohannem Emmanuelem regis cubicularium' (a comic begging-ode to the royal chamberlain, 1495/9), in Sousa, *Provas da Historia Genealogica*, VI ii, pp. 179–88 (182–3). In the same passage, Cataldo claimed to have 'brought light to the benighted through all the cities of Italy'; he refers to his attempts to cadge a post in Bologna, Rome, and Ferrara. On Cataldo Parisio see A. da Costa Ramalho, *Estudos sobre a Epoca do Renascimento* (Coimbra, 1969) and *Estudos sobre o Século XVI* (Lisbon, 1983).

50. A. Moreira de Sá, *Humanistas portugueses em Itália* (Lisbon, 1983); Silva, *Humanismo e Direito em Portugal no Século XVI*, pp. 112–75.

his knotty *Rod'* – an obscene pun on the title of Rombo's grammar, *Stick for the Blind*. This did not deter Rombo, who became rector of the university; it was his demise in 1533, and the impact of the novel weapon of printing, introduced in Portugal and Spain with powerful royal subventions,[51] which at last assured the tardy triumph of the humanist method. Outside the university walls, humanist classicism was already flourishing. Manuel I invited the Flemish scholars Clenardus, Vasaeus, and Fabricius to Portugal to teach the ancient languages. In the 1530s, John III put in motion the reforms which led to the removal of Lisbon university to Coimbra (1537), where in 1543 was inaugurated the celebrated Colégio das Artes. This, staffed in 1548 by a series of distinguished humanists brought in from Bordeaux including the Gouveia brothers, Diogo de Teive, and the Scot George Buchanan, was intended to be the nucleus and powerhouse of Portuguese humanist scholarship.[52]

Cavaleiro's admiration for Antonio of Lebrixa (known as Nebrija, *Aelius Antonius Nebrissensis*, 1444–1522) reflects the intellectual influence which Castile, the dominant political and cultural power in the Peninsula, now exercised over her neighbours east and west. Like Cataldo Parisio, Nebrija arrogated to himself the title 'conqueror of barbarism' (*debelador de la barbarie*). Nebrija, however, had in him the stuff of a genuine culture hero. A native Spaniard educated at the Spanish College in Bologna, he was the intellectual match of any Italian; his pioneering work on the pronunciation of Greek is held in esteem by classical

51. See the introductions by Sheppard and Painter in British Museum, *Catalogue of Books Printed in the XVth Century, Part X*, and F. J. Norton, *Printing in Spain, 1501–1520. With a Note on the Early Editions of the "Celestina"* (Cambridge, 1966) and *idem, A Descriptive Catalogue of Printing in Spain and Portugal 1501–1520* (Cambridge, 1978). In Portugal, the earliest press to print in types other than Hebrew was financed almost entirely by John II and his consort Eleanor, and later by her brother Manuel I (Norton, *Descriptive Catalogue*, pp. 491–501), and by the grant of the first *privilégios*, or copyright monopolies. In Spain, where output was higher and more diverse, and presses were spread out over a huge country, the role of the Crown was relatively less preponderant, but quantitatively no less important; Isabel protected certain favoured native presses by import tariffs, decrees, financing of editions, *privilégios*, and fiscal and military exemptions to masterprinters.

52. On Cavaleiro's *Nova grammatices ars* see Ramalho, *Estudos sobre o Século XVI*, pp. 125–51. Cataldo's epigram 'Ad Cavalerium' on Rombo's *Baculum cecorum* is in Sousa, *Provas da Historia Genealogica*, VI ii, p. 275. On the development of Portuguese humanist scholarship see J. Sebastião da Silva Dias, *A Política Cultural da Época de D. João III* (Coimbra, 1969); on Buchanan and his companions at Coimbra, I. D. McFarlane, *Buchanan* (1981), pp. 122–58.

scholars.[53] Besides, Nebrija played a real role in the institutional reform of Spanish university education. Nevertheless, as in the case of Cataldo, we must not forget the part which rhetorical self-fashioning, as well as a considerable dash of wit, played in Nebrija's assiduous creation of his own legend. This started with the substitution of his humble Spanish name, Antonio Martínez, by the impressive-sounding *Aelius Antonius Nebrissensis*, concocted by identifying his Andalusian village Lebrija with the *Nebrissa Veneria* mentioned in a poem by Silius Italicus (*Punica*, III, 393–5), and from some ancient lapidary inscriptions to unknown Aelii and Aeliani found in the fields near his birthplace – archaeological evidence, as Nebrija affected to believe, that he was related to his fellow-Spaniards the emperors Aelius Hadrian and Aelius Trajan.

It was part of Nebrija's carefully-nurtured image never to acknowledge predecessors. Yet his affinity to the native tradition going back to Cartagena is striking. He must have known Palencia, who was a familiar of Nebrija's first patron Archbishop Fonseca of Seville; and been acquainted with Margarit's *Lost Chronicles* and Cartagena's *Recapitulation*, both of which were printed in 1545, presumably from copies among Nebrija's personal papers, by his son Sancho (*Xanthus Nebrissensis*). Nevertheless, Nebrija omitted to mention any of these in his own *Sample of a History of Spanish Antiquities* (Burgos, 1499), a short Castilian foretaste for Isabel I of a promised five-volume Latin work. The *Sample* began with a list of sources suspiciously reminiscent of a similar list in Margarit's book, with the difference that Nebrija named sixteen new sources – three of them genuine. In a later reference to the still forthcoming *Antiquitates*, he blustered that his five tomes would soon disprove 'the theories of all those who have ever written anything

53. For biographical and bibliographical studies of Nebrija see P. Lemus y Rubio, 'El Maestro Elio Antonio de Lebrixa', *Revue Hispanique*, 22 (1910), pp. 459–506, and 29 (1913), pp. 13–120; the editor's introduction to Antonio de Nebrija, *Gramatica de la lengua castellana (Salamanca, 1492). Muestra de la istoria de las antigüedades de España. Reglas de orthographia en la lengua castellana*, ed. I. González-Llubera (Oxford, 1926); F. G. Olmedo, *Nebrija (1441–1522): Debelador de la barbarie, comentador eclesiástico, pedagogo, poeta* (Madrid, 1942), and his *Nebrija en Salamanca (1475–1513)* (Madrid, 1944). On Nebrija's contribution to classical scholarship there is much to be done, but the keystone has been laid by Rico, *Nebrija frente a los bárbaros*; in English we have I. Bywater, *The Erasmian Pronunciation of Greek and its Precursors: Jerome Aleander, Aldus Manutius, Antonio de Lebrixa* (Oxford, 1908), and the brief but acute remarks in. G. A. Padley, *Grammatical Theory in Western Europe 1500–1700: The Latin Tradition* (Cambridge, 1976). The studies by Rico, Gil, and Codoñer in *Nebrija y la introducción del Renacimiento en España* give a taste of the excellent Spanish scholarship now in progress.

whatever on this subject'.[54] The pugnacious boast was intended to damn to outer darkness not only Cartagena, Margarit, and Palencia, but also a living rival, the Spanish-domiciled Sicilian scholar Luca di Marinis (*Lucius Marineus Siculus, c.* 1444–1533), whose *On the Glories of Spain* had appeared in Salamanca in 1496.[55] Despite this contempt for his uncouth rivals, Nebrija shared with them a tendency to glorify pre-Roman Spain at the expense of Roman (and hence Italian) civilization, and an allegiance to royal ideology. When invited to become one of the royal historians by King Ferdinand (1509), Nebrija did not hesitate to begin his *Decades of the Deeds of Ferdinand and Isabel of the Spains* with the forged classical documents of Giovanni Nanni's gloriously irresponsible *rifacimento* (1498) of the introduction to Arévalo's *Compendious History*. He applauded the king's choice of a native historian (himself) rather than the expected Italian with a quotation from Cato about the influence on Rome of effeminate Hellenes, 'which we may apply to the Italians: "as soon as these fellows teach us letters, we shall be utterly corrupted".' Notorious republicans ('sectarians of some *sham* of liberty'), Italians would very likely belittle Spain's imperial greatness out of envy.[56] As we have seen, this parallel between cowardly Italians and mendacious Greeks had occurred to Diego de Burgos as long ago as 1460. In the prologue to his Spanish-Latin dictionary of 1494, Nebrija's boast that his aim in travelling to Italy had been, 'by the law of retribution (*por la ley de la tornada*), to restore their lost homelands to the Latin authors who have so long been exiled from Spain' was merely a variation on the hoary anti-Italian topic of the *translatio studii*.

Soon after his return from Bologna in 1470, Nebrija set out for Salamanca with the intention, as he tells us in a celebrated passage, of 'bearding barbarism in its den'; and in 1481, he published his *Latin Introductions*, a textbook on Latin grammar which was designed to replace the medieval manuals then in use in the Salamancan lecture halls. The success of the *Introductions* was phenomenal; they were immediately reprinted (1482), issued in a bilingual edition for Queen Isabel (*c.* 1487), revised and expanded several times (notably in the

---

54. 'Preface' to *Aenigmata iuris civilis* (1506), published in Antonio de Nebrija, *Léxico de derecho civil*, ed. C. H. Núñez (Madrid, 1944). The *Muestra de la historia de las antigüedades de España* is in Nebrija, *Gramatica de la lengua castellana*, ed. González-Llubera.

55. C. Lynn, *A College Professor of the Renaissance: Lucio Marineo Sículo among the Spanish Humanists* (Chicago, 1937). Marineo taught at Salamanca 1484–96; by 1488, he was complaining of Nebrija's enmity in letters to his fellow-countrymen Peter Martyr and Cataldo Parisio.

56. On the *Rerum a Ferdinando et Elisabe Hispaniarum regibus gestarum Decades* see Tate, *Ensayos sobre la historiografía peninsular*, pp. 183–211. Nebrija went on to edit a volume of Nanni's *Opuscula* for the press (Burgos, 1512).

*recognitio* of 1496), again reprinted, and exported all over Iberia and Europe. The second edition was republished, for example, in Venice in 1491, and the most extensive version, of over 400 pages, appeared in Lyon in 1524; the book was much used in England. At a stroke, the *Introductions* overshadowed all the other efforts of humanistically-inclined Iberian pedagogues.[57]

To open the definitive *recognitio* of this famous book is a strange experience for the modern reader, indoctrinated by centuries of adulation and by Nebrija's own fanfares into expecting a wholly innovative work. What he finds are hundreds of closely printed columns of Gothic black-letter text, in which bare grammatical rules, some of them couched in traditional doggerel verses for memorization, are surrounded by a sprawling gloss. The obsolete features of Nebrija's book were indeed pointed out by some dissident contemporaries. Lucio Marineo found the *Introductions* so unwieldy to use in his classes for the sons of the nobility (by 1495, they had reached over three hundred pages) that he wrote his own counterblast, *A Brief and Handy Grammar* (dedicated to Isabel I *c.* 1496; printed 1532), a primer of some sixty-seven leaves which taught the rudiments by short examples from classical authors. Marineo summed up his purpose in a sentence: 'I beseech you, grammarians all, not to spread over five years what can be taught in as many months.' By the 1530s, the Erasmian Cristóbal de Villalón was to suggest ironically that Nebrija's *arte* was itself the serpent responsible for 'the original sin of barbarism' in Spain.[58]

Villalón, however, was writing in a Spain which had already had fifty years to absorb the impact of Nebrija's teaching. Back in the 1480s, as Nebrija explained in the prologue to the *recognitio*, the old-fashioned verses, which were not used in the first version, had to be reintroduced in the second in order to smooth ruffled feathers within

---

57. Rico, *Nebrija frente a los bárbaros*, gives a succinct account of the reform of Latin grammar in Spain; Codoñer, in *Nebrija y la introducción del Renacimiento en España*, pp. 105–22, assesses Nebrija's originality. For the bibliography of the *Introductiones Latinae* see A. Odriozola, 'La caracola del bibliófilo nebrisense, o la casa a cuestas, indispensable al amigo de Nebrija para navegar por el proceloso de sus obras. Extracto seco de bibliografía de Nebrija en los siglos XV y XVI', *Revista de Bibliografía Nacional*, 7 (1946), 3–114.

58. The critiques of *Antonio* (as Nebrija's grammar became known by antonomasia) in the generation of Juan de Valdés and Cristóbal de .Villalón were affected by Erasmianism and anti-Andalusian prejudice: see E. A. de Asís, 'Nebrija y la crítica contemporánea de su obra', *Boletín de la Biblioteca de Menéndez Pelayo*, 17 (1935), pp. 30–45; J. M. Sola-Solé, 'Villalón frente a Nebrija', *Romance Philology*, 28 (1974), pp. 35–43; and E. Asensio and J. Alcina, "*Paraenesis ad politiores litteras adversus grammaticorum vulgum*" *(s.l., 1529): Juan Maldonado y el humanismo español en tiempos de Carlos V* (Madrid, 1980).

the bastions of traditional institutional pedagogy.[59] It was the incidental remarks in the prefaces and ever-expanding gloss of the successive editions of the *Introductions*, and above all his steadfast refusal to countenance the speculative linguistic theories of scholastic *modistae* who derived grammatical rules not from classical usage but from logic, which encapsulated Nebrija's findings on the phonology and accidence of the classical language. The dynamite of his ideological position was declared in a brilliant series of *repetitiones* (Latin orations traditionally delivered by a professor on St Luke's Day at the opening of the academic year at Salamanca) on points of humanist scholarship. The most famous is the *Repetitio secunda*, delivered and published in 1486, subtitled *On the Corrupt Pronunciation of Certain Letters by Ignorant Spaniards* (reprinted in an expanded version as *On the Force and Power of the Alphabet*, 1503), in which, in the course of various disquisitions on the digamma, Nebrija fustigated the medieval barbarism of Spanish scholarship, and outlined the ideal of the humanist *grammaticus* as a polymath whose deep knowledge of Latin language and letters made him the arbiter of all the academic disciplines. This predated Politian's celebrated statement of the same idea, the *Praelectio 'Lamia'* (1492), by a decade.[60] All sciences, Nebrija argued, are based on language, which only the humanist grammarian is capable of purifying and systematizing; *ergo*, the humanist is the expert of final recourse in all sciences. To borrow the vocabulary of the eighteenth-century Enlightenment, Nebrija's *grammaticus* – now fancifully transformed from the despised medieval choir-school dominie into the torchbearer of a whole culture – corresponded not to the *grammairien*, but to the philosopher *encyclopédiste*.

Nebrija's *Repetitio secunda* represented a return to the debate addressed in Cartagena's *Declinationes*, set in the Salamanca of half a century before. Cartagena argued against Bruni that Ciceronianism must be subject to philosophical rigour; Nebrija, in common with most

---

59. Rico, *Nebrija frente a los bárbaros*, pp. 46–7, cites Nebrija's words on the mixed reception of the first edition ('hominibus carmini Alexandrino [*i.e.* Alexander of Villedieu's *Doctrinale*] assuetis non multum placebant'). Some surprising products of Nebrija's pen – his edition of the despised medieval school-texts of the *Libri minores* and excerpts from hymns and catechistical matter, and perhaps his edition of Giovanni Nanni – were hack works which the great scholar undertook at the importunate bidding of unenlightened patrons.

60. On the *Repetitio secunda*, on *Repetitiones* in general, and on the influence of Politian's ideal of the *grammaticus* see J. Alcina, 'Poliziano y los elogios de las letras en España (1500–1540)', *Humanistica Lovaniensia*, 25 (1976), pp. 198–222; Rico, *Nebrija frente a los bárbaros*, especially pp. 48–56; *idem*, '*Laudes litterarum*: humanisme et dignité de l'homme dans l'Espagne de la Renaissance', in *L'Humanisme dans les lettres espagnoles*, ed. Redondo, pp. 31–50; and L. Gil, 'Nebrija y el menester del gramático', in *Nebrija y la introducción del Renacimiento en España*, pp. 53–64.

humanists of his time, tacitly accepted the limitation upon Ciceronianism, but fell back on Bruni's stronger point, that philosophy must be subject to philological rigour.[61] The rest of Nebrija's many-sided career may be understood as a practical demonstration of the philosopher-grammarian's task, applied not only to the etymology, accentuation and pronunciation of the classical languages, and to his pioneering work on the grammar of the vernacular,[62] but also to the vocabulary of law, cosmography, astronomy, and – most important of all – Holy Scripture.

But Nebrija was only one of the men who contributed to the great project of biblical scholarship initiated by Cardinal Archbishop Francisco Jiménez de Cisneros (formerly known in English as Ximenes, 1436–1517), which resulted in the foundation of the Trilingual College and university of Alcalá, and in the publication of the six volumes of the renowned Complutensian Polyglot Bible (1514–1517).[63] In Nebrija's lifetime, droves of Italians and Sicilians visited Spain, while Alcalá and Salamanca were endowed with more than their fair share of fine native scholars. The anti-Aristotelian Fernando Alonso de Herrera (1460–1527), editor of Valla's *Elegantiae* and Trapezuntius's *Rhetoric* and author of several treatises on tricky grammatical points, upheld the humanist against the scholastic approach to philosophy. His friend the Italian-trained Hellenist and textual critic Hernán Núñez de Toledo (El Comendador Griego, *Ferdinandus Pincianus*, 1475?–1553) and the Sicilian Lucio Flaminio were perfect types of the humanist philologist, explaining knotty passages in those knottiest of authors, Pliny

---

61. Anti-Ciceronianism in Iberia predated Erasmus's *Ciceronianus* (1527). Nebrija himself regarded linguistic purism as an empty goal; boys should be brought up, he affirmed, on the Christian Latin poets such as Sedulius, Prudentius, and Baptista Mantuanus as well as the pagan poets (preface to his edition of *Prudentii opera*, Logroño, 1512) – though it is hard to believe his heart was in this particular affirmation. A more hostile anti-Ciceronianism was the rule, as we see in the preface 'Ad iuvenes studiosos bonarum artium' which Nebrija's friend Aires Barbosa prefixed to his edition of Arator's *Historia apostolica* (Salamanca, 1516). For an excellent and nuanced study of this question see V. García de la Concha's article in *Nebrija y la introducción del Renacimiento en España*, pp. 123–43.

62. For a brief summary on Nebrija's work in the field of Spanish grammar see the editor's introduction to Antonio de Nebrija, *Gramática de la lengua castellana*, ed. A. Quilis (Madrid, 1980).

63. On the Complutensian university (thus called from the Latin name of Alcalá de Henares), inaugurated in 1498 and opened in 1508, whose *Constitutions* were promulgated in 1510, see A. de la Torre y del Cerro, 'La Universidad de Alcalá: datos para su estudio. Cátedras y catedráticos desde la inauguración del Colegio de San Ildefonso hasta San Lucas de 1519', *Revista de Archivos, Bibliotecas y Museos*, 20 (1909), pp. 412–23; 21 (1909), pp. 48–71, 261–85, 405–33; M. Bataillon, *Erasmo y España: Estudios sobre la historia espiritual del siglo XVI*, 2nd. ed., trans. A. Alatorre (Mexico–Madrid–Buenos Aires, 1966), pp. 10–22.

the Elder and Pomponius Mela. Hernán Núñez was also a Greek scholar; with the brothers Vergara (Francisco's Greek grammar, the first written by a Spaniard, appeared at Alcalá in 1537), Politian's Portuguese student Aires Barbosa (*Arius Barbossa Lusitanus, c.* 1465–1540), and Aldus's Cretan friend Demetrios Dukas, he was responsible for the first ornaments of Iberian Hellenism.[64] Though Nebrija was the leader of this circle, he did not bring it into existence; for that, and for the stunning impact of the new humanist pedagogy in Spain, the active economic and political patronage of the Crown and of powerful sections of the Church and nobility continued to be responsible, thereby ensuring that Iberian humanism kept its characteristic stamp as a creature of the ruling monarchist and aristocratic ideology.

A further indication of the spread of the new tastes in ambits beyond Nebrija's immediate circle is the impact of humanist genres on Castilian vernacular literature. This began before Nebrija's day, in the 1460s and 1470s, with close and rather formal adaptations. The subject matter of *On the Happy Life*, a dialogue written in Rome in 1463 and dedicated to Henry IV of Castile (printed 1483 and 1499) by the *converso* secretary Juan de Lucena (*c.* 1430–1506?), was taken bodily from Bartolomeo Fazio's Ciceronian dialogue *On the Fortunate Life* (1446), a Stoic attack on Valla's Epicurean *Voluptuary*. But Lucena replaced Becadelli, Guarino, and Lamola, the interlocutors of Fazio's work, and its setting in Guarino's house in Ferrara, with his own patrons and friends, the heroes of the first generation of the new learning in Castile ('our Petrarchs', as he called them), Santillana, Cartagena, and Mena; and set the scene in the Castilian royal court. Lucena's colourful prose, powers of characterization (praised by the Erasmian Juan de Valdés in 1535 as 'wonderfully accommodated to the *dramatis personae*'), and eye for local Castilian detail (including some savage anti-clerical satire) make this a more fascinating work than its Latin original. Lucena was also one of the earliest Spaniards to state, in his *Epistle Encouraging Literary Study*, the connection between the revival of letters and the spiritual reform of the inner man; in 1503, he became the first of the long and

---

64. I do not count Jeroni Pau, whose works were written in Italy. A general study of the Salamancan and Complutensian classical scholarship of this time is an urgent desideratum. Some inkling can be gained from Olmedo, *Nebrija en Salamanca*; J. López Rueda, *Helenistas españoles del siglo XVI* (Madrid, 1973); and monographs such as A. Bonilla y San Martín, 'Un antiaristotélico del renacimiento: Hernando Alonso de Herrera y su *Breve disputa de ocho levadas contra Aristótil y sus secuaces'*, *Revue Hispanique*, 50 (1920), 61–197; M. D. de Asís, *Hernán Núñez en la historia de los estudios clásicos* (Madrid, 1977). Portugal is better served, for instance by Dias, *A Política Cultural da Época de D. João III* (on Aires Barbosa see I, 213–28).

distinguished line of Iberian humanists to fall foul of the Inquisition.[65] A few years later, we find in the Castilian *Letters* (printed 1486) of another *converso* secretary, Palencia's bosom-friend Hernando del Pulgar (*c.* 1425–1500?), a successful adaptation of another favourite humanist Latin genre, the familiar epistle.[66]

However, the culmination of humanist influence in Castilian letters is the *Comedy of Calisto and Melibea*, an erotic comedy begun between 1492 and 1496 by an unknown author of whom all we can say is that he was a member of a humanist coterie at Salamanca at the height of Nebrija's popularity. As in Italian universities and courts, the custom of reading (and later performing) Latin comedies on feast-days such as Corpus Christi had probably been instituted among Salamancan students by humanist professors; the anonymous *Comedy*, at any rate, shows an easy familiarity with the latest fashions of this humanist *commedia erudita* of rogues and trollops.[67] The *Comedy* was left incomplete; in 1498, the MS was discovered and the play completed by a *converso* law-student at the same university, Fernando de Rojas (*c.* 1475–1541), and shortly afterwards printed to great acclaim. The *Tragicomedy*, as Rojas renamed the work in a second and expanded

---

65. For the *De vita felici* and *Epístola exhortatoria a las letras* see *Opúsculos literarios de los siglos XIV á XVI*, ed. A. Paz y Melia (Madrid, 1892), pp. 103–217; on its relation to Fazio's work, M. Morreale, 'El tratado de Juan de Lucena sobre la felicidad', *Nueva Revista de Filología Española*, 9 (1955), pp. 1–21. On Lucena's Pre-Erasmianism see R. Lapesa, *De la Edad Media a nuestros días* (Madrid, 1967), pp. 123–44, and A. Alcalá, 'Juan de Lucena y el pre-erasmismo español', *Revista Hispánica Moderna*, 34 (1968), pp. 108–31.

66. J. N. H. Lawrance, 'Nuevos lectores y nuevos géneros: la epistolografía en los albores del Renacimiento español', in *Literatura en la época del Emperador. Actas de la Academia Literaria Renacentista (v–vii)*, ed. V. García de la Concha (Salamanca, 1988), pp. 81–99, where Pulgar's predecessors and successors in this genre are also discussed.

67. The school drama is documented in Salamancan statutes only from 1530 (Shergold, *History of the Spanish Stage*, pp. 143–4, 168–74); but in the prologue to a Salamancan edition of Leon Battista Alberti's comedy *Philodoxus* dated 1502, Bachelor Quirós describes play-readings in his house: Gallardo, *Ensayo de una biblioteca española*, IV, §3559; C. Grayson, 'La prima edizione del *Philodoxus*', *Rinascimento*, 5 (1954), 291–3. Likewise the vernacular adaptations of Plautine works by the humanist Francisco López de Villalobos (1473–1549), though published in 1515, were composed during his student days at Salamanca at the turn of the century. Terence, with Donatus's scholia, was printed in Barcelona in 1498; we know that Arnao Guillén de Brocar obtained a royal licence to print Nebrija's edition of the *Comedies*, with the humanist commentaries of Jouvennaux and Badius Ascensius, in 1511: Olmedo, *Nebrija (1441–1522)*, p. 152. The school-drama tradition continued to flourish, with plays by humanists such as Fernán Pérez de Oliva (1494?–1531), Juan Maldonado (1485?–1554), Juan Pérez (*Johannes Petreius*, 1512–45), Francisco Sá de Miranda (1481–1558), Diogo de Teive, and most famously António Ferreira (1528–69), whose Portuguese *Tragédia de dona Inês de Castro*, complete with classical chorus and *ekkyklema*, was performed in Coimbra about 1557. Around the mid-century, the practice was taken over by the Jesuits: see, for example, N. H. Griffin, *Two Jesuit Ahab Dramas* (Exeter, 1976).

version a year or two later, completely transcended its humanist models; it was not only the greatest book written in Spanish up to that time, but also the first to achieve European fame, being printed, translated, and adapted (under the humanist title *Celestina*) into Italian, French, German, English, and Latin from 1506 onwards.[68]

# III

By the second decade of the sixteenth century, therefore, the impact of humanism in Spain was no longer confined to a number of individuals in small literary circles around the court. Within a short time, in fact, the term 'humanist' itself became outdated. To be sure, a second generation of distinguished academic philologists followed the first, notably Francisco Sánchez de las Brozas (El Brocense, *Franciscus Sanctius Brocensis*, 1523–1600) whose *Minerva; or, The Elegance and Causes of the Latin Language* (1562; revised 1587), widely read and printed throughout Europe, is now recognized as one of the most significant Renaissance contributions to theoretical linguistics; but this was not the all-embracing humanism which Nebrija had fought for.[69] But most humanist-educated men chose a career in the bureaucracy, as they always had. By the mid-1520s, pure classical humanism on the Italian *quattrocento* model was in crisis, moved down the agenda to make way for more urgent affairs of society and government, in particular the spiritual reforms of Erasmianism and the equally impressive reform and revival of Catholic theology associated with the Thomist School of Salamanca led by the Dominican Francisco de Vitoria (1485?–1546) and his followers Domingo de Soto (1494–1560) and Melchor Cano (1509–60), which first clashed with the Erasmians at the celebrated *junta* of Valladolid in 1527. We must be careful to distinguish between the classical philologists and these men, who are sometimes called 'humanist lawyers' and 'humanist theologians' – they were, properly

---

68. On humanistic comedy see A. Stäuble, *La commedia umanistica del Quattrocento* (Florence, 1968); on the debt of the *Tragicomedia de Calisto y Melibea* to humanist sources, and on its European diffusion down to the Latin translation *Pornoboscodidascalus* by Kaspar von Barth (1624) see M. Bataillon, *"La Célestine" selon Fernando de Rojas* (Paris, 1961); A. D. Deyermond, *The Petrarchan Sources of "La Celestina"* (Oxford, 1961); M. R. Lida de Malkiel, *La originalidad artística de la "Celestina"* (Mexico, 1962).

69. A. F. G. Bell, *Francisco Sánchez el Brocense* (Hispanic Notes and Monographs VIII: Oxford, 1925); for El Brocense's place in the history of linguistics, and his indebtedness to Scaliger and Ramus, see the editor's introduction to Francisco Sánchez de las Brozas, *Minerva (1562)*, ed. E. del Estal Fuentes (Salamanca, 1975); Padley, *Grammatical Theory in Western Europe*, pp. 97–110. Simply by saying *theoretical* linguistics we admit that El Brocense was the opposite of a 'humanist' in Nebrija's sense: Rico, *Nebrija frente a los bárbaros*, pp. 131–3.

speaking, lawyers and theologians who had a training in humanist Latin and classical literature. The situation was summed up by a Complutensian professor of rhetoric of the next generation, Alfonso Garcia Matamoros (*Alphonsus Garsias Matamorus Hispalensis*, 1510?–72) who, in his patriotic history of Spanish letters from Tubal and the Scipios to his own day, *The Claims of Spanish Scholarship* (Alcalá, 1553), remarked that whereas the age of Cartagena had been 'slightly more cultured (*aetas paulo eruditior*)', and the reign of the Catholic Monarchs the backdrop to Nebrija's 'fierce and bloody battle with the barbarians', a decade or two later the time had come 'when it was not so much an ornament to know Latin as a disgrace not to know it'. Matamoros then let the humanist side down by listing the Salamanca scholastics and jurists among his examples of this brave new Latinate world.[70]

In Iberia, the transition from the humanism of the manuscript-seekers and grammarians to the hybrid style we call High Renaissance is clearly illustrated in vernacular literature. After the zenith of Rojas's *Tragicomedy of Calisto and Melibea*, humanist influence on Castilian letters is represented by Fray Antonio de Guevara, bishop of Mondoñedo (1480?–1545). Guevara was educated, probably by Lucio Marineo, at the court of the Catholic Monarchs. His *Familiar Epistles* (1539; expanded 1541) are a gossipy sequel to Pulgar's *Letters*; his *Golden Book of Marcus Aurelius* (1518, printed 1528; expanded as *Dial of Princes*, 1539) crams sententious classical lore into a biography of Marcus Aurelius supposedly translated from a Greek MS discovered in the library of Cosimo de'Medici. But Guevara's florid style, immensely popular all over Europe, represented humanism in its putrescent state. His learning was entertaining, but bogus; much of it, such as the Roman emperor's racy letters to the Great Whores of Antiquity, invented by the worthy bishop himself. By Guevara's day the influence of the *quattrocento* revival on vernacular literature was being superseded, notably by the pastoral *Eclogues* and Horatian epistles of Garcilaso de la Vega (1501?–36), the great-nephew of Santillana, which were written not in Spain but at the viceregal court of Naples. Garcilaso was the Wyatt of Spanish letters, introducing the Petrarchist mode into Spanish poetry; the dominant influence on his verse was not humanism (though he did write Neo-Latin poetry), but the Italian sonneteers Bembo, Tansillo, Tasso, and Sannazaro. In 1532 Garcilaso's companion Joan Boscà published his translation of an Italian masterpiece by a visitor to the Spanish court, Baldassare Castiglione; Garcilaso declared that Boscà's *El Cortesano* (1534) was 'perhaps the first work written in

---

70. A. Garcia Matamoros, *Apología "Pro adserenda Hispanorum eruditione"*, ed. J. López de Toro (Revista de Filología Española, Anejo XXVIII: Madrid, 1943), pp. 196, 198, 204.

Spanish worthy of a learned man's attention', implying that a work like the *Tragicomedy of Calisto and Melibea*, penetrated through and through by the grand outlook and style of *quattrocento* humanism, was to his delicate palate old-fashioned and medieval. For the next half century, the influence of humanism on literature in Iberia came to be filtered through the dark glass of Renaissance Italian poetry.[71]

To argue that the impact of humanist scholarship and the revival of antiquity were overtaken or overlaid by broader Renaissance influences in the 1530s is not to deny that Iberia would continue to produce distinguished scholars in the pure humanist tradition – Spain's greatest and most influential classical scholar, Antonio Agustín (1517–86), was barely walking when Nebrija died.[72] But, as intellectual leadership was taken over by the Thomist School of Salamanca, classical philology was put to pasture in the glades of academe. Nebrija had tried to claim for philology a position over all the arts and sciences; Francisco de Vitoria now stated drily that 'the office of the theologian is so wide that no argument, dispute, or subject is beyond his remit', and put down Erasmus with heavy-lidded irony as 'that *grammarian* who thinks himself a theologian'.[73]

The crisis and decline of humanism is dramatically exhibited by the fate of Erasmianism.[74] The tendency of many historians to suppose that humanism and Erasmianism were the same thing displays, it is true, a serious misunderstanding of both movements. The impact of Erasmianism in Iberia was due not to humanism but to the desire for religious reform, a desire which had its roots in antecedents very different from Renaissance philology. *Devotio moderna*, Franciscan

---

71. It is true that early signs of Petrarchism appeared in the Neo-Latin poetry of Nebrija's friends Lucio Flaminio (1503) and Juan Sobrarias (1506), but Alcina's essay in *Nebrija y la introducción del Renacimiento en España*, pp. 145–56, shows that these were superficial, and uninfluential. Neo-Latin poetry on Christian and panegyric themes flourished mightily in academic circles, but with little effect on the vernacular: see Alcina's 'Tendances et caractéristiques de la poésie hispano-latine de la Renaissance' in *L'Humanisme dans les lettres espagnoles*, ed. Redondo, pp. 133–49.

72. On Agustín's 'deep influence on the antiquarians of the late seventeenth century' see A. Momigliano, 'Ancient History and the Antiquarians', *Journal of the Warburg and Courtauld Institute*, 13 (1950), 285–315; for a sketch of his work, particularly on the textual criticism of Roman law, F. de Zulueta, *Don Antonio Agustín* (VIIIth David Murray Lecture: Glasgow, 1939). Though Agustín was educated and lived much of his life in Italy, the range of his interests – jurisprudence, epigraphy, numismatics, and the abstruser grammarians and lexicographers – placed him foursquare in a peculiarly Hispanic tradition of classical studies, which has survived unchanged from Nebrija to the present day.

73. For these quotations, and pointed comments on the old view of Vitoria as a 'humanist', see A. Pagden, *The Fall of Natural Man: the American Indian and the Origins of Comparative Ethnology* (Cambridge, 1982), pp. 25–6, 60–1, 66.

74. M. Bataillon, *Études sur le Portugal au temps de l'humanisme* (Coimbra, 1952); *idem*, *Erasmo y España*.

mysticism, and the Observant movements are three forms of reforming zeal whose indifference towards humane letters springs to mind. But Spanish and Portuguese reformers were often led to Erasmus's brand of humanism by their reforming interest in Scripture and the Fathers. This was notably the case of Cisneros, whose foundation of the university of Alcalá was not a gesture of classical enthusiasm, but 'the installation of a complete organism for ecclesiastical education'.[75] The episode of Nebrija's involvement with the publication of Cisneros's Complutensian Polyglot is therefore full of significance for our story.

From the early days of his professorship at Salamanca, Nebrija had been attracted by the example of his hero, Lorenzo Valla, to the question of the philological criticism of the Bible. Even before the famous declaration of his intention to dedicate himself exclusively to divine letters in 1495, he began to compile vast dossiers of lexical and textual notes on the Scriptures. This predated by many years Erasmus's publication of Valla's *Annotations* (1505); it was in line with the general tenor of humanist scholarship in Spain, where critical editions of religious writers such as Sedulius, Prudentius, Arator, and Baptista Mantuanus outnumbered those of classical authors, and where the old anti-Italian jibes about the 'frivolity' of pagan poetry still retained much force. The first sign of the likely reception of Nebrija's Biblical studies was the confiscation of his papers by the Inquisitor Diego de Deza in 1505/6 but in 1507 Deza was replaced by Cisneros. Nebrija was now actively encouraged by the cardinal to begin his Biblical studies again; and in 1507 he published in Logroño his *Third Fifty* (an ironical reference to Deza's two attempts to prevent their appearance) of essays on disputed words in Holy Scripture, together with an *Apologia* addressed to Cisneros defending the grammarian's duty to submit the text of Scripture to philological scrutiny. The *Apologia* shows Nebrija at his scintillating best, both in the side-splitting excoriation of his barbarous opponents, and in the brilliant demonstrations of critical acumen and solid scholarship with which he pinpoints errors and proposes emendations to celebrated Biblical *loci conclamati*.[76]

Despite, or perhaps because of, the impact of the *Third Fifty* (reprinted in 1514, and again, in Paris, in 1520), Cisneros did not immediately involve Nebrija in the project for the publication of the Complutensian Polygot, which was then going forward amidst the building works in Alcalá. In 1513, however, as the moment for the final revision of the texts drew nearer, the Cardinal invited Nebrija, whose

---

75. Bataillon, *Erasmo y España*, p. 10.

76. On the *Tertia quinquagena* and *Apologia* see Bataillon, *Erasmo y España*, pp. 24–34; Rico, *Nebrija frente a los bárbaros*, pp. 62–72; J. H. Bentley, *Humanists and Holy Writ: New Testament Scholarship in the Renaissance* (Princeton, 1983), pp. 80–8.

outspoken views had finally lost him his Salamancan chair, to apply for a post at Alcalá. The new professor was not required to lecture; his job was to cast an eye over the proofs of the Bible as they were brought in to his lodgings from Arnao Guillén de Brocar's printing-shop next door. From his own palace nearby, the cardinal could stroll each morning for a chat at Nebrija's downstairs window, and to check that Mrs Martínez was keeping the professor's addiction to the wine bottle under control. Within a short time, Nebrija discovered that Cisneros's editorial team, far from adopting his own radical critical principles, had on the cardinal's express instructions opted merely for a 'purified' text of the canonical Scriptures, based on the oldest MSS that could be found, but without textual emendations, even where the Vulgate offered plain mistranslations. Worst of all, the edition was to include glossaries based on precisely those medieval 'barbarian' grammarians whom it had been Nebrija's mission to drive from Spain. Nebrija refused to be associated with the Complutensian Polyglot unless the whole job was done afresh.

Cisneros did not give way to Nebrija's tantrum. In a delightfully civilized interview, he informed the recalcitrant professor that the Bible would be printed as it stood, though Nebrija was quite free to publish his philological researches elsewhere. True, the Bible had by this time been set up in type after twelve years of labour, but so footling an objection could never have weighed with the stern and mighty Cisneros. We must accept the less obvious explanation: that the cardinal considered Nebrija's intellectual arguments, and rejected them. In retrospect, this seems a decision of fateful significance to the story of humanism in Spain. The greatest monument of Spanish humanist scholarship would be published without the participation of Spain's greatest humanist scholar. Cisneros had shown, gently but firmly, that he accepted Nebrija's ideal of the humanist as the arbiter of all disciplines in theory, but not in fact. It was not a spiritual or theological objection which defeated Nebrija, but an intellectual one. Humanists might study the Scriptures, but they could not challenge the orthodoxy established by weightier disciplines. The circle was thus complete: Cisneros's position was essentially that of Cartagena in the *Declinationes* of 1431. Nebrija had failed to persuade the people who mattered that philology must be taken seriously.

The inevitable resignation of Nebrija from the Complutensian project, tendered in a letter of regretful self-justification which is one of his most convincing works, unwittingly presaged the way in which the Politianesque ideals of his youth would be overtaken (though no one could have foreseen this at the time) by the great tide which was to rack Europe with religious war in the coming decades. Significantly, the letter was written not in Latin, for the humanist market, but in

Spanish, 'so that I may have more witnesses to the fact that I warned your Worship of this matter in good time'.[77] The double defeat, personal and national, implied in these words was made concrete in 1516, when Erasmus published in Basel his *Novum Instrumentum*, a radical humanist translation of the New Testament conducted on just the lines Nebrija had proposed. Spain's bid to become the powerhouse of biblical humanism in Europe had suffered a major setback, irrespective of the fact that, with the arrival in Spain of the Flemish court of the first Habsburg king of Spain in 1516, Erasmianism was poised to embark on its meteoric Spanish adventure. The situation was revealed by the shrill and chauvinistic attack on the *Novum Instrumentum* presented in the *Annotations against Erasmus* (1520) of Diego López de Zúñiga (*Didacus Lopidis Stunica*), one of the editors of the Alcalá Polyglot. The only effect of Zúñiga's intemperate squib (whose publication Cisneros forbade as long as he lived) was to convince Erasmus and learned Europe that Spain would not, after all, join the humanist revolution. The episode deterred Erasmus from ever setting foot in Spain.[78]

Though the calibre of scholarship in Iberia in the brilliant imperial period of Emperor Charles V (I of Castile and Aragon, 1516–58) remained high, the record of Spanish and Portuguese humanism was on the whole depressing. The best classicist, the Valencian *converso* Juan Luis Vives (*Ludovicus Vives*, 1492–1540), was forced into exile by the racist Inquisition. After the trauma of the *comunero* revolts, brutally put down in 1520–23, many brilliant minds went abroad, or compromised themselves deeply with the imperial machine, writing witty and elegant imitations of Erasmian and Lucianic dialogues, Livian histories, and Ciceronian epistles in defence of such glorious acts as the Sack of Rome (1527) and the massacre and deportation of Moorish insurgents in the kingdom of Granada (1568–70). This was because after the crisis of the Council of Valladolid (1527), the Erasmian majority of humanistically-inclined scholars saw that allegiance to Charles was the only guarantee of their spiritual ideals. The age-old dependence of Iberian humanism on the Crown, its uneasy inferiority to scholasticism in the universities, its narrow chauvinism – factors which had dogged it ever since Cartagena's day – were now coming home to roost. Consequently, when the backlash against Erasmus came with the Inquisition trials of the

77. Antonio de Nebrija [ed. R. Chabás], 'Epistola del maestro de Lebrixa al Cardenal quando avisó que en la interpretación de las dicciones de la Biblia no mandasse seguir al Remigio sin que primero viessen su obra', *Revista de Archivos, Bibliotecas y Museos*, 8 (1903), pp. 493–6. For the date and significance of the letter see Bataillon, *Erasmo y España*, pp. 35–9; Bentley, *Humanists and Holy Writ*, pp. 88–91.

78. Bataillon, *Erasmo y España*, pp. 91–6, 115–32.

1530s and the *autos de fe* of 1557–62, it had grave, and even desperate, consequences for humanism. In the recently founded College of Arts at Coimbra, the pride of Portuguese classicism was decimated by the anti-Erasmian purges of 1550; the inquisitorial Indices of prohibited books (1551 and following) completed the job. In Spain, Inquisitor Valdés's Index and Philip II's decree (1559) forbidding his subjects to study in foreign universities other than Bologna, Naples, Rome, and Coimbra set similar limits to the horizons of Spanish humanism.[79] Henceforth, classical education in Iberia was to be controlled by the rising Jesuit order.

A parallel to the fall of Erasmian-tainted humanism is provided by the last great endeavour of Iberian humanist scholarship in the Fernandine and Caroline period: the description and justification of the Iberian empire in the New World. The role which classical philology may have played in stimulating the discoveries has been debated; a dispassionate view suggests that it was small, though not necessarily negligible.[80] Be that as it may, we have seen how the Portuguese expansion and exploration in Africa and the Indian Ocean attracted the attention of Italian humanists in the mid-fifteenth century. The role which the discovery of the New World and circumnavigation of the globe played in stimulating humanist endeavour and discussion was, however, of a different order from that of the African and Asian explorations. America was not merely a region of the known world which had not been visited or conquered by Alexander, but a whole unknown world which had no right to exist at all if the ancients knew anything about cosmography, and which therefore demanded attention from classical scholars. Besides, the humanist profession was inescapably involved in early discussions of the American experience because classical science and rhetoric were amongst early modern Europe's chief intellectual resources for facing the challenge to imagination, reason, and political ideology posed by the New World.[81] Both of these factors are epitomized in the first major humanist work on the discoveries written in

---

79. M. Brandão, *A Inquisição e os Professores do Colégio das Artes*, 2 vols (Coimbra, 1969); H. Kamen, *Inquisition and Society in Spain in the Sixteenth and Seventeenth Centuries* (1985), pp. 62–100.

80. For example, F. Rico, 'El nuevo mundo de Nebrija y Colón', in *Nebrija y la introducción del Renacimiento en España*, pp. 157–85 reviews the participation of humanists such as Nebrija in discussions of cosmography in the Iberian courts at the end of the fifteenth century, where newly-recovered texts of Ptolemy, Pomponius Mela and Strabo may have fostered interest in exploration. But it is hard to believe that this motive was as important as commercial greed.

81. For what follows, I am indebted to Pagden, *The Fall of Natural Man*, and Á. Gerbi, *Nature in the New World: From Christopher Columbus to Gonzalo Fernández de Oviedo*, trans. J Moyle (Pittsburgh, 1985).

Spain, the *Decades on the New World* of Pietro Martire d'Anghiera (*Petrus Martyr ab Angleria Mediolanensis*, 1457–1526), who was appointed official chronicler of the newly-founded Council of the Indies in 1510.[82] Martyr, a sound classical scholar, was invited to Spain in the 1480s by Santillana's grandson Iñigo López de Mendoza III, count of Tendilla. He remained close to the Spanish court for the rest of his life, apart from a brief but significant sojourn in Cairo in 1501/2. He was thus in a unique position to interview many of the explorers on their return to Spain, and was later officially charged with examining the reports, artefacts, maps, and humans brought back by the caravels to the Council of the Indies's offices. It is he who is credited with the first use of the terms 'New World' and 'Western Hemisphere', in the letters in which he published the news of Columbus's landfall (1494). After these first fine careless raptures, Martyr began to slot the marvels into the schemes of his classical education; at the same time he managed to convey a sense of wonder, pride, and gratification at the novelty and grandeur of his subject-matter, beside which 'the exploits of Saturn or Hercules pale into insignificance'. He deduced, correctly, that the naked, disorganized, and backward cannibals of Columbus's *Letter* were distinct from the Moslem barbarians he had studied in Egypt; he therefore transformed them into a race of handsome, fair-skinned savages in a state of nature, inhabiting a lush paradise unencumbered with 'the evil curse of Mine and Thine', free of laws, clothes, war, and envy.

The vivid hues of Martyr's Utopian vision derived from the classical myth of the primeval Golden Age. Each new wonder was checked for classical parallels: coolly dismissive of Columbus's conjecture that the land he had stumbled across was the Biblical Ophir or part of Cathay, Martyr was more excited by the reports of tribes of cannibals and warlike virgin huntresses, since the testimony of the ancients made the existence of these *anthropophagi* and Amazons inherently probable (though Martyr eventually dismissed the Amazons as a fable). Accounts of huge fish or seamonsters were dutifully filed under references to Arion's dolphin and the Tritons. Even when Martyr's comparisons were purely rhetorical, they revealed a cast of thought; in his mind's eye, the native women in their nude beauty were nymphs and dryads,

---

82. An instalment of the *De orbe novo* was printed – with a famous woodcut map of the West Indies – among Martyr's *Opera* at Seville, 1511; but the first *Decade* had probably been completed by 1501, and appeared in an unauthorized Italian translation as early as 1504. In 1516, a revised edition of the first three *Decades* appeared at Salamanca; this had been seen through the press, and a glossary of *vocabula barbara* appended, by Martyr's friend Nebrija. It is therefore misleading to give '1530' (after Martyr's death) as the date of this work; that was when the complete text of eight *Decades* eventually appeared in the official edition printed by Miguel de Eguía. Martyr has until recently been dismissed as a 'journalist'; see now Gerbi, *Nature in the New World*, pp. 50–75.

the Spanish sergeants were 'decurions', and the Indian who betrayed a plot to her Spanish lover was Fulvia, the Roman lady who betrayed Catiline.

Columbus's emphasis on the abject brutishness and cowardice of the natives he encountered was not disinterested scientific observation, but a gambit designed, like his exaggerations of the vegetable and mineral wealth of the islands, to persuade the Spanish Crown that the conquest and evangelization of these pathetic people was necessary, easy, and profitable. Martyr, on the other hand, idealized the Indians because he wished to glorify the Spanish achievement in discovering and conquering 'our New World', as he called it – an aim betrayed by his decision to omit all account of Spanish atrocities. This he masqueraded as a courteous deference to his addressee, Pope Leo X, who, though he might delight in the firm breasts and wanton protervity of Indian maidens, would surely recoil from the rehearsal of bloody horrors. But Martyr also regarded the Indians as worthy of scientific speculation and analysis, because he had access to the recently rediscovered perspectives of ancient ethnography. Though Martyr never doubted that Christianization was a prime objective in the Indies, his classical studies enabled him to recognize that a pagan society could function successfully, and even legitimately, on its own terms.

Martyr's enlightened approach had one drawback: it was out of tune with the conquistadors' assumption that Indians were fair game for rape, pillage, and enslavement. Even as Martyr and other humanist publicists poured forth their encomiums of the new-found lands, their words were being undermined by a grim reality. It was not their image of the noble Indian, but their image of the savage Spanish conquistadors which was seriously astray. When Fray Antonio de Montesinos's condemnation of the *encomienda* system came to attention in the homeland in 1512, there was an outcry. The *junta* of Burgos convened by Ferdinand to discuss the problem was not led, however, by humanists, but by the theologians and legists of the grand old scholastic faculties. It was a Scottish theologian at the Sorbonne, John Mair, who had brought Aristotle's *Politics* into the debate on the vexed question of whether the Indians, as barbarians, could be classified as 'natural slaves'. When the royalist lawyer Juan López de Palacios Rubios drew up his *Brief on the Islands of the Ocean Sea* in 1513, he portrayed the Indians much as Martyr had, as primitives. But he was not drawn to conclude that American society was a classical Golden Age; instead, his scholastic training led him to deduce from various shockingly unnatural features of this primitivism – communal living, nakedness, sexual promiscuity, matrilineal descent – that Indians were irrational, uncivil, and hence naturally slavish in Aristotle's sense. Palacios Rubios's brief was to provide a watertight case for exploiting the natives while retaining the fiction that they were, as the Papal donations and imperial policy declared, 'vassals' of the Spanish Crown.[83]

With the discovery and conquest of Mexican, Mayan and Incan civilizations, the question of natural slavery assumed a new urgency. These were societies which could not easily be dismissed as primitive, and were indeed similar to the civilizations of the classical world. Nevertheless, Bartolomé de las Casas and Francisco de Vitoria were moved to make their contributions on the ensuing 'question of the Indies' not by humanism, but by theology. Once the question of the Indies had become a matter of state, the humanists were forced to take a back seat. At most, they might be asked to formulate the classical authorities for a predetermined imperial policy. The position had significant parallels with that which Nebrija had run up against in the matter of the Complutensian Polyglot; the old disciplines and authorities were to have the last say.

We see this in the work of the last Spanish classical scholar to fall within the bounds of this chapter, Juan Ginés de Sepúlveda (*Johannes Ginesius Sepulveda*, 1490–1573), whose *Second Democrates; or, on the Just Conquest of the Indians* was submitted to the royal censors for its *imprimatur* in 1547. Sepúlveda had spent much of his life in Italy, first at the Spanish College at Bologna, where he is supposed to have met Pomponazzi, Paulo Giovio, and Manutius, and then in the customary bureaucratic post, as royal chaplain and chronicler. Admired as a Latinist by Erasmus, Antonio Agustín, and other competent authorities, his works included Aristotelian translations and treatises on history, ethics, and politics. But, even before the inquisitorial trials of Hellenists such as Juan de Vergara in the 1530s,[84] Sepúlveda had sensed the danger in the connection between Greek studies and Lutheranism; one of his first works was an attack on Luther, *On Fate and Free Will*, where he mused whether it might not be the case that 'study of eloquence and humane letters brought this pernicious plague of heresy upon our heads'.[85] Now he tried once again to sense which way the wind was blowing, and penned an attack on the ideas of the turbulent priest Bartolomé de las Casas, whose pamphlets on the Crown's neglect of the rights of its Indian vassals were giving the Emperor a headache. Sepúlveda's work marshalled classical authority and Aristotelian argument to prove that the enslavement of the Indians was just, holy, and politic. His pamphlet, from its hyperbolical rhetorical style to the jaunty dialogue format in which Democrates, the author's *alter*

---

83. Pagden, *The Fall of Natural Man*, pp. 27–56.

84. Bataillon, *Erasmo y España*, pp. 438–70.

85. L. Gil Fernández, *Panorama social del humanismo español (1500–1800)* (Madrid, 1981), pp. 209–13; Bataillon, *Erasmo y España*, pp. 407–9.

*ego*, is given all the good arguments against the villainous Lutheran stooge Leopoldo, was thoroughly humanist. The *Second Democrates* was thus sadly inappropriate to the stern level of technical scholastic discourse which had been set in these matters by Vitoria and his followers, who were convened to evaluate Sepúlveda's work in a *junta* of 1548, and who unanimously condemned it as the meddlesome work of a man who had 'studied more in languages than theology'.[86] In the debates between Sepúlveda and Las Casas which ensued in Valladolid in 1550–51, the humanist was made to pay for having couched his work in the language of classical rhetoric; his arguments were picked over and submitted to a roasting as if they were the questions, propositions, and distinctions of a scholastic treatise, instead of the elegant commonplaces of an orator. Indeed, Sepúlveda's lack of theological expertise had led him into the trap of Lutheran heresy.[87] The question rumbled on for a decade, doubtless because Sepúlveda's pretty arguments for condoning the atrocious behaviour of the Spanish colonists were too useful to dismiss out of hand. Intellectually, the theologians had swept the board.[88]

86. The quotation is Sepúlveda's own rueful assessment: Pagden, *The Fall of Natural Man*, pp. 109–18; *idem*, 'Dispossessing the Barbarian: the Language of Spanish Thomism and the Debate over the Property Rights of the American Indians', in *The Languages of Political Theory in Early-Modern Europe*, ed. A. Pagden (Cambridge, 1987), pp. 79–98.

87. Q. Skinner, *Foundations of Modern Political Thought*, 2 vols (Cambridge, 1978), ii, p. 142; Pagden, 'Dispossessing the Barbarian', p. 93.

88. I record with gratitude the cordial encouragement of Denys Hay and Brian Tate, *migliori fabbri*; and the unstinting help of Nigel Griffin, Clive Willis, Gordon Kinder, Joseph Bergin and Antony Pagden, who strove manfully to offset my shortcomings – *Herculeum opus; sed Dis aliter visum.* I cannot blame any of them for my shameful ignorance of Portugal, which deserved a better treatment.

*Chapter Eleven*

# Humanism in England

## GEOFFREY ELTON

### I

Overwhelmed as at present we are by students of humanism in Tudor England – by art historians, literary historians, ordinary historians – we fail to remember how relatively recent that outburst is.[1] Until the 1940s, Frederic Seebohm's barnacle-encrusted study, first published in the year of the Second Reform Bill,[2] was still being cited as not only authoritative but actually dominant; even in 1959 the second edition of Conyers Read's bibliography did not include a section specifically on this topic. Instead it scattered relevant material among such headings as 'Ecclesiastical history – general' or 'Education'.[3] By 1968, the situation had changed sufficiently for Mortimer Levine to devote a section of his bibliography to intellectual history; this accommodated most of the proper studies, by then much increased in number.[4] Until the war, two convictions governed inherited wisdom. One was that English humanism should be approached from Italian

---

1. This chapter does not pretend to exhaustive coverage; of necessity it will deal with the main developments only.

2. F. Seebohm, *The Oxford Reformers* (1867; revised edn 1869).

3. Conyers Read ed., *Bibliography of British History: Tudor Period 1485–1603* (2nd edn, Oxford, 1959). The works listed under general Church history (pp. 173–4) included a good deal on humanism, most of it remarkably venerable. The appearance of W. G. Zeeveld's book (n. 8, below) in the general political section suggests that the compilers read only its title.

4. M. Levine ed., *Bibiliographical Handbooks: Tudor England 1485–1603* (Cambridge, 1968), pp. 92–100. Here, too, religion usurped part of the relevant publications.

origins; the other believed that its career ended with the defeat of the papal Church in England. The first notion produced an interest in such lesser figures as William Grocyn and Thomas Linacre, generally rather overrated as pioneers; the second resulted from a devout belief in John Fisher and Thomas More as the greatest lights of English humanism, a belief much encouraged by the canonizations of 1935. In his extraordinarily influential biography of More, R. W. Chambers linked both streams: he emphasized More's derivation from Ficino and Pico, and he decreed that with the death of his hero humanism had died in England.[5] Erasmus was not forgotten, but he tended to appear as the pupil of Colet and associate of More. Seebohm's inclusion of him among, of all things, the Oxford reformers set a scene: he was, so to speak, absorbed into the English manifestation of humanism, a step behind the tragic victims of Henry VIII whose disappearance closed a glorious chapter in the nation's intellectual life and initiated the dark days of Protestant bigotry.

A new era in the study of humanism opened in the later 1940s. One of the innovators was Denys Hay whose work on Polydore Vergil, begun in 1937, reinforced the tendency to look towards Italy but reached a different level altogether of scholarship and insight.[6] His splendid edition of that part of Vergil's *Anglica Historia* that dealt with the reign of Henry VII had shown him that the Roman Catholic tradition of humanism in England ignored far too many other influences of a strictly secular sort.[7] His Vergil emerged not just as a papal collector who happened to dislike Wolsey and kept a chronicle, but as a highly productive man of learning and of influence, a man who shared the concerns of Erasmus, though he lacked the Dutchman's originality. Hay thus drew attention to the density of humanist activity in England; he got behind the front men and taught us to look also at the second rank. The same lesson was taught, even more effectively, by Gordon Zeeveld's study of a group of young English scholars gathered around Reginald Pole at Padua.[8] Zeeveld's innovations, seemingly unsuspected by himself, proved powerful. In the first place, he demonstrated what no one in this field of research had previously grasped: for humanist writings, evidence in print alone does not suffice and the historian must also look at treatises left in manuscript. This recognition greatly enlarged the available material as well as the company of humanists to

5. R. W. Chambers, *Thomas More* (1935). Read, in one of his absurd annotations (see his no. 481) called the book 'scholarly but partisan'. In fact, its partisanship gained strength from sizeable defects in scholarship.

6. D. Hay, *Polydore Vergil: Renaissance Historian and Man of Letters* (Oxford, 1952).

7. Denys Hay ed., *The Anglica Historia of Polydore Vergil A. D. 1485–1537* (Royal Hist. Soc., Camden 3rd Series LXXIV, 1950).

8. W. Gordon Zeeveld, *Foundations of Tudor Policy* (Cambridge, Mass., 1948).

be studied. Secondly, Zeeveld opened up the possibility that intellectuals might have exercised a direct influence on national policies. And thirdly, without remarking on it, he helped to put an end to the Chambers doctrine according to which English humanism died in 1535. This point had previously been made by Douglas Bush,[9] but his voice had failed to drown the popish message.

Since the early 1950s, studies of humanism in England have in the main followed four different lines of enquiry. The bulk of the work has concerned itself with particular individuals – men of learning and men of affairs. Out of these investigations there came by stages the realization that among the foremost characteristics of English humanism was the ambition to apply the results of learning to the service of social amelioration. Later there arose unexpected doubts about the old hero figures in this landscape whose right to be counted humanists became less certain than it had been. Lastly, very recently, the supposed 'Erasmian' coherence of the movement in England has been questioned. I propose now to track these four different groups of writings, though, of course, I recognize that they must not be thought strictly delimited one from another. Perhaps, then, we shall be able to see where at present we stand and where we should go from here. Despite the flood I mentioned, there is certainly no cause to think that the chase is over.

## II

The great figures of the earlier analysis have received further attention. John Fisher has not had much of it because his share in the resistance to Henry VIII's first divorce has shut out an investigation of his purely scholarly work, but the large compendium put together by Edward Surtz will at least prove a good starting point for future scholars.[10] The book comprises a fairly detailed analysis of Fisher's many writings and tends to demonstrate that, thanks to the Lutheran Reformation which roused him to a passionate defence of the existing order, he should chiefly be regarded as a traditional theologian. It was in that guise that he impressed his contemporaries in Europe. However, he also fulfilled some of the conditions of the humanist stereotype, especially in his support for the study of Greek and Hebrew and in his services to education. His involvement with Cambridge, of which he was chancellor for thirty-one years (1504–35), where he presided over two Colleges (Michaelhouse and Queens'), and where he became instru-

---

9. D. Bush, 'Tudor Humanism and Henry VIII,' *University of Toronto Quarterly*, 7 (1938), pp. 162–77.

10. E. Surtz, S. J., *The Works and Days of John Fisher* (Cambridge, Mass., 1967).

mental in the founding of two more (Christ's and St John's), constitutes his best claim to the title of humanist. A little conference held there to commemorate his death very properly concentrated on that aspect of his life and never got around to the issues that came to terminate his life.

As Surtz showed, in 1535 the European face of Fisher easily outshone that of Thomas More, but it did not take long for their standing to be reversed. Nor has More retired from the champion's place. On the contrary, the last thirty-five years have raised him ever higher, thanks especially to two very different enterprises. Founded and dominated by the Abbé Germain Marc'hadour at Angers, a gathering of the devout calling themselves *Amici Thomae Mori* have been keeping the laurels green by means of a journal. *Moreana* contains an extraordinary mix of matters (I cherish the memory of a set of verses entitled 'A posthumous poem by St Thomas More'), but in more recent years it has also published a number of sensible articles and reviews. Since both Marc'hadour and his company started from the fixed position that More was a saint of the Church and therefore beyond criticism, *Moreana*, adding much detail, has not greatly developed our knowledge of the man; more particularly, it has hampered the study of his humanism because his criticism of the Church has had to be played down.

The other enterprise also sprang from feelings of piety but produced vastly more substantial results. This is the great edition of More's *Complete Works*, published by the Yale University Press. It was initiated by Richard Sylvester who until his sadly premature death in 1978 remained its general editor and driving force.[11] Most of the fifteen volumes so far published do not throw light on More the ·humanist because the bulk of his own massive production was directed elsewhere (against heretics and concerning the after-life), but three books do contribute, being in fact the essence of his claim to the humanist accolade. More's cooperation with Erasmus in producing translations of Lucian throws the clearest light on his endeavour to train himself as a humanist scholar;[12] his incomplete but immensely influential account of Richard III displays an idiosyncratic but also humanist ambition to write a new kind of history;[13] and *Utopia* remains, of course, his chief claim to fame in that role.[14] The great edition has stimu-

---

11. *The Complete Works of St Thomas More* (hereafter *CW*), ed. Richard Sylvester and others (New Haven, Conn., 1963– ). It now appears that financial problems will after all prevent this edition from being complete, but the things to be omitted are indeed of little significance.

12. *Translations of Lucian*, ed. Craig R. Thompson (*CW* 3/I, 1974).

13. *The History of King Richard III*, ed. Richard Sylvester (*CW* 2, 1963).

14. *Utopia*, ed. J. H. Hexter and E. Surtz (*CW* 4, 1965).

lated much work on the man, some of it in the introduction to those volumes, some in separate books, and more in articles of which two useful collections have appeared. The first contributes little to More the humanist, being more concerned with his activities as a public figure and with his last transformation into a budding saint;[15] the other assembles a gathering of very varying quality in which a number of pieces analyse mostly linguistic problems arising from More's humanist works.[16] The notable edition of his letters also, of course, includes material bearing on his notions of scholarship and learning, especially his rebuff to Oxford's traditionalists and his battle with Martin van Dorp who had dared to decry Erasmus.[17]

More's history of Richard III has not attracted as much study as one might hope, especially if the production of the king's self-appointed champions is ignored which usually confines itself to abuse of Sir Thomas. A sensible assessment of the book as a piece of history is found in Charles Ross's recent biography of the king.[18] Ross refuses to go all the way with Alison Hanham's cheerful conclusion that More was really composing 'a satirical drama': 'To adopt her arguments *in toto*,' he says with unwonted severity, 'tends to lead to the conclusion that More did not believe a word of what he was writing.'[19] Even if it did – and I think the stricture exaggerated – one may ask, why not? Hanham offered a more convincing reconstruction of More's mode of composition than did Sylvester in the introduction to his edition, and she displayed greater independence in the face of More than is usual; and she made a strong case for her views. There is indeed much dramatic construction, much stage-play *modo Italiano et modo Moreano*, which is where its link with More the humanist shows much more clearly than in some conventionally high-minded denunciation of tyranny. The evil of tyranny was a general humanist *topos*, no doubt, but when More tackled it he did so with his usual searching irony and with a verve which turned the conventionally abstract into a positive human experience.[20]

However, More the humanist was above all the author of *Utopia*, and the battles of scholars continue to rage around that book. *Utopia*

---

15. *St Thomas More: Action and Contemplation*, ed. Richard Sylvester (New Haven, 1972).

16. *Essential Articles for the Study of Thomas More*, ed. R. S. Sylvester and G. P. Marc'hadour (Hamden, Conn., 1977).

17. *The Correspondence of Sir Thomas More*, ed. Elizabeth F. Rogers (1947).

18. C. Ross, *Richard III* (1981), pp. xxvi–xxxi.

19. Ibid. p. xxvii, n. 22; A. Hanham, *Richard III and the Early Historians 1483–1535* (Oxford, 1975), ch. 7.

20. D. B. Fenlon, 'Thomas More and Tyranny,' *Journal of Ecclesiastical History*, 32 (1981), 453–76, makes some interesting points in the course of too pious an argument.

from the date of publication has always offered to every reader that which he sought in it. The great debate was reopened by J. H. Hexter who in a slender book of 171 small pages and a big essay of 151 large pages laid out four propositions, the first three of which have rightly never been contradicted.[21] He firmly disposed of various earlier attempts to read *Utopia* as either a tract for modern times (socialism and democracy before their day) or a medieval song of praise for the life monastic; he worked out the history of its composition, showing that the description of the island with its ideal society preceded the writing of the framework in Book I; he drew attention to what he called 'the Dialogue of Counsel', the separate argument concerning the scholar's role in public life, which concludes the first book; and he developed his theory of More as 'the first modern radical'.[22] He saw More as a strictly Christian humanist but held that to its author Utopia, a country which had ordered its existence without ever receiving the gospel message, even so represented the true Christian way of life which More positively wished to bring into existence.

This last part of the interpretation has led to much argument. Though Quentin Skinner expressed himself as fully convinced,[23] Dermot Fenlon seized on the suggestion that by inventing a truly Christian commonwealth for the nonexistent island of Nowhere More meant to express a strong criticism of the half-hearted and pussyfooting views of other Christian humanists, especially Erasmus. While they expected to create a good Christian society on earth without calling for any revolutionary transformation, More – so Fenlon argued – wished to show them that on earth there was no hope of their ambitions being realized.[24] Hexter held that More believed Utopia to be not only the right ideal but also obtainable if the necessary effort – that marginally modern revolution – were but faced; Fenlon reversed this by arguing that More outlined what indeed he regarded as the ideal society in order to demonstrate its unattainability. However, the latest review of the

<hr/>

21. J. H. Hexter, *More's Utopia: the Biography of an Idea* (Princeton, 1952); and the introduction to *CW* 4 (above, n. 14).

22. J. H. Hexter, 'Thomas More: on the Margins of Modernity,' *Journal of British Studies*, 1/1 (1961), pp. 20–37.

23. See his review of *CW* 4 in *Past and Present* 38 (1967), pp. 153–68. Hexter's interpretation lies at the heart of Skinner's assessment in his *Foundations of Modern Political Thought* (Cambridge, 1978), I, pp. 255–62. Stop-Press: Professor Skinner has now revoked his agreement with Hexter in his latest contribution to the debate on *Utopia* – see his 'Sir Thomas More's *Utopia* and the language of renaissance humanism,' *The Languages of Political Theory in Early-Modern Europe*, ed. A. Pagden (Cambridge, 1987), pp. 123–57.

24. D. B. Fenlon, 'England and Europe: *Utopia* and its aftermath,' *Trans. of the Royal Hist. Soc.* 5th ser., 25 (1975), pp. 115–35. I in effect accepted that interpretation in *Reform and Reformation: England 1509–1558* (1977), pp. 42–6.

work on which More's reputation as a great figure among humanists must rest has rather tended to return to an earlier and less sophisticated tradition. Brendan Bradshaw enabled himself to take this journey into the past by rejecting all efforts to solve the mysteries of the book by calling in aid More's ironic temper: he asks us to take More's words at their ostensible meaning.[25] In his view, therefore, More did believe in the virtues of the structure which he had created for Utopia – in the community of property, the precisely ordered existence, the political hierarchy, the deference to age, and all the rest – but by introducing the conversion of the islanders at the end he expressly denied that their commonwealth had been a Christian one. As regards More's judgement as to the practicality of such propositions, Bradshaw rejected both Hexter's More, looking for revolution, and Fenlon's, putting forth a pessimistic denunciation of idealistic dreams. Bradshaw reads the fictitious More's argument with Hythloday, the man who has actually been to Utopia, as an attack on the uncompromising absolutism found in Plato (whose views Hythloday is used to represent) – the absolutism of all or nothing. Better acquainted with real life and circumstances, More was willing to accept piecemeal and halfway answers. He neither sought revolution nor despaired of betterment; convinced that reform was both necessary and possible, he allowed that service to the common weal must involve statecraft and diplomacy and compromise which will secure that available measure of reform which is better than none.

There is something basically agreeable about Bradshaw's interpretation, but it does not really stand up. Like others before him, he takes More to express his opinion straightforwardly where it suits the thesis but to hide it where it would confuse the thesis. More is made to switch his irony on and off: once again, the reader sees what he wants in that infuriatingly ambiguous book. I have to admit that to me all recent commentators have seemed rather overawed by the reputation of author and book and thus seek profundities not of More's making.[26] Did More expect that his little book, started as a *jeu d'esprit* among friends and not intended for publication, would be taken to sum up his inmost feelings on human society, the State and the ways of God? As his *Richard III* proved, he liked to write fiction with a message, and *Utopia* is his masterpiece in that genre. More also loved to make pointed jokes, and *Utopia* is full of them. So it certainly deserves some

---

25. B. Bradshaw, 'More on Utopia,' *Historical Journal*, 24 (1981), pp. 1–26.

26. My short life of More in *Studies in Tudor and Stuart Politics and Government*, III (1983), pp. 355–72, represents my previously most recent and most considered assessment. I apologize for drawing attention to a piece in a foreign language: it was written for a German collection.

of its fame: it lovingly presents a splendid invention, swiftly and elegantly worked out with spirit and manifest delight. It made More famous on the continent of Europe where nothing like it had been seen; there it was rapidly reprinted several times. In England, on the other hand, where people had heard his kind of criticism made before, it seems to have had no noticeable impact until Ralph Robinson published his translation in 1551, and until the growth of the More cult tended to be regarded for what it was – fiction. John Foxe disparagingly called it poetry. Nowadays it regularly receives praise for its supposedly penetrating and original analysis of contemporary life especially in England. This praise ignores the fact that More's analysis very unoriginally concentrated on the standard complaints of the day, regularly mentioned, for instance, in the preambles to acts of Parliament. He adds memorable formulations: More was a writer of genius, but a modestly interesting thinker. Everybody remembers the sheep devouring men; nobody bothers to recall the acts against depopulating enclosure which had long since made the point – and which, incidentally, mistook the causes of agrarian unrest. Social critics from William Langland to Edmund Dudley had thought as deeply on these matters as Thomas More. Unlike him, they had not been able to think of a cure, but it must be said that the Utopian arrangements which More prescribed deserve rather more adverse criticism than they have received. More's recipe involved putting mankind into universal straitjackets. His island commonwealth lacks genuine liberty because men, being sinful (greedy and proud), will always pervert liberty into licence. It also happens to lack all privacy and would not have pleased the More who found the peace of the monk's cell in prison, twenty years later. In Utopia, a reasonably good life is offered to all in exchange for submission to a stringent system and constant supervision. That the system has some attractive features, such as restricted working hours and the absence of serfdom, is true enough; every restrictive regime has always paraded such minor bonuses as sprats which draw the mackerel of independence into the net.[27]

Every reading of *Utopia* ultimately comes up against the question whether More really meant us to believe what he said. Irony pervades the book – the kind of irony which leaves its import very unclear. Did More think community of property ideal (as Hythloday makes out), or absurd (as Morus objects)? Did he approve the Utopians' pleasure

---

27. Others have recognized the totalitarian aspect of *Utopia* but seem more willing than I am to allow More his little foibles. See J. H. Hexter, 'Utopia and Geneva,' *Action and Conviction in Early Modern Europe* (Ft. Harbison), ed. T. K. Rabb and J. E. Seigel (Princeton, 1969); J. Colin Davis, *Utopia and the Ideal Society: a Study of English Utopian Writing 1516–1700* (Cambridge, 1981), ch. 2.

in sexual intercourse or their contemptuous jokes at its expense? Did this essentially conventional Christian really think that a truly pious life could be lived without knowledge of the gospel? And how can we even put such questions to an author who gives his philosopher and guide, Hythlodaeus, a name which translates as either the enemy of nonsense or the purveyor of nonsense?

Nevertheless, the student of humanism has to make up his mind on at least some of these puzzles. For myself, I now reckon that More did think Utopia an ideal society in the double sense that life cannot be better ordered on earth, and that it was unrealizable in actual fact. I agree with Bradshaw that More wished to help improve the condition of earthly commonwealths and for that purpose accepted the need to come to terms with the facts of life at the courts of princes. I agree with Fenlon that More liked to show to his fellow humanists that scholarly vapouring about reform was as pointless as all refusals to compromise on abstract principles. I agree with no one when I maintain that quite enough ink has been wasted on *Utopia*. More meant to amuse, shock and bewilder, all of which he achieved; but he would have been greatly surprised by all those solemn debates about his meaning that still continue.

Naturally enough, no other humanist has attracted as much attention as Thomas More. Among those well known to an earlier generation of scholars, Thomas Elyot already stood assured of his position as a writer on political thought, thanks to the rather outdated discussion provided by H. H. S. Croft in his edition of Elyot's *Governor*.[28] In the new wave of humanist studies, a much better account of the man was offered by Stanford Lehmberg who also reviewed his very varied writings;[29] shortly afterwards, John M. Major, analysing Elyot's production, somewhat predictably raised him on a pedestal as a Platonic thinker – a moralist and educator, of real and original influence on his age.[30] It would meet the case better to treat him (as Lehmberg hints he was) as a prolific populariser with occasional original ideas largely produced by what Elyot, in jaundiced moods, regarded as undeserved ill fortune. Alistair Fox has picked on two short pieces written in the 1530s in protest against the collapse of his career in the king's service as his most original and revealing writings.[31]

---

28. Thomas Elyot, *The Boke named the Gouernour*, ed. H. H. S. Croft (1883) with a biographical introduction.

29. S. E. Lehmberg, *Sir Thomas Elyot, Tudor Humanist* (Austin, Texas, 1960).

30. J. M. Major, *Sir Thomas Elyot and Renaissance Humanism* (Lincoln, Nebraska, 1964).

31. A. Fox, 'Sir Thomas Elyot and the Humanist Dilemma,' *Reassessing the Henrician Age*, ed. A. Fox and J. A. Guy (Oxford, 1986), ch. 3.

Pursuing individuals: Zeeveld's signpost pointing to Padua has not gone unnoticed. Too little has so far been done about Reginald Pole himself, a personality so ambiguous that he might almost have been invented by Thomas More. The brief study by William Schenk is commonplace about the man's thought, while the important work of Dermot Fenlon concentrates on Pole's participation in the reforming movement within the Church of Rome in Italy.[32] There is a *terra nova* waiting to be explored. It looks as though Thomas Mayer will be the one to travel there, having already succeeded in altering our view of Pole's companion, Thomas Starkey. Mayer has reconsidered the dating and purpose of Starkey's manuscript treatise on government; he concluded that it was written before Starkey had any idea about seeking service with Henry VIII, that he meant it for the instruction of Pole above all, and that so far from being a premature constitutionalist Starkey wished to set up the kind of aristocratic control over monarchy which some fifteenth-century noblemen had hoped to erect.[33] Among lesser figures one might notice Roger Ascham who has attracted a careful new biography with little new to say.[34]

Is there anything to hold all these thinkers together? The one umbrella that floats above them is held there by a conviction which – to judge by his work on Polydore Vergil – must have somewhat surprised Denys Hay. Increasingly we have been taught to distance English humanists from their once universal Italian ancestry and to seek the unifying principle in the role and influence of Erasmus – *supra omnes et ˙omnium praelector*. In 1965 there appeared a book which gave comprehensive expression to this growing conviction: James McConica's study of three generations of scholars, and indeed of public figures, who were all said to owe their world of ideas to Erasmus and no one else.[35] McConica deserved full appreciation for helping to demonstrate that the age of the early Reformation in England witnessed a major and principled manifestation of general reformist thinking; here he added weight to the argument that English humanism not only survived the year 1535 but mattered far more after the disappearance of Fisher and More than before. On the other hand, as we shall see, the thesis of a lasting and protean Erasmianism does not fit the facts; these had to be placed under a distorting glass to create that image. Nevertheless, for some decades the rule of Erasmus endured. With an exception: every herd has to have its maverick. In this case, the part was played by

---

32. W. Schenk, *Reginald Pole, Cardinal of England* (1950); D. B. Fenlon, *Heresy and Obedience in Tridentine Italy: Cardinal Pole and the Counter Reformation* (Cambridge, 1972).

33. T. F. Mayer, 'Faction and Ideology: Thomas Starkey's *Dialogue*,' *Historical Journal*, 28 (1985), pp. 1–25.

34. L. V. Ryan, *Roger Ascham* (Stanford, 1963).

35. J. K. McConica, *English Humanists and Reformation Politics under Henry VIII and Edward VI* (Oxford, 1965); cf. my review in *Historical Journal*, 10 (1967), pp. 137–8.

Stephen Gardiner whom earlier scholars never treated as a humanist at all. As a lawyer, and as a champion of a discredited pronunciation of Greek, he seemed to have nothing to do with the 'new learning'. Thus Peter Donaldson's speculative but to me convincing identification of Gardiner as a careful student of Machiavelli came as something of a shock to those who could not suppose that a champion of the old religion would go to that source for his ideas.[36]

## III

Rather more interesting than this continued conventional study of individuals (always excepting Thomas More) is another development which derived from Zeeveld's look at the role of humanist thinkers in the practical planning of reform. The recognition that English humanists, unlike their continental colleagues, tended to agree with Morus rather than Hythlodaeus in bringing their minds to the service of the common weal was not, of course, entirely new, though previously historians had mainly investigated the ideas and activities of educators. After all, the founding of St Paul's school formed Colet's chief claim to membership of the humanist circle. Though F. Caspari's book claimed to be concerned with what he called the social order, it was really about the educational programmes (education of the ruling elite) put forward by a diverse body of writers, from Erasmus, More and Starkey to Sidney and Spenser; even at the date of its appearance it carried a rather old-fashioned look.[37] More comprehensive analyses of the penetration of humanist concepts into schools, universities and private tutorships were supplied by Joan Simon and Kenneth Charlton who at any rate established the far-reaching changes that came to permeate English education in the course of this century.[38]

However, a novel recognition of a practically active humanism arose from the pursuit of scholars not into schoolrooms but into government service. Naturally enough, since he was the most eminent humanist to make this move, Thomas More has been set up as the presiding deity of this enterprise, but this theory errs. More entered Henry VIII's service in 1517 and stayed there for fifteen years:[39] small wonder that

---

36. P. S. Donaldson ed., *A Machiavellian Treatise by Stephen Gardiner* (Cambridge, 1975); for doubts about the ascription see Fenlon's review in *Historical Journal*, 19 (1976), pp. 1019–23.

37. F. Caspari, *Humanism and the Social Order in Tudor England* (Chicago, 1954).

38. J. Simon, *Education and Society in Tudor England* (Cambridge, 1966); K. Charlton, *Education in Renaissance England* (1965). W. T. Costello, *The Scholastic Curriculum at Early Seventeenth-Century Cambridge* (Cambridge, Mass., 1958) attempts to deny the influence of humanism, but he misleads because the innate scholasticism of theological study, with which he was concerned, is by no means the whole of Tudor education.

39. G. R. Elton, 'Thomas More Councillor,' *Studies*, I, pp. 129–54.

his claque expected the author of *Utopia* to put at least some of his reforming notions into practice.[40] However, the supposed evidence is illusory. Scarisbrick ascribed to More a detailed programme of projected reforms which I had identified with the circle of Thomas Cromwell,[41] and we have both turned out to be wrong. The paper came from Christopher St German, the foremost legal writer of the day; it entered history and effect through being submitted to Cromwell and had nothing whatsoever to do with More.[42] A most thorough investigation of More's career in the king's service has been unable to discover any genuine reforming activity; even in his court of Chancery he at best consolidated and systematized the innovations introduced by Cardinal Wolsey.[43] On the other hand, St German's emergence as a planner of reform is very important. A man close to seventy when he began to show himself in that role in the 1520s, he cannot at all be accommodated under the humanist umbrella and is therefore a very necessary reminder that the humanists participated in a general movement for reform rather than inspired it.

As Zeeveld had discovered, the urge to help the community to a better living came from the second generation of English humanists, many of whom, for the same reason, also sought reform in Church and religion. He singled out Thomas Starkey, Richard Morison and Richard Taverner, all of whom were promoted into service by Thomas Cromwell. Indeed, the pull offering its chance to the push originated with the man who, it was later remembered, 'loved not the men who pedantically boasted their reading, but that rationally made use of it',[44] a memory well supported by a personal archive full of reform proposals some of which he found the time to promote.[45] Typically, in that atmosphere redolent of humanism, Cromwell took a serious interest in educational reform; in fact, he seems deliberately to have looked for servants of the state among university graduates, adapting the earlier reliance on a trained clergy to the needs of a lay-governed State. Out of this policy came the careers of men like William Cecil. At the same time, university dons increasingly offered their learning for employ-

---

40. J. J. Scarisbrick, 'Thomas More: the King's Good Servant,' *Thought*, 52 (1977), pp. 249–68.

41. G. R. Elton, *Reform and Renewal: Thomas Cromwell and the Common Weal* (Cambridge, 1973), pp. 71–5.

42. J. A. Guy, *Christopher St German on Chancery and Statute* (Selden Society, 1985), pp. 62–3, 127–35. Cf. also Guy's further essays on St German in *Reassessing* (above, n. 31), chs. 5, 7, 8.

43. J. A. Guy, *The Public Career of Sir Thomas More* (Brighton, 1980).

44. D. Lloyd, *State-Worthies* (new ed., 1766), I, 78.

45. The reform activities of Cromwell and his circle form the theme of my *Reform and Renewal*. Cf. also my 'The Political Creed of Thomas Cromwell' and 'Reform by Statute: Thomas Starkey's *Dialogue* and Thomas Cromwell's Policy,' *Studies*, II, nos. 31 and 32.

ment in affairs, the outstanding examples being Sir John Cheke and Sir Thomas Smith. Known at one time mainly as 'Erasmians' seeking to promote classical studies at Cambridge, they have more recently emerged as leaders of an unsystematic movement of social and political reform that rested on humanist principles. Smith, regius professor of laws at Cambridge and principal secretary to both the duke of Somerset and Queen Elizabeth, has some right to the champion's title: his analysis of the economic problems of mid-century England represents a level of insight and understanding not matched again for the best part of a century.[46] Arthur Ferguson's wide-ranging survey of what was less a movement than a general intellectual and political fashion, though short on the practical effects of it all, satisfactorily established this socially involved face of English humanism.[47] Even so, he was too ready to engrave the features of Erasmus and More on that face.

## IV

The discovery of post-Reformation humanism has, perhaps not surprisingly, been accompanied by growing doubts about their pre-Reformation predecessors. This has particularly affected our views of the great pillars of the past. No one questions the description as humanists of such less influential persons as William Grocyn, teacher of Greek, or Richard Pace, civil servant and diplomatist.[48] The standing of Colet, Fisher and even More is less secure.

In part, of course, such debates depend on a definition of humanism, Christian or otherwise, and one quickly becomes aware how slippery that term is.[49] Criticism of the Church, for instance, was not confined to humanists, nor even was devotion to the classics, often enough found in the so-called Middle Ages.[50] Certainly, humanists insisted on the purification of Latin as well as the study of Greek and the intro-

---

46. M. Dewar, *Sir Thomas Smith: a Tudor Intellectual in Office* (1964); *idem*, ed., *A Discourse of the Commonweal of this Realm of England* (Charlottesville, 1969). On the other hand, the reformers of Edward VI's reign, none of them humanists, have been shown up as legendary in my 'Reform and the "Commonwealth-men" of Edward VI's Reign,' *Studies*, III, 234–53.

47. A. B. Ferguson, *The Articulate Citizen and the English Renaissance* (Durham, N. C., 1965).

48. Pace has recently, a bit surprisingly, entered into the discussion: Fox, *Reassessing* (n. 31), pp. 41–3.

49. For a sensible discussion see ibid. pp. 31–2, 34–5 where the best use of the term is made to rest on the techniques of study and exposition.

50. Differences from the Renaissance are emphasized in R. W. Southern, 'Medieval Humanism,' *Medieval Humanism and Other Studies* (Oxford, 1970), pp. 29–60; they are regarded as less clear-cut by R. Thomson, 'John of Salisbury and William of Malmesbury: Currents of Twelfth-Century Humanism', *The World of John of Salisbury*, ed. Michael Wilks (Oxford, 1984), pp. 117–25.

duction of Hebrew to a degree not found before: above all, they were philologists rather than philosophers. They broke with the investigative techniques of the scholastic tradition, replacing logic by rhetoric and the syllogism by the dialogue. In all Erasmus's vast output, perhaps the most typical production – the one that only a humanist would write – is his textbook on style, *De Copia Verborum*. Thus humanists can up to a point be identified by their principles as students and teachers: humanism was above all an educational movement. However, there is surely one characteristic a man had to display in order to join the club: he must think *humaniter* and believe in a human ability to control human fate. Not all of them need to have fully subscribed to the slogan, 'homo mensura'; it was possible to doubt that man is the measure of all things and to allow for the work of God's grace in men nevertheless endowed with free will. What no one properly to be called a humanist could adhere to was an Augustinian belief in the total and helpless depravity of fallen man, or to Lutheran solafideism, or to a clericalist view by which a priesthood acted as the sole channel of grace, or to a total denial of free enquiry. Measured against these principles, the membership of that established trio does become questionable, especially when all are ranked under the Erasmian banner. For it remains correct to regard Erasmus, who fulfilled all the conditions, as the prototype and leader.

Erasmus several times acknowledged his debt to John Colet from whom he learned methods of enquiry and discourse, though the most recent review of that relationship demonstrates that any similarity of thought was confined to Erasmus's earliest writings.[51] Colet also displayed his credentials when he created in St Paul's School an example of reformed teaching centred upon the classics and the return to the sources. Nevertheless, it is difficult to call a man a humanist without very severe qualifications who held the lowest opinion of fallen mankind, demanded full submission to the canon law, wished to educate only the clergy, and preached the superior virtue of the clerical estate provided it returned to primitive asceticism.[52] As has been said, his 'whole career was a protest against worldliness', and he showed really quite insufficient interest in the reform of the laity to make the grade.[53] Certainly he resisted scholasticism and knew his Plato and

---

51. P. I. Kaufman, 'John Colet and Erasmus' *Enchiridion,*' *Church History*, 46 (1977), pp. 296–312.

52. H. C. Porter, 'The Gloomy Dean and the Law: John Colet, 1466–1519,' *Essays in Modern Church History* (Ft. Sykes), ed. G. V. Bennett and J. D. Walsh (1966), pp. 18–43.

53. P. I. Kaufman, 'John Colet's *Opus de sacramentis* and Clerical Anti-clericalism: the Limitation of "Ordinary Wayes",' *Journal of British Studies*, 22/1 (1982), pp. 1–22.

Plotinus, but the distinctly humanist Colet of tradition owed his character to Erasmus's description which, as was usual with that scholar, pictured the assessor far more than the assessed.[54] Much the same doubtful verdict must be passed on John Fisher. He too enjoyed the friendship of Erasmus and proved himself a convinced progressive in matters of education, though even in these his successor as chancellor of Cambridge, Thomas Cromwell, possibly did more to promote a humanist reign in the university. Fisher, of course, like Colet, was primarily a theologian – the only notable theologian on the English bench of bishops in his time. And here the two great campaigns of his life – against Luther and against Henry VIII's first divorce – proved him to be a committed adherent of tradition and of Thomas Aquinas (whom Colet disliked). Fisher wrote his Latin treatises in the manner of the past; he evaded the innovations in discourse and presentation which we rightly associate with humanism. He was a man of great and varied learning, a man of principle and purpose, but being a friend of Erasmus and More is not sufficient proof of his attachment to humanism which must at the least be reckoned intermittent and in the last part of his life invisible. He calls for more work.[55]

On More, on the other hand, the work has been plentiful, quite apart from the debates about *Utopia* already outlined. The trouble started, I think, when I found myself growing doubtful whether hagiography had a place in history and asked some impertinent questions about that supposedly humanist scholar who gave so much of his time to routine employments in the king's service where he promoted no reforms, who displayed such a tendency for disputing the human power for good, and who became such an exceptionally determined persecutor of heretics.[56] I showed cause why we should not simply trust one of the chief foundations of the inherited image of More, namely William Roper's notes assembled twenty years after his father-in-law's death and designed to smooth the path towards canonization. And, somewhat embarrassingly, I drew attention to More's manifest preoccupation with matters sexual, on which Erasmus had actually remarked only to be ignored down the ages. More, like Luther, preferred Augustine to

54. J. B. Trapp, 'John Colet and the *Hierarchies* of the PS-Dionysius,' *Religion and Humanism* (Studies in Church History 17, ed. K. Robbins; Oxford, 1981), pp. 127–48. Colet's use of the ancients is investigated in Leland Miles, *John Colet and the Platonic Tradition* (1962), but the author's attachment to Rome has produced a book in the medieval style, calling for an exegete or glossator.

55. The problems emerge from Surtz's study (above, n. 10) which takes Fisher's humanism for granted but tends to reveal the difficulties of believing in its existence.

56. See my *Studies*, I and III, nos. 7, 8, 45, and Reviews (c); also my 'Persecution and Toleration in the English Reformation,' *Persecution and Toleration* (Studies in Church History 21, ed. W. J. Shiels; Oxford, 1984), pp. 163–87.

all other Fathers of the Church; More, again like Luther, believed man to be totally depraved as a consequence of the Fall. True, unlike Luther he tried to rescue free will, though not (I still think) altogether convincingly.[57] His chief difference from the reformer, however, lay in his unswerving allegiance to the Church Universal to which he ascribed a total authority well out of step with normal humanist principles. I pointed out that the traditional and humanist More appeared to be constructed exclusively out of what he did and wrote before about 1521; the image-makers had ignored the next twelve years of his life and the bulk of his writings. To me it thus became doubtful whether More could be called a humanist after the time that he turned his mind solely to the defence of the Church and the demolition of heresy.

Since I first entered my comprehensive *caveat* two large and important books have appeared which express similar doubts, though possibly in more measured tones. Alistair Fox was the first scholar to use the whole corpus of More's writings in an attempt to understand the man and his intellectual development.[58] While professing a greater respect for More's personality and thinking than I had done, he came to much the same conclusions on More's inner psychology (the psychology of a man exceptionally conscious of the fact of evil in this world) and also held that the onset of the Reformation terminated More's humanist phase. Instead, his diagnosis put before us a More who tried to reconcile a belief in God's goodness with the evidence of misery in a world created by God. In the end, More came to treat human history as a sequence of temptations to desert an all-demanding God who, however, would reward humble obedience and unquestioning submission with salvation at the last. Nothing very humanist about that. Even more critical of More the humanist is the large biography by Richard Marius, the only member of the Yale team to have resisted saint-worship.[59] Marius, who had won his spurs by a brilliantly convincing analysis of More's faith in the authority of the Church,[60] added one further, rather crucial, item to the question of

---

57. Cf. e.g. *Confutation of Tyndale* (*CW* 8, 1973), pp. 502–3, where More refutes Tyndale's Lutheran doctrine of God's unsolicited grace by calling it absurd that men should be compelled to 'sit even still and do nothing toward it'. The Lutheran doctrine does not stop men from seeking grace but denies that such a manouevre will persuade God to grant it, a point which is not met in More's display of angry irony. More seemingly did believe in grace bestowed freely and not bought by works, but I do not see that he ever succeeded in resolving the incompatibility of predestination by God's decree with human free will. Not that he has been alone in this.

58. A. Fox, *Thomas More: History and Providence* (Oxford, 1982).

59. R. Marius, *Thomas More: a Biography* (New York, 1984).

60. In his contribution to the introduction to the *CW* edition of the *Confutation*, III, pp. 1271–1363.

More's humanism when he disproved the ancient legend of an exceptionally close and long-enduring friendship between More and Erasmus. So far as real evidence goes, it now looks as though relations between the two men were really intense only in about the three years surrounding the production of *Utopia* (about which Erasmus was as hesitant as More was about his friend's *Praise of Folly*); after 1521, the signs of a growing distance are really clear enough. Not that they quarrelled, but they went their different ways, so that it will not do to make More's humanism depend solely on a likemindedness with Erasmus. In the end, Erasmus's first reaction to More's ultimate fate not only lacked true sorrow but also indicated that in his view More had long left the fold. 'I wish he had never dabbled in so perilous a business and left theology to the theologians,' was all that the prince of scholars could find to say about his supposed bosom friend.[61] Though it is true that a week later he had collected himself sufficiently to lament more convincingly,[62] it is plain enough that in Erasmus's opinion More had ceased to be one of the gang.

The most recent attempts to restore More firmly to the ranks of the humanists either concentrate, once again, exclusively on *Utopia* (already discussed) or sound a trifle bewildered. Craig Thompson decided that 'as a humanist More was essentially Erasmian', a verdict which, of course, highlights Marius's subsequent critique of the later More. When their relations can be shown to be less than those of David and Jonathan, Thompson rather feebly sees only 'minor matters of imperfect sympathies and misunderstandings'. And while acknowledging David Knowles's remark about More changing through life as all men change, he concluded that the continued quality of his writing proves him to have remained a humanist to the end.[63] That does seem a weak last resort – not to mention that it calls for a charitable assessment of the style of most of More's anti-heretical writings. I rather share C. S. Lewis's low opinion of the literary quality of More's controversial works, the *Dialogue concerning Heresies* alone excepted.[64] However, this is unquestionably a debate that has not yet ended.

61. 'Utinam periculoso negocio se nunquam admiscuisset, et causam theologicam cessisset theologis' (*Opus Epistolarum Des. Erasmi Roterodami*, ed. P. S. Allen, XI, p. 216).

62. Ibid., p. 221: 'In Moro mihi videor extinctus.'

63. C. R. Thompson, 'The Humanism of More reappraised,' *Thought*, 52 (1977), pp. 233–48;.D. Knowles, *The Historian and Character* (Cambridge, 1963), p. 7. Thompson was sufficiently ambiguous for Fox to read him as saying that in the Tower More *had* ceased to be a humanist (*Reassessing*, 10). But I think that Thompson meant to apply this only to the last devotional works.

64. *English Literature in the Sixteenth Century, excluding Drama* (Oxford, 1954), p. 174. The somewhat critical assessment in Rainer Pineas, *Thomas More and Tudor Polemics* (Bloomington, 1968) has found little favour with the More brigade.

## V

This is where quite a short while ago the story terminated and the matter could be left to rest. We might be arguing about this and that, but we were essentially agreed that a group of learned men who acknowledged Erasmus as their leader thought and wrote in early-Tudor England about the issues, and in the manner, appropriate to humanists. But about a year ago a rather formidable cat from New Zealand landed among the cooing pigeons. Having firmly put Thomas More in his place, Alistair Fox next found himself very dissatisfied with an analysis which treated English humanism as a single 'movement' any participant in which shared the fundamental convictions and the outlook on the world entertained by all the rest. Thus, in two short essays, he broke up the scene and put forward a new interpretation which still awaits development in the fires of debate.[65] To Fox it has become plain that English humanism constituted 'a multifarious phenomenon'. Multifarious but not totally fragmented: he finds a key in the different uses to which different men wished to put their learning outside the mere cause of learning. They shared a respect for the revival of classical literature: thus his ignorance of it eliminates St German from the ranks. They also shared a conviction that their philosophy carried implications for the betterment of men's condition, especially for men charged with the exercise of government. But where Caspari (n. 37) reduced all problems of 'social order' to a general programme for educating the ruling elite, while McConica (n. 35) lumped all ideas together under the title of Erasmianism, Fox saw the need for fundamental distinctions.

In effect, Fox identified three possible reactions to the demands the world made upon the scholar. Erasmus held to the rather naive view that an exposure to good letters and moral maxims would suffice to bring about a better common weal. He was the Hythloday of reality, determined upon absolutes which had to be spelt out and maintained in perfection, even if in consequence the good world could exist only in the imagination. Erasmus is thus described as a pessimist since the ends of his optimistic dreams could never achieve reality, but I would think it more pointful to term him an opti-pessimist because experience seems never to have persuaded him out of his ethereal position. More differed from his friend, whose innocence he criticized in *Utopia*, by an explicit pessimism based upon his despair of mankind; he understood that comprehensive or fundamental reform was out of the question and resigned himself to piecemeal reform (or in practice none).

---

65. 'Facts and Fallacies: Interpreting English Humanism' and 'English Humanism and the Body Politic' in *Reassessing* (above, n. 10), pp. 9–51.

The third choice available to the humanist escaped 'from both the Erasmian and Morean pessimism' by positively tackling the problems of society – of taking action on the basis of remedies worked out by reason and experience. The prototype of this 'optimistic' stance, Fox argues, was Thomas Starkey, and the humanism that prevailed in England from the 1530s onwards opted mainly for this kind of participation in government. More (this is an addition of mine to the thesis) had no real disciples until Utopian writers like Harrington picked up some of his message in the next century. The only true Erasmian among English humanists (this *is* Fox) was Thomas Elyot who shared both the master's belief in the power of learned instruction and his total ineffectualness in practice. One question now to be pursued concerns possible later Erasmians, that is humanists distinguishable from the likes of Thomas Starkey and Thomas Smith, but even at first sight, before the review of the whole scene by means of this analysis has progressed further, the underlying ideas carry a great deal of conviction.

They seem especially convincing because Fox throws in one insight that he has not yet had a chance of following up. Recognizing the strain to which the Lutheran explosion exposed a generation of thinkers whose anthropology had always tended to be superficially hopeful, he notes that 'there was always, therefore, an incipient fracture in the Christian-humanist synthesis'.[66] The Christian view of man as sinful and corrupt could not really be reconciled to the humanist hopes that men could and would help themselves to a better life. Theocentric Christianity and humanocentric humanism could form an alliance only by ignoring the abyss between them. The Reformation brutally acquainted Erasmus with those facts of life that he would not admit destroyed his constructs, while with equal brutality it demonstrated how right More had been in his ingrained pessimism about the role of good letters in a fallen world. Luther in effect rendered Erasmus irrelevant, and More, who seemed to see this, discarded his earlier humanism in order to fight for that form of Christianity which to him constituted the sole hope of salvation. The third set of humanists for the time being found it possible to maintain their cheerful belief in Thomas Cromwell and the virtue of secular action; most of them, though not Thomas Starkey, regarded the new faith as congruent because it demolished the barrier between the service of God and the service of man. But – and here we part company with Fox – this new synthesis could only be temporary. It did well in Cromwell's decade when the power of the State encouraged the practical participation of the humanist scholar. And though the example was to be fitfully

---

66. Ibid., p. 30.

followed later, the ways began to show signs of a new parting. The failure in government of Thomas Smith differed from that of Thomas Elyot only in that the latter, guided by Cromwell, accepted his relegation to the study, whereas the former never quite understood why he had got no further as a statesman.

The fundamental trouble lay in the fact that the reformed religion, as it was preached in the sixteenth century, in its essence rejected the teachings of the humanists. The humanists had won their sole victory when they conquered the territory specifically reserved to education, for even there it proved easier for Thomist Jesuits than for Calvinists to absorb the new form of classical education. From the 1550s onwards, no Englishman who passed through the hands of teachers escaped a system built on the return to the ancient authors and a training of the mind in the techniques of rhetoric and literature. With this went a respect for man's potential which continued to serve practical statesmen engaged in facing the problems of society – such men as William Cecil. But if the educated scholar opted for the service of God – especially, if he entered the clerical profession – he found himself compelled to a view of man as totally sinful and totally dependent on God's unpredictable grace. Double predestination marches ill with any form of humanism. Though Calvin himself could cope with his humanist training by relegating everything not consonant with it to the realm of God's mysteries which it is not the function of reason to examine, others proved less relaxed; the reformed religion that sprang from him set up manifest and often intolerable tensions within the minds of men educated by the humanists and committed to a predestinarian faith. In the end, it was the second that gave way and largely disappeared in its stringent form; by about 1660, at any rate, the main part of thinking Christians among Englishmen had insensibly surrendered to the triumph of the humanist view of the world.[67]

---

67. For a first attempt to set out the problem see my 'Auseinandersetzung und Zusammenarbeit zwischen Renaissance und Reformation in England,' *Renaissance – Reformation: Gegensätze und Gemeinsamkeiten*, ed. A. Buck (Wiesbaden, 1984), pp. 217–25. There are some interesting pointers in R. M. Douglas, 'Talent, and Vocation in Humanist and Protestant Thought,' *Action and Conviction* (above, n. 27), pp. 261–98.

# Index